COMMANDO

Also by James Owen

A Serpent in Eden:
The Greatest Murder Mystery of All Time

The Voice of War:
The Second World War by Those Who Fought It
(with Guy Walters)

Nuremberg: Evil on Trial

Danger UXB:
The Heroic Story of the WWII
Bomb Disposal Teams

COMMANDO

WINNING WORLD WAR II BEHIND ENEMY LINES

JAMES OWEN

Little, Brown

LITTLE, BROWN

First published in Great Britain in 2012 by Little, Brown

Copyright © James Owen, 2012

The moral right of the author has been asserted.

All rights reserved.
No part of this publication may be reproduced, stored in a retrieval system, or transmitted, in any form or by any means, without the prior permission in writing of the publisher, nor be otherwise circulated in any form of binding or cover other than that in which it is published and without a similar condition including this condition being imposed on the subsequent purchaser.

A CIP catalogue record for this book is available from the British Library.

Map copyright © John Gilkes

ISBN 978-1-4087-0302-1

Typeset in Bembo by M Rules
Printed and bound in Great Britain by
Clays Ltd, St Ives plc

Papers used by Little, Brown are from well-managed forests and other responsible sources.

MIX
Paper from
responsible sources
FSC® C104740

Little, Brown
An imprint of
Little, Brown Book Group
100 Victoria Embankment
London EC4Y 0DY

An Hachette UK Company
www.hachette.co.uk

www.littlebrown.co.uk

In memory of M.R.D. Foot (1919–2012),
soldier and historian of secret warfare,
and of those he briefed for Operation
AQUATINT in September 1942

DUDLEY PUBLIC LIBRARIES	
000000548834	
Bertrams	03/10/2012
940.541241	£20.00
	DU

CONTENTS

CHRONOLOGY

CORDITE – Rhodes, Greece, March 1941

AMBASSADOR – Northern France, June 1940

EXPORTER – Litani River, Syria, June 1941

FLIPPER – 'Rommel's HQ', Libya, November 1941

ARCHERY – Vaagso, Norway, December 1941

POSTMASTER – Gulf of Guinea, West Africa, January 1941

CHARIOT – St Nazaire, France, March 1942

JUBILEE – Dieppe, France, August 1942

DRYAD – Casquets, Channel Islands, September 1942

MUSKETOON – Glomfjord, Norway, September 1942

ANGLO – Rhodes, Greece, September 1942

AGREEMENT – Tobruk, Libya, September 1942

JV and FRANKTON – Boulogne, France, April 1942 and Bordeaux, France, December 1942

TARBRUSH – Northern France, May 1944

FLOUNCED – Vis, Yugoslavia, June 1944

OVERLORD – Normandy, France, June 1944

INFATUATE – Walcheren, The Netherlands, November 1944

TALON – Kangaw, Burma, January 1945

ROAST – Lake Comacchio, Italy, April 1945

ECLIPSE – Northern Germany, April 1945

ACKNOWLEDGEMENTS

This book is in truth what the Commandos used to call a combined operation. No author can write a work of history like this without drawing on the expertise, advice and memories of dozens of people, and I am profoundly grateful to all of them for their generosity in sharing those, and for their willingness to trust me with their knowledge and experiences.

I want particularly to thank the veterans and their families who talked to me or who allowed me to use photographs or quotations from memoirs. These included Jonathan Clogstoun-Willmott, Roxana Courtney, Luke Griffiths, Will Davies, Alexander and Edward Haig-Thomas, George Walkley, Rorie Smith, Miles Whitelock, Billy Moore, Stan Scott, Gerald Bryan, Elizabeth Lane, Desiree Roderick and the late M.R.D. Foot.

Geoff Murray and Pete Rogers of the Commando Veterans Association were unfailingly prompt and kind in answering my questions, in suggesting lines of enquiry and in helping me to make the most of a memorable weekend at Fort William. André Heintz and Gérard Fournier coped heroically with my attempts to quiz them in French, and Édith Germain at Orep was good enough to put me in touch with them. James Dorrian, Peter Stanley and Alan Ogden guided me in the right direction when it would have been easy to have gone astray.

My thanks must also go to the patient and dedicated staff of the

National Archives, the Imperial War Museum, the Liddell Hart Centre at King's College, London, the National Army Museum, the Second World War Experience, the British Library and the London Library. The contribution that institutions such as these make to preserving our history, and to enabling authors to write about it, rarely receives the appreciation it deserves.

My editors Richard Beswick and Iain Hunt were the personification of coolness under fire, Philip Parr drilled my prose into shape, Linda Silverman provided close support in picture research, and my literary agent Julian Alexander coped heroically with the heavy flak that came his way. I could not have undertaken the challenge of writing this book without their unfailing encouragement, or that of those closest to me. They all deserve medals.

LIST OF ILLUSTRATIONS

Micky Burn covertly signals 'V for Victory' with his fingers while a PoW at St Nazaire

Commandos returning from the Dieppe raid with a German prisoner *(IWM)*

Coming ashore on D-Day from a landing craft, as perfected in training *(IWM)*

Recruits cross a rope bridge at Achnacarry as a shell explodes to simulate combat conditions *(IWM)*

Roger Courtney as Commanding Officer of 2 SBS in 1942 *(George Walkley)*

Nigel Willmott, who led the COPP clandestine reconnaissance teams *(Clogstoun Family)*

Section II

Joe Houghton and Graeme Black commanded Operation MUSKETOON *(Mrs Desiree Roderick MBE and Commando Veterans Association)*

Dick O'Brien was one of the few commandos to return from MUSKETOON *(IWM)*

The Glomfjord power plant, which was the target of MUSKETOON *(National Archives)*

Members of Force B before the disastrous attack on Tobruk in 1942 *(IWM)*

SBS officer Tommy Langton walked back to his own lines after the failure of Operation AGREEMENT *(Getty Images)*

Gerald Montanaro proved that attacks could be made successfully by canoe *(Liddell Hart Centre, King's College London)*

Cockleshell Hero: 'Blondie' Hasler mounted one of the boldest and costliest missions of the war *(Royal Marines Museum Collection)*

John Durnford-Slater, the first officer to raise a Commando, briefs General Montgomery in Italy, 1943 *(IWM)*

Anders Lassen served with the Commandos, SOE, the SAS and SBS, and was awarded a posthumous VC *(IWM)*

John Barton carried out daring missions behind the lines in Yugoslavia and Italy *(Barton Family)*

After being captured on a reconnaissance operation shortly before D-Day, George Lane was interviewed by Rommel himself *(Lane Family)*

Royal Marine commandos move inland from Sword Beach, Normandy, on 6 June 1944 *(IWM)*

French troops from 10 Commando march through the streets of Flushing during the battle for the fortress island of Walcheren in 1944 *(National Archives)*

3 Commando Brigade take it easy during a break from the campaign against the Japanese in Burma *(IWM)*

George Knowland VC broke up a Japanese attack by firing a mortar from the hip at Kangaw, 1945 *(IWM)*

Patrick Dalzel-Job was said to be the model for James Bond and served with a unit set up by Ian Fleming *(Liddell Hart Centre, King's College London)*

The Queen Mother dedicates the Commando Memorial at Spean Bridge, Scotland, in 1952 *(Popperfoto/Getty Images)*

Commando Operations, 1940–1945
R.Litani
EXPORTER
FLIPPER
Tobruk
AGREEMENT
TALON
Kangaw
Gulf of Guinea
POSTMASTER
Lofoten Islands
Narvik
Glomfjord
MUSKETOON
0 100 200 300 miles
0 200 400 km
SWEDEN
Gulf of Bothnia
FINLAND
Trondheim
Vaagso
ARCHERY
NORWAY
Bergen
Oslo
Helsinki
Leningrad
Stockholm
Tallinn
Achnacarry
North Sea
Riga
UNITED KINGDOM
DENMARK
SOVIET UNION
Copenhagen
Baltic Sea
Minsk
Hamburg
NETHERLANDS
Bremen
ECLIPSE
London
Amsterdam
Berlin
Walcheren
INFATUATE
Warsaw
Boulogne
TARBRUSH
DRYAD
Casquets
JV
COLLAR
Brussels
GERMANY
Kiev
Guernsey
AMBASSADOR
OVERLORD
Dieppe
JUBILEE
Frankfurt
Prague
NORMANDY
AQUATINT
Paris
Nuremberg
St Nazaire
CHARIOT
CZECHOSLOVAKIA
Munich
Vienna
HUNGARY
FRANCE
SWITZ.
Berne
AUSTRIA
Budapest
Bordeaux
FRANKTON
Milan
Trieste
Venice
ROMANIA
ITALY
Belgrade
Bucharest
Marseilles
L. Comacchio
ROAST
YUGOSLAVIA
Florence
BULGARIA
FLOUNCED
Vis
Adriatic Sea
SPAIN
Sofia
CORSICA
Rome
Istanbul
Tirana
Salonika
Naples
Salerno
ALBANIA
SARDINIA
TURKEY
GREECE
Mediterranean Sea
Palermo
Athens
Algiers
SICILY
Tunis
MALTA
Rhodes
CORDITE
ANGLO
NORTH AFRICA

PROLOGUE

CORDITE

It was an hour after dusk when the submarine surfaced. As it began to recharge its batteries, the hush of the night air gave way to a raucous throb. Every pulse of the engines, reverberating through the hull, jarred the nerves of the two men waiting below. Never had danger felt so real before.

From the voice pipe came the words they had been expecting, spoken quietly but with urgency. They climbed a ladder into the conning tower, then another down onto the wet deck, its casing almost level with the water and speckled with foam. After days in the cramped confines of the submarine, the moonless sky above them seemed vast. The darkness was as soft as velvet and smelled of the sea.

Beyond the gun platform, a lone figure crouched on the slim fin of the starboard fore-hydroplane. With one hand, the Special Boat Section corporal clung to a steel stay meant to stop mines from fouling the craft. With the other, he held in place the two-man canoe which had been brought up through the forward hatch and lowered over the side. The prow heaved under his grasp, rising and falling on the swell.

Dressed only in a thick sweater and long-johns, the first paddler let the canoe ride up towards him and stepped across awkwardly into the front seat. The boat lurched and clattered against the submarine as the kneeling corporal tried his best to steady it again. Then the second man vaulted athletically in behind, placing his palm flat on the canvas and levering his heavy frame into place. The satisfied grin showed even through the boot polish that covered his face.

Working swiftly, senses alert for the glare of a searchlight or the roar of an E-boat, a naval rating passed the men double-ended paddles, a Thermos flask and two small boxes. These were an infra-red transmitter and receiver, newly invented and highly secret. Already stowed in the canoe were a machine-gun and a 0.38 revolver, wrapped in the best waterproofing available – a cellophane envelope.

Then they were away, easing off with their paddles and dipping their shoulders in the purposeful rhythm that would bring the canoe in a mile to land. Behind them, the submarine drew back into the night. Ahead lay the coast of Rhodes, and thousands of enemy troops. Operation CORDITE was on.

By early 1941, Britain's position in North Africa looked much more promising than it had done a few months earlier. A series of offensives mounted by General Sir Archibald Wavell had shattered the Italian forces in the region and he was able to turn his attention to the other end of his Middle East command. At Churchill's insistence, Wavell had previously sent troops to help Greece in its fight against Italy, yet though the mainland still resisted the Dodecanese Islands had fallen to the invaders. Already the Italians and their German allies had flown sorties from the airstrips there and the threat presented by them to Britain's possessions in the Eastern Mediterranean, and perhaps even to the Suez Canal, was clear.

Wavell now proposed to secure this flank by seizing the largest of the Dodecanese, Rhodes. The attack – codenamed CORDITE – was to be executed in April by an infantry division, supported by tanks, which was to be put ashore by a naval contingent under Rear Admiral Harold Baillie-Grohman. More specifically, responsibility for the convoy releasing the landing craft at the right place and on time rested with its thirty-year-old navigating officer, Lieutenant Commander Nigel Willmott.

Willmott had visited Rhodes in peacetime, but his view of his task was shaped more by what he had witnessed in Norwegian waters earlier in the war. Many of the vessels lost on both sides at Narvik in April 1940 had foundered on unseen obstructions, grounding amid uncharted shoals or holing themselves on rocks marked on no map. And those ships had had expert navigators. Willmott was only too aware that few of the landing craft which he would be dropping four miles offshore, at night, had compasses, and that none of the officers steering them would be trained in pilotage.

For, despite Britain's long military and naval traditions, the truth was that it still had a great deal to learn about cooperation between the two arms. Willmott's uncle had taken part in the last major amphibious landing, at Gallipoli in 1915, where the assaulting troops had been slowed by barbed wire hidden in the surf. Now Willmott worried that he could give the landing craft no information about what they might find if they actually reached their designated beaches.

Aerial reconnaissance only showed half the picture. It would not reveal the sandbar that might convince a helmsman he was in the shallows, only for soldiers laden with kit to plunge off the ramp into deep water. Nor could the survey of Rhodes's coast which Willmott had recently made through the periscope of a submarine tell him whether sand at a particular spot lay fourteen inches deep – enough to bear the weight of armour – nor where the enemy had concealed their pillboxes.

The Navy was Willmott's career and accordingly he made decisions cautiously. Yet there was a side to him that was open to possibilities which eluded others. As a young midshipman, he had had his fortune told by an old woman in Ceylon. She had predicted that a great war would come but that he would survive it in the desert. His shipmates had laughed, pointing to his sailor's uniform, but here he was with a cushy berth on the Staff in Cairo. It was this same willingness to look beyond the obvious that now persuaded him that – whatever his superiors thought – CORDITE would fail, and with catastrophic loss of life. The only way to avoid that was for him to see the beaches for himself.

When Willmott first suggested this to Baillie-Grohman he was rebuffed. He knew far too much about the operation to risk being captured. Yet he was sure that sooner or later the Army would want better intelligence about the places where it was to land. So certain was he that, although he disliked swimming, he started a training routine. In the early mornings, while the sun was still below the Pyramids, he did twenty-five laps of the Cairo Club Baths, practising sliding silently through the water as if approaching a beach watched by sentries.

The call came earlier than he had anticipated. There was a panic on: the plans had changed and the Army needed to know if they could land tanks below the town of Rhodes itself. By the next day, Willmott was in Alexandria, negotiating passage in a submarine. His intent was to row between it and the beach in a rubber dinghy, swimming the last hundred yards or so for greater stealth. The flotilla commander pointed out straight away that a dinghy would not fit through a submarine's hatch. Instead, he had another suggestion.

A few weeks earlier, a large and rather mysterious body of troops had disembarked in Egypt and they were now encamped north of Suez at Kabrit. They were commandos. There had been much talk about this new organisation since its formation six months before, but no one seemed to know what commandos actually did, or indeed how they might be used in North Africa. One of their sections, however, had contacted the submariners to explore the feasibility of making clandestine landings by canoe. They were currently training on the Great Bitter Lake, where Willmott was introduced to their leader, Captain Roger Courtney.

The two men proved to have very different temperaments. Willmott had an ancestor who had won the Victoria Cross in the Indian Mutiny, but he did not see himself in the heroic mould. He achieved results through planning and dedication. Courtney was, by contrast, in the words of one of his men, 'a grown-up boy' with the adventurous outlook of an Elizabethan privateer.

Now nearly forty, Roger Courtney had abandoned a job in a bank to seek his fortune in Kenya. There he had become a white hunter, helping wealthy visitors to shoot big game and acquiring the nickname 'Jumbo'. He had then paddled the length of the Nile in a canoe, armed only with an elephant spear and living off a sack of potatoes. The journey had left him with two shillings in the world and in need of work, so he made his way to Palestine and signed up as a colonial policeman.

The Arab Revolt of the mid-1930s had taught him much about irregular warfare. He had seen how a handful of guerrillas could pin down a larger force using rapid movement and camouflage. When the insurgents began to snipe his barracks, Courtney was sent up a clock-tower with binoculars to spot their muzzle flashes. The bullets kept coming out of nowhere. Not until later was it discovered that the flash was being masked by wet sacks hung in front of the rifles.

Courtney had had a spell in the Army as a young man, and several months before war broke out in 1939 he joined up again. He had got married a year earlier, and had spent his honeymoon travelling down the Danube to the Black Sea in a collapsible German-made canoe. The locals called it a *folbot* – a folding boat; Courtney and his wife called it *Buttercup*.

In skilled hands, Courtney realised, canoes were fast and silent. He came to think that they would be perfect for carrying out reconnaissance and sabotage at close quarters, but like Willmott he failed at first to persuade more conventional minds of his idea's merits. Yet where Willmott had waited to be proved right, Courtney had resorted to direct action. In the late summer of 1940 he made a bet with his commanding officer that he could board a ship at night and get away again, even if the crew was forewarned. A few evenings later, the CO was hosting a drinks party for the other officers when the French windows opened abruptly and in stalked Courtney, naked apart from a pair of sodden swimming trunks. Without a word he flung down the breech-blocks and covers from the ship's anti-aircraft guns and left the way he had come. Daylight revealed a line of crosses chalked on the hull where there would have been limpet mines.

Challenged to repeat his feat against a submarine depot vessel, Courtney and a comrade again succeeded in placing their canoe undetected alongside the ship and making their chalk marks. They were then tempted by a dangling rope-ladder – only to find a master-at-arms and two marines with fixed bayonets waiting for them at the top. Yet Courtney had made his point, and when the commandos sailed for the Mediterranean, their Folbot Troop went with them.

The 'folboteers' would soon be given a more anonymous name to disguise their activities – the Special Boat Section (SBS). Courtney quickly found, however, that no one on Wavell's staff knew what to do with them. He was therefore delighted to be given the chance to demonstrate his worth by helping Willmott carry out his reconnaissance. One of his NCOs, Jimmy Sherwood, was equally excited to be told that he too had been selected for the SBS's very first operation.

They had a fortnight to prepare. 'For several nights we practised approaching the shore in folbots, with the object of getting ashore without being seen,' Sherwood later remembered. 'There were people on the beach trying to spot us.' A canoe seen bow-on has a narrow silhouette and usually they were only sighted at the last moment. They were happy enough with this since the Italian patrols on Rhodes would not be actively looking for them, and the sound of the waves would help to cover any noise they made.

The two officers also spent hours in games of hide and seek. 'Generally speaking, it's surprising what one can do at night if one keeps low to the ground or water and quiet,' Willmott wrote afterwards. Courtney had a hunter's eye, but after ten days Willmott was able to swim ashore in the dark and circle behind him twice as often as he was caught. They also found that as long as Willmott remained motionless in the sea, a torch shone on him would dazzle Courtney rather than illuminate Willmott.

The latter had sheathed the torch in a contraceptive to keep the water out, and the rest of their kit was equally makeshift. They might have to stay submerged for hours, and in an age before wet-suits the best protection against the cold that Willmott could devise was a submariner's thick jersey and woollen leggings soaked in periscope grease. On top of this he wore an inflatable Gieves waist-coat to add buoyancy. Even so, the clothing was heavy and uncomfortable, and did not stop Courtney from catching a bad chill which for several days put an end to their training.

The folbot did not inspire Willmott with confidence either. He soon learned the rudiments of paddling, but the canoe had been made for the pre-war leisure market rather than to military specifications. There were no spray caps and the boat risked being swamped in rough water. It was also prone to tip over in all but the lightest of winds. In fact, the sole piece of high technology that they had laid their hands on was the infra-red transmitter. Its rays were visible only when seen on the screen of the receiver, and most nights they practised homing in on the beacon being flashed by Sherwood from the base of Alexandria's lighthouse. Without the device, their chances of returning safely to the submarine would be remote.

In the last week of March 1941, the trio sailed for the Dodecanese aboard *Triumph*. 'I'd never been in a submarine in my life,' said Sherwood. 'I thought it was romantic, not dangerous!' They saw little sign of enemy activity on the surface, although they spotted much in the air; far to the west, the Navy was eviscerating the Italian fleet in the battle of Cape Matapan. On the night of the 30th, Sherwood helped to launch the folbot a little over a mile from the northern tip of Rhodes.

Willmott was to make the first recce, and after they had closed to within a hundred yards of the beach, he slipped as silently as he could into the water. The canoe was floating in a small bay, separated from the main harbour by a promontory. Shingle sloped steeply up from the shallows to a sea wall, beyond which lay the

Hotel des Roses. Once a fashionable resort, it was now the headquarters of the Axis forces on the island.

The sea was so cold that it took his breath away, and Willmott quickly started to swim towards the narrow crescent of sand. Almost instantly, he saw that it would be impossible to land tanks there. The foreshore was too rocky and the gradient was too stiff. He then began to check whether it was suitable for troops, stretching his toes down to see how the sand shelved under the surf. As he did so, he heard someone speaking in German.

On the road behind the wall at the back of the beach, two sentries were stamping their feet to warm themselves. One was having a surreptitious smoke while the other hawked and wheezed. Willmott focused on the sound of the water around him. Then, moving in time to the noise made by each breaking wave, he began to crawl up the shingle on his elbows.

He had got halfway to the wall when he saw one of the soldiers looking at him. He froze. The hours of practice with Courtney had taught him that if he stayed absolutely still he resembled nothing more unusual than a rock in the dark. Through his wet clothes he felt a breeze coming from the sea, and he clamped his teeth together to stop them from chattering. The sentry turned his head again and moved away.

Peering over the wall, Willmott realised that the Germans were no more than ten yards from him. A truck passed between them, and the headlights revealed two others stationed further up the road. His limbs felt tired and numb, and he did not relish going back into the water. Digging deep into his reserves of willpower, he dragged himself back down to the sea and began methodically to explore the shallows.

Within a few minutes he found a sandbar, some fifteen yards out. If the landing craft came to rest on this, their cargoes would be sitting targets. He traced its course, noting carefully where it ended so as to be able to direct the boats around it. Then he headed for the last of his objectives – the Hotel des Roses itself.

There might be hidden gun emplacements here, and he crept

slowly round the edge of its lawn, keeping to the shadows, until he was only fifty yards from the building. Satisfied that there were no tank traps or machine-gun nests, only tamarisks and bougainvillea, he retraced his steps downhill. Grabbing a few pebbles from the beach as geological specimens, he braced himself for the icy coils of the sea.

Three hours had passed and the Benzedrine tablets he had taken to keep himself alert had worn off. Fatigue began to wash over him as he held his torch aloft, two hundred yards from the shore, praying that Courtney would see his signal. It took all his concentration to keep flashing 'R' in Morse code and after ten minutes he started to worry that the commando had been captured. Or perhaps he had lost his bearings in the dark and been carried out of position by the current.

Willmott felt a blissful exhaustion overwhelming him. He lost sensation in his feet, and then in his legs as it crept up him. His eyes closed, but he willed them to open and as he did so heard the sound of a blade parting water. Up came Courtney, and with a final effort Willmott pulled himself over the stern of the canoe. So cold was he that he could not feel the whisky that Courtney poured down his throat, but the hot coffee revived him a little and they began to paddle out to sea to rendezvous with the submarine. A thick mist came down, but once through it they were able to begin transmitting with the infra-red equipment, watching in turn for *Triumph*'s own beam. They did not have long to wait before they saw her rise from the water.

The next night, Willmott went onto a beach south of Rhodes town. There he found an unmarked reef below the waterline which would have holed any landing craft. Pushing his luck, he worked his way through barbed wire and got onto the esplanade of the town itself. No sooner had he begun to swim for the canoe than he saw a group of sentries with torches combing the area where he had just been. By now his strength was spent, and after resting for two days in the submarine he agreed to Courtney's suggestion that he let him make the third and final recce.

It was the nearest they came to getting caught. The beach was twenty miles down the east coast, and while Courtney was ashore Willmott paddled off to take depth soundings at another. When he returned four hours later there was no sign of Courtney. The minutes passed and Willmott began to fear that something had gone wrong.

Then out of the dark came the frantic barking of a dog. It was a high, angry snarl warning of an intruder. There was a guard hut close to the water, and Willmott expected at any moment to be picked out by a searchlight and to see tracer arcing towards him. Instead, all he heard was a long, muted whistle. Was it Courtney? Or was it a ruse to lure Willmott in? If he was captured, the entire invasion would be compromised. Yet the outcome would be the same if he left Courtney there. Willmott presumed that it was the commando's presence which was disturbing the animal, and cradling his tommy-gun in the crook of his arm he slowly nosed the canoe right in to the beach.

The whistle sounded again, and then Courtney came floundering loudly through the surf. He was unable to swim, having seized up with cramp after mapping more than half a mile of enemy defences. The dog had followed him much of the way, growling from the other side of the fence. Stroke by stroke, Willmott backed the folbot out to sea, keeping his weapon levelled at the beach all the time, until they could hear the barking no more.

The mission had achieved all of Willmott's ambitions for it. He had acquired vital intelligence and shown that many of the charts on which the planners of CORDITE had relied were wrong. As he put it later: 'There had been natural misgivings at Headquarters about the practicability of this sort of snooping . . . but the venture proved the possibilities.' But when *Triumph* returned to Alexandria they learned that all their efforts had been for nothing. Germany had invaded Greece on 6 April, so Wavell's priority was now to reinforce the mainland. The attack on Rhodes was cancelled.

None the less, it would seem clear that Willmott had demonstrated beyond doubt the value and potential of covert beach reconnaissance. He and Courtney had also shown what could be accomplished by enthusiastic cooperation between the Army and the Navy, and that a few men might by foresight, surprise and daring succeed where a more orthodox approach would not. Yet their reward was to be ignored by those who should have made best use of just such a lesson.

Roger Courtney was awarded the Military Cross for his courage on Rhodes but within three months the Commandos in the Middle East would be disbanded, and by the end of 1941 the SBS in the Mediterranean had been absorbed into other units. Similarly, Nigel Willmott was appointed to the Distinguished Service Order (DSO), but not for another year and a half did his superiors think to make use of his unique experience again. In the meantime he found himself evacuating British troops from other beaches in Greece, and teaching navigation in the desert.

It is a mark of the legendary status that the Commandos have attained in the seventy years since they were founded that so little of what is commonly thought about them is true.

When they were set up in 1940 Britain's fortunes were at a low ebb. After Dunkirk, its armed forces appeared permanently on the defensive, and even the Battle of Britain was a victory won on the back foot. The public was ready to be inspired by any organisation which took the fight to the enemy, and the media was willing to do its bit to raise morale. So was born the image of the commando, dagger between his teeth, striking night after night in a carefully coordinated campaign of sabotage and raiding. By and large, that has remained the heroic picture of them cherished by successive generations.

The reality was considerably more complex. In fact, for much of their wartime existence, the Commandos were regarded by those in charge of military strategy not as a major asset but as a nuisance. Occasionally they were treated by the rest of the Army from whose ranks they originally came, and by the other armed services, with undisguised hostility. As Willmott discovered after CORDITE, this was partly due to the suspicion within the higher ranks of the Staff of anything untried and irregular. The Army is an institution, and a vast one, and it functions most efficiently when running on straight lines. Yet the failure of the Commandos to win greater approval from the High Command was also self-inflicted.

Their early raids were described by their greatest supporter, Winston Churchill, as 'silly fiascos'. But even once fully trained, they endured years of frustration as political in-fighting, the high-handedness of their commanders and resentment at the resources given them led to the cancellation of operation after operation. From July 1940 until June 1941 they carried out just one attack of any significance, and before March 1942 only two more of real importance. So much for 'hitting back'.

Moreover, when they were given an opportunity, the raid often ended in failure or at an almost recklessly high cost in blood if it managed to achieve its aims. Three men out of thirty-four came back from FLIPPER, the attack on Rommel's supposed headquarters. More than two-thirds of those who went to St Nazaire were killed or taken prisoner, while the fledgling Special Service Regiment was annihilated at Tobruk. Four from twelve survived Operation MUSKETOON, two from the original party of twelve returned after ANGLO, and just two of the ten 'Cockleshell Heroes' lived to tell of FRANKTON. The toll on officers was especially high. The five who went on BASALT in the autumn of 1942 won between them a Victoria Cross, the DSO and six Military Crosses (MCs), but none saw the end of the war.

Nor were their successful raids indispensable to Britain's survival. At a strategic level, such exploits were of questionable value, drawing off highly skilled troops who might have been better used elsewhere. Their early operations made for good propaganda, perpetuated by numerous films after the war, but that has led to their effect being overestimated in the years since.

It has also coloured the public perception of the Commandos' role. Their time as coastal raiders was in fact brief. By 1942, they were already being envisaged – when used in large numbers – primarily as assault troops. It was as this spearhead that they were deployed from 1943 on the beaches of Italy and later of Normandy, side by side with the newly formed Royal Marine Commandos, whose adoption of a name and tradition created by the Army at first caused much resentment.

Even in this new role, though, it could be argued that the wrong lessons were drawn about their abilities. Certainly, the Commandos did all that was asked of them as flank guards and amphibious warriors in the push to the Po and the drive to the Rhine. The evidence suggests, however, that they were largely wasted on the tasks they were allocated, and could have done more if handled with greater flexibility and imagination. Pertinently, many of the objectives assigned to the elite Commandos were accomplished as well by ordinary regiments of the line. It was not the Commandos but the 8th Infantry Brigade which supplied the first troops to storm ashore Sword Beach on D-Day.

It was only in the decades after the war that the more important achievements of the Commandos came to be appreciated and acted on. For there is no doubt that the approach of some of them to combat, especially of those ever-smaller units which specialised in raiding, has had a profound effect on the art of war. It is no coincidence that the Parachute Regiment, the SAS and the SBS all sprang directly from the Commandos. Indeed, the very idea of 'special forces', now such a feature of modern warfare, is their legacy.

The particular methods and feats of a few individuals on a handful of occasions have often been taken to stand for the tactics and deeds of the Commandos as a whole. That was not the case. One of the aims of this book is to reveal the wide variety of commandos' experiences, and the diversity of formations the term encompassed. Some commandos, for example, saw very little fighting. For many, it came in intense bursts rather than as the prolonged slog endured by regular soldiers. Perhaps the most famous Commando leader, Lord Lovat, spent about a week on the front line in the course of the war, the great majority of it – until he was severely wounded – in the period after D-Day.

The soldier's job is to win battles. That of the historian, seated safely at his or her desk, is to set the record straight. No one's memory is honoured by the repetition of myths or by the sensationalising of events in which men lost their lives. To show that things sometimes go wrong, however, is not to denigrate the courage of those who served in the Commandos, nor to overlook the pride with which they wore the green beret. Those virtues were common to all commandos, as was a shared ethos of self-belief and self-reliance that frequently allowed them to wield influence in war far out of proportion to their number. That standard military training now aims to instil in every recruit those Commando qualities, and often by using the techniques they first developed, is the most enduring tribute to the reputation they won for themselves during the Second World War.

Many books have already been written about the Commandos. Most concentrate on a particular unit or operation, or just on the original Army Commandos and not on their comrades (as they were from 1942) in the Marines. Meanwhile, the previous general histories, largely written by an earlier generation, tend to favour the wider military context over the viewpoint of the individual soldier.

This book is, I think, the first to try to tell the full story of the Commandos in the words of those who were there, and to do so by focusing on the most important or representative of their missions. It is written for a wide readership rather than for the scholar, but I hope that even those who already know something about the Commandos will find in it much that is new to them.

Among the little-known and first-hand accounts in the archives on which I have drawn is that of Gerald Montanaro's waterborne raid on Boulogne harbour – Operation JV – which pre-dated 'Blondie' Hasler's overly bold attack on Bordeaux by nine months. There are also insights from the only other survivor of FRANKTON, Bill Sparks, and reminiscences by Tommy Langton of his epic walk to safety after the debacle of AGREEMENT, when commandos dressed as German soldiers tried to seize Tobruk.

Other chapters include new material on the extraordinary

assassination of a German commandant in Yugoslavia by a commando disguised as a shepherd, and the even more remarkable assignment he was then given personally by Field Marshal Alexander. The tensions behind the façade of unity maintained by two of the Commandos' leaders, Lord Lovat and Robert Laycock, are laid bare in their private letters, while one written by a prisoner-of-war sheds light on the fate of two officers executed in a concentration camp on Hitler's orders. Another chance find means that the suspected treachery of a member of 62 Commando (the Small-Scale Raiding Force), who became an agent for the Gestapo, can now be revealed.

Above all, this is a book about the impact of war on men, and the impact they had on war. The Second World War continues to fascinate us because we wonder how we would cope if we faced such a test. These are the stories of those who did so for real.

1

AMBASSADOR

5 June 1940 was a fine summer evening, but the cloudless skies did little to dispel the gloom in the War Office. From a corner room on its second floor, the head of the British Army was looking thoughtfully up Whitehall to Trafalgar Square. Barrage balloons rode above Nelson's Column and over the road a stream of government messengers hastened in and out of the Admiralty. He watched the scene for a minute or two and then turned to the officer sitting on the other side of his desk. 'We must', he said, 'find a way to help the Army exercise its offensive spirit again.'

Twenty-four hours earlier, the nation had heard its prime minister, Winston Churchill, give Parliament the news of the Army's retreat from France. He had promised that Britain would never surrender, but there were many who did not share his optimism. Returning home that night from the War Office, Lieutenant Colonel Dudley Clarke began to ask himself what other countries had done in the past when their main force had been driven from the field. By the time he reached his flat on Piccadilly he had his answer. For a career soldier, Clarke was unusual in being something of an intellectual. He was less interested in hunting and shooting than he was in books and music. He had a sharp mind and an imaginative streak that ran in the family; his brother later wrote many of the Ealing film comedies.

While he had been walking through the West End, Clarke had been thinking about South Africa's history. He had been born there during the Boer War, and he remembered how after their armies had been defeated the settlers had formed small bands of horsemen who for two years had harried and eluded a British force ten times their number. The Boers' word for them was 'Kommando'.

On one side of a sheet of writing paper Clarke jotted down his idea. 'With the resources we have,' he wrote, 'there seem enormous possibilities of creating untold havoc among enemy air bases and communications if we resort to guerrilla warfare on a big scale.' Perhaps the Kommandos could be reborn under another flag.

Like Roger Courtney, Clarke had seen irregular warfare at first hand in Palestine, where he had served as a staff officer under Sir John Dill. When Churchill appointed Dill as the new Chief of the Imperial General Staff at the end of May 1940, Clarke went with him to the War Office. Every commander of an army needs an aide who knows how his mind works, and even as Dill was looking across the rooftops of Whitehall Clarke was pulling the sheet of writing paper from his pocket.

Dill was immediately enthusiastic. He told Clarke to expand his notes into a briefing paper which he could take to the Cabinet meeting the next morning. By lunchtime, the plan was approved, and that afternoon Clarke found himself in charge of all raiding operations, with orders to strike at German positions across the Channel as soon as possible. The Commandos had been transformed from a historical memory into Britain's newest weapon in less than forty-eight hours.

The uncharacteristic speed with which the wheels of government had turned owed everything to one fact: Churchill had been brooding on exactly the same problem. 'The completely defensive habit of mind, which has ruined the French, must not be allowed to ruin all our initiative,' he wrote to his principal military adviser, Major General Hastings Ismay, on 3 June. 'How wonderful it would be if the Germans could be made to wonder where they were going to be struck next instead of forcing us to try to wall in the island.'

Churchill understood how vital it was to raise both military and civilian morale quickly after the shock of Dunkirk, and two days later he urged the matter again on Ismay: 'We have got to get out of our minds the idea that the Channel ports and all the country between them are enemy territory. They must become no man's land. Enterprises must be prepared,' he insisted, 'with specially trained troops of the hunter class who can develop a reign of terror down these coasts ... The passive resistance war, which we have acquitted ourselves so well in, must come to an end.' That same evening, Clarke echoed those thoughts to Dill, and Churchill at once gave the Commandos his approval. He had, after all, seen at close range how effective they had been in their original incarnation when a war correspondent in South Africa.

Yet, encouraging though it was to have Churchill's backing, Clarke was being asked to do much more than just form a new unit. In its four-hundred-year history, the British Army had never incorporated a permanent body of irregular troops; and if he was to succeed, Clarke would also have to change the military mindset. There had been rare examples of commanders conducting guerrilla campaigns, such as T.E. Lawrence in Arabia and Orde Wingate during the troubles in Palestine, but both had made use of local and largely unprofessional forces. Even the Boers had been defeated eventually, and their example had had no impact on the training and tactics prescribed by the General Staff.

During the First World War, all three armed services had famously combined to mount just such a raid as Churchill now envisaged. Eight Victoria Crosses were won in the attack on the Belgian port of Zeebrugge, which the Germans were using as a U-boat base, but in the years since then little attention had been paid to developing a doctrine of amphibious operations. Air power was the coming thing, and the assumption was that it would make landing troops directly from ships (as was the standard method for waterborne assaults) almost impossible.

Only late in the 1930s had the War Office set up a department to study ungentlemanly warfare. It was staffed by just two officers,

Colin Gubbins and J.F.C. Holland, both veterans of the strife in Ireland and sharing a common interest in subversion. At their suggestion, in the spring of 1940 volunteers from the Territorial Army had been formed into ten 'Independent Companies' tasked with sabotaging the enemy's lines of communication. Under Gubbins, some had taken part in the fighting in Norway, yet in a portent of things to come they had been used by the generals not in their intended role but as an infantry reserve.

None the less, the Independent Companies were the most obvious remedy for Dudley Clarke's first headache. Dill had made it clear that, with an invasion expected at any moment, no existing unit was to be diverted from defensive duties to provide recruits for the Commandos. Five Independent Companies, however, were merely doing garrison duty in Scotland, so Clarke told two of their COs to pick a hundred men and bring them south for a raid in a fortnight's time.

Meanwhile, Clarke got on with planning it. He decided that the chances of keeping it quiet would improve if he did not hold meetings at the War Office. Accordingly, he based himself at the Belgravia home of the former ambassador in Berlin, Sir Horace Rumbold. Sworn to secrecy, Sir Horace's butler gamely answered the door to a series of beefy men ill at ease in civilian clothes who told him that they had come about the 'Charity Committee'.

The minutes of the meetings were kept by Rumbold's daughter Constantia. Other members of the team were also recruited out of Clarke's own address book rather than from the civil service. Marian Marling, known as 'Buster', was a relation of a friend of Clarke, and put herself and her car at his disposal. Joan Bright, a girlfriend of Ian Fleming and afterwards a key figure in Churchill's administrative staff, came over from Intelligence to organise the filing cabinets. As liaison officer between his department – now christened MO9 – and the Commandos themselves, Clarke settled on the debonair form of David Niven, who had held an Army commission before becoming a film star.

The creation of this little empire did not go unnoticed in

Whitehall. The higher echelons of the War Office had squirmed in their seats when Clarke unveiled his radical plans for the Commandos to live out of barracks and to draw weapons from a central store as needed. Eyebrows were raised even at the use of a Boer term for their name. Within a week of Clarke's appointment, the service ministries moved to reassert their control over what they regarded as their own resources.

Anthony Eden, the Secretary of State for War, wrote to Churchill emphasising the War Office's need – or at least desire – to coordinate all aspects of irregular warfare. The same day, Clarke learned that responsibility for directing raids was to be handed to a senior officer, Lieutenant General Alan Bourne, the Adjutant-General of the Royal Marines. He was to report to the Chiefs of Staff and the Prime Minister and head a combined staff from all three services, to be housed in the Admiralty.

Clarke's position in this new set-up appeared uncertain. He was reassured by Bourne that for the time being he would concentrate on securing help and facilities from the ministries, while Clarke looked after policy and continued to organise the first raid. But Clarke could see trouble ahead. If the Commandos fulfilled their potential, the Chiefs of Staff would find that in Bourne's organisation they had created a rival to their own power, and one with the Prime Minister's ear.

Churchill had talked in terms of turning five thousand soldiers into commandos, with ships at their disposal night and day. Neither the War Office nor the Admiralty would relish losing such a quantity of men and equipment when they were already hard-pressed to meet demands on other fronts. Dunkirk had left them with even larger shortfalls. It seemed most unlikely that they would give the Prime Minister's new venture their enthusiastic cooperation. For the moment, however, Clarke kept his reservations to himself and turned his attention to a map of the French coast.

In the first flush of excitement at Clarke's scheme, the War Office had turned its own mind to the question of how to find recruits for the Commandos. On 9 June, a letter went out to each of the Army's regional Home Commands, asking them to collect the names of officers who could raise volunteers for a new unit 'specialising in tip and run tactics'. The officers were to have personality, tactical ability and imagination. A few days later the letter reached the desk of the adjutant of the 23rd Medium and Heavy Training Regiment of the Royal Artillery.

John Durnford-Slater had been in the Army for a decade, but while he had enjoyed life with it in exotic India, garrison duties back in Britain had bored him. He had planned to resign his commission until the Munich Crisis in 1938. War seemed inevitable to him afterwards and he had decided to stay in. Sturdily made, energetic and red-headed, with a rather high and breathless voice which others mimicked behind his back, he was eager to have a taste of real soldiering. 'I was tired of training men for action,' he said later, 'I wanted action for myself.'

He applied for the job of raising a Commando unit, wrote his own recommendation, had an interview at the War Office, and on 28 June received a telegram promoting him from captain to lieutenant colonel at the age of just thirty. He was to lead 3 Commando, the first to be formed, making him – as he proudly recalled – the first commando.

From the start, the Commandos were not organised into the standard formations of battalions and regiments. Each Commando would consist of five hundred men – less than the strength of a regular battalion – divided into ten troops. Since they were to operate in small groups there would be a higher proportion than usual of junior officers. It was a measure of Durnford-Slater's vigour that within a week he had interviewed dozens of candidates in headquarters towns across Southern Command and chosen the thirty-five he needed.

'What I was seeking and what I obtained', he wrote later, 'were men of character beyond normal.' Mental and physical toughness was important, but he prized keenness over sheer size. He also looked for cheerfulness and confidence. All would help build the spirit which would enable soldiers to overcome difficulties and danger.

That it was left to Commando COs to choose their own officers, rather than the Army doing so, set the tone for the new force. Much that was to be unique about it stemmed from that one peculiarity, born largely of the haste with which the organisation was created. It made it as much a club as a military unit. Above all, the pride taken by men and officers alike in having been picked to join them gave the Commandos immediate *esprit de corps*.

One of the first young officers chosen by Durnford-Slater was John Smale. The son of a well-to-do farmer, he had shown more enthusiasm for the rugby pitch than for his lessons while at Haileybury, and in 1936 he had joined the Lancashire Fusiliers. His battalion had fought three engagements in the retreat from Brussels to the beaches at Dunkirk, where he had been confronted by the sight of a general having a breakdown and asking him why he wasn't wearing a hat.

When he returned to Britain, he realised that it might be another two years before recruits were trained to replace those killed in France and the battalion went to war again. He was twenty-four, and full of self-confidence despite his recent experiences. 'We'd fought the Germans and felt we were just as good as them,' he said years later. 'The feeling was among those who had come back that we wanted another go at them . . . So when the offer of joining the Commandos cropped up, I jumped at it.'

Durnford-Slater told him that the officers were in turn to select their own men from volunteers, and sent him to make the rounds of the 4th Infantry Division with another second lieutenant and Dunkirk veteran named Peter Young. Neither had any qualms about the guerrilla methods that the Commandos were to use. 'You would be attacking German soldiers, and it was their job to defend themselves, it was fair play,' thought Smale. Young would take to raiding with such zest that by 1945 he would be a brigadier with a DSO and three MCs.

'We chose a number of what you would call old soldiers, fully trained infantrymen,' recalled Smale of their recruiting process.

> In addition, quite a number of younger chaps who had been called up, young businessmen mostly. They were a very different type in that from the weapon-training point of view they didn't compare, but on the other hand they were young, fit and probably had more flexible minds . . . We hoped they would be quicker thinkers in an emergency.
>
> We also enlisted quite a lot of Artillery men and those from the Tank Corps . . . a smattering of Royal Engineers who were trained in explosives, and quite a number from the Royal Army Service Corps who were trained in vehicles. We were a hotch-potch lot. When you saw us on parade we all wore our own head dress. We didn't have the green beret yet so, what with a few tam o'shanters, we were a pretty mixed bunch to look at.

Those who had been picked were told to report to Durnford-Slater at Plymouth and on 8 July, just over a week into its existence, 3 Commando held its first training exercise. It consisted of rowing a small boat borrowed from the Navy round and round the harbour. It was hardly a dashing entrance into the war, but it was a start.

The first Commando raid, however, was not to be carried out by the Commandos. Quick off the mark as Durnford-Slater was, Churchill's impatience for an early sortie meant that this had already taken place four days before 3 Commando came into being. The troops involved were the 115 men of the Independent Companies summoned from Scotland by Clarke.

Led by Major Ronnie Tod, they were divided into four groups and carried across the Channel in RAF air–sea rescue launches from Dover, Folkestone and Newhaven. They reached France in the early hours of 24 June and were put ashore at four spots near Boulogne.

One of the officers in the party that landed at Le Touquet was Ronnie Swayne. A rugby Blue at Oxford, he had joined No. 9 Independent Company from the Herefordshire Regiment. They had been briefed to go to Norway, but had merely got as far as embarking on a ship to take them there.

The main aim of the night's raid was to capture prisoners. Swayne's target was the Merlimont Plage Hotel, which it was thought was being used as a barracks. But from the start things went wrong. They arrived at their beach late, when the short summer night was already ending. Swayne managed to locate the hotel, only to find that it was empty and – since the doors and windows were boarded up – had apparently been so for some time.

Having 'wandered around a bit, looking for Germans', he decided that as time was running out they should head back to the crash boat. Except that at the beach there was no sign of it. 'The boat was hanging around off shore,' he recalled, 'and we couldn't make contact with it.' It was at this point that two German sentries stumbled on them.

Swayne levelled his revolver at close range and pulled the trigger twice. Nothing happened, and it was then that he remembered that he had forgotten to load it. He grappled with one of the soldiers and hit him on the head with the butt of his gun, while his batman bayoneted the other.

As it turned out, Swayne's carelessness proved to be a stroke of luck. The Germans had been killed silently, whereas shots would have alerted a larger patrol soon seen making its way across the dunes. By then, Swayne had lost his patience and swum out to the launch. His temper was not improved by the water which filled his baggy breeches and made the boat seem further out still.

When he reached it, he abruptly informed the naval officer in charge that he was being demoted, replaced him with the coxswain, and took the vessel in to pick up the rest of his soldiers. Most of their weapons, however, had to be left behind. 'We got everybody off, but it was a rather amateurish affair,' he admitted.

Two of the other three groups had not done any better. One had got several hundred yards inland without encountering opposition and had then come home. The second had tried to sabotage a seaplane anchorage, but their boat had almost been swamped by an aircraft taking off. The last group was commanded by Tod himself, accompanied by Dudley Clarke. Tod had invited him along at the final meeting of the 'Charity Committee'. Clarke knew perfectly well that members of the War Office staff had no business blacking up their faces and creeping up on German guard posts, but he convinced himself that MO9 ought to send an observer with the raid. He was thrilled when Bourne gave him permission to go, providing he stayed in the boat.

Everything remained calm ashore at Stella Plage until Tod came back to report that so far he had found nothing. At that moment, a German bicycle patrol came riding silently along the water's edge, where the sand was firmest, and so slipped unnoticed past Tod's lookouts. Tod himself did spot the patrol, however, and he was unable to resist such a tempting target. Snatching up his new tommy-gun, he brought it to bear on the cyclists but he had never used the weapon before and in cocking it dislodged the magazine. It fell noisily to the ground, the Germans opened fire, and Clarke was knocked out by a violent blow to the side of his head.

When he came round, the firing had stopped. He could feel an acute pain in his hip and it took him a while to realise this was just the result of having crushed his silver cigarette case as he fell on the deck. In the meantime, Tod had gone to find the rest of his men in case the Germans returned in strength, and a long half-hour later Clarke saw shadowy figures wading quietly out towards the boat. Closer and closer they came, with bayonets fixed, until Clarke suddenly wondered with horror if they were his own troops.

'Give the password!' he croaked. His voice was so tense that he did not recognise it as his own. The nearest figure halted a few yards away, but the answer he gave was quite incomprehensible. For a minute they remained rooted to the spot, each as frightened as the other, until Clarke heard an NCO say his name and the strain was broken.

As dawn broke, Clarke saw the others in the boat looking at him with worried faces, and found to his shock that his head and coat were caked in blood. A bullet had almost severed his ear. The near loss of the Commandos' founder was by far the most notable event of a dismal night.

Operation COLLAR, as the raid was called, had been a complete failure. No intelligence had been gathered, no prisoners captured, and no damage done to the German forces except for the sentries killed by Swayne. Even then, he had neglected to take their identity papers, and an attempt to tow the bodies back to England had ended in rather grim farce when they were lost in mid-Channel.

Naturally, none of this was revealed in the bland press release put out the following day by the Ministry of Information. The spin it gave to 'successful reconnaissances of the enemy coastline' was seized on by newspapers eager for positive news. 'The point is', trumpeted a leader in *The Times*, 'that this incident shows the offensive spirit, which is exactly what the public wants.' Churchill had certainly judged the popular mood correctly.

The lesson was not lost on Clarke. 'Publicity will play a very big part in exploiting the moral value of a raid,' he observed later in some notes on how to plan them. 'Good publicity may easily extract a great deal of moral effect from a raid which achieved few concrete military results – in fact, the less achieved, the more important to boost it! On the other hand,' he urged, 'the moral effect of one fiasco will outweigh that of several successful raids.' It was sound advice, but it would be a long time before it was taken to heart.

As 3 Commando began to assemble in early July, Durnford-Slater was briefed on its first operation by Niven, who to his surprise proved to have none of the showy manner of a film star. AMBASSADOR would take place in just a week's time. Despite the evidence from Boulogne, the frame of mind at the top was still one of hurry – of being seen to do something – rather than of prudence. Tod's troops were to be handed the chance to redeem themselves, together with forty of the new commandos.

The target was Guernsey, which had been occupied by the Germans on 4 July. It was thought that the aerodrome at Le Bourg might be used as a base by the Luftwaffe, and the raiders were to prevent this by destroying its underground fuel tanks. An officer originally from the island had been landed by submarine and cleverly learned from the baker who supplied the German garrison that it numbered 469 soldiers. Most were based in the capital, St Peter Port, from where reinforcements could reach any part of Guernsey within twenty minutes.

Durnford-Slater decided to take with him H Troop, as it contained many regulars who had fought in France, including Joe Smale and Peter Young. On the evening of 14 July, the commandos boarded buses for Dartmouth and there embarked on the destroyers *Saladin* and *Scimitar*. Durnford-Slater was still recovering from shock as he made his way up the gangway. A few minutes earlier he had learned that his men had asked untrained fifteen-year-old naval cadets to help load the magazines of the Troop's few precious Bren guns. 'We were completely raw,' recalled Smale, but they were not the only ones.

The commandos' role in the operation was to provide a diversion. They would land on the Jerbourg Peninsula in the south of Guernsey while the Independent Companies came ashore near the airfield and attacked it. As they neared the island, Tod's one hundred men disembarked into RAF crash boats which had been towed behind the destroyers and headed in two groups for their beaches.

None arrived. Some of the craft developed engine problems, others became swamped even before they set off. In one of them was Ronnie Swayne, who found himself being constantly transferred between a series of boats as each began to fail. By dawn, he was sitting in a launch with water up to its gunnels. Fortunately, they were spotted by their destroyer and picked up.

'We weren't remotely ready,' he concluded. 'We didn't know what kind of boats we wanted, we didn't know how to do it, and there wasn't a proper planning body to prepare for these raids. In any case, there was a fearful shortage of weapons.'

One group had gone right off course. After sailing east for several hours, they came to an island which they assumed must be their destination, but its landmarks did not agree with their map. In fact, it was Sark; they had missed Guernsey altogether. Only afterwards did the Navy realise that the electric field of degaussing coils newly installed in boats to counter magnetic mines was interfering with the compasses.

Oblivious to the shambles taking place out to sea, Durnford-Slater ordered his men to scramble down the nets into their launches at twenty minutes past midnight. There was no moon and the water in Telegraph Bay was calm. The boats sped towards land, but the first sign that things might go wrong came when they grounded not on smooth sand, as predicted, but on rock some way out from the beach.

Undaunted, Durnford-Slater set an example by leaping briskly over the side. He found himself chest deep in water, at which point a wave hit him from behind and knocked him over. He came up spluttering and soaking, as did everyone else. All of their weapons had received a dunking, too. Standing on the shore, with the sea flooding out of his battledress, he saw ahead of him a flight of steps which led to the top of the cliffs. He set off at a fast run, but there turned out to be 250 of them and he was soon exhausted. Behind him he could hear the squelch of wet boots plodding up the steps rather more slowly.

The Troop then divided in two. Durnford-Slater headed along a path towards a machine-gun post and the German barracks. Smale's job was to set up a roadblock to stop reinforcements from arriving. 'There was a bungalow at the top of the cliffs so we thought we'd better have a look.' His Troop's commander, Vivian de Crespigny, broke down the door, but when he began to question the only person inside, an old man, all he got from him was a piercing series of shrieks. 'De Crespigny said he was mad,' remembered Smale. 'He wasn't mad, he was just scared completely out of his wits, poor chap. De Crespigny said: "You'd better lock him up in case he bolts." So we locked him in the lavatory, and there he stayed.'

Meanwhile, Durnford-Slater was creeping up on the gun emplacement. He sent another officer, Johnny Giles, around the back and readied his pistol. Jumping over the sandbags, he found himself looking down the barrel of Giles's tommy-gun. The post was empty, and de Crespigny soon found that the 'barracks' contained no Germans either.

Back at the road, Smale had made a makeshift barricade from the bungalow's rockery. They had brought a roll of barbed wire with them for this purpose, but it had proved too heavy to carry up the steps. His sentries then reported that there was someone coming along the path. Smale had been told to presume it would be the enemy and he should shoot first without challenging. He decided instead to shout out the password – 'Desmond!' – and discovered that it was Giles, coming to say that it was time to get back to the boats.

Durnford-Slater was surprised not to have heard any explosions from the direction of the airfield, and disappointed not to have encountered any Germans. None the less, he knew that the destroyers were under orders to leave them behind if they failed to make the rendezvous at 0300. He herded his men down the steps, but then lost his own footing and tumbled head over heels to the bottom, dropping his cocked Webley. The gun went off with a shattering noise, finally waking a nearby German position which started to fire tracer wildly out to sea.

Down on the beach, there was a decided air of anticlimax. This changed to alarm, however, when it was realised that the crash boats were unwilling to come in and risk the rocks that were now covered by the risen tide. The commandos would have to swim for it.

Three of the men now chose this moment to admit that they did not know how to. 'We'd done a swimming test at Plymouth,' recalled Smale, 'but they must have got someone to do it for them and give in their names. One of them I knew quite well, Corporal Dumper of the East Surreys.' Struggling to contain his anger, Durnford-Slater told them to go and hide themselves and he would arrange for a submarine to pick them up the next evening. 'Well, I'm not sweating on it, sir,' said Dumper with a shrug of resignation.

All the weapons were piled into a dinghy, which began to make trips between the beach and the boats. But on its fifth journey it capsized in the heavy surf and the guns were lost. There was now nothing for it but to swim the hundred yards out to the launches. Durnford-Slater went first, doing his best to hold his silver hip flask and cigarette case above the waves. But the sea was much rougher now, and though Durnford-Slater was impressed by his troops' discipline, many of them quickly became exhausted. Joe Smale was a strong swimmer but found his grenades weighed him down, and as he reached the boat he began to founder. 'I sank twice and the third time panicked,' he said later. 'I thought: "Well, I won't come up this time," so I shouted, "For Christ's sake, get me out!" And a naval officer jumped in fully clothed and pulled me out. He saved my life.'

All the other men reached the boats safely, although to his annoyance Durnford-Slater let slip his flask and case as he was being hauled aboard. His watch had stopped working and he was appalled to discover that it was half past three. Assuming that the destroyers would already have sailed, he flashed a torch towards the appointed meeting place, and was relieved to see *Saladin* reply. Dawn was fast approaching, but despite the danger this brought of air attack, the captain had decided to make one final search for the launches.

Sitting around in the hats and football jerseys used to clothe the survivors of shipwrecks, the veterans of AMBASSADOR grinned sheepishly at one another. The raid had been a 'ridiculous, almost comic failure', admitted Durnford-Slater, and he and Tod resolved to learn from their mistakes. Joe Smale accepted that 'if that garrison had been there . . . we would have been massacred', though he blamed the Navy and the planners for the cock-ups. He had found the experience 'thrilling but very frightening, mainly because you didn't know what was going to happen'. He was still too young to appreciate that his exploits might provoke the same emotion in others: 'Durnford-Slater took the attitude that we might as well be on leave, and I was home within a day. Mother asked me in the dining room what I'd been up to and I said, well, I'd been in Guernsey last night. The horror on her face!'

Churchill's reaction to the raid was sheer rage. The first he knew of it was when other ministers came to a Cabinet meeting saying they had read about the operation in the evening paper. His initial response was to demand that the officer responsible for having staged it lose his commission, until Eden said that he thought it rather a good show.

Nevertheless, Churchill remained dissatisfied with MO9's work so far. 'It would be most unwise to disturb the coasts of any of these countries by the kind of silly fiascos which were perpetrated at Boulogne and Guernsey,' he told Eden the following week. 'The idea of working all these coasts up against us by pin-prick raids and fulsome communiqués is one to be strictly avoided.'

The Prime Minister's anger was understandable enough, but it was not entirely justified. At least in part it stemmed from the different conception that he and Clarke had of the Commandos. From his conversations with Alan Bourne, the new Director of Raiding Operations, it seems that from the start Churchill wanted the attacks to be conducted in great strength. He urged Bourne, for instance, to seize Calais and hold it for twenty-four hours, and to Eden indicated that he wanted to see raids involving up to ten thousand men.

Clarke had always thought in much smaller terms. In any case, he was restricted by the resources that the Army and – crucially – the Navy were willing to make available when they were already overstretched. Not for the only time in the war, Churchill's vision was at odds with what could actually be done. But the failure of AMBASSADOR, and his continued personal interest in the Commandos, was to have far-reaching consequences for them.

The events on Guernsey may have helped to confirm his instinct that subversion abroad should be directed by other hands. On 17 July, the Special Operations Executive (SOE) was formed and told to 'set Europe ablaze', with Colin Gubbins as its deputy chief. Its remit was in theory different from that of the Commandos, since its agents would operate for much longer periods behind enemy lines. But as the war went on, the two organisations came regularly into conflict, often competing for the same resources and targets.

Churchill had also decided that the scholarly looking Bourne lacked the experience, and the aggression, needed to forge the Commandos into the strike force that he wanted them to be. Instead, he turned to an old friend.

He was irritated not to have been consulted about Bourne's appointment, and as early as 7 July told Eden: 'My own judgement turns strongly on Sir Roger Keyes.' The admiral was known throughout Britain as the hero of the Zeebrugge raid, which he had planned and led in 1918. Yet he was now approaching seventy, and within the Navy he had a reputation for demanding his own way rather than listening to the opinions of others. Churchill saw him as a man who made things happen, and Keyes agreed. Bourne was persuaded to stay on as his deputy at the new Combined Operations Headquarters, but Clarke and MO9 were finished. In late 1940, he was sent out to Cairo with the task of deceiving the Germans about the strength of British forces and their strategy in North Africa.

For the Commandos he had left behind there was to be no such fun. Only long months of hard work lay ahead.

2

EXPORTER

For forty days and forty nights the two commandos had evaded capture in the wilderness of the Libyan desert. Tomorrow would be Christmas Day, 1941. A few hours earlier they had spotted troops they believed to be British. When dawn came, they would try to get close to them without being seen and confirm their identity.

Both were too excited to sleep. Despite their very different backgrounds, they had got on well enough throughout their ordeal. Rank and class had meant little when hunger had driven them to dig up the entrails of a goat previously rejected as inedible even before they had rotted. Yet regaining the safety of their own lines held rather different prospects for each man. The sergeant would return to a world where he had proved himself an exceptionally reliable soldier but where he took orders from those who were not. At least, however, he would not have to listen any longer to the officer passing the time by reading out loud to him. They had just one book with them – *The Wind in the Willows*. His commander, meanwhile, would have much explaining to do. Not only had their mission ended in catastrophe, but the two-thousand-strong force he had led a mere six months earlier had been reduced to two men sharing a tattered blanket borrowed from a Bedouin. Professional ruin and personal humiliation were staring him full in the face. It was not the destiny he had seen for himself when he had sought so eagerly to join the Commandos.

From birth, Robert Laycock had been expected to succeed and had enjoyed every advantage to help him do so. His father Joe, who had won the DSO in the Boer War and was a renowned sportsman, had superb social connections. He had travelled back from South Africa in 1900 with Churchill, and for many years had been the lover of the Countess of Warwick, also mistress to Edward VII. When his son came to marry, it was to one of the daughters of Freda Dudley Ward, who had a lengthy affair with the future Edward VIII in the 1920s. After Eton and Sandhurst, Bob Laycock had joined the Royal Horse Guards in 1927 and by September 1939 he was working at the War Office. A few minutes after learning that war had been declared, he was summoned to a meeting about anti-aircraft defences and told that the Germans were expected to launch an immediate aerial offensive. At that very moment the wail of the air-raid siren floated through the window.

'In accordance with strict regulations we all trooped sheepishly down to the shelters in the shored-up, air-conditioned sub-basement,' he wrote later. 'There was a certain amount of banging going on overhead and a few of the more senior officers who had served in the 1914–18 war were heard to observe, rather over heartily, that it was exhilarating to hear the sound of gunfire again. We found out later that the noise was made by workmen busy strengthening the floors above us.'

Laycock would come to be characterised by some who served with him as no brighter than those officers in the shelter, a 'society cavalryman'. But he was far more able than that term implied. He certainly carried himself with all the nonchalant assurance of a school prefect, yet few others who did so during the war were reading Bertrand Russell's *Introduction to Mathematical Philosophy*. Staff officers with an interest in the sciences were rare in the Army, and by mid-1940 Laycock found himself designated an expert on chemical warfare and bound for Headquarters in Cairo.

For most soldiers such a posting would have represented another step up the ladder. But for Laycock it was a dead end. At thirty-three, he had the vision, energy and ambition to make his name if given the right opportunity, and that would mean seeing action. With the possibilities of that limited after Dunkirk, he set his heart on being chosen to command one of the ten new Commandos. He was rebuffed.

Dudley Clarke had been keen to have Laycock, but the stumbling block was the War Office. GHQ Middle East needed an anti-gas staff officer and Laycock was to proceed to Egypt as ordered. However, it was now that his contacts came into play. His friend David Niven urged that he be given another chance, and Clarke agreed, providing Laycock somehow found a substitute for his staff job. Within two days he had done so and begun to raise 8 Commando; within three years he would be the youngest major general in the Army.

The legend is that Laycock recruited his junior officers at the bar of his club, White's. In fact they were sifted from those who volunteered, but the application forms do reveal that he was not looking to cast his net wide. Laycock was not searching for supermen but for those in whom he could put his trust, and often that equated to those in his social circle. The first qualification that candidates were asked about was whether they rode. Of course, many officers did, but the question perhaps indicated more about the conventional mindset that still prevailed at MO9 than it did about the abilities that would be needed by commandos.

Among those who were successful were Robin Campbell, the son of an ambassador, an ex-Reuters journalist and judged 'a very good type'. He was soon joined in Laycock's unit by Earl Jellicoe, Viscount Milton, the Lords Sudeley and Stavordale, a pair of heirs to press empires – Gavin Astor and Julian Berry – and the Prime Minister's son, Randolph. Laycock had taken the latter as a favour to Churchill, while his own wife Angie had spent the early months of the war staying in Hampshire with Berry's family, the owners of the *Daily Telegraph*. A third of 8 Commando's thirty-four officers were, like Laycock, Etonians.

Those whom they were to command underwent a more stringent initial selection process. Much could be taught to them, but some qualities needed to be inherent. Few had experienced combat yet, but a desire to take on the Germans was one attribute for which officers looked. More important, however, was the capacity to make decisions without being told what to do, unusual in an Army where soldiers had everything organised for them. Even before Laycock met one group of Scots Guardsmen they were being thinned out by their own CO. 'No drive', 'not sufficiently quick or intelligent' and 'not tough enough' were his candid assessments.

By contrast, Jimmy Sherwood had the adventurous spirit that Roger Courtney – 'white hunter', noted Laycock, 'extremely hard and fit' – wanted to see. While working as an office boy in a flour factory, Sherwood had dreamed of joining the RAF. Having failed the eye test, he found himself instead driving lorries for the Royal Army Service Corps. Courtney was already thinking how he could make use of his folbot and was interested to learn that Sherwood had done some canoeing as a young man in Ireland. He sent him up to Inveraray, on Loch Fyne, where 8 Commando was mustering.

Such was the freedom given Commando leaders at first that they were allowed not only to hand-pick their recruits but also to train them according to their own ideas. There were no manuals for the new commanding officers to follow, nor did they all agree on the best ways to achieve results. Nevertheless, as Sherwood quickly discovered, a high degree of physical fitness was thought to serve a number of purposes. Soon after arriving the men were formed up wearing all their combat kit, including rifles, steel helmets and respirators. Randolph Churchill, looking fat and unfit, took his place at the head of the column and then 'we belted out along the road northwards by the loch, going hell for leather'. They marched for an hour, rested for ten minutes, then turned back again. It was the return trip that seared itself into Sherwood's memory.

'It was absolute agony,' he recalled, having done little marching in boots during his time as a driver. 'We were almost doubled up, and I just about managed to hobble back to camp.' To the surprise of many, so did Randolph, sweating profusely and shouting at the men to pick up their step: 'He was told to bugger off . . . Only afterwards did it dawn on us what the point was, to weed out those who could stick it – or make themselves stick it.' Those who had had enough were not disciplined, just 'returned to their units'. RTU was to become the main tool used to mould the commando, and a mark of shame that most volunteers would do their utmost to avoid bearing.

Laycock told his troop leaders that the men were to adopt 'the lightning, destructive and ruthless methods of the gangster'. Above all, they were to practise moving silently at night, developing as raiders unencumbered by heavy weapons the advantage that 'the burglar possesses over the unsuspecting householder'. Yet he still laid great emphasis on drill, smart turnout and good discipline, without which he thought the unit would deteriorate into a rabble.

Despite such strictures, when Evelyn Waugh joined No. 8 from the 'austerity and formality' of the Royal Marines, he was surprised at the country house ways which Laycock had allowed to prevail in the officers' mess.

'I found a young troop leader wearing a military tunic and corduroy trousers,' he wrote. 'He was reclining with a white Pekingese in his lap, a large cigar in his mouth and a large glass of Grande Marnier in his hand.'

The officer had won an MC, so Laycock's smart friends did not lack courage, but other COs were more obviously imaginative in their choice of recruits and methods. 3 Commando had also moved to the west coast of Scotland, basing themselves in the seaside town of Largs. There Durnford-Slater opened up 'a completely new world of training', thought Joe Smale. Looking back, he saw how restricted had been the curriculum in his infantry battalion. 'Now we learned cliff climbing, which we'd never heard of before. We learned crossing wire obstacles, and street-fighting – which I'd never come across in the peacetime Army.'

Meanwhile, Durnford-Slater ruthlessly disposed of those not up to the mark, including one fantasist who boasted of having shot

German officers in a raid on the casino at Le Touquet: 'He hadn't, nor had anybody else.'

'We were gradually pulling together and becoming more professional,' agreed Ronnie Swayne, whose Independent Company had become 1 Commando.

> We got rid of the officers and men who we didn't think up to scratch, either not fit enough or a bit wet, or we just didn't like them. The Commandos tended to be clubs . . . each had its own character.
>
> In mine, there was a lot of very tough discipline. And I think with our Welshmen and boys from the farm it was probably not a bad idea . . . But they weren't badly behaved. They were very good lads who occasionally had a few too many beers on pay night, but they weren't savage thugs at all, just the opposite.

It was precisely this lack of ferocity which concerned Laycock. 'The average Englishman needs mentally toughening for the somewhat drastic actions demanded of Commando soldiers,' he wrote. That could not be done simply by route marches. It called for more specialised knowledge, and unconventional teachers.

The Special Training Centre came into being almost by chance. In April 1940, a sabotage team dispatched to Norway by MI(R) – the subversion department headed by Holland and Gubbins – had been forced to abort their mission when their submarine narrowly survived an attack by a U-boat. Among its members was a Scottish landowner, Bill Stirling. While the party was staying on his estate and awaiting new orders, he suggested that they set up a school to pass on their skills and so give future operations a greater chance of success.

The scheme was approved and a house commandeered at Lochailort, in the rugged and remote Moidart area of the Western Highlands. Many of its instructors were destined to become key figures in the development of irregular warfare. Stirling's brother David – later to found the SAS – taught fieldcraft, as did their cousin Shimi, Lord Lovat. Ian Fleming's brother Peter was in charge of signals, while the future Chindit leader Mike Calvert handled demolitions.

Their first pupils were the Independent Companies, but by the autumn of 1940 they began to accept large groups of commandos for month-long courses. Ghillies took them up on the hill to learn stalking and camouflage, with wary deer standing in for German sentries. There were games of hide and seek, and a competition in which two soldiers had to hunt each other.

Lochailort's resident experts included George Murray Levick, who had been on Scott's expedition to the South Pole and taught survival techniques. 'He tried to make us live on pemmican – a mixture of animal fat and dried meat,' recalled Swayne. 'We all pretended we did, but we used to go off and get a good meal of venison down in the village afterwards.' Murray Levick's aim was to encourage soldiers to 'broaden their outlook' on food when in remote places. 'I knew a man who always cut a hole in the skull of a seal as soon as he shot it and sucked out the nice warm brains,' he told them. 'Young foxes and dogs are quite palatable, but they are improved with Worcester Sauce or Tomato Ketchup.'

Most of his pupils were more taken with the shooting of Olympic marksman Cyril Mackworth-Praed. Soldiers were normally considered up to standard if they got off fifteen shots a minute from their Lee Enfield rifles. Using his third finger on the trigger and his second to work the bolt, Mackworth-Praed could fire thirty, and put them all in or beside the bull's eye of a target three hundred yards away.

Undoubtedly the greatest impression, however, was created by the close-quarter combat team. 'Suddenly at the top of the stairs appeared a couple of dear old gentlemen,' remembered Second Lieutenant Ronald Hall of the Dorset Regiment, who had been sent to do the Lochailort course. 'Both were wearing spectacles, both dressed in battledress. They walked to the top of the stairs, fell, tumbling, tumbling down the stairs and ended up at the bottom, in the battle crouch position, with a handgun in one hand and a fighting knife in the other – a shattering experience for all of us.'

The two 'dear old gentlemen' were William Fairbairn and Eric Sykes, recently returned from China, where they had spent years policing the crime-ridden slums and opium dens of colonial Shanghai. They were now in their late fifties. 'The senior detective', recalled a fellow instructor, Peter Kemp, 'had the manner and appearance of an elderly amiable clergyman, combined with the speed and ferocity of a footpad: lulled by his soft tones and charmed by his benevolent smile, we would be startled to hear him conclude some demonstration with a snarled: "Then you bring up your right knee smartly into his testicles."'

The pair had perfected a system of self-defence that struck many of the commandos as ungentlemanly in the extreme. Like all the training at Lochailort, however, it was intended to prepare them for the reality rather than the theory of war. They were taught how to gouge eyes, break ear drums and slit mouths by jamming their thumbs into the corners and ripping upwards. Similarly, Fairbairn had developed an instinctive method of pistol shooting that prized speed above accuracy. It was based on his experience that most exchanges of fire took place at short range. 'Instead of holding the gun out in front of you,' learned Joe Smale, 'you had to keep it central and shoot immediately a target appeared.' Fairbairn had turned a warehouse in Shanghai into the first range where policemen were taught to react to targets as they popped up unexpectedly, and this was now replicated at Lochailort.

But Fairbairn and Sykes's most famous innovation was the Commando dagger. Concerned that the standard-issue sheath knife was more of a tool than a weapon, they designed a seven-and-a-half-inch-long stiletto which was manufactured for the Commandos by blade-makers Wilkinson Sword.

'They taught us how to kill a sentry by creeping up behind him, putting an arm round his neck and jabbing the knife in,' Smale recalled. The fighting knife, and the ruthless image it evoked, was instantly adopted by the Commandos as their symbol and endlessly played on by the press in the years to come. Yet, as Smale remembers it, the dagger made more of a contribution to psychological warfare than it ever did in the field: 'It got a lot of publicity, but Durnford-Slater would not allow them to be issued. He felt that there would be a pub brawl and someone would lose their life. The only time I saw a knife in 3 Commando was when it was being worn by the girlfriend of an officer which somehow she had got hold of. I never handled one.'

Weeks of intensive lessons in hand-to-hand combat, sniping and explosives, topped up by endurance marches over mountains once traversed by Bonnie Prince Charlie, brought the commandos to a peak of fitness. Now all they wanted was to put their training to use. But their commanders were finding that unexpectedly hard to do.

The fall of France left Britain facing invasion, but its consequences continued to shape the war even after the RAF had averted the immediate threat of a German landing. The planning for all three armed forces had been based on the assumption that, like the First World War, any future conflict would take place in Europe. Instead, the Navy and the Air Force now found themselves in the front line of defence, while the bulk of the Army was bottled up at home. Even returning to the Continent, let alone defeating Germany, would require disembarking on a hostile shore.

As later became apparent, the only solution lay in a joint effort by the three services. This would require a complete change in thinking by senior officers accustomed to putting the needs of their own branch first. Patience would be vital in appreciating the demands of each arm, and tact called for in forging an entirely new relationship between them. Unfortunately, the burden of these twin challenges fell chiefly on someone who possessed neither of those virtues.

Roger Keyes had made his reputation with exploits reminiscent of the age of Nelson. During the Boxer Rising in China in 1900, he had blown up the magazine of a rebel fort and been among the first over the walls into the besieged British Legation in Peking. His admirers saw him as a hero, but many of his contemporaries in the Navy viewed him as the loosest of cannons.

His leadership of the Zeebrugge raid was further evidence of his courage, but he was too young to be given high command during the 1914–18 war. By 1939, when he was sixty-seven, he was thought too old, but this was not an opinion shared by Keyes himself. He rapidly came to believe that the mistakes of the earlier conflict – as he saw it, principally a failure of nerve – were being repeated, and used his position as an MP to criticise those he held responsible. On 7 May 1940, dressed in his admiral's uniform, he made a dramatic speech in the Commons condemning the handling of the Norway campaign which contributed to Neville Chamberlain's downfall the next day.

Keyes accordingly thought of his appointment by Churchill as Director of Combined Operations in July as a vindication of his ideas about the conduct of the war, especially by the Navy. He also appears to have assumed, largely due to the hazy definition of his role, that the post ranked him above the heads of the three services, at least in matters relating to combined operations. Instead of trying to win the cooperation of the Chiefs of Staff, Keyes from the start was on a collision course with them.

The first problem he had to address was transport. COLLAR had shown that using improvised landing craft and crews risked the entire operation. Specialised equipment would have to be developed almost from scratch, but in the meantime several fast cargo ships and cross-Channel ferries were converted into carriers for the Commandos. Any raids that they made, however, would depend for crews and escort vessels on the Navy's goodwill. But Keyes made little effort to win over the planning staff at the Admiralty who had to facilitate his requests, while his relationship with the First Sea Lord, his onetime friend Sir Dudley Pound, had been severely strained by his criticisms of the Navy. As each proposal by Keyes was scuppered by the services, tensions with them grew.

Matters came to a head in December 1940 over Operation WORKSHOP, a plan for two and a half thousand commandos to seize the tiny Italian island of Pantelleria, strategically sited between Sicily and Tunisia. It was exactly the type of coup which appealed to Keyes and he pushed hard for it to be approved.

The Commandos did not help their cause when the dress rehearsal for the attack, carried out at night on the Isle of Arran and watched by the top brass, became a shambles after the officer ordered to wake 3 Commando in time for it overslept. What sealed the operation's fate, though, was the refusal of the Chiefs of Staff to spare the air and sea power needed to hold Pantelleria afterwards.

Keyes was livid with rage and appealed to Churchill. Although he had encouraged Keyes to develop WORKSHOP, the Prime Minister did not want to be drawn into a divisive struggle with the Chiefs of Staff and made it clear that the operation was off. But, trading on their long friendship, Keyes invited himself to Chequers in order to change his mind. 'He was greeted by an indignant PM,' wrote Churchill's private secretary, Jock Colville, in his diary. 'We were all thunderstruck by his audacity: he carries the Zeebrugge spirit too far into private life.' This time that spirit failed to sway the Prime Minister.

Colville regarded Keyes's behaviour as megalomania, but behind it lay his genuine concern for the commandos. Many had been training hard for a raid for six months. Like athletes, they had been brought to a pitch of readiness, and it would become more difficult to keep them motivated if they were continually stood down. Their parent regiments were also proving reluctant to release more of their best men to be trained as commandos. They had been promised their volunteers back after they had taken part in a few operations in the autumn, but as yet there had not even been one.

So it was with excitement that Jimmy Sherwood learned, after returning to Arran from leave in late January 1941, that all communication with the mainland had been cut off. With the other members of the Folbot Troop, he was told to pack up his gear and board one of the converted 'Glen' cargo ships, the *Glenroy*. When he and the rest of 8 Commando woke the next morning, they were already in the Atlantic, where a Force 9 gale was whipping the sea into a heaving fury.

Accommodation was makeshift. The troops slung their hammocks in the hold and the lavatories were 'merely long rows of seats facing one another down a long alley with water running underneath. It was as primitive as they come and all very matey,'

Sherwood recalled. 'Luckily everyone was feeling so seasick that they couldn't have cared less where they sat.'

A few days earlier, Laycock had been promoted to colonel and appointed commander of Force Z, made up of sixteen hundred men from 7, 8 and 11 Commandos and bound for North Africa. Charles Haydon, the head of the Special Service Brigade, into which the Commandos had now been grouped, sounded a note of caution in his instructions to proceed overseas: 'No information is available with regard to the scale of any tasks which you may be called upon to undertake . . . It will be your duty to explain the size, organisation and administrative state of the Force to the General Staff.' It did not sound as if firm plans had been made for the raiders, but if anyone had doubts they were forgotten in their enthusiasm at finally being on their way.

Keyes's own son Geoffrey was serving with No. 11, and after seeing them off the admiral wrote to another proud father: 'I saw the last of the three Commandos who sailed in the "Glens" on Friday, the envy of all those who were left behind. I gave your love to Randolph, who is delighted to be one of the lucky ones. So many of our mutual friends have sons in that splendid party. It is the flower of my striking force.'

All too soon the flower would start to wilt. 'Layforce', as it was then renamed, had been sent to Egypt when the Italians were being routed and it seemed likely to have the freedom of the Mediterranean. By the time it had rounded Africa and was steaming for Suez, Rommel had arrived in the Western Desert. From being in a position of comfort, Wavell found himself stretched, and worryingly so when the Germans invaded Greece at the start of April.

One idea had been to send the Commandos to Rhodes to carry out CORDITE, for which Nigel Willmott duly reconnoitred the beaches. But with Tobruk and Athens now threatened, and fears growing that the oilfields of Persia and Iraq might fall into German hands unless garrisoned, Wavell was suddenly short of troops. Nor could he spare the fighter cover and destroyer escorts needed for

Layforce to strike in the Dodecanese, or anywhere else. The Commandos had become a luxury for which he had no use.

As the Staff in Cairo made plain to Laycock, in any case they had never asked for the Commandos: they had been forced on them. Once they arrived, no one at Headquarters knew quite what to do with them. Laycock tried his best to get permission for raids but his badgering of staff officers older yet junior to him did not go down well, and they were wary of Randolph's presence, too. The commandos' lack of equipment and the consequent need to scrounge everything except their personal kit from other troops was another source of irritation.

'We had expected to go into action immediately,' Sherwood recalled. Instead, he learned that 'Wavell didn't know why we were there. We were very taken aback. It was a shame because we were the best kind of soldiers – all volunteers.'

And when a raid was organised for them, it did not go well. In mid-April, 7 Commando was sent by sea to attack the Italian-held port of Bardia, in eastern Libya. Things went badly from the start. The landing had to be postponed because of poor weather – a hazard that was to become a recurring feature of operations. In the interval, no one realised that the bulk of the enemy forces were being withdrawn. The assault then went in late, not all of the Commando craft were released by their carriers, and of those who were put ashore seventy were stranded on the wrong beach and left behind. Some damage was done to coastal batteries but it did not justify the risks taken and the men lost. Any chance of the Commandos impressing Wavell on their own terms had gone.

On 5 May 1941, Laycock expressed his frustration to one of the few sympathetic figures at Middle East Command, Lieutenant General Arthur Smith:

> Our situation is now becoming desperate ... Unless we are actively employed soon I anticipate a serious falling-off in morale which at one time was second to none. The effect on the troops may be summed up by an inscription found written

on the partition in the mess decks of one of the Glen ships: 'Never in the history of human endeavour have so few been buggered about by so many.'

Worse was to come. Three weeks later, German parachutists rained down on Crete. Desperate for manpower to contain them, Wavell hurriedly sent No. 7 to the island together with 50 and 52 Commandos, two irregular units which had been raised in the Middle East and added to Layforce after seeing action in East Africa and the Greek islands.

Led by Laycock himself, their orders were to cover the retreat southwards of the main body of Allied troops, who were to be picked up by the Navy. They carried out their task skilfully but the choice of them for this role showed how little Cairo understood the Commandos. As Laycock pointed out later, a rearguard needs to engage the enemy at a distance and hold them there. Yet his lightly armed raiders lacked the heavy firepower of machine-guns and artillery which would have enabled them to do this effectively. Most landed in Crete equipped only with rifles, and though a bayonet charge at Sphakia stemmed one breakthrough, the majority of the force was cut off and taken prisoner when German superiority ended the evacuation prematurely. Of the eight hundred commandos committed to Crete, just two hundred returned, among them Laycock and his intelligence officer, the novelist Evelyn Waugh.

Once again, Layforce had been mishandled and had suffered grievously as a result. So it was all the more unexpected when only a week later they were given the chance to show what they could really do. This time, it promised to be the perfect Commando operation.

A month earlier, the war had seemed very remote to Tommy Macpherson. As the train carrying 11 Commando had rolled slowly through the orchards of Palestine, there had even been time to jump down and stuff his shirt with oranges and grapefruit before clambering back on board. Now, as his landing craft prepared to drop its ramp on a Syrian beach, for the first time he steeled himself for battle.

Just a few days before, on 2 June, his Commando unit had been told by Headquarters in Jerusalem to prepare for a mission. Although it was all rather short notice, it was far preferable to the garrison duty in Cyprus that they had been doing for the past weeks. Their objective would be the bridges over the River Litani, which runs through a deep wooded gorge to the Mediterranean coast south of Beirut, in what today is Lebanon but was then part of Syria. Since 1918, the country had been administered by the French, and since Germany's entrance into Paris its high commissioner had been collaborating with the Axis. Its airfields had been used to supply the pro-Nazi government in Iraq, and the prospect of it coming further under German control now prompted the British to invade.

One obstacle to an advance north from Palestine was the Litani. The main bridge over it, at Qasmiye, was known to be defended by strongpoints manned by two battalions of French colonial troops from Senegal. The commandos were to seize and hold the crossing, allowing an Australian infantry brigade to pass over.

Three months before, at the start of March, 3 and 4 Commandos had staged a raid on the remote Lofoten Islands in northern Norway. They had destroyed factories used to produce fish oils, an important source of vitamins for U-boat crews, and had also captured German Navy code books and rotors for an Enigma encoding machine. Yet, though Operation CLAYMORE had been a success, like Layforce's attack on Bardia it had faced no real opposition. On both raids, the only casualties had been self-inflicted.

EXPORTER – the name given to the Litani plan – would be the first time that the Commandos had made a full-scale assault on a defended position, and perhaps the first true test of their worth. It was one that No. 11's CO was wholly confident it would pass. Drawn from Scottish regiments, the unit had been trained remorselessly by Dick Pedder at Galashiels and on Arran. He was known for his fierce temper and insistence on self-discipline, but he was not without imagination.

At one aerodrome, then on full alert for a German invasion, the guards on the main gate had found themselves subjected to an impromptu lecture on their slovenly dress by two officers who had arrived in a staff car. So distracted were they by this that they missed the tall girl from the WAAF and the burly charlady who passed behind them and began to throw unfused grenades into the control tower. A busload of 'workmen' then piled through the entrance, while another group cut the perimeter fence and pretended to massacre the pilots as they spilled out onto the strip. In thirty minutes, 11 Commando had the whole field in their hands.

Pedder had expected his prospective officers to accept standards no lower than his own, and the attrition rate among them had been high. Those who remained included his second-in-command, Major Geoffrey Keyes, the admiral's eldest son and in his sister's words 'determined to do him credit'.

Tommy Macpherson also had someone to look up to. His brother Phil had captained Scotland's rugby team to their first Grand Slam in 1925. At nineteen, Tommy was the baby of the officers' mess, but he had already shown his own athletic prowess in taking eight seconds off the school record for the mile at Fettes College. The onset of war had interrupted his plans to go to Oxford, and like many of his contemporaries he wondered if he would ever see his native hills again after joining up. 'We had been brought up at the knees of our fathers and uncles involved in the First World War in the certain belief', he reflected, 'that the lifetime at any battle front of a second lieutenant did not exceed three weeks.'

Five of the officers shared a house, including Gerald Bryan and his fellow Irishman Blair Mayne, known, perhaps inevitably, as 'Paddy'. Mayne had played rugby for the British Lions and been heavyweight boxing champion of the Irish Universities. His housemates' favourite game was to place him in the middle of the room and then hurl themselves at him from the four corners simultaneously. They never managed to bring him down.

For all his immense strength, Mayne was aggressive only when confronted with an enemy, or when drunk. At Hogmanay 1940, Bryan had been duty officer and called on Mayne, who had turned down the chance to go with the others to a party. Feminine company tended to leave him tongue-tied. Bryan found him sitting on the floor, drinking alone, and as he was busy declined to fetch the jug of water that Mayne wanted. As he walked back across the gravel, shots shattered the windows of the house, and Bryan had to duck and weave his way to safety. The next morning he found Mayne still slumped on the floor, with thirty-six miniature bottles of liqueur lined up in front of him.

Together, the junior section officers comprised a powerful group of personalities: rather stronger, thought Macpherson, than the troop leaders above them. For Pedder's forceful temperament meant that his immediate subordinates tended to nod agreement rather than think for themselves. Litani would show whether that might prove to be a weakness in an emergency.

Pedder's plan was straightforward. 11 Commando would be divided into three parties – X, Y and Z – which would land from the sea in the early morning of 8 June. The main force, under Keyes, would secure the bridge, which was known to be mined, while Pedder's group a mile away in the centre would head over the dunes and deal with the French barracks on a plateau behind. A mile further to the north, Captain George More would lead a reserve tasked with keeping any reinforcements at bay and capturing a second bridge over a wadi on the road to Sidon.

Speed would be vital to their success. Surprise would enable them to overcome the potential dangers of a fortified position. Then the prompt arrival of the Australians and their armoured support would allow Pedder to hand over to troops better equipped to hold the bridge against a counter-attack. As it proved, No. 11 was to be deprived of all these requirements.

When the *Glengyle*, carrying the 27 officers and 456 men of the Commando, dropped anchor four miles off the Syrian coast, the beaches showed white with surf. A west wind was blowing, and a local policeman who knew the area well undertook a reconnaissance and advised that the sea was too rough for the flat-bottomed landing craft to make the hour's journey to land in safety. The launch from which he had observed the beaches was chased by a patrol boat, and it was apparent that with the moon gleaming bright behind her the

Glengyle must be visible ashore. The ship returned overnight to Port Said, where it came as no surprise to learn that the French had blown the Qasmiye bridge. Nevertheless, the Commando was ordered to turn around and try once more the next night.

As the Assault Landing Craft (ALC) headed in, this time over calm water, the officers aboard them tried to hide their anxiety. They had got away later than intended from the *Glengyle* and already the protection that darkness gave them was fading. In silence they tried to still their fears about how they would react under fire by concentrating on their drill. Pedder had trained them again and again to race off the ramp as fast as they could. When the ALCs carrying the northern group grounded with a judder, jerking Macpherson from his thoughts, the first two men obediently exited the craft at the double. Only when they disappeared from sight did it become clear that two of the squadron's three ALCs were stuck on sandbars some forty yards offshore. Z Party's first action in enemy territory was to make a human chain to carry men and weapons to the beach. It was then they realised that they had been landed south rather than north of the Kafr Bada wadi, from which machine-guns now opened up on them as they advanced. The only option was a frontal attack.

'The distance was about three-quarters of a mile,' remembered Macpherson. 'I am bound to say it seemed longer at the time.' Sporadic firing was coming from a ring of machine-gun nests around the bridge and the commandos headed for these in a series of zigzagging rushes. The Lebanese French troops manning the posts proved to have little appetite for a fight, and several other prepared positions were found abandoned or captured without the loss of any casualties.

At one point an ambulance approached from the north, and the commandos ceased firing to allow the French wounded to be treated. It was with some surprise that they saw a heavy mortar being unloaded instead, but its team soon decided that the range was too short for them to bring it into action and drove away again. By 0630 the bridge and numerous prisoners were under Macpherson's control.

What proved to be more troublesome was that the Troop had contrived to drop both their wireless sets in the sea and neither now worked. No. 11's adjutant, George More, found a motorcycle and set off to find Pedder's group to the south, but the bike was shot from under him by machine-gun fire and he narrowly escaped injury.

As the morning passed, Z Party mopped up pockets of resistance while dodging the wild shelling of two French frigates which had appeared offshore. A battery of howitzers was found hidden in a valley to the east, but as Macpherson was taking the surrender of the Senegalese artillerymen their sergeant lunged at him with a bayonet. A rapid burst from Sergeant Charlie Bruce put paid to him, although not before a deep cut had been scored across Macpherson's wrist.

By noon it was obvious to Macpherson that there had been a hold-up to the south as the Australians had not arrived. Eight French armoured cars then attacked from the north, but failed to push Macpherson's men off the high ground around the bridge. Another half-dozen armoured cars nosed in from the east, and as dusk settled infantry began to work their way round the commandos' flank.

At 1730 Macpherson received a message from More to retire to a rendezvous point across the river. He remembered afterwards being 'somewhat handicapped in this manoeuvre by the fact that no officer other than George More himself had a map'. He had studied the area too, but had not anticipated having to follow the route they were now given. A sub-section failed to keep a meeting with them in a wood, so he set off looking as confident as he could, 'the other ranks following with an air of unrelieved pessimism and disbelief'. Further knots of French troops were encountered along the way, but they gave little trouble and were sent out into the night without their weapons, trousers, socks or boots.

Crossing the Litani posed greater difficulties, as it was fast-flowing and twenty yards wide. It proved fordable, but two of the Troop panicked, lost their footing and disappeared rapidly downstream in the dark. Macpherson dived in and hauled them out under fire from a French post alerted by the men's shouts, but several rifles and a Bren gun were lost in the crossing. After gaining the far bank, the commandos marched inland and arrived at an Australian bivouac 'where we were warmly welcomed to what appeared to be a continuous beer party'. It was clear, noticed Macpherson ruefully, that they had no intention of advancing that day.

For all his disappointment, he had had more luck than his comrades elsewhere. During the withdrawal he had lost contact with More's group, which tried to make its way along the shore. Shortly after midnight they got caught at close range between barbed wire and a machine-gun. Five men were killed, three wounded, and the survivors taken prisoner.

Meanwhile, Pedder's three Troops had been under fire from the moment they beached. A bullet had also put their radio set out of commission, so X, Y and Z parties now had no means of communicating with one another. Although they took casualties in doing so, Paddy Mayne's Troop first pushed along the coast road before turning inland and working their way south to support Keyes's party. When they reached the Litani, they were fired on several times by the Australians and one man was killed, even though they waved a white flag to show that they were friendly forces.

Pedder's No. 1 Troop had gone straight for the barracks and taken it. A battery of four 75mm guns stood close by and the Senegalese crew of the nearest was routed by a bayonet charge. Many of Bryan's men had been in the Royal Artillery and they now hauled the captured piece round until it pointed at the other three guns. The first shell smashed into an ammunition dump and blasted its gun into the air. A few more shots silenced the other two.

There was little time to enjoy their triumph. Pedder wanted to take a section forward to a ridge from which mortars were starting to find their range. Bryan was to cover them, but as his men moved up to do so they came under attack from a concealed machine-gun. A sergeant got up to run, and was sent reeling by a shot from another direction. They were being targeted by a sniper. Bryan rapidly ordered a retreat to cover. Another sergeant was shot through the throat as he stood up, and a moment later Bryan himself was hurled to the ground. He realised he had been hit, and decided not to die only when he saw that it was in his legs. He hauled himself into a dip in the ground and lay there bleeding, not daring even to reach for his water bottle in case he was shot again.

Pedder was already dead. As his men advanced towards the high ground, bullets started to crack past them from positions in the trees ahead. Then machine-guns joined in. He told his section to go back down the gully from where they had come, but as he turned to follow them a bullet punched through him from behind. He barely had time to shout, 'I'm shot!' before he died.

Within minutes the steep-sided ravine had become a death trap. Both of the other officers with Pedder were also killed, leaving the incapacitated Bryan the only one of the four in the Troop still alive. Its sergeant-major took command, but although the half-dozen survivors were able to hold out until late afternoon, they were eventually surrounded and forced to surrender.

The first sign of trouble for Keyes's X Party came a few minutes after it landed at 0450. Dawn was breaking, and it outlined the masts of native feluccas to their left instead of to the right. The river was still between them and the French. In the dark, the crew of their ALCs had missed the mouth of the Litani, which was hidden by a sandbank, and put them ashore on the wrong side of the blown bridge. Expecting to advance through positions held by the commandos, the troops of the 21st Australian Brigade were surprised to be woken by Keyes's men walking through theirs.

A small party of Australians with some collapsible boats was waiting on the riverbank, but as Keyes approached them a red Very light shot up from the French lines. At once the entire area was bombarded by heavy and accurate fire from 75mm guns, 81mm mortars and machine-guns on the crest beyond. For the next few hours, they were pinned down by the barrage and by sniper fire which killed several men. 'Extremely unpleasant,' wrote Keyes in his diary later.

He had taken cover behind a bush, and admitted he was loath to leave this in order to confer with another officer, George Highland. With his batman, Private Ness, he began crawling inch by inch along the ground, taking almost half an hour to travel thirty yards.

'Feels like a billiard table and several bullets very close,' he noted. Told that it was even more exposed further on, 'Ness and I start running but I trip up after three paces, as I am heavily laden. Fall down on the bank and Ness, the idiot, gets down too, even more exposed. We got badly sniped, so I told him to run on ... I gave them 10 minutes to forget me and do it in two bursts. Inspect Woodnutt and Jones on the way, both dead.' Soon after, Lieutenant Eric Garland – known, of course, as 'Judy' – deliberately exposed himself to the sniper's fire, spotted his position and riddled it with a Bren gun.

When the Australian artillery belatedly began to shell the French batteries, the commandos were able to get down to the rushes by the river and send Garland and six men across in a boat. Having cut their way through barbed wire, they lobbed grenades into the redoubt overlooking the bridge and captured it.

Highland was able to send another boatload over, but Keyes then learned that some of his Troop had been ordered to withdraw by the Australians' brigadier, who had been told that all the commandos by the river were dead. A company commander had also decided that it was too dangerous for the Australians to advance after one of them was wounded by a shell splinter.

In the redoubt on the far side, Garland noticed that the gun which had targeted the Australians was prevented by its embrasure from traversing onto the positions which the French had held. He too decided to use Vichy's weapons against them, and sent four rounds from the 25mm anti-tank gun in the post straight through the slit of the other fortification more than a thousand yards away. 'Good shooting settled his hash,' recorded Keyes with satisfaction.

The Australians were now able to cross a pontoon bridge, and over the course of the next day forced the remaining French troops to throw down their arms and release those commandos who had been captured. Keyes was not impressed by his allies' conduct, however. That morning he had found that the haversacks of his dead had been looted by Australian scavengers. 'They don't intend to do anything as long as someone else is there to do it for them,' he wrote bitterly. An Australian colonel told him that the commandos' bravery had made him ashamed of his own men, although he explained that they had not been in action before. 'Neither had mine,' retorted Keyes.

'My cavaliers took a bad knock, though everyone was splendid,' he told his father in his next letter home. He had been shocked to hear how bad their losses were. Forty-five commandos were dead, including their CO and three other officers, and seventy-five men had been wounded or were missing. A full third of those who had landed were casualties, including Gerald Bryan, who was to lose a leg in hospital in Beirut. Three weeks after his twenty-fourth birthday, Geoffrey Keyes found himself in command of 11 Commando.

They had accomplished their mission, but paid a high price. After the disasters on Crete and at Bardia, Layforce was rapidly being bled dry. Too often their fate was not of their own making. At Litani, they had been let down by poor navigation, weak intelligence about the French positions and the Australians' caution, even if Pedder had arguably been too impetuous in the face of unexpectedly strong resistance. Yet, while their courage was not in question, Tommy Macpherson felt that they had made costly mistakes which should have been avoided.

'Whatever else we were good at in the Commandos at the time,' he wrote to Bryan many years later, 'we were quite extraordinarily bad in the information bit of orders . . . I, and I think most of the other junior officers, only had the sketchiest idea of what was going on.' On the battlefield, that lack of certainty could be fatal. As Macpherson also noted, it was a failing which was to be repeated with tragic consequences in their next – and final – operation, this time in the Libyan desert.

3

FLIPPER

'Am twenty-one today!' wrote Tommy Macpherson excitedly in his diary. But he would long remember the occasion for another reason as well. 'A red letter day!' he noted at the foot of the page. 'Today Geoffrey found a great idea and we began to put it over – it will be a fight.'

The four months since Litani had seen major changes made to the Commandos both at home and overseas. Although Wavell had been replaced by Sir Claude Auchinleck, Middle East Command was still overstretched and in mid-July 1941 the decision had been taken to break up Layforce. There was little chance of more amphibious operations being mounted in the Mediterranean in the near future, and in any case the COs of hard-pressed regular units in the region were not willing to lose their best soldiers to bring the force back up to strength.

The news that they were to be disbanded angered many of Laycock's men. For all their tribulations, they had forged a strong bond together and still believed in the Commandos' potential. 'It's as raiding units that their real value lies,' insisted Laycock – a sentiment with which at least one other officer in No. 8 wholeheartedly agreed. Already David Stirling had been touting to the generals his idea for attacking the enemy's lines of supply with paratroops. Now he began to recruit a few dozen similarly frustrated members of Layforce for his own band of raiders, codenamed L Detachment, Special Air Service (SAS).

Many of the other commandos returned to Britain, while 120 volunteered to train guerrillas in the Far East. Evelyn Waugh tried to expedite his transfer back to his original unit, the Royal Marines, by buttonholing a colonel on the Staff, only to be told peremptorily to put the request through the proper channels. He saluted, turned on his heel and left, reappearing a moment later having strode smartly through the wrong door.

Randolph Churchill secured a job at Headquarters, and it did not take long for his father to learn of Layforce's fate. 'The Commandos have been frittered away,' the Prime Minister complained to the Chiefs of Staff, ordering that they be reconstituted as soon as possible. By mid-October, Auchinleck had complied, but Laycock was disappointed by the make-up of his new Middle East Commando. He had wanted it to be a powerful, elite force like that he had brought out from Arran. Instead, he lamented, its strength of just 250 consisted 'in the main of Jews, Arabs, a few Spaniards, together with the remnants of British units from which most of the best officers and other ranks have already been withdrawn'.

Although its six Troops included the newly born SAS, and Courtney's SBS, the bulk of it was drawn from Palestinian soldiers and refugees from Franco's regime who had served in 51 Commando. There were also sixty men of No. 11 who had stayed with Geoffrey Keyes. 'We are thousands of men short of our own requirements for infantry battalions,' Laycock was told by his ally General Smith. He would simply have to do his best with what was available.

His pleas for more resources had also been undermined by another development. During the summer, relations between Roger Keyes and the Chiefs of Staff had deteriorated, but more importantly so had his friendship with Churchill. Mistakes made during Exercise LEAPFROG, a rehearsal for a raid on the Azores, had been all the more embarrassing as they had been witnessed by George VI himself, and in September the Chiefs tried to strip Keyes of any control over operations.

Keyes protested repeatedly to Churchill. 'I know I am destined to play a decisive part in helping you to win this war,' he blustered, but his confidence even as he neared seventy was no longer shared by the Prime Minister. When he refused to accept a more limited role, Churchill told Keyes in mid-October that he had no option but to replace him. His successor was to be another ambitious naval officer, though one who had made his reputation for dynamism in *this* war, the forty-one-year-old Lord Louis Mountbatten.

While his father battled to save his command, Geoffrey Keyes had been confirmed as CO of No. 11. Yet his wispy pencil moustache could not hide his youth, nor was the jealousy of older officers mollified by the white-and-purple ribbon of the MC he had worn since Litani. 'For a major of forty-two in an office to see me walk in aged twenty-four is like a red rag to a bull,' he told his father. 'I have met two of my instructors from Sandhurst . . . who looked pretty sideways at me.'

He was under no illusions that if the Middle East Commandos were to retain any control over their own use, and if he was to stifle the muttered accusations of favouritism that followed him as Keyes's son, they would have to vindicate themselves with a truly audacious raid. Macpherson, now his second-in-command, agreed: 'It means convincing brass hats that we can do special jobs and do them well.'

What Keyes had in mind was more than that: a knockout blow in the fight for control of North Africa. He would lead a small force to a villa 250 miles behind the German lines and there assassinate the Afrika Korps' commander – Field Marshal Erwin Rommel himself. For the time being, however, he shared few of the details with anyone else, and the first that Macpherson knew it was being considered by the Staff was when one morning in late October he was ordered to report to the submarine base at Alexandria. Once aboard *Talisman*, he was told that under no circumstances would he be allowed to disembark. Instead, still wearing just his ordinary uniform of drill shorts and a khaki sweater, he was to recce a beach whose location he was not allowed to know. He would be taken ashore by the SBS.

On the night of the 24th, Macpherson and Corporal Andy Evans clambered into their folbot and began to paddle hard for the beach – at Ras Hilal, about midway between Tobruk and Benghazi. In a second canoe were an officer Macpherson knew from 11 Commando, Lieutenant Trevor Ravenscroft, and Captain James Ratcliffe, who had a week or two's seniority over Macpherson and so was in command.

While getting through the surf, Ravenscroft dropped the party's signalling torch, but as they had a compass bearing for the rendezvous with *Talisman* the next night this did not seem a serious problem. They hid the boats in a cave and headed straight up the steep escarpment to the plateau. Macpherson assumed that he would be coming back with a larger group, so committed to memory the location and routines of two patrols they saw. They spent the day in the cave and that evening set off in good time for the meeting with the submarine.

All night they criss-crossed the area where she was supposed to be but there was no sign of her. When dawn came, they decided to spend the day in the folbots and wait for *Talisman* to surface after dark. The only rations that they had were a ham sandwich each, but so confident was Macpherson of being picked up that he gave his to the others.

Night fell eventually, and at 0130 they heard an engine noise and saw the red light which the sub was to show. It had to be *Talisman*. They raced through the water towards her but when they were only ten yards away realised that the sound was coming from a caique full of German troops. Fortunately the recce party was not spotted, and they headed for land after agreeing that there was no point in waiting any longer for the Navy. They were right about that; *Talisman* had gone to the wrong bay.

The wind had risen, and when Ratcliffe and Ravenscroft's folbot ran onto rocks the only compass the group had was smashed. They had not been allowed to bring a map, so to stand any chance of finding their way to Tobruk on foot they would have to follow the coast. They split into pairs to increase their chances of evading capture, but the two SBS officers were soon taken prisoner by the Italians and more patrols were sent out to look for Macpherson and Evans.

For three days they managed to escape detection, but on 1 November hunger drove them to seek food. All they had had since the day in the boat was a vile soup they had made in a tin on the beach from rainwater and wild broccoli. When they came across a camp in the dark, they watched the sentries make their rounds and then crept through the perimeter. Macpherson looked first for the cookhouse but soon decided it would be quicker to see what he could find in one of the tents. Leaving Evans to keep a lookout, he began to tiptoe between the rows of bunks filled with sleeping Germans. On the shelves below the beds he could see loaves of bread, and as quietly as he could reached for one and slipped it into his shirt. As he did so, he heard what sounded like a pistol shot. Evans had got cramp and dropped the flap of the tent. There were shouts in German, and someone switched on a torch and began to shine it around. Macpherson stayed rooted to the spot as the beam was played on him by a sleepy corporal. 'He raised a scream fit to bring the roof down,' he wrote later. Grabbing Evans, he ran into the night and towards the hills. Their last sight of the camp was of the sentries shooting at each other in the confusion.

There seemed to be no pursuit but, after a couple of hours, Evans became convinced that they were being followed. They stopped and listened. Sure enough, coming closer and closer was the sound of heavy breathing, and then out of the darkness a Doberman sprang straight at Macpherson. There was just enough light for him to see its gaping jaws, and just enough time for him to draw his knife before the dog landed on him. It dropped dead on the spot, having impaled itself on the blade.

Their luck held for a few more days until they came across a military telephone exchange under a culvert near Derna. They vandalised it, not realising until afterwards that this gave away their location. They were quickly traced by the Italians. Thinking that they would hear any vehicles approaching, the pair were walking through scrub when they were suddenly surrounded by a large patrol mounted silently on bicycles.

Macpherson was disarmed but not before he managed to slip the spare magazine for his Colt into his pocket. He made his first attempt to escape a few hours later while being interrogated. One of the *carabinieri* asked him to demonstrate how the gun worked, thinking it was empty. Macpherson had just loaded it and turned the tables when he was stricken by cramp and quickly overpowered.

Several days later he made another run for it. Left alone to wash, he dropped straight out of the bathroom window and onto a motorcycle in the yard outside. It started 'like a bird', he remembered, 'but unfortunately stopped with equal suddenness within 20 yards'. This time he was caught while still looking for the petrol switch. It was to be his last taste of liberty for two years.

It was a sign of how much Keyes was prepared to stake on the raid that Macpherson's failure to return from the recce made almost no difference to its planning. A week after his capture, sixty commandos left Alexandria in *Talisman* and *Torbay*. Not until two days into the voyage were they told what their mission was.

The men were drawn largely from No. 11, but there had been some last-minute additions to the personnel. Robin Campbell, the ambassador's son who had been in 8 Commando, was summoned straight from a desk job at Headquarters in Cairo because he spoke German. Another recruit was David Sutherland. He had been in the same house as Keyes at Eton, and had been in 3 Commando until he had failed to wake Durnford-Slater in time for the night exercise on Arran. He had since transferred to No. 8, and offered to teach the raiders about demolitions in return for a place on the operation.

With him was Fred Birch, a meat porter in Liverpool before the war, who had joined No. 7. So far he had taken part in the messy raid on Bardia, where one of his officers had been shot dead after failing to give a password, and the disaster on Crete. Birch had got away from there on an abandoned landing craft, celebrating his twentieth birthday on board before it beached in Egypt after ten days at sea.

Promoted to lance sergeant, Birch had been showing Keyes's men how to use plastic explosive until one of them was found to have scabies the day before departure. The six men sharing the soldier's tent were quarantined as in the close confines of a submarine the disease might easily spread. 'So they were six men short of doing the job,' Birch later recalled. 'They came to us and they said: "Well, we're afraid we're going to have to press you into service. You're volunteers."'

The attraction of Operation FLIPPER for Auchinleck was that it dovetailed with a plan of his own. The raid would take place on the eve of his CRUSADER offensive, intended to relieve the pressure on Tobruk, and was to be coordinated with other attacks, including the SAS's first mission. Keyes's group would hit four separate targets, among them the Italian intelligence and communications network, as well as the house near Beda Littoria which had been identified by Arab sources as Rommel's HQ. Attempting such a coup would be not only daring but highly dangerous. 'Even if initially successful,' feared Laycock, 'it meant almost certain death for those who took part in it.' Yet so important did he think it might be to all their futures that he decided to accompany the operation himself.

Although he took care to appear confident, Keyes was also pessimistic about their chances of returning home again. Although the commandos enjoyed the novelty of the crew bringing them breakfast in their bunks, there was little to do in the submarine except write letters. Keyes had done his best to make his father proud since he was a small boy, and he regularly sent him all his news. They had developed a code to use in their correspondence, and Geoffrey's innocent-seeming letters from Norway in 1940 had contained details of mistakes being made in the campaign, providing ammunition for the admiral's criticism of the government.

Now he concealed nothing from him. He may not yet have

heard of his father's replacement by Mountbatten, but just before leaving port Geoffrey had been shocked to learn from his girlfriend that she had become engaged to someone else. Like a knight of old, he was more than ever determined to prove himself or to perish in the attempt. In a letter to be sent to his family if he failed to return, he wrote:

> It is dirty work at the cross roads with a vengeance, on the old original conception of the Commandos. It may be perfectly alright, in which case this won't get posted, but I am not happy about the future really. If the thing is a success, whether I get bagged or not, it will raise our stock a bit and help the cause. So don't worry about me, even if this does arrive . . . This is a hell of a chance.

Just after dark on the evening of 14 November, *Torbay* broke the surface twenty miles west of the beach reconnoitred by Macpherson. The change of landing spot was the one concession to his capture. While fourteen two-man rubber dinghies were placed on the combing and inflated with a foot pump, an SBS folbot was sent to check if FLIPPER's reception party was waiting ashore. The reassuring flash of light that pierced the inky darkness announced that they were.

Fred Birch was in the dinghy next to Keyes. The drill was that *Torbay* would trim down and they would float off, but the wind and swell were increasing by the minute. Birch was given a hand down from the hydroplane into his boat, which was already laden with a four-gallon tin containing food, ammunition and explosive. 'My mate didn't come in at the same time,' he remembered, 'and then the submarine went up. There were two sailors holding on to the lines to the dinghy. It turned sideways and I nearly went into the water, but fortunately managed to hold on.' Eventually he got away, but he had had better luck than most. The sea had swept four of the boats off the superstructure and washed one man overboard. In the worsening conditions it took hours to recover them. During a second attempt to launch the dinghies, some were swamped and others overturned. Lieutenant Tommy Langton of the SBS estimated that he had to dive into the water fifty times in the next six hours until all the commandos were dispatched, far behind schedule.

Many of the boats broached in the freezing surf as they reached the beach, soaking their occupants to the skin. They had been warned that they would be shot out of hand if they so much as lit a cigarette once off the submarine, but the first thing that most saw ashore was a bonfire which had been built to warm them up.

Meanwhile Laycock, unable to account for the delay, was fretting aboard *Talisman*. By the time that his party's turn came, three hours late and well after midnight, the wind was strengthening to a Force 7 gale. The strong easterly current was also making it hard for the submarine to hold position, and as she started to trim down to let the boats off she grounded and rolled.

David Sutherland was chatting to Laycock in the adjacent dinghy and the first he knew that something was wrong came when he saw his commander's jaw tighten. The giant wave surged beam-on over the casing, pitching men and equipment into the billows of the sea. With the boats scattered, most of the commandos instinctively swam back to *Talisman*. One man was never seen alive again and only Laycock and seven others reached the shore.

Sutherland had managed to cling on to a steel hawser as the water enveloped him, but it proved impossible to launch any more of the inflatables. The wind simply pushed them out to sea instead of towards land. He and the rest of Laycock's group remained aboard *Talisman*, and when the weather deteriorated the following day they returned to Alexandria. Keyes had calculated that he needed six officers and fifty-three men to give his raid a chance of succeeding. Now he was deep inside hostile territory with little more than half that number.

Although Keyes was in command of the operation, it seems to have been Laycock who took the decision to press on as planned rather than wait to see if *Talisman* could disembark reinforcements the next day. He was influenced by the risk of being discovered if they waited, and by instructions from Cairo that the attack on Rommel would be of most help if carried out in two nights' time. Doing his best to look cheerful, Keyes modified his plan and divided the party in three. A small detachment, under Lieutenant Roy Cooke, would cut Italian communications by blowing up a telegraph pylon near Cyrene, where several lines connected. Most of the remaining commandos, led by Keyes and Campbell, would go after the field marshal. Laycock and three men were to stay behind at the rendezvous.

That evening they set off up the escarpment. Their local guides were supplied by John Haselden, the Arabic-speaking intelligence officer who had been waiting for the group on the beach. Wearing native robes over his battledress, he had made his way on foot for more than one hundred miles to keep the appointment and reconnoitre the terrain over which Keyes was now to march. It was his informants who had tipped off the British about Rommel's visits to the villa at Beda Littoria. Two Senussi tribesmen had been recruited to take Keyes there, but they had never made it ashore from the submarine so Haselden had found a shepherd to show the way.

After a steep climb, the party marched inland all night, stumbling along sheep tracks strewn with rocks. The weather in recent days had been unseasonably hot and humid, and the rain that began to fall steadily indicated that a storm was building. At first light they wrapped themselves against the cold in damp blankets and tried as best they could to sleep. Their guide had deserted them soon after midnight, despite being threatened by Keyes at gunpoint, but during the day they were discovered by other locals who soon offered their services. Speaking through Keyes's Palestinian interpreter, Corporal Avishalom Drori, they agreed – for a fee of one thousand Italian lire – to lead the group to a cave where they could rest the next night. One enterprising boy said that he could fetch cigarettes from a nearby Italian canteen, and duly returned with several packets a couple of hours later.

They left after dark, marching in single file through the drizzle with Keyes at their head. It took two and a half hours to reach the cave, which was about five miles from the villa. 'Apart from an appalling smell of goats,' thought Campbell, 'it was an ideal place to spend the rest of the night and the following day.' The Arabs gave them a meal of kid, and the next morning Keyes sent the resourceful boy to spy out the land at Beda Littoria.

While he was away, the most spectacular storm in local memory lit up the skies above the cave. 'It started to rain,' remembered Birch, 'rain and rain and rain: I had never seen rain like it.' Campbell saw the countryside they would have to cross that evening turn to mud before his eyes. Dry wadis became foaming torrents: 'Spirits were sinking – I know mine were – at the prospect of a long, cold, wet and muddy march before we even arrived at the starting point of a hazardous operation.' Keyes's hopes were lifted, however, by the information that the boy was able to provide. This allowed him to draw a detailed map of the town from which to brief everyone. The challenge was to be 'Island'; the password 'Arran'.

At 1800 they swapped their boots for plimsolls and set off, slithering and slipping in the rain and mud. 'The travelling was so bad', Birch recalled, 'that we had to hang on to the man in front for balance.' Regular halts had to be called whenever someone fell or there was a danger of those at the back losing touch in the dark with the rest of the column.

At 2230, they reached the foot of the slope beneath the town. They had a brief rest and then began to scrabble slowly over the wet turf. About halfway up, one man fell, striking his tommy-gun against a rock. The sound was immediately echoed by the barking of a guard dog, and then the door of a house was flung open and light poured out. 'As we crouched motionless, hardly breathing, we heard a man shouting at the dog,' wrote Campbell. 'Finally the door closed, and we resumed our way upward.'

They were now at the edge of the town. Cooke's party of seven, including Birch, peeled off towards the crossroads where they were to cut the wires. Keyes went forward to scout with Jack Terry, who at nineteen was already a sergeant. He had been at Litani and, as neither Macpherson nor Sutherland had made it this far, was one of the few in the party whom Keyes knew well enough to trust.

As the pair vanished into the gloom, the others tried to shelter from the downpour against the walls of the souk. Then one of the commandos tripped over a can, alerting another dog. A voice began screaming in Arabic in a nearby hut, and after a couple of minutes two men in uniform approached the group. One was an Italian sergeant-major, the other an Arab. They wanted to know who the men were and what they were doing. Drori translated this to Campbell, who replied coldly in German: 'Tell them we are German troops on patrol, and to go away and keep that dog quiet.' This they did, bidding the group '*Gute Nacht*', which the commandos thought very funny.

Just then Keyes returned. He told Campbell that with Terry they would form the main assault party. They would take Drori and two men to watch the exits from the villa. The remaining soldiers were to assume positions around the perimeter overlooking the guard tents and a small hotel, and prevent anyone from interfering. The attack would go in at midnight. Keyes's recce had established that there were no sentries in the garden of the house or among the tall cypress trees which lined the drive. Perhaps the rain had driven the patrols indoors.

Keyes led Campbell and Terry through a gap in the hedge at the back of the villa, where he had hoped to find an open door or a window. Yet they all proved to be barred and shuttered. The three men waited until the one light that was showing went out, and then Campbell banged loudly on the carved wood of the front door and demanded in German to be let in.

There are several versions of what happened next, some of which changed over time and none of which agree on the key details. What is certain is that the door was opened by a powerfully built German private wearing an overcoat and steel helmet. Keyes pointed his Colt at him, but the guard seized the muzzle and they began to wrestle. Before Campbell could get behind them, the German pulled Keyes with him inside the entrance and began to shout. Instinctively Campbell fired several shots with his revolver. As Terry explained later: 'That's what raised the alarm.'

They found themselves in a large hall with a stone floor, from which a staircase led to the upper floors. 'We heard a man in heavy boots clattering down the stairs though ... he was hidden by a right-hand turn,' wrote Campbell later. 'He was shouting: "What goes on there?"' A burst from Terry's tommy-gun sent him scurrying back up again.

In the meantime Keyes was searching the rooms off the hall. The first two were empty, but the third was not. 'As I was standing behind Colonel Keyes he fell to the ground after being struck,' said Terry. 'I immediately sprayed a burst of tommy-gun fire round the room and Captain Campbell came and threw grenades over my shoulder. Enemy resistance outside appeared to be big so we withdrew from the house dragging Colonel Keyes.' Campbell felt for Keyes's heart but it was no use: he was dead.

The commandos on watch in the garden had done their job. Two Germans had been killed, one in his pyjamas after emerging from a tent and another as he was fleeing the house. Running round to investigate what had happened, Campbell had his leg broken by what Laycock afterwards described as 'a stray burst of fire'.

With both their officers now down and the Germans roused, Terry obeyed Campbell's order to lead the group back to the beach. No one suggested trying to find Rommel. Some of the men offered to carry Campbell, but he told them to leave him behind. There was no chance of his crossing a dozen miles of rough terrain in time to make the pick-up. He gave Terry his map, and then lay in the rain waiting to be found. The guards who discovered him deliberated in German for some time whether they should finish him off. He understood every word they said.

Covering their withdrawal by blowing up the villa's electricity generator, Terry led the downhearted survivors back towards the coast. In the dark, he failed to find a cave where they had dumped dry clothing and rations, and so after a short nap he marched the group through the day, aware that the enemy would be looking for them. At 1700 that afternoon, he met Laycock close to the beach and gave him the news of Keyes's death.

There was no sign of Roy Cooke's party. Their task had been to destroy the communications pylon and so prevent help from being summoned to Beda Littoria. They soon realised that it was miles farther to the crossroads than they had expected, and they were already exhausted from their approach march. Two of the men were holding up the others so Cooke told them to make their own way back and decided to hijack the first vehicle that came along.

Soon they saw the headlights of a car, but it failed to stop when they showed their weapons and then it slewed off the road. Its Italian driver ran away after they had shot at him, and it proved impossible to get the car out of the ditch. They eventually arrived at their target hours behind schedule and soaked through. Birch's mood was not improved by discovering that even though he had carefully wrapped his matches in a waterproof condom, his wet hands made them useless when he tried to light the charges placed on the pylon. They did as much damage as they could with an incendiary bomb, and then headed for the coast.

Two days later they were lying up in a cave, having met some friendly seeming Arabs, when they were surrounded by Italian troops who threw in smoke grenades. They had little choice but to surrender. At Cyrene, Cooke was separated from his men, but they quickly worked out that the 'South African' soldiers in their cell who asked so many questions were actually Italians in disguise. Soon Birch was on his way to a PoW camp at Benghazi.

The main group's attempts to escape had not gone any better. *Torbay* appeared in the bay on time but Laycock then found that the dinghies they had hidden by the beach had been moved by Arabs. He tried signalling the submarine to make alternative plans, but his torch was not designed for the purpose and his Morse code messages were garbled. Nor did he properly understand those that were flashed to him. He thought he was being told that the sea was too rough to attempt a pick-up, when in fact *Torbay* was signalling that the weather meant they could not send in a folbot with the supplies he had requested.

The submarine's commander, Anthony 'Crap' Miers, then offered to place *Torbay* close to a nearby spit of land so that the men could swim out. Laycock thought they were so tired that some would inevitably drown, so, despite Miers's reservations about the dangers involved, they agreed to rendezvous again the following evening.

At daybreak, Laycock posted sentries to watch the approaches to the caves where the force was sleeping. An Arab had stumbled across them earlier and Laycock was worried that he might give away their location. Then, towards midday, he heard shots to the west. A group of *carabinieri*, made up of Italians and Arabs in red headscarves, was advancing across the hillside opposite. The commandos returned fire and attempted to work round their flank, but by 1400 German soldiers had appeared as well and they were soon within two hundred yards of Laycock's position. He decided that he could not hold them off until nightfall, and ordered the men to split into twos and threes and make a run for the hills to the east.

Laycock paired himself with Terry. The first half-mile was across open country and Laycock later described the going as 'unpleasant', but the enemy's marksmanship was poor and they broke through the cordon. That was as far as most of the men got, though. When Tommy Langton paddled in cautiously to the beach that evening, looking in vain for a torch signal, all he could see was the glow of cigarette ends. He deduced correctly that no commando would be smoking on a hostile beach, and that the raiding party had been rounded up.

But Laycock and Terry had not. For the next six weeks, the Old Etonian and the one-time butcher's boy helped each other to survive against the odds. They first made for two alternative rendezvous but these were guarded by patrols evidently looking for them. Knowing that CRUSADER must have begun, they walked steadily eastwards, hoping sooner or later to run into their own troops.

'Living behind the enemy lines is very unlike any other form of soldiering,' Laycock later reflected. 'One can never feel quite at ease. One is continually on the alert, since there is danger on every side.' His greatest fear was of being stalked by the *carabinieri*'s Arab trackers, and once or twice they had close brushes with them. Yet they were not in the desert proper but on a coastal range covered in scrub and thorn bushes which gave good cover, and which was honeycombed with caves in which to hide.

'Only once did we get careless,' Laycock recalled, 'when both of us were dozing in a cave together. I had left my revolver and field-glasses near the mouth of the cave and Sergeant Terry had taken off his equipment. To our great consternation, there was a rustle at the mouth of the cave and we suddenly became aware of the bottom half of an Arab who was clearly about to enter.' Laycock assumed that the man would be only too eager to earn the reward that the Germans were offering for information about them, and he knew that the Arab was much closer to his gun than he was. 'After what seemed an interminable age,' he recounted, 'during which Terry and myself lay like logs, feeling rather like rats caught in a trap, the Arab ducked down and entered the cave and very nearly jumped out of his skin.'

However, it soon became clear that their visitor was willing to help, as were the other Senussi they encountered, all of whom shared what little food they had. Nevertheless, Laycock calculated that his total intake over the final five weeks of their journey was about the same as he usually consumed in a single day. Often their entire ration was a piece of unleavened bread about the size of a walnut, occasionally supplemented by wild mushrooms or arbutus berries. During the first week, they had to drink water from stagnant pools, but thereafter it rained frequently, so at least they were never thirsty.

Aside from Terry having to endure hearing the adventures of Mr Toad over and over again, their chief affliction was a craving for sugar. When they finally met up with British troops on Christmas Day they fell on the marmalade offered to them and ate a pot each.

The relief that they felt at having reached their own lines could not disguise that the raid had been a calamitous failure, however.

It was hoped that the others would make it back, too, but only Bombardier John Brittlebank did. For another six months, Geoffrey Keyes's family did not know for certain that he was dead, and they consoled themselves with the black Highland bonnet he had left behind in the submarine. Then, in June 1942, a letter from Campbell, written in a PoW camp, brought confirmation of their worst fears. Campbell himself had had his leg amputated because of his injury.

By then, there had been time for those with something still at stake to reflect on what had happened during the raid. Their disappointment had only deepened when they learned that Rommel was not even in the villa that night, but at a fiftieth-birthday party held for him in Rome. Laycock recorded the news in his official report, written early in 1942. Yet five years later, replying to a query by the Royal Artillery's regimental historian for information about Jack Terry, he wrote of the attack that 'Rommel had left the night before and did not return until a few days later.' In fact, as was by then well known in military circles, Rommel had been in Italy for the preceding three weeks. Moreover, he had not visited the villa for some months; at the time of the raid, the quartermaster staff of a *Panzergruppe* was using it as their HQ.

The dissemination of myths about the operation therefore started early. For instance, Laycock, who had thought the mission potentially so important – or glorious – that he had accompanied it, queried in his accounts why it had been necessary for such a senior officer as Keyes to risk leading it at all. There was perhaps little that Laycock could have done from the beach to influence the assault itself once he had decided it should proceed, but in his reports he glossed over his difficulties with the Morse signals and avoided taking the blame for the raid's unhappy outcome.

He was not the only one to have made mistakes. Haselden's sources reported that the Italians had learned where Laycock's group was from maps found on two prisoners (perhaps the men sent back by Cooke), on which was marked the location of the beach. But then Haselden's tips were not always accurate. 'I was informed by the Arabs that Lt-Col Keyes . . . had shot three German officers . . . all better than majors,' he reported after the attack. 'Four German Other Ranks were killed in a fight outside the house.' In reality, there had been only four German casualties in total, with the highest ranking a lieutenant. 'We lost one Other Rank killed,' Haselden's informant continued. 'One officer was wounded but got away.'

The truth is that the raid relied far too much on intelligence from Haselden which had not been independently verified. The tremendous risks inherent in the mission were only worth taking if Rommel was definitely at the villa. As he was not, the survivors of the operation began to embellish what had happened to make it more palatable. Laycock's only source for the events at the house was Terry, and his description of Keyes's heroic death does not square with the careful detail of Campbell's account, suggesting that something had gone awry.

In fact, the only dependable report on FLIPPER was that written by the Germans the day after the raid. It contains one crucial revelation: both Keyes and Campbell were hit by shots fired by their own side. The 'stray burst' that wounded Campbell came from a commando posted at the back of the house who was expecting Germans to run out of it. And the only time that Keyes could have been shot by one of his own men was as he struggled at the door with the shouting guard. Geoffrey Keyes was killed by those instinctive shots from Robin Campbell's revolver.

No doubt feelings of guilt, loyalty and consideration for Keyes's father prompted the subsequent cover-up. Not for the first time, it was made official by the awarding of medals. Jack Terry, whose tenacity and initiative had shown what commandos were capable of as individuals, received the Distinguished Conduct Medal, while Campbell got the DSO. And Geoffrey Keyes finally made his father proud by becoming the first commando to win the Victoria Cross. His adjutant, Tommy Macpherson, thought that Keyes's death 'was actually what he had been looking for all his life. He would not have made a good CO long-term – he didn't have the qualities for that – but he was a most determined leader.'

Keyes was buried by the Germans with military honours in the cemetery at Beda Littoria, on a hill that looks south towards the Sahara. In the autumn of 1943, his brother Roger, by then a sub-lieutenant in the Navy, found the wooden cross marking his grave. The verger told him that the German colonel who had presided over the funeral had placed his own Iron Cross on the coffin.

The raid had been extraordinarily daring, and news of it no doubt did give British morale a lift. But it accomplished nothing of substance beyond hastening the end of the Commandos in the Middle East. The SAS – whose own raid that night had also gone very wrong when high winds blew them off course – took over most special operations in the theatre, working closely with the Long Range Desert Group. Larger raids there in the future were to be supervised by SOE, while the remnants of Laycock's force were absorbed into a variety of different units. He himself was ordered back to London.

Roger Keyes died at Christmas 1945, having repaired his friendship with Churchill after the row over his management of the Commandos. 'I would far rather have Geoffrey alive than Rommel dead,' the Prime Minister had told him. Five years later, he unveiled a tablet in the crypt of St Paul's Cathedral commemorating both father and son.

Their passing marked the end of an era of gallant amateurism in raiding, a cast of mind much too common in the early years of Britain's war. In North Africa, it would be replaced by the professionalism of Montgomery, and at Combined Operations by the vigour of Mountbatten.

For eighteen months, much had been expected of the Commandos and very little achieved. Now it was high time to make good on all that promise.

4

ARCHERY

Roger Keyes's fall, and the ill treatment of Layforce, had revealed the tensions between those responsible for the day-to-day conduct of the war and those with longer-term objectives. The former could ensure that the Axis was kept at bay, but ultimate victory would require an invasion of Europe, with all the planning and equipment that entailed. Churchill had reluctantly agreed that Keyes was not the man to accomplish that task, but he was also aware that he could not allow so fundamental an ambition to be sidelined.

So, from the start, Mountbatten's remit was wider than that given to his predecessor. At first his role as Adviser, Combined Operations, and in the relatively junior naval rank of commodore, appeared more narrowly defined and therefore more limited than Keyes's had been. Yet he made better use of the scope it gave him, and appreciated that organising raids was only the first step in a programme of combined operations that would inevitably bring him greater powers.

None the less, when he took over in October 1941, he faced a struggle to carry out even his most basic duties. Combined Operations Headquarters (COHQ) in Whitehall then had a total staff of twenty-three, including typists and messengers. It had no regular Air Force or Navy officers (only reservists) and not one signals specialist, Mountbatten's own field of expertise. Since the days of Dudley Clarke, many of its personnel had felt their primary loyalty lay with their parent service rather than with COHQ. Quoting Churchill himself, Keyes told Parliament in mid-1942 that he attributed his failure to the 'negative power of those who control the war machine in Whitehall'. Certainly the service ministries, such as the Admiralty, were no keener to see Mountbatten build a rival power base.

Several factors contributed to his success in doing just that. Undoubtedly he benefited greatly from America's entry into the war only six weeks after he took up his post, for the military and industrial might of the United States made it far easier to contemplate a second front. Indeed, a COHQ mission was in Washington to ask President Roosevelt for a loan of landing craft when news broke of the Japanese attack on Pearl Harbor. The British would eventually use hundreds of US-built LCs in the Normandy landings, with the vessels modelled on those used in the swamps of Louisiana.

Mountbatten's personality also helped him to get his way. His evident ambition – in part desire to vindicate his father, Prince Louis of Battenberg, who had been forced by anti-German feeling to resign as First Sea Lord in 1914 – repelled some with whom he had dealings. Yet his comparative youth, energy and enthusiasm for science made him seem modern, and helped to draw the best out of the inter-service staff now recruited to COHQ.

Above all, Mountbatten had Churchill's backing. To retain that, however, he had to demonstrate that he could preside over raids that at last made a significant impact. The Mediterranean had not proved the happiest of hunting grounds, and with its options limited COHQ began to look across the North Sea at the long coast of Norway.

The first successful Commando raid had taken place there the previous March. The fish oil factories of the Lofoten Islands were not heavily defended by the Germans and had been a soft target. The raiders from 3 and 4 Commandos had met with so little opposition that their Navy press officer had been able to go skiing on the hillside above the landings. 'And one of our sillier officers,' recalled Joe Smale, 'a chap called Dick Wills, went to the post office and got them to send a telegram to "A Hitler, Berlin".' It read: YOU SAID YOUR LAST SPEECH GERMAN TROOPS WOULD MEET THE ENGLISH WHEREVER THEY LANDED STOP WHERE ARE YOUR TROOPS? Wills's message may not have been much above the level of a schoolboy's taunt, but it expressed the spirit of defiance that Mountbatten was seeking. Soon after his appointment, three more raids were planned against Norwegian towns. However, the first provided an unwelcome reminder of the habit of disaster which had dogged the Commandos up to that point.

On 9 December 1941, a force chosen from 6 and 12 Commandos sailed from Scotland for Florø, a centre of the herring trade. The press was invited to accompany Operation KITBAG and during the voyage one soldier was persuaded to bend the rules and fuse a grenade for publicity photographs. When it exploded below decks, half a dozen men were killed and twice as many injured. Despite the accident, the mission's naval commander opted to press on, but as the convoy neared Florø its navigation went awry and, unable to locate the fjord on which the town was sited, the ships had to turn back.

The disappointment of yet another cancelled raid made it all the more vital that the two which were to follow went ahead without a hitch. ANKLET, a diversionary attack which was to revisit the Lofotens, was to be carried out on Boxing Day and No. 12 was to have a second chance to show its mettle. Meanwhile, the main operation – ARCHERY – was entrusted to No. 3 and Durnford-Slater.

Their destination would be Vaagso, another important fishing town about a hundred miles north of Bergen. The raid would again take aim at economic targets – shipping and processing plants – but this time No. 3 would also deliberately seek a fight with a German garrison. 'At long last,' thought Durnford-Slater, 'we would learn if our training had made us the fighting and killing force we were intended to be.'

*

For a year now, No. 3 had based itself at Largs, a small town on Scotland's west coast popular with holidaymakers from Glasgow. One of the peculiarities of the Commandos was that the troops did not live in Army barracks but in accommodation that each soldier found for himself and which was paid for from a daily allowance. This arrangement encouraged initiative, spared the men the usual cleaning and maintenance duties, and let the unit move at short notice. Seaside resorts, among them Weymouth, Hastings and Paignton, were popular choices as billets by COs since they had plentiful supplies of B&Bs. 'The soldiers did rather well,' thought No. 3's adjutant Alan Smallman. 'Many of them were able to get landladies on their side by chatting them up and so forth, so they didn't have to spend their per diem of 6s 8d. Most of the officers had to spend all of their 13s 4d living in hotels.' For all the comparative informality of the unit, evidently some assumptions persisted.

Eric de la Torre had first joined No. 8, but he sprained his ankle jumping off the bus in the blackout while home in London on leave and had to stay behind when Layforce sailed. He then transferred to No. 3. When the Commando went to Arran for training, de la Torre was the last off the boat, and seeing that all the seafront cottages were already taken, he and two pals headed uphill. The owner of a large bungalow where they tried their luck turned them away at first, but then called them back on the condition that they learned to play bridge and helped her with the housework. Both her servants and her playing partners had gone back to the mainland. 'We ended up with a better billet than the officers,' recalled de la Torre. 'The trouble was that you'd get back after a hard day's training and she'd get the cards out and it might be one o'clock before you were in bed.'

The administrative arrangements in Largs for the Commando were primitive. The main offices were housed in Nardini's, the local ice-cream parlour, while the Troops established their HQs in a gasworks, a coal yard and a cigarette kiosk on the front. Smallman did better with his accommodation, as he, Peter Young and

Durnford-Slater were put up by Lord Glasgow at his home, Kelvin Castle. In return for the peer's hospitality, Durnford-Slater offered to blow up an old tree stump, and assured him that they could do so without harming a nearby plantation of saplings. He left it to his great friend Lieutenant Charlie Head, a vet in peacetime, to organise the demonstration. Smallman was among those invited to lunch at the castle to watch it: 'Charlie was no expert in demolition, and overdid the explosive charge by about ten times. The tree rose vertically in the air, and fell plumb on top of all those that Lord Glasgow was seeking to protect.' Some weeks later a letter arrived listing all the collateral damage that had been caused by the blast, including the breaking of every window in the castle. 'He added as a PS that when one of the maids had pulled a chain in the downstairs servants' loo the cistern had come off the wall, which we felt was perhaps stretching it a bit.'

Durnford-Slater took rather more care over the arrangements for the raid. A detailed scale model of Vaagso was constructed, which he brought back up from London by train in a reserved compartment after briefing Mountbatten on his progress. The Commando force would consist of some 575 men, with No. 3 bolstered by two Troops from No. 2 and a detachment of Norwegians who had been on the previous Lofotens raid. They would be accompanied by a powerful flotilla of warships led by the cruiser *Kenya*, and for the first time COHQ's planning made provision for coordinated air cover. ARCHERY would be a truly combined operation.

Durnford-Slater had told only a few of his officers about it, and even his second-in-command, Major Jack Churchill, was unaware of the target. The first that ordinary commandos such as George Peel knew of the raid was when they were told to draw ammunition and board two converted Belgian ferries, the *Prince Charles* and the *Prince Leopold*. At Scapa Flow, they picked up *Kenya* as escort but still had no word as to where they were going. 'And then the storm started,' recalled Peel. 'They'd given us pork for lunch and it wasn't very long before that was in the sea.' By the time they reached the Shetlands, on Christmas Eve, there was water to a depth of fourteen feet in the for'ard hold of the *Prince Charles* and the operation was delayed for a day while she was pumped out. The commandos were able to have their lunch of turkey, and shortly before sailing on Boxing Day were told their destination.

Reveille on 27 December was at 0400. Breakfast was an hour later, weapons were checked and then the troops were called up on deck. As they stood quietly together for a while, getting used to the dark, the air felt bitterly chill even to those wearing roll-neck sweaters and thick leather jerkins. Durnford-Slater had made sure to put on clean underwear to reduce the risk of infection if he was wounded. 'You knew there were going to be casualties,' thought George Webb, 'but you hoped it wouldn't be you. If it was you, you hoped you would go out cleanly.'

At 0700, the lead destroyers picked up a beacon from the submarine *Tuna*, stationed at the entrance to Vaagsfjord to prevent any navigational difficulties. An hour later the commandos began to take their places in the LCs. As early glimmers of light began to brighten the snow on the steep slopes above the water, the lookout at Husevaagso spotted the convoy. He telephoned the battery on the island of Maaloy which guarded the approaches to the port. The duty orderly was busy polishing his commander's boots, and so ignored the shrill ringing. The lookout persisted and eventually got his warning through to the harbour master at South Vaagso, only to be told that he must be drunk.

The LCs were lowered and at 0845 began their run-in to the sound of birdsong ashore. As they did so, a flight of Hampdens roared in only a few feet above them and started to bomb the German defences. Three minutes later, a star shell soared over Maaloy. Away to the right, those in the LCs could see pieces of the barracks there being tossed into the air as *Kenya* and her flotilla of four destroyers bombarded the tiny island with more than four hundred shells in less than ten minutes. Meanwhile, the LCs were rapidly closing on the beach, and with just a hundred yards to go Durnford-Slater fired ten red Very lights as a signal to stop the barrage and for the Hampdens to lay smoke.

At that moment, one of the planes was struck by anti-aircraft fire from an armed trawler, and as the pilot lost control it dropped its sixty-pound phosphorus bomb on one of the landing craft. Durnford-Slater had already had a narrow escape when engulfed by a sheet of fire from an explosion on the beach. It had set light to both his sleeves but he had beaten the flames out with his leather gloves. Others were less lucky. George Peel heard the screams of agony of those in the LC hit by the burning phosphorus: 'They jumped into the water to put it out, but it made no difference.' There were at least twenty casualties, with half of 4 Troop killed or wounded.

With several targets to aim at, Durnford-Slater had divided his force into five groups. He would lead the largest, numbering two hundred men, into the main town of South Vaagso. To his left, 2 Troop were already dealing with the small garrison at Hollevik – most of its members still being at breakfast in Vaagso – while on the right 5 and 6 Troops, under Churchill, were heading straight for the coastal battery at Maaloy.

Some of the men had a last swig of water (into which a few had poured their rum ration the night before) as machine-guns opened up on them from the island. These were countered by a far more ancient weapon of war – the skirl of bagpipes, played by Churchill.

By 1941, 'Mad Jack' was already a near-legendary figure. Even by the unorthodox standards of the Commandos, he was acknowledged to have peculiar habits and an insatiable thirst for adventure. He and his brother Tom (who would later act as Laycock's principal staff officer in Italy) had grown up in Hong Kong as the sons of a colonial civil servant, and after being commissioned in 1926 he spent a decade with the Manchester Regiment in Burma. He devoted one leave to crossing India on a motorcycle, until he crashed into a water buffalo.

Peacetime soldiering in Britain bored him, so in 1936 he left the Army, aged twenty-nine, and used his pension to finance a grand tour of Europe. When the money ran out, on the island of Capri, he decided to walk home, making ends meet by playing the bagpipes for an Italian dancer to whom he had taught the rudiments of the Highland Fling. After reaching Paris, still wearing his claymore, he worked as a bodyguard to a playboy who pretended to be the Crown Prince of Siam. 'I think the war coming when it did was probably the best thing that could have happened to me,' he later reflected.

He fought with the BEF in France in 1940, winning the MC for holding up a German advance and extricating his men through the enemy lines in the dark. The campaign also spawned the most enduring legend about him – that he was the first British soldier since the days of Agincourt to kill one of his foes with a bow and arrow. Churchill was a world-class archer, a talent he had displayed before the war in Hollywood films such as *The Thief of Baghdad*, and he recalled that it had long been his ambition to put his skills to use on the modern battlefield: 'I said if I can shoot a chap, and surprise somebody, I will bloody well do so.' However, as he later admitted to a fellow officer – who had watched him fire an arrow through a thick barn door – he had been denied his wish. 'We went into this village one night to ambush a German patrol but the driver reversed the pick-up into a wall and buggered up my bows,' he confessed, 'so when the Jerries did come I had to shoot them with my rifle.'

Now, in Norway, as the melody of 'Frimley' floated across the water to him, Durnford-Slater asked: 'Which bloody fool is that?'

'We all knew it was Mad Jack,' recalled de la Torre, one of whose boyhood heroes had been the piper Daniel Laidlaw, awarded the VC in 1915 for inspiring his comrades at Loos. Churchill's piping seemed to put new heart into his men, too, and as the naval bombardment ended and the ramps of the barges came down, he dashed ashore – brandishing his claymore.

Determined not to be beaten to his objectives, Peter Young had also raced onto the beach and made for the barracks. Through the screen of white smoke that covered everything there suddenly appeared a German soldier. 'I and L/Sgt Connelly shot him,' recorded Young. 'He screamed with pain and surprise, spun round and fell.'

His Troop spread out and began to search the buildings. 'We ran into two Germans and I threatened one of them with my rifle and bayonet,' Young later recalled. Expecting the man to surrender, he had to pull his gun away smartly when instead he made a grab for it. Young and Lance Corporal Harper then shot him as he ran away, but in the meantime another German had taken aim at Young's back: 'At that moment Trooper Clark came round the corner of the building and shot the German and Harper turned round and gave him a burst.'

By now fire had taken hold of the battery offices, and when told that he too was alight Young threw himself out of the window and into the snow. Uninjured, and having set up a temporary HQ, he then set off to find Churchill. He passed one of his men, minus the false teeth that he had left on the *Prince Charles*, bringing in the first of a sizeable group of prisoners. It included two prostitutes who had been attending to the garrison's needs. Very soon it was apparent that the whole island was already under the commandos' control. Young looked at his watch and saw that the entire attack had lasted less than ten minutes.

Crouching on his heels in his LC, immediately behind Durnford-Slater, Eric de la Torre was awaiting his own taste of action. The only man who could see over the sides was the sailor who was steering. As they reached the shallows he warned them that a lorry was coming down the road and that a gun was being trained on them: 'Then a stream of tracer flew over the barge – it didn't look any more lethal than fireworks.'

De la Torre had joined the Commandos from an accounts section in the Ordnance Corps because 'I wanted to get where the action was.' Now he had a pistol in each pocket – and a fifty-eight-pound wireless set on his back. As HQ Troop spilled out onto the beach, two yellow-nosed Me 109s came screaming over the mountain tops and cannon shells hammered into the rocks around them. 'It was absolutely miraculous that none of us were hit,' admitted de la Torre. Yelling, 'Come on, No. 3!' the giant figure of Captain Johnny Giles led the charge towards the wooden houses of South

Vaagso. With him was George Peel, who had joined up at twenty because 'like all stupid young men I wanted excitement'.

Giles used grenades to clear houses near the churchyard one by one. After shooting at three Germans who had been firing at him, he rushed at a door, burst inside – and fell to the ground in front of Peel. 'He was hit straight between the eyes,' Peel remembered. 'When you see your CO shot dead in front of you, your whole mentality changes. You're no longer a boy. You get mad. It ceases to be a game and you're out to kill – you become a real soldier. You do everything to survive and to kill the enemy.'

Slipping on the ice, Peel ran forward again with a small group, taking casualties all the time. 'We kept on going, got to this house, jumped over the fence and crashed in through the back door.' The six of them threw themselves to the floor, keeping as low as they could as bullets tore through the wooden walls of the building. Despite his terror, Peel could not help but notice the incongruity of his surroundings: 'The whole place was looking wonderful. It had been prepared for Christmas, with a tree and presents. We thought: "What are we doing here?"'

Because of their seasickness, most of them had not eaten for more than a day, so they reached up from beneath the table to help themselves to the fruit and cake that lay on top of it. Peel also saw a small silver casket with a cross on it standing on the sideboard:

> Inside were tiny tissues of paper, and I realised by looking at them, even though it was Norwegian, that they were parts of the New Testament. I thought: 'I need God right now, to look after me, perhaps if I put this in my pocket he'll look after me a bit more.' So I put it in my pocket, I don't know why. Then there was a god-almighty scream.
>
> Outside there was a young soldier screaming his head off with pain. He'd been hit by a machine-gun. We grabbed his epaulettes and pulled him inside. We cut off his trousers and the whole of his leg had been shattered.

Peel and his mates took a door off its hinges to use as a stretcher, then tossed a coin to see who would carry it. Peel lost. As he began to back out into the cold air, bullets pockmarked the snow around him and he had to resist the urge to run. 'I thought: "I'm going to get it any moment now."' Somehow, though, they managed to reach the edge of the little rise on which the house stood and pushed the door down to where medics were treating the wounded. In his pocket, Peel fingered the silver casket. 'I thought: "This little box has saved me."'

The fighting was now from house to house, but Peel's section was also caught between snipers in a wood and a howitzer on the other side of the fjord. 'You go forward, observe, then wave the next man on, until you hit trouble,' he remembered. 'The Germans were everywhere. All you were doing was killing as fast as you could . . . you're fighting and fighting and killing and killing. You think you're not going to survive this, but you do.'

As Peel struggled to take in Giles's death, Captain Algy Forrester led the remnants of 4 Troop up the town's narrow main street, firing his tommy-gun from the hip. Two of his fellow subalterns had already been wounded and it was clear that the German resistance was far stiffer and more skilful than anticipated. The commandos had been told that the garrison numbered 150, but it had been substantially increased by seasoned troops on Christmas leave. And, as luck would have it, more than seventy German soldiers had been forming up for a march through the town when the attack started. Some made use of the excellent natural cover on the hillside to harass the commandos as they pushed up from the beach, while others turned the Ulvesund Hotel into a strongpoint. This commanded the entrance to South Vaagso, and in the face of fire from it the raiders' advance faltered.

Determined to regain the momentum, Forrester pulled the pin on a grenade and made a dash for the hotel's front door. As he did so, it opened, one of the defenders shot him, and he fell on his own grenade. At once Captain Martin Linge, leading the Norwegian section attached to 4 Troop, took over and led a second charge, only to be fatally shot through the chest as he reached the building. Within twenty minutes, the leaders of 3 and 4 Troops had both been killed and most of their other officers had been put out of action. The attack was stalling.

The news of these losses rocked many of the commandos. 'I was very surprised when told that Captain Forrester had just been shot,' recalled George Webb. 'I just thought he was capable of doing anything – he was very single-minded.' Meanwhile, at the HQ set up near the beach, de la Torre had heard the bursts of automatic fire up ahead. 'Then Drain, who was Johnny Giles's wireless operator, came running back white-faced and said: "Captain Giles is dead." He was a giant of a man, played rugby for Herefordshire and boxed heavyweight for the Commandos. The thought that he was dead was a real shock.'

De la Torre and Durnford-Slater had set up their signals post in the first house they had come to. There was no sign of its inhabitants, but the stove was still warm and when they tried the bedroom door it was locked. De la Torre tried to get the radio going but because of the mountains around Vaagso he was unable to raise any of the other sections. With Durnford-Slater increasingly concerned to learn what was happening elsewhere, de la Torre decided to see if he could get a better signal up the hill behind them. 'Something flew over my head,' he said later, 'and a split second later I heard the crack of a rifle. There was a German up there!' He hid behind a large rock and cautiously lifted his helmet above it on the point of his pistol. There was another shot. Lying flat on his stomach, he wriggled back to the house and gave Durnford-Slater the bad news. If he wanted to discover what had happened to the attack, the colonel would have to go forward and find out himself.

It was now about 1000. As Durnford-Slater walked briskly towards the main street he could see how the terrain – hills close by on one side, and the fjord on the other – had made it difficult for his men to outflank the defenders. Although he could not contact the Troops ahead of him, he was in communication with the head of the Special Service Brigade, Charles Haydon, who was on *Kenya*.

Suspecting from the firing he could hear that fresh impetus was required, Durnford-Slater now asked Haydon to commit the reserve which until then had been kept aboard ship.

One of its officers was Lieutenant Graeme Black, a thirty-year-old Canadian who had been in Norway back in 1940 with an Independent Company before joining No. 2 Commando. He and the rest of 4 Troop had assumed that they were being sent on a course when they went up to Thurso at Christmas, and only realised they were bound for Vaagso when Norwegian interpreters joined their ship.

Looking over a low stone wall, Black saw the street and quayside ahead shrouded in black smoke. He pushed a pair of scouts across the side of the hill to flush out any snipers and then beckoned to his men to follow him up the left side of the road. There was a dead German in the first house they reached. The next shelter was 150 yards away and Black ran hard towards it, holding a Bren in front of him in case of trouble.

His Troop then shuttled from house to house, finding only frightened civilians in their cellars. But a little further on they came across a group from No. 3 held up by the concentration of fire beyond. Black dashed across the snow to the nearest house, and from the dining room spotted three figures about a hundred yards away, behind the main street. Knowing from their greatcoats that they must be Germans, he loosed off his pistol at them. Then he grabbed a rifle and lined up a shot at a man holding a Schmeisser submachine gun. An instant later he reeled back from the window. His intended target had fired first and put three bullets through Black's forearm and wrist, smashing his watch. When later asked his opinion of the value of the Schmeisser as a weapon he quipped: 'I reckon a two-inch group at 100 yards isn't too bad.'

Despite the pain, once patched up he was able to relay fire directions from spotters to the Bren gunners now sited either side of the house. They were to give covering fire while another group rushed a cottage where the Germans were massing for a counter-attack. Fortunately Black insisted on trying the three tommy-guns that his men were going to use. None of them worked: their return springs had frozen solid.

The Germans' weapons had no such problems. Bullets zipped through the thin walls of the house, shredding the bells and tinsel on the Christmas tree. Black suffered another wound in the arm, while in the wooden boards just above Sergeant Bill Challington's head there were soon more than fifty holes. Challington ignored them, asking only for the small-arms ammunition from the casualties' pouches to be loaded into Bren magazines for him. Soon his steady nerve began to calm the others.

In the meantime Durnford-Slater was searching busily for 3 and 4 Troops. Charlie Head advised him to keep an eye out for snipers as they entered the town. 'Lookout nothing,' he snapped back, 'I'm in a hurry.' At the water's edge he was reunited with Peter Young, who was coming ashore with his men after being summoned from Maaloy to help.

To give themselves some protection from the Germans on the hillside, Young decided to work his way forward through the closely grouped warehouses along the wharf. Moving in single file through the soft snow, his men ran into another party commanded by Lieutenant Denis O'Flaherty. Bounding from building to building like stepping stones, together they had reached a large woodpile when two men fell, one shot through the lungs and dying. There was no sign of the sniper. All too aware of how exposed the commandos were, Young ordered them to run to a red-painted warehouse some sixty yards away. He took the lead and was within ten strides of the doorway when a smartly turned-out German stepped into it and threw a stick grenade at him. Young swerved to his left, fired from the hip, and ducked as a second grenade followed. Reaching the wall of the building, he flattened himself against it with only a large crate between himself and the door. He was soon joined by Sergeant George Herbert and several others. As they fumbled with cold fingers for their Mills bombs, a third German grenade landed about eight feet from them. Young had time to brood on the damage it would do to his legs before he realised it had failed to go off.

The warehouse was large, so Herbert hurled about ten grenades into it. 'I then ran into the building shouting "Hande Hoch!",' wrote Young later, 'thinking that they had been done for. I was immediately shot at from an inner door, returned the fire, and came out.' It was dark within and it seemed too risky to attempt a frontal assault. Then inspiration struck Young. The depot was made of wood: they could burn it down.

But while he started to organise this, O'Flaherty and Trooper Sherington – both armed with tommy-guns – ran inside and up the stairs. Young angrily followed them in and heard two shots. 'Sherington had been hit in the leg,' he wrote, 'and O'Flaherty looked as if he had had a plate of strawberry jam flung in his face.' A bullet had gone through his eye, down into his mouth and out the side of his neck. Their lone foe could have finished both men off but instead he let them stagger out. 'Although I detest Jerry,' said Herbert, 'this one must have been a gentleman, and what a fighter.' He needed to be dealt with, however, so Herbert splashed petrol up the walls and within a few seconds the whole building was burning fiercely. Young left one man to attend to the German when the smoke and heat forced him out, and continued up the road.

Bitter street fighting of this kind was now going on everywhere in the town. After a few minutes, Young met up with Durnford-Slater again. Seeing a car outside one house, they suspected that it might be the billet of the garrison commander. Young shoved open the door and searched inside. Lying on his bed they found Hauptmann Schröder, brought there to die after being hit by a shell. Young was all for rousing him but Durnford-Slater told him to leave the man be.

Gathering what was left of their sections, the pair now advanced in waves down the main street. Young dashed from door to door, but Durnford-Slater disdained cover and simply strode swiftly onwards, pistol in hand. Suddenly Herbert halted and pointed, and Young heard an explosion as Durnford-Slater vanished from sight. A German sailor had opened a door on the fjord side of the road and lobbed a grenade which had come to rest between the colonel's feet. He happened to be standing on a corner and flung himself around it. The only injuries he suffered were grazes to his knuckles, but his batman and another soldier were badly wounded.

The sailor who had thrown the grenade then walked out with his hands up. But Sergeant Joe Mills's blood was up. 'He shouted "Nein, nein" to Sgt Mills,' recalled Young, 'who however replied "Ja, ja" and shot him.'

'Yeah, well, Mills,' said Durnford-Slater laconically, 'you shouldn't have done that.'

Mills was awarded the Military Medal after the raid. The responsibility shown by him and other NCOs, such as Herbert and Challington, during it was to become one of the characteristics of the Commandos; indeed, more of their officers than usual would come through the ranks. The Army's hierarchy inevitably reflected the class divisions in society, but in the Commandos respect for officers tended to be earned rather than simply given.

When Forrester and Linge were killed in rapid succession trying to storm the Ulvesund Hotel, it was Corporal Ernest 'Knocker' White who rallied the remnants of 4 Troop. He had no experience of command, but as he stood up, gave orders and saw them obeyed he grew in confidence. A few moments earlier, none of the others had had any appetite for battle. Now they reloaded, took their places at his shoulder, and turned their vengeful fury on the Germans.

Soon after, Sergeant Ramsey and the mortar section appeared. He landed a direct hit on the hotel roof with his third round, and then dropped another ten through the hole. Grenades were thrown in and a rapid fire kept up to prevent anyone escaping. When Durnford-Slater later passed the ashes of the building he counted more than a dozen bodies inside.

Satisfied that the work of demolishing the oil factories was now well in hand, the colonel began to make his way back to his HQ through the blazing streets. The sky was filled with a blizzard of labels from the canning plants which soon smothered everything that was not alight. A young German soldier lay in the snow, close to death. He waved Durnford-Slater over and, in place of a common language, offered him his hand to shake.

At 1250 the signal was given to withdraw.

The fighting had died down in most places but there were still pockets of lethal resistance. Graeme Black waited half an hour to ensure that the troops pulling back on his right could not be outflanked, then he was helped through the fence to the house behind. Here there were a number of wounded men and no officers in charge. He started to send the injured to a sunken courtyard by the post office some eighty yards away, but as the men paused to lower themselves down to it two were picked off by snipers. When Black arrived, he dived in head first despite his wounds and was copied by those behind him.

He soon realised that the injured could not scale the hill between them and the boats. First he sent runners to ask for a pick-up where they were but when the men did not return he accepted that they too must have been hit. So he set off himself, dodging from door to door. Behind one he heard a noise and burst in: it had been made by three locals hiding under a pile of oilskins. Further on, fire forced him up the hillside, stumbling through slush, his breath coming fast as he used his injured arm to lever himself awkwardly over waist-high wire fences. At the landing area he found Durnford-Slater, who agreed to send an LC to collect the wounded.

George Peel was also still in close contact with the enemy. He had received the order to withdraw and was standing on the porch of a house when its door began to open towards him. 'I thought: "It can't be a Norwegian, they wouldn't be that stupid, it must be a German." I kicked the door like mad, saw a body there, and pulled out my knife and put it straight in his middle. I let it go and saw the body collapse.' It was a German officer. 'Having done it for the first time, it appalled me. You have no idea what it feels like to put a knife in someone. I didn't want anything to do with that knife any more. I saw the man: he looked at me.'

By 1445 re-embarkation was complete. In the dwindling light, the convoy headed for Scapa Flow, carrying 98 prisoners and 77 volunteers for the Norwegian forces in exile. Some 130 Germans had been killed for the loss of 17 commandos and the Norwegian Captain Linge. Two naval ratings had also lost their lives. While the soldiers had been ashore, two destroyers had sunk nine vessels in the sound beyond Maaloy, despite the stout fight put up by a twenty-five-ton trawler, *Fohn*. Her officer had been killed by a shell as he was about to drop the ship's code books over the side. They contained the call signs for all enemy shipping in northern waters, including France, and would prove a valuable source of intelligence.

The RAF had also seen through its part in the synchronised plan to prevent the Germans intervening during the raid. It had put the runways at Herdla and Stavanger out of action, and Blenheims and Beaufighters had maintained top cover over the operation from dawn until dusk. But eleven aircraft had been lost, overmatched against the Luftwaffe's nimbler machines. 'It was a terrible sight to see them hit the mountains and bounce like balls of fire down the cliffs into the sea,' wrote Haydon's brigade major, the novelist Robert Henriques.

> The sight was particularly painful for us, because we saw it from the bridge of the *Kenya* where the RAF controller was trying desperately to warn the Blenheims that German fighters were on their tail. We had warned the RAF again and again that unless they took part in our planning and communications exercises their radio links from ship to aircraft could not possibly work. But the RAF had refused to participate at any stage . . . and the deck-to-air link was never even tested before we sailed.

It was a painful lesson to learn, but otherwise Henriques thought ARCHERY a triumph for COHQ's planning. 'I have never been in a battle where such perfect control was maintained, so far as the naval and military forces were concerned,' he noted. The Command Group on *Kenya* had maintained an air of calm detachment throughout the engagement, even when bombs fell near by in a rare German attack. Henriques had looked up from the deck to see a batman staring down at him reprovingly, the tray and cups still in his hands: 'Hot soup, sir?'

Peter Young spent the voyage to Scotland interrogating German prisoners, but some found other ways to keep busy. The two prostitutes had been put in the cabin of the ship's doctor, but after helping themselves to his pyjamas they began to wander the corridors. A couple of sentries were detailed to keep them in their room. The next time that the captain passed by he saw two rifles with fixed bayonets leaning against the door.

The medics had their hands full treating the fifty-seven wounded soldiers. Those who did not pull through were buried at sea. 'It brought home to you what war was about,' thought Eric de la Torre as he watched the coffins slide into the grey deep.

That became all the more evident when they arrived back in Largs several days later. 'As we drew in,' recalled Alan Smallman, 'we were met by quite a number of wives anxious to know what had happened to husbands. The landladies had been happy for men to have their wives up, but in retrospect we shouldn't have allowed it. I had the sad task, as one or two others did, of explaining to wives whose husbands had been injured or killed that that had happened.' Among those in the crowd on the platform was Johnny Giles's mother, who had come with his brother to welcome him home. 'That was sad,' said Smallman. 'After that we had a rule that no wives should join the throng.'

Next morning on parade Durnford-Slater made a speech to the Commando in which he paid tribute to the fallen of both sides. He also said that one or two had not proved up to the standards he demanded and would be RTUd. Then he announced that every pub in Largs had agreed to stand the men free beer on New Year's Eve. 'Can you imagine what a night that was!' remembered George Peel. 'They were wonderful people.'

The CO himself held a party to celebrate the success of the raid. Some thought it inappropriate and him callous, but when his landlady brought Durnford-Slater a cup of tea on New Year's Day she found him crying. 'I had been thinking about my friends who died in the long, snowy street,' he wrote. 'These gallant dead would not be with us for battles to come. Without them we should not have done so well at Vaagso.'

Many of those who had come through were proud of what they had achieved. 'We'd been blooded,' thought Peel, 'we were commandos.' Back in Bristol on his first leave after the raid, he noticed that it had given others a lift, too. When he walked into the Mauretania pub, wearing his uniform and Commando shoulder-titles, he was bought drinks all night.

'It was a big morale booster,' agreed George Webb. 'It made us think we'd done something that the country wanted. Otherwise we were just bumbling along from one disaster to another.'

Among those delighted by ARCHERY was Mountbatten. 'I am basking in your reflected glory,' he told Haydon, for the raid had strengthened his hand by proving what could be accomplished. Within two months he was to be elevated from mere Adviser to Chief of Combined Operations. Remarkably, he was to sit as an equal with the Chiefs of Staff whenever matters within his sphere of action were discussed. He was promoted to acting vice-admiral, and given the equivalent honorary rank in the other two services. It was a testament to both his political skill and his charisma that Mountbatten's appointment was approved by the Chiefs themselves. COHQ was here to stay.

The most important lesson of Vaagso had been that tri-service planning paid off. 'It had never been achieved before with British forces,' stressed Henriques, 'and it was a pattern for the rest of the war.' Ideas that had seemed novel – the importance of flexibility, the use of a floating reserve and diversionary air attacks – now became standard, as did leaving control of a raid to the commander on the ground. Ultimately, the cooperation achieved at Vaagso became the blueprint for all future amphibious operations. Indeed, after the TORCH landings in North Africa exposed the chasm of understanding between the US Army and Navy, Henriques was sent to help Major General Lucian Truscott with the planning for HUSKY, the invasion of Sicily.

So keen did Truscott become to promote integration between the services that he made naval and army counterparts share bedrooms and sit next to each other during meals.

The expansion of COHQ which followed ARCHERY had long-term consequences for the Commandos as well. From now on, Mountbatten's focus was not so much on the results of individual attacks but on what could be learned from them. The Commandos would remain the cutting edge of Combined Operations. Yet, where they had been at its core, where originally *it* had been created to service *their* needs, they now became the research arm of an organisation with a rapidly enlarging portfolio of other interests. From 1942, Commando raids in any strength were in essence dry runs for D-Day.

This switch in emphasis from the tactical to the strategic benefits of raiding was not without irony, given the impact of ARCHERY on the German High Command. There is little firm evidence to support the widespread belief that Hitler and his advisers considered the Commandos (and indeed most resistance activity in Northern Europe, including the work of SOE) to be a major threat to their control of occupied territories. Attacks did dent their prestige, and outrage the Führer, but their effects were short lived, often localised and did not, in themselves, exert decisive influence on German planning for the war.

Perhaps the only exception was in Norway. Its fifteen-thousand-mile coastline – six times that of France and by far the longest in Europe – was impossible to guard and Hitler thought it a 'zone of destiny'. 'If the British go about things properly,' he said after ARCHERY and its companion raid ANKLET, 'they will attack northern Norway at several points . . . and thus exert pressure on Sweden and Finland. This might be of decisive importance for the outcome of the war.'

Although ARCHERY had been no such thing, Hitler feared it was the precursor to a full-scale landing. Even before Vaagso, Norway had been placed under a state of emergency and the local populace subjected to SS jurisdiction. After the raid, the German Navy assessed the garrison as having 'feet of clay' and much of the fleet's offensive capacity was diverted to the country's defence. Vast numbers of troops were also transferred there. Although many were second-line soldiers in fortification battalions, by 1945 up to three hundred thousand German soldiers were in Norway rather than in North-West Europe.

Yet, for all the care taken over its planning, ARCHERY might have gone the way of the raids in the Mediterranean. The intelligence had been faulty again and the commandos faced a larger and more experienced German force than anticipated. So what had made the difference this time?

Durnford-Slater had no doubts. When he came to brief 3 Commando in 1943 for the invasion of Sicily, he cited as the standard he expected an earlier example of leadership. 'Algy Forrester's performance at Vaagso, by going like hell down the main street, really won that battle,' he told them. 'You can't just say, "Nip along there, I'll be along in a minute."'

Joe Smale fully appreciated what was expected of him and his fellow officers:

> John [Durnford-Slater] was an artillery officer commanding what was essentially an infantry unit, and he looked at tactics in a different way from how an infantry officer would . . . One of the main things he instilled into us was that officers must lead. He felt they were the best people to do it, that the men knew them and would follow them. If it was left to the underlings it would take longer, and require more covering fire, which we hadn't got. There had to be officer power in front . . . That was what you were there for. If you didn't like it, you could go back to your regiment, and to conventional warfare.

But Smale also acknowledged that over time making officers the spearhead veered close to recklessness. At one anniversary reunion, he talked to a soldier who told him that 'the good thing about

No. 3 was that we had officers who led from the front', as Durnford-Slater himself did. 'That's why we lost three troop commanders at Vaagso,' Smale pointed out. 'Well, you could do that if you had one or two raids a year, but it wouldn't do for a long campaign. In ordinary infantry warfare you couldn't afford to lose three senior officers each time you went into action. But that's why you joined a Commando.'

Denis O'Flaherty won the DSO for his leadership at Vaagso, but he too queried the long-term viability of headlong heroism. The raid established the effectiveness of the tactics of fire-and-movement that were later to become the signature of the Commandos, but by 1944, 'quite rightly they had lost the blind dash that I thought was remarkable in the minority who were actually engaged at close quarters at Vaagso. I have never seen that equalled in any Army since.'

There had been no lack of dash at Litani or on the Rommel raid, but at Vaagso everything had at last come together. Backed by air and sea power, acting with ruthlessness and professionalism, the raiders could afford to take risks, to feel sure of themselves even when the going was hard.

'Before Vaagso, late in 1941, the Germans had taken no real beating on land,' wrote Durnford-Slater. 'Now, I felt, all our arduous training and my merciless rejection of the unsuitable and the unfit had been justified.' The Commandos had finally come of age.

5

POSTMASTER

On the dunes at Dunkirk a young British officer was waiting for a ship. All around him lay the chaos of defeat. As he crouched alone in a shell hole in the sand, watching for Stukas in the sky above, he was sent sprawling by a blow which hit him hard on the back. 'This is it,' he thought, 'they've got me.' Then he heard a voice stammer in his ear: 'I say, I f-f-feel a b-b-bloody coward. How about you?'

There was much about Commando raids that was new. Unlike most military operations they did not aim to take and hold territory or to engage and destroy a significant part of the enemy's forces. Yet, while this affected their training and tactics, the majority of their attacks were in many ways more conventional than is commonly thought. Far from being made by small groups dependent largely on stealth, they often sought to overpower smaller garrisons with weight of numbers, as at Litani and Vaagso. Both of those assaults also took place in daylight.

Nevertheless, a handful of units did come to specialise in raids which relied on guile and the daring of a few men. If, like the SAS, these units did not always remain within the Commando fold, they almost always had their roots in it. Although little known even at the time, among the most successful and influential was the force which had its beginnings on that beach at Dunkirk.

Geoffrey Appleyard struck many who met him as the perfect soldier. From boyhood in Yorkshire he had been high-spirited and active, and by the time he went up to Cambridge he had become a world-class skier. He arranged to spend Christmas 1936 in Italy in the shadow of the Matterhorn. While there, he climbed over the Swiss frontier, skied down the glacier to Zermatt and made the return journey the same evening by moonlight. As a test of endurance it was considered so foolhardy that no guide would accompany him. In 1938, aged twenty-two, he captained the England ski team to victory against Norway and, but for the outbreak of war, would have competed in the 1940 Winter Olympics.

As it was, he joined the Royal Army Service Corps. 'Funny how relative everything is,' he wrote to his parents, 'you don't really appreciate a holiday til it's over. The same way you don't really appreciate your liberty until it's threatened. But I'll *never* be *made* to say "Heil Hitler". I'd sooner die.'

By the time that he found himself at Dunkirk, he had already been mentioned in dispatches for defusing an ugly situation when a French officer had threatened to shoot him unless allowed to jump the queue of traffic retreating towards the coast. Handsome, straightforward and a devout Christian, there was something about him that reminded others of one of King Arthur's knights. All he lacked was a leader to serve.

Gus March-Phillipps also seemed to be a figure from a more romantic past. 'M-P is a very stout fellow,' Appleyard wrote later, comparing him to Francis Drake, 'a great lover of the open air, of country places and, above all, of this England of ours and all its unique beauty and life.' He was a professional soldier in the Royal Artillery, a novelist, and an accomplished horseman whose scarred mouth only improved his looks in the eyes of his admirers. But where Appleyard was a team player, M-P was an individualist who did things his own way, and went white with stuttering rage when not allowed to. 'He was one of the two men I met during the war who frightened me the most,' recalled the historian M.R.D. Foot, then an intelligence officer at COHQ. The other was the similarly unpredictable Paddy Mayne.

Shortly after returning from France, March-Phillipps joined 7 Commando as a troop leader. He soon recruited Appleyard as one of his subalterns, the two men having become friends following their alarming meeting in that shell hole at Dunkirk. 'Of course, it's absolutely terrific – it's the grandest job in the Army one could possibly get,' an excited Appleyard told his parents. 'Just pure operations, the success of which depends principally on oneself and the men one has oneself picked to do the job with you.'

In the autumn of 1940 they were sent up to the Highlands. Among those training with them was a recent Oxford graduate and fellow veteran of Dunkirk, Jan Nasmyth. One rainy afternoon he wrote an essay on the philosophy of raiding. In the English fashion, it made its way to his former tutor at Balliol, from there to the Vice-Chief of the Imperial General Staff, and finally into the hands of Colin Gubbins, then helping to set up SOE. Gubbins was impressed by Nasmyth's ideas, and with SOE still in its infancy he was in need of a core of experienced soldiers who could carry out missions for it. Many of its first agents had been brought in for their knowledge of foreign countries and their language skills, but they were often more intellectual than military types, and it would take time to train and infiltrate them into Europe. By January 1941, SOE had arranged for March-Phillipps and a group of his commandos to be put on its books as instructors – and as its specialised raiding team.

They had a varied workload. At the start of April, Appleyard embarked on the submarine *Tigris*, bound for the Bay of Biscay. One of his colleagues was André Desgranges, formerly a diver in the French Navy. The force's task was to pick up the first Free French agents that SOE had managed to drop into France. Operation SAVANNA had aimed to ambush Luftwaffe pilots as they travelled by bus from their billets to Meucon airfield in Brittany. Five French soldiers led by Captain Georges Bergé had landed by parachute in mid-March but had soon learned that the Germans' travel arrangements had changed, making an attack impossible. Instead they had headed south to the sands of Les Sables d'Olonne, near La Rochelle, to await extraction.

On the first night, Appleyard and Desgranges each paddled a two-man folbot a couple of miles to shore but there was no sign of a light or of Bergé's men. In the darkness, Desgranges was carried by the current onto a rock and, having abandoned his holed canoe, returned to the sub in Appleyard's. When they surfaced again on the next appointed evening, there was a heavy sea running and *Tigris*'s captain tried to dissuade them from landing. But Appleyard thought he had seen a signal on land and insisted on having the two remaining canoes prepared. However, as they were being readied on deck, one was swept away by a wave. Repeated attempts were then made to get the final canoe away but it kept capsizing, throwing Appleyard into the freezing water. Eventually he managed to battle his way to the beach, but still there was no one waiting there.

He had been warned to be back by moonrise at 0300. Knowing that time was fast drawing on, Appleyard now threw caution aside. Waving his torch, he began to shout at the top of his voice as he ran up and down the sand. Then, just as he had decided to get back into his folbot, three men came out of hiding. They were Bergé, Joël Le Tac and Jean Forman, who until that moment had themselves been under observation from German coast watchers. The other two members of the party had failed to make the rendezvous.

There was no way that all four men could fit into the canoe. Le Tac volunteered to stay behind and waded into the pounding surf to hold the head of the folbot steady. His two comrades then squeezed themselves in behind Appleyard. During the three-mile journey back to *Tigris* their combined weight repeatedly threatened to sink the craft. Waves broke over them again and again, swamping the boat, and only a combination of steady bailing and vigorous paddling brought them to the sub just as she was submerging. They had all been given up as lost.

Le Tac made his way to Paris and when Forman was infiltrated back into France the pair carried out SOE's first major act of sabotage – blowing up a power station near Bordeaux. Bergé went on to link up with David Stirling in the desert and to found the French Squadron of the SAS.

Appleyard received the MC for this exploit, but March-Phillipps was already making plans for larger operations. SOE would need time to build up networks in Occupied Europe, but in the meantime it was keen to mount amphibious missions of its own. Accordingly, in March 1941, March-Phillipps had bought *Maid Honor*, a sixty-five-ton fishing trawler with a wooden hull and the reddish-brown sails characteristic of her home port of Brixham. She would need a crew of about a dozen. Appleyard was chosen as second-in-command, and in turn brought on board his childhood friend Graham Hayes, who had experience of sailing to Australia on a four-masted grain ship. Hayes was now in 2 Commando and persuaded his sergeant, Tom Winter, an able engineer, to join Maid Honor Force with him. Other recruits included Desgranges, valued as much for his cheerfulness as for his mechanic's skills, while from 7 Commando came the newly commissioned Leslie Prout as supplies officer.

There was also a tall, fair-haired, twenty-year-old Dane, assessed initially by SOE as 'the weakest character of the party . . . the black sheep of a good family who has run away from home and become a sailor'. Yet soon Anders Lassen's athleticism and expertise as a hunter, as well as his evident hatred for the Germans, impressed his instructors so much that he was recommended to Gubbins as a potential crew member for the *Maid Honor*. When he reported to the ship, March-Phillipps turned to Prout and said: 'Unless I am very much mistaken, that youngster will go a long way.' Within four years Lassen would become the most highly decorated commando of the war.

By the summer of 1941 the force was based at Poole, in Dorset, but its ultimate area of operations was to be much farther afield. The situation in the Mediterranean meant that much Allied shipping heading for Egypt, as well as for India and the Far East, now passed along the west coast of Africa. But losses to U-boats were becoming so severe there that convoys from Britain were beginning to be routed to the Cape of Good Hope via Brazil, turning a brief cruise into a six-week voyage. The Admiralty suspected that the submarines were refuelling at bases in Equatorial Africa, largely under Vichy French control, and SOE was ordered to gather intelligence on them.

So, in August, *Maid Honor* set course for Sierra Leone. Such an adventure was considered too hazardous to risk all of the crew and much to Appleyard's frustration he was ordered to travel out separately with Prout. He worried constantly about the small trawler's ability to cope with the vast ocean but five weeks later she sailed proudly into Freetown. The only moment of anxiety had come when she was challenged by a British cruiser.

For the next few months Appleyard and March-Phillipps combed the mangrove swamps of French West Africa without finding any trace of a U-boat. Boredom with the heat and the mosquitoes had just begun to set in when the SOE station in Nigeria identified a new potential target. Twenty miles out in the Gulf of Guinea lay the island of Fernando Pó. It was a Spanish colony, and so a neutral haven for three Axis ships which had been anchored there for more than a year. The largest was an eight-thousand-ton Italian merchantman, the *Duchessa d'Aosta*, bound for Genoa when Italy's entry into the war had forced her to take refuge in the port of Santa Isabel. Her valuable cargo included several million pounds (by weight) of wool, hides, copra and coffee, as well as copper ingots. Already moored in the harbour when she arrived were two smaller German vessels which had fled British plantations in the Cameroons – the tug *Likomba* and a diesel-driven barge, *Bibundi*. Noting that 'they had an 80 per cent incidence of VD, no money and little food', the island's British Consul reported that the forty-strong crew of the *Duchessa* appeared to have little interest in fighting for Mussolini. But her radio had been left unsealed by the Spanish authorities and might be used to report the movement of Allied convoys. Meanwhile, the *Likomba* had taken on a supply of oil and looked as if she might be readying herself for sea. Somewhat reluctantly, the Foreign Office agreed that SOE should try to hijack all three ships, providing that their activities could not be traced back to the British government and so compromise relations with Spain.

Throughout the autumn, work went ahead on preparing the coup. Once a week the SOE agent who had suggested it, Leonard Guise, made the journey from the mainland to Fernando Pó in an ancient and leaky launch. He was posing as a diplomatic courier but all the while was noting the shoals, currents and buoys of the harbour approaches. Meanwhile, the British Vice-Consul at Santa Isabel, who also worked for SOE, got on friendly terms with the pilot of the Spanish Governor's private aircraft. The souvenir photographs of his flights over the island included some admirably detailed images of the ships below.

Initially, the Governor had been suspicious of these joyrides and put the British Consulate under surveillance. Then SOE had a stroke of luck:

> On a hot afternoon . . . our Vice-Consul had the good fortune to discover the Governor beguiling the boredom of the siesta by giving one of his native mistresses a shower-bath from a watering can. Blackmail would be too strong a word for the delicacy with which the Vice-Consul conveyed to the Governor that this pastime, if widely publicised, might injure his reputation on the island; but it remains a fact that the severity of his restrictions against the Consulate was relaxed, and from that hour.

Meanwhile, at Lagos, the assault party was being assembled. To minimise the chances of British complicity being discovered, they would have to strike with great rapidity. The force would enter the port on a moonless night, seize control of all three ships, disable the wireless, blow the mooring chains with explosives and tow the vessels out to sea. All this was to take no more than fifteen minutes.

Much would depend, however, on what opposition was encountered. A scheme was already being hatched to lure the crews to a dinner on the night of the attack, fixed for 14 January. Yet in case some remained on board it was thought sensible for the raiders to number at least thirty. The local branch of SOE could only spare four of its staff and their thoughts turned to the eleven commandos on *Maid Honor*: 'We were very pleased to find such a party of delightful, enthusiastic and courageous men prepared to face any task allotted to them, no matter what the odds.'

Less cooperative were the British colonial military authorities, who refused to loan any of their troops for what they regarded as an act of piracy. Only at the last moment were another seventeen volunteers found among Nigeria's police and civil service. Most assumed that they would be trekking overland to French territory – one guess was that they were going to kidnap the Governor of Dahomey (now Benin) – and spent their last twenty-four hours ashore practising marching in heavy boots.

Maid Honor herself was not suitable for the mission so the colonial administration lent the force two tugs, *Vulcan* and *Nuneaton*. Under the cover of darkness they were stocked with ammunition and weapons, explosives packed in two Bergen rucksacks, and a supply of detonators kept in waterproof tins. March-Phillipps then briefed his men, making it clear that secrecy was essential. 'Gus's threats as to what he would do to anyone who talked made the thought of falling into enemy hands seem almost pleasant,' recalled one of the SOE agents, Major Desmond Longe. The ships left Lagos in the dead of night on Sunday 11 January, steering west under the waning moon to fox any watching eyes until they were well out to sea.

It was not the most comfortable of voyages. As *Nuneaton* could not carry enough fuel for a round trip, she was towed by *Vulcan* at two cables' length, wallowing in the swell like a naughty puppy on the end of a lead. Longe recorded of those aboard that 'many of the volunteers (not being seafaring men) suffered sadly . . . in the rollers of the South Atlantic'. The galley stoves had been commandeered for heating and moulding the plastic explosive into shaped charges, so at first there were no hot meals, either.

The daylight hours were spent sunbathing, sharpening knives and taking pot-shots at the sharks which followed the tugs. Graham Hayes also trained several of the party to paddle folbots, which were to play an important role in the operation. While practising this, Bill Newington, normally a district commissioner, capsized when he made the mistake of shifting his considerable bulk abruptly as he turned to look behind him. He swam nonchalantly back to *Nuneaton* still wearing his pork-pie hat and with his pipe clenched between his teeth, pushing the canoe in front of him. None of the frantic cries and gestures from the boat could induce him to speed up his return, and it was only when he was pulled from the water that he realised there had been a large dorsal fin behind him all the way.

There was a more serious alarm when an especially large wave caught the nose of *Nuneaton* and pulled it under. She had been shearing off at an angle, so the crew had lashed her helm in order that they could take turns firing the Bren gun from the stern. Now she began to ship water and list sharply to starboard. Crates of beer, lengths of hawser and the crew's suitcases slid off the deck into the sea, there were shouts for help from the rapidly flooding engine room, and it was clear to all watching from *Vulcan* that the other boat would soon sink under the strain of the tow.

The only man to react was Anders Lassen. He rushed from *Vulcan*'s wheelhouse and severed the tow line with an axe. At once the danger was averted but *Nuneaton* had virtually turned on her side and although the crew managed to right her, water had got into the engine and it began to give trouble. This was a serious problem. At a key moment during the attack it might fail. To carry on was to run even greater risks than the force had already accepted – but without any hesitation March-Phillipps decided to do so.

Just before midnight on the 14th, both ships were in position two hundred yards outside the crescent-shaped harbour of Santa Isabel. There was a last shake of hands and a mug of rum was passed round.

Across the dark water, the lights of Fernando Pó shone like fireflies. Precisely at midnight, as if by magic, they all vanished. SOE had bribed the wife of the chief electrician of the power station with a diamond bracelet and she had arranged for one of her admirers to be on duty at the plant that evening.

The crews of the three target ships had meanwhile been invited to a select gathering at the casino. 'His Majesty's Government's funds for this night reached even the proprietor of the local brothel,' Longe revealed, 'whose ladies were enlisted to add to the attractions of shore-going.' March-Phillipps received word that the party was in full swing by means of a red torch lodged in the upper window of a house on the edge of town. It belonged to an Anglican missionary. He had reconnoitred the ships for SOE in the guise of enquiring after the sailors' welfare.

With a muffled chug of her engines, *Nuneaton* began to grope her way into the port under the lee of the cliffs. A little earlier, *Vulcan* had almost collided with her and March-Phillipps's excited voice had come bellowing through the darkness: 'Will you get a b-b-b-bloody move on or g-g-g-get out? I'm coming in!' Determined to stick to the agreed plan, the skipper of *Nuneaton* had responded by swinging hard across the other tug's bows and stopping dead. A volley of furious comments was exchanged before common sense prevailed and *Vulcan* drew back to wait her turn.

The night before, Hayes's folbots had made a mock-raid on *Vulcan* and had proved to be almost invisible. Now *Nuneaton* lowered one from each side and soon they faded away into the blackness. The two German tugs were moored about seven hundred yards west of the *Duchessa*, and when the first canoe came alongside *Likomba* it was challenged by a native watchman. The raiders bought time by replying in Pidgin English, convincing him that it was the ship's master returning. He allowed the visitors to board, paused in wide-eyed horror on seeing their tommy-guns, and then flung himself over the side.

By then, *Nuneaton* had sneaked up on her prey from behind, and two more boarders began clambering over to make fast the tow.

From below came a belated warning that the charges on the hawsers had just been fired, and then both men were blown into the air. One had a grenade ripped from his hand by the explosion, while the other cracked a rib. *Likomba* began to drift away but Guise was able to scramble across from *Nuneaton* and secure the towing cable. The only other casualty of the blast was a cat that had been asleep in the anchor locker.

Meanwhile, as *Vulcan* crept towards the *Duchessa*, Appleyard could see a line of light marking her portholes, showing that not all the crew had gone ashore. Indeed, a torch was shone on the tug as it drew near, but no challenge came. When the helm was swung about, the first boarding party prepared to jump from a plank mounted alongside the wheelhouse roof. Five men, among them March-Phillipps, landed silently on the forward well deck. The two ships touched hard, *Vulcan* recoiled, and as they came together again the second group leapt.

Dressed in dark clothes and plimsolls, their faces blackened with cork, the strike force now split into five sections. Longe ran at full speed along the ship and scrambled down a ladder to the aft well deck, only to be knocked off his feet by what he assumed was a fleeing Italian sailor. In fact it was one of two pigs kept by the crew (and soon to be eaten by the raiders). Having picked himself up, he and another SOE operative began to lay three charges on each of the six cables at the stern and to link their detonators so that they would explode simultaneously.

Prout had gone to the engine room, March-Phillipps headed for the bridge, while Appleyard and Winter began to shepherd the crew into cabins at gunpoint before readying the charges on the forward anchors. The senior surgeon of the Nigerian government had by now also made his way over a rickety bamboo ladder to the *Duchessa*, but the only potential case for treatment was a hysterical elderly stewardess. Assuming from the commotion that the crew had returned from the party the worse for drink, she had barricaded herself in her cabin, fearing their intentions.

Because of his immense strength, Lassen had been given the most physically demanding task. This was to carry *Vulcan*'s towing cable onto the freighter and fix it securely to the fo'c'sle. But it proved to be even heavier than anticipated and almost all the others had to go forward to help him. March-Phillipps was alerted once it was done, but before he could give the order to fire the detonators an explosion erupted from the opposite side of the harbour. This was the sound of Hayes's men setting off the charges on the *Likomba*.

Vulcan responded with a long blast on the steam whistle, the Italians were vigorously encouraged to take cover, and a blinding flash lit up the whole island. There was a momentary lull, then the British officials watching the drama from the balcony of the Consulate heard the silence pierced by a very English voice saying: 'I am laying another charge.' Appleyard had seen that one had not gone off and sprinted forward to place another with a very short fuse. A shattering roar followed, and the anchor finally parted. 'There goes the principal lace in her stays,' said the skipper of *Vulcan* with satisfaction. By now bugles were sounding ashore and headlights could be seen hurtling down the mountain road. The raiders redoubled their efforts and to the alarm of *Vulcan*'s African stokers the ship's engineer screwed down the safety valve and sat on it. With the steam pressure dangerously high, the tug took the strain of the *Duchessa*.

Inch by inch she began to draw away from the wharf as a crowd came running around the side of the cathedral and down to the water. Longe covered the harbour front from the stern with a tommy-gun while most of her Italian crew stood disconsolately on the jetty. From the remarks he caught, it was clear they thought that their shipmates had mutinied and were making their escape without them. 'The Italian captain could be seen on the quay,' said Longe, 'calling, with gesticulation, for his ship: or failing his ship, for an explanation.'

The searchlights which probed the sky and the occasional boom of a gun suggested that the Spanish believed they were under attack from the air. Even under full steam, *Vulcan* and her prize were making just three knots, but the coastal defences remained silent as the pair headed slowly but unerringly down the narrow channel that led to the open

ord Lovat (left) briefs Robert Laycock after leading the storming of the Hess Battery at Dieppe in 1942. (Imperial War Museum (IWM))

Dudley Clarke: founder of the Commandos. His inspiration was the Boer horsemen who had harried the British in his native South Africa. (IWM)

Family pride: Geoffrey Keyes won the VC but lost his life in the attempt to assassinate Rommel at his desert base. (IWM)

His father, Admiral Sir Roger Keyes, also had a reputation for courage but overstepped the mark as the first head of Combined Operations. (Getty Images)

ıergy and charm: with
ɾd Louis Mountbatten
(centre) fighting their
corner in Whitehall,
he full potential of the
ommandos began to be
realised. (Time Life Pictures/
Getty Images)

'arehouses ablaze in
e snow at Vaagso, a
rning point for the
ommandos in 1941.
eel helmets, not
oollen caps, were worn
ı most operations.
etty Images)

Three musketeers: the core of Maid Honor Force – (left to right) Gus March-Phillipps, Geoffrey Appleyard and Graham Hayes. None survived the war.

The Italian merchantman *Duchessa d'Aosta* photographed secretly in the neutra harbour of Fernando Pó, West Africa. Her hijacking by March-Phillipps caused diplomatic incident. (IWM)

The 500-yard long *Normandie* dock at St Nazaire, built for the great ocean liner, but also able to shelter the *Tirpitz*. (Time Life Pictures/Getty Images)

The *Campbeltown* after ramming the dock – and before the charges hidden in the bows exploded. Despite the shell damage, the attack was detected only at the last moment. (Popperfoto/Getty Images)

Micky Burn captured on German newsreel covertly signalling 'V for Victory' with his fingers to indicate the success of the St Nazaire raid.

A defining image: commandos returning from Dieppe with a German prisoner. Although they accomplished their mission, the landings that followed ended in disaster. (IWM)

Clear the beach: commandos charge ashore in Normandy. It was vital to exit landing craft as quickly as possible and much time was spent practising. (IWM)

From 1942, training was centralised at Achnacarry Castle, near Fort William. Live rounds were used to prepare recruits for the dangers of combat. (IWM)

Roger Courtney (centre) commanding 2 SBS in 1942. He realised that canoes were ideal for stealthy missions after paddling one the length of the Nile. (George Walkley)

Nigel Willmott trained teams of swimmers in the clandestine reconnaissance of invasion beaches after he and Courtney had pioneered the technique on Rhodes. (Clogstoun Family)

sea. Within a few minutes they had cleared the harbour and left Fernando Pó behind. *Nuneaton*, towing both *Likomba* and *Bibundi*, followed in their wake. The entire operation had lasted just thirty-five minutes.

However, it was not over quite yet. The raiding parties grabbed some sleep, but first light revealed that Hayes and the *Nuneaton* were well astern of *Vulcan*. In fact, she was still within sight of the island, and her engine had begun to sputter. The *Duchessa* was also playing up. March-Phillipps had hoped that she could proceed under her own steam, but it seemed that her own engines had been idle for too long. He was also worried that the flotilla might become a target for U-boats if it continued to sail so slowly and ordered that several yachts which were being dragged along behind the main prizes should be cut loose.

The twenty-nine Italians still on the *Duchessa* had soon got over their shock and offered to cook for their captors. By the time that they were digesting a lunch of pork washed down with green Chartreuse – it turned out there was no fresh water on board – *Nuneaton* had dropped over the horizon. March-Phillipps decided to go to look for her in *Vulcan*. Crouching on the rail of the *Duchessa*, he leapt for the plank alongside the wheelhouse of the tug – and was thrown into the air like a spinning top when he landed on it just as she rolled. Down he dropped, straight between the hulls of the two ships, and it seemed impossible that he would not be crushed. But once they had parted, he bobbed up out of the sea like a cork and was swiftly fished out.

So as to maintain the fiction that the ships had not been seized in Spanish territory, the plan was that they would rendezvous on the 15th with a British corvette, *Violet*. This would then claim to have intercepted them in international waters. When March-Phillipps finally caught up with *Nuneaton*, however, it became clear that she would have to make her own way to the meeting place as best she could. *Vulcan* and her tow pressed on and arrived on time, intending to head back to *Nuneaton* with the warship. But after forty-eight hours there was still no sign of the Royal Navy.

Violet's smoke was eventually sighted off the low hump of Cape Formoso on the afternoon of the 18th. March-Phillipps was not in the best of tempers and ignored her signal to him to heave to. When a shot was then fired across his bows he began to get angry. A little later, the arrival of an armed boarding party, and the attempts of the young officer in charge to disarm the commandos, was the final straw.

'I'll take over here,' said the officer.

'No, you bloody won't!' replied March-Phillipps, so furious that his stammer vanished. Swearing freely, he demanded to know why the corvette was late – she had run aground – and what their behaviour meant.

'You speak remarkably good English for an Italian,' said the puzzled sailor, 'where did you learn it?' *Violet*'s captain, it transpired, had not confided the truth about the *Duchessa* in anyone, and the young officer had believed a BBC report that her crew had mutinied.

In the meantime, Hayes had had a trying few days fretting about the seaworthiness of *Nuneaton*. Until the 17th, even when the engine was working, she was able to make no more than a knot and a half and the current carried her steadily back towards Fernando Pó. Rations aboard began to run short, and things only improved when she was spotted by a passing British collier which telegraphed to Lagos for help. On the 20th, *Nuneaton* was herself taken in tow by the merchantman *Ajassa*.

The next evening, as dusk gilded the waters of Tarquah Bay, the *Duchessa* made a triumphant entry into Lagos harbour. A large crowd had gathered to meet her, and standing on the landing stage with a whisky and soda in his hand, cheering loudest of all, was the Governor of Nigeria himself. None the less, amid all the excitement, March-Phillipps and Appleyard remained anxious about the fate of *Nuneaton* and the two German tugs, which they had last seen almost a week earlier. It was only as the *Duchessa* was being backed into her berth that they spotted Hayes's ship moored near by. He had beaten them home after all.

Flushed with pride and relief, the two raiding parties met up again in the *Duchessa*'s saloon. As bottles of beer were passed round, telegrams of congratulation were read from Gubbins, Eden (who by now was Foreign Secretary) and Churchill himself. In the meantime, SOE's representatives dispatched a cipher to London: 'All Post Masters arrived here 2000 today. Casualties our party absolutely nil. Casualties enemy nil with the exception of a few sore heads.'

The next morning, the chief pilot of Lagos called on the head of station to congratulate him. He confessed that previously he and his friends had wondered what to make of the SOE men. 'Up til last night,' he admitted, 'we thought you were a bunch of bloody missionaries!'

By then, the crew of the *Duchessa* had already been interned, and those involved in her cutting out sworn to secrecy under pain of dire repercussions. The civil service volunteers were sent at once to South Africa on leave, while Maid Honor Force prepared to return to Britain. On Fernando Pó itself, suspicion was rife as to the part played in the raid by the consular officials, but when one of them was drunkenly assaulted by the German captain of the *Likomba* they had the satisfaction of first thrashing him and then extracting an apology for his behaviour.

SOE's main agent on the island was questioned by the authorities, but his cover held up long enough for him to make his getaway by canoe, across the straits to the Cameroons, at the start of March. All the while, the Foreign Office maintained the line that the *Duchessa* had been captured some days after its departure from Santa Isabel. This did little to placate the furious Spanish government, but privately Whitehall was impressed by an exploit which was compared to Francis Drake's singeing of the fleet at Cadiz.

'You will be glad to learn that POSTMASTER has done SOE a great deal of good with the FO etc.,' London told its Lagos station. It helped as well that the combined value of the *Duchessa* and her cargo was assessed at £355,000 (some £13 million today). The total cost of the operation had been just £5000, much of it spent on the diamonds which had won round the chief electrician's wife. In

1950, by way of a thank-you from a grateful Admiralty, the participants in the raid each received a cheque for £44 2s.

POSTMASTER was the first significant example of a successful collaboration between the intelligence services and a special forces team, drawing on the strengths of each. It should have served as a blueprint for future similar missions. Yet such cooperation was to become progressively rarer, replaced instead by a mutually harmful rivalry.

For the time being, however, Maid Honor Force could enjoy the acclaim which now came its way. On March-Phillipps's recommendation, Appleyard and Hayes were awarded the MC, while he himself received the DSO. He also suggested that Lassen had shown sufficient leadership potential for him to be commissioned in the field. This promotion made the Dane probably the only Commando officer never to do Commando – or indeed officer – training.

The only downbeat note was sounded by SOE's Leonard Guise. While preparations were being made for the operation, doubts had been raised several times about March-Phillipps's gung-ho style of leadership. Even in retrospect, Guise thought that 'certain of our seniors showed at intervals a very detached conceit'. He acknowledged the commandos' courage, but pointed out that had there been even 'any mild form of resistance' the raid might have ended in disaster. Too much faith had been put in the reports that there would be no opposition, and too much disregard shown for the risks which might follow. On another night, it might not go so well.

Yet, for Appleyard, accepting such dangers was part of an outlook which had now given his life purpose. 'It isn't a spirit of "Safety First",' he wrote to his family, 'but it's a spirit of adventure, of gibing instead of getting, of clean living and physical fitness, of comradeship and unity, and above all it's God's spirit. Of that I'm sure.' In Maid Honor Force, he had found a band of brothers beside whom he could happily fight and die; and in Gus March-Phillipps a leader he would follow to the end.

6
CHARIOT

The boost which the raid on Vaagso had given to Combined Operations was surpassed just two months later by a still more spectacular success. At the end of February 1942, the new Parachute Regiment – converted from the original 2 Commando – made a highly audacious raid on a radar station at Bruneval, near Le Havre. Landing on the cliff tops, they surprised the sentries, snatched the top-secret Wurzburg apparatus and made their escape by sea almost before the Germans could react.

Mountbatten was cock-a-hoop. He was soon to be given parity with the Chiefs of Staff and intended to set the seal on COHQ's revival with its most ambitious operation to date. It had shown that it could carry the fight to the enemy, and achieve tactical victories. But it had not yet made a major strategic contribution to the war; nor had it taken on the garrison of a large port, as it was thought any future invasion must. A sterner test had to be found.

The choice of its next target was determined by the main threat then facing Britain. For months, its supply lines across the Atlantic had been ravaged by U-boats and German warships. Among their most important bases was St Nazaire, sited at the mouth of the Loire on France's western coast. Workmen had been imported from Spain to build seven new slipways for submarines in late 1941, but more worrying still for the Admiralty was the port's great dry dock, the Forme Ecluse. Built to house the ocean liner *Normandie*, at almost five hundred yards long the dock had been the largest in the world when opened in 1932. Ten years later, it was one of the few capable of housing the greatest remaining German surface raider, the *Tirpitz*, and as it was 250 miles from Britain it was the only one not within easy reach of the RAF. After the sinking of her sister ship *Bismarck* in 1941, *Tirpitz* had been hidden away in Norway. If the Forme Ecluse could be put out of action, she would probably have to remain there, neutralising her as a menace to Atlantic shipping.

The obvious precedent was the assault on the submarine base at Zeebrugge in 1918, led by Roger Keyes. Yet whereas the Belgian port could be struck at directly from the sea, St Nazaire lay six miles up the Loire. Any attack along the estuary would have to be made in the teeth of murderous fire.

Planning for the raid began as early as the summer of 1941. From the start it was seen as a joint operation by the military and the Navy, and it was also acknowledged that losses would be severe. Indeed, so heavily would the mission depend on surprise for success that the whole idea was initially rejected by its designated naval supervisor, the Commander-in-Chief Plymouth, Sir Charles Forbes. SOE was then asked to help but decided that it would be impossible for it to smuggle into the port the amount of explosive required to demolish the lock gates of the dock. (This would allow tidewater to flow through and eventually silt it up.) So, early in 1942, COHQ turned to 2 Commando.

Although it had had to endure the cancellation of several raids for which it had prepared, No. 2's CO, Charles Newman, had gained a reputation as a particularly inventive and effective trainer. The time that the attacking force would have ashore at St Nazaire to complete their task was likely to be short before the Germans brought superior resources to bear, so they would need to rehearse their plan thoroughly. And that plan would have to be so bold that it would catch the Germans completely off guard.

When Newman arrived in London from his HQ at Ayr, Haydon

presented him with the outlines of just such a scheme, codenamed CHARIOT. The key objective of the raid was to destroy the outer gate of the dock basin, and the only way to do this for certain was for it to be rammed at speed by a large ship. This would be disguised as a German vessel, and to give her an even better chance of evading the estuary defences she would avoid the main channel up it. Instead, she would pass at night over the surrounding mud flats, carried on an exceptionally high spring tide.

The ship would carry a group of commandos and be accompanied by sixteen motor launches (MLs) carrying others. Once landed at the port, they would blow up the dock's pumps and cause as much damage as possible to the U-boat pens before escaping in the MLs. The attack would be preceded by an RAF raid on St Nazaire intended to divert the Germans' attention from any activity at sea. All the other details were to be left to Newman and his counterpart as leader of the naval force, Commander R.E.D. Ryder. Given a room to share at COHQ, the two men sized up each other, liked what they saw, and set to work.

The first priority was to find their Trojan horse. Almost immediately the plan hit a snag, however, when Forbes refused to allow them to use one of his destroyers, as COHQ had hoped. He suggested that a submarine be substituted for it, but Newman thought his men would hardly be ready to spring into action after a voyage of three days inside one. The Admiralty eventually yielded and produced an obsolete destroyer lent by the Americans and renamed *Campbeltown*.

Changes to her funnels would make her resemble a large German torpedo boat, while armour plates bolted to the deck would give the commandos some protection during the run-in. Her bows were to be strengthened for the ram, and a hidden chamber would be packed with three tons of explosive primed to go off two hours after hitting the lock gates. As insurance, a motor torpedo boat (MTB) would also try to destroy the inner gates with delayed-action torpedoes. By early February, Mountbatten had secured approval for the attack. Its date was set for late March.

Without yet knowing their destination, some 250 commandos had already begun to train for the raid. The demolition parties would be made up of volunteers from half a dozen units, while No. 2 would supply about a hundred more as protection for these and as assault teams to knock out the port's defences.

Newman's great gift was for instilling confidence in his men, and showing that he had it in them. He was not a professional soldier but a keen Territorial who owned a firm of building contractors; he had been doing a construction job for the London *Evening Standard* at its printing works when war was declared. At thirty-seven, and already bald, he was still an enthusiastic racing driver, a handy middleweight boxer and a first-class rugby player. If all this was conventionally hearty, more unexpected was a fondness for musicals and his hobby of writing show tunes.

Newman had used both hard exercise and his imagination to bind the Commando together. While in billets on the Dorset coast, he had challenged the men to set a world endurance record by speed marching from Paignton to Bridgwater – a distance of sixty-seven miles – in less than twenty-four hours. Eating as they walked, with none of the customary ten-minute breaks every hour, they had done it in ten minutes short of a day. By the end, some were still feeling fit enough to seek out the girls at the local dance hall.

They had spent much of 1941 in Scotland, where Admiral Keyes had come to see how they lived off the land. Subaltern John Roderick organised a meal of pigeon for Keyes and his two Wren drivers, which all three pronounced delicious. Only once the guests had left did Roderick learn from his supplier that the meat had actually been farmyard cat.

Tough as it had become, the Commando had seen little action together. Newman himself had experience of leading an Independent Company in Norway, while one and a half Troops had gone to Vaagso as reserves. The wrist wound that Graeme Black had suffered there would prevent him from commanding one of the assault groups at St Nazaire, so Newman recalled another veteran of the earlier raid, David Birney, even though he was on sick leave, too.

One of his few other officers to have been under fire was Micky Burn. Even by the sometimes quirky standards of the Commandos, his path into them had been unusual. He had left his studies at Oxford after only a year and in the early 1930s began to drift about Europe, going first to the French resort of Le Touquet (which had been developed by his mother's family) and later to Florence, where he stayed with Alice Keppel, one of Edward VII's mistresses. It was his time in Germany, however, which was to affect him most deeply.

In Munich, he mixed with fellow Englishmen studying for the Foreign Office exams, including Donald Maclean, already a Communist agent. Yet Burn was soon more impressed by the apparent achievements of another political system closer to hand. 'I am ashamed that I was taken in for a short time by National Socialism,' he later admitted of his flirtation with the Nazis. 'What made me sympathise was that there were two million unemployed in England. I had seen that in the coalfields and it sickened me. I thought that anyone who cures that was a good person.' In 1935, he went to a Nazi rally at Nuremberg. There he met Adolf Hitler, who signed Burn's copy of *Mein Kampf*. With his friends Unity Mitford and her sister Diana Guinness (shortly to be Mosley), he also visited the concentration camp at Dachau. When he returned to Britain he joined *The Times*, whose editor then favoured appeasing Germany.

Yet Burn's main role for the paper was to uncover details of the increasingly scandalous relationship between the new King, Edward VIII, and Mrs Wallis Simpson. This he was well placed to do as his father was solicitor to the Duchy of Cornwall – the source of the King's private income – and friendly with his adviser Walter Monckton. At the same time, the shyly handsome Burn was having to come to terms with his own forbidden liaisons: he was attracted to men, and for a decade had been having an intermittent affair with another of the future defectors to Moscow, Guy Burgess.

Believing that war was inevitable, Burn joined the Territorials in 1937 and served with an Independent Company in the ill-fated Norway campaign. He had found it a dispiriting experience, alleviated only by the relatively informal relations in the unit between officers and men. Such a command structure chimed with his growing interest in socialism and his belief in the working man's capacity for self-improvement, so he was delighted when it 'was developed much more in the Commandos'.

> It was something quite unforgettable. It was one of the best things in the war, perhaps one of the few good things. A lot of them came from poor, uneducated backgrounds, and I learned what capabilities they had if encouraged to develop their own initiative. There wasn't much time for that in Norway, but there was during our Commando training. That was very revealing. It was sad, it never seemed to be developed after the war. What wasted capabilities there were – and no doubt still are.

To increase his troops' self-confidence, Burn devised an exercise in which they had to respond instantly to unexpected scenarios handed to them without warning in an envelope. 'Three nuns are approaching – this was at the time when the Germans were supposed to be dressing up as nuns – and they look rather unshaven. What are you going to do? Then the men thought of situations for us . . . The training was always on the assumption that everyone above them would be killed and they would have to take over themselves.' Grim as such predictions were, their value was to be fully borne out at St Nazaire.

Eric de la Torre's first hint that something was in the wind came when Durnford-Slater sent him on a dock demolitions course, 'with the chance of a bit of fun at the end of it'. There he met two of the officers largely responsible for suggesting the raid, Bob Montgomery and Bill Pritchard. The latter's father had been the dockmaster at Cardiff, while Montgomery had spent time in St Nazaire itself during the retreat from France in 1940. They trained de la Torre at the King George V Dock in Southampton, which had a very similar layout to the Forme Ecluse. 'The Commando was split into small teams of five or six,' remembered de la Torre. 'We were blindfolded and had to feel our way down the stairs to the pumps and lay charges. They said when you get to your target there may be no electric light, so you need to learn to work in the dark.' Once they had mastered this, they were allowed to use torches but timed against a stopwatch. When he got back to his billet, de la Torre slept with the plastic high explosive stored in a shoebox under his bed.

Ronnie Swayne, with his sergeant Tom Durrant, had also been selected to lead a party of twelve men from 1 Commando. They practised blowing up the harbour at Newport, and also at Cardiff. 'We learnt how to lower sacks of explosive against the lock gates at the points where it would do most damage,' Swayne explained. 'And we learnt how to deal with the big metal caissons – empty narrow chambers which slot into the locks to close them. And also with the pumping machinery, the impeller pumps and the workings required to empty a lock and to transfer water in the lock system.'

When the course finished, they were put on a train and assumed they were returning to their base. But dawn revealed the Cornish coast, and at Falmouth they were marched off the train and straight onto one of the converted Belgian ferries to be briefed. The first thing they saw was a marvellously detailed scale model of St Nazaire, though only one officer, who had been there on holiday, recognised where it was.

'I remember when Charles Newman gave the orders out and we realised what a dangerous operation it was going to be, one of my two subalterns, Tom Peyton, gave a gasp of excitement,' recalled Burn. 'It's extraordinary in retrospect how delighted people were to be about to do something which was very likely to lead to their deaths.' Peyton was just twenty; only two years earlier he had been a schoolboy at Eton. Now he was to help Burn command an assault group in one of the most hazardous missions of the war.

After receiving an outline of the operation, Swayne and the other officers were handed more detailed notes to read. His were forty pages long and, since it was the only quiet place on the ship, he settled down with them in the lavatory. After ten minutes there was a furious knocking on the door. It was Newman, who wanted to use the place for its proper purpose. Swayne apologised and went back to his cabin, only to realise to his horror that he had left the secret orders behind: 'I got the biggest ticking off of my life!'

The implications of the plan now began to sink in. De la Torre had discovered that he was to cross the Channel in one of the wooden-hulled Fairmile motor launches. These were preferred to landing craft for the raid because the troops could be concealed below deck if the boats were spotted from the air, but they required extra fuel tanks to be mounted astern to enable them to make the round trip. De la Torre said later:

> We were told we were all volunteers, we had the option to pull out – but no one did. Many of us thought it was sheer suicide, however. I thought the suicidal bit was having to go five or six miles up the Loire, especially in a small boat. I'd had a look at our ML. It just had an Oerlikon [machine-gun] fore and aft, the boat was made of mahogany, and I thought about all the coastal batteries they'd shown us on the model. I thought: 'If a shell hits us, we're finished' – let alone getting into the docks.
>
> You know a lot of you aren't going to come back but you push it to the back of your mind and talk about something else . . . I did think: 'If I get a bullet, I hope it's a quick one and I'm finished not wounded.'

His feelings were shared by Ronnie Swayne, who confessed to 'frightful apprehension' despite (or perhaps because of) his prior experiences raiding the French coast and Guernsey. 'I think few of us thought we'd get back by sea. I certainly didn't think so. I was relying on the fact I could speak French fluently to get through the town and get to open country and walk home. I don't think an insurance company would have been very interested in us.'

Micky Burn had found it difficult enough to choose ten men for his protection party from his Troop of sixty. Everyone had their group of four or five pals who could not usually be separated, and those who were not selected for the raid were miserable. Burn himself was able to shut out from his mind any thought of his own fate, but he realised early on that his dependable sergeant, Bill Gibson, had had a premonition of his death.

'Well, dad, dearest,' Gibson wrote in a letter to be sent to his father if he was killed, 'I will close now, don't be too unhappy, remember what you always told me, keep your chin up. I'll have done what chance has made my duty and I can only hope that by laying down my life the generations to come might in some way remember us and benefit by what we have done.'

On the morning of 26 March, in brilliant sunshine, Mass was celebrated on the ship's foredeck. Among those who took Holy Communion was Bertie Hodgson, who was leading a protection group and sharing a cabin with John Roderick, the officer who had dished up the cat to Keyes. 'I was wondering if it really did make any difference to talk to God and ask for a safe return,' Hodgson confided to his diary. 'Probably not, but nevertheless it's a wee bit comforting.' At midday, the troops left the ferry, boarded their launches and prepared to sail. 'Well, here it is,' wrote Hodgson, 'the day we've been looking forward to for two years ... Everyone in high spirits all the time ... I still pray that we are allowed to touch land and have a scrap – if we don't, the men will go crazy, poor devils.'

Almost the only detail that Newman had not passed on was Mountbatten's remark that he did not expect any of them to come back. But as he stood on the bridge of *Atherstone*, one of the escorting destroyers, and looked back at the two columns of launches creaming along behind, he was also conscious of Mountbatten's parting words that CHARIOT was no ordinary raid but an operation of war. It was a responsibility he was determined the Commando should shoulder, and one which justified the dangers it was about to face.

The ships set a course west of Brest and out into the Bay of Biscay. At dawn the next day, the White Ensign was hauled down and replaced by German flags. A few hours later, a shout from aloft alerted Newman to the presence of a U-boat, which was chased and depth-charged. Although it got away, it reported only the two destroyers which had pursued it. The convoy also crossed paths with two French trawlers whose crews were taken off to prevent them giving any warning of the attack. When darkness fell, the flotilla veered east towards the mouth of the Loire.

All bar one. The engine of the motor launch carrying Hodgson and his team packed up just at that moment, and there was a hectic scramble to transfer men and kit to another of the Fairmiles. They lost contact with the others, and spent the best part of the next two hours trying to catch up. 'Watching till the eyes ached,' Hodgson noted. 'Somehow I couldn't believe I could be cheated of this job at the crucial moment.' Their task was made harder by the mist which had come down and cut visibility to two miles.

At 2200, Newman saw the flashing of a dim red light ahead and soon they slid by the partially submerged submarine *Sturgeon*, stationed as a navigation beacon to guide them in. From the conning tower came the hail of 'Goodbye – and Good Luck.'

'We have at last sighted the MLs and hope to get back into position again for the attack,' wrote Hodgson. 'Lovely moon and conditions perfect. Have now really arrived in position as before. Submarine and destroyers left behind. Here we go, "nearer St Nazaire to thee". I feel so relieved now that most of my apprehensions and fears have gone.' At a speed of ten knots, the flotilla entered the Loire.

One thought was uppermost in everyone's mind, felt Newman: 'How far could we proceed up the river before we were spotted?' He and Ryder had transferred to the small gunboat *MGB 314*, which was leading the formation. Behind them came *Campbeltown*, still under German colours, and ranged astern of her the pairs of motor launches. An MTB brought up the rear. The hope was that the RAF's bombing raid would occupy attention ashore, and from midnight bright flashes could be seen on the horizon and loud firing heard inland. It seemed to those watching to be very intense.

'Suddenly . . . two vivid beams of light shot out – a searchlight on the bank of the river swept the water lines and with a sigh of relief it was seen that they had just missed us,' recalled Newman. 'Against these beams one could see the whole force silhouetted and, for the moment, safe. On we went.'

Until 0122, eight minutes before zero hour and a mile from the dock, they remained undetected. Yet the garrison commander at St Nazaire had become suspicious of the behaviour of the Wellington bombers overhead. The low cloud meant that few had dropped their payloads, but their continued presence in the area made him think they were trying to divert attention from a landing elsewhere. An alert went out to the coastal batteries, and a searchlight stabbed down the main Charpentier channel, picking out *Campbeltown*.

'From that moment the entire force was floodlit,' Ryder reported afterwards, 'but for what seemed like five minutes no fire was opened.' Using call signs taken from the code books captured at Vaagso, the MGB signalled that two ships damaged by enemy action were proceeding to the harbour. On and on *Campbeltown* steamed, the altered rake of her funnels fooling the batteries, until one flak position called her bluff and opened up.

At once she made the international signal for friendly fire. 'Up went her Boche flares,' remembered Newman, 'and for a moment it seemed as if they were going to accept them.' More precious time was bought. 'Then, without warning, the whole bag of tricks let loose. The noise was terrific – tracers of every colour seemed to pour into our fleet – the *Campbeltown*'s side seemed to be alive with bursting shells.'

The White Ensign was hoisted once more, and Oerlikons, Brens and mortars spat fire at the searchlights. A flak vessel was silenced, and some of the batteries put out of commission, yet the British casualties were rising quickly. On both sides fear and confusion spread.

'People often ask what you think about at such moments and as far as I can remember my mind was a complete and frightened blank,' recalled Stuart Chant, who was lying on the deck of the destroyer, only partially shielded by the new steel plating. 'The *Campbeltown* was immediately the main target of the enemy guns and was hit repeatedly. A fire raged on the for'ard deck . . . about 75% of the Commandos had been wounded and I had been hit in the arm and the leg.' Nevertheless, by now they had reached the outer part of the port.

Through what seemed an eternity of shellfire, Newman peered over the armoured bridge of *MGB 314*, looking for landmarks. At first it all seemed so different from the model he had spent hours studying. Then, suddenly, he saw the long line of the Old Mole. Right ahead were the gates of the dock, and hard behind them was *Campbeltown*, her engine room ablaze but still making nineteen knots. The MGB swung hard to starboard and on went the warship – 'going fast and shooting hard'.

She cut through the anti-submarine boom without a tremor, and then in the glare of a searchlight they lost sight of her. But the sound of her crashing into the dock could be heard even above the shattering noise of gunfire, and when the sparks and smoke had cleared they could see her embedded slap in the centre of the gates. *Campbeltown* was just four minutes behind schedule, and already CHARIOT had accomplished its main objective.

There was just time for a quick handshake with Ryder and then Newman was over the side and standing on French soil. He had decided to make his HQ near the Old Entrance to the port, not far from the dock gates, and expected to see his regimental sergeant-major, Alan Moss, and the reserve already in place there. That there was no sign of them was his first indication that not everything had gone to plan.

As he turned the corner of the house he had chosen as his headquarters, he literally bumped into a German coming the other way. Newman's first instinct was to say 'Sorry!' and his second to jab his gun into the man's ribs. His prisoner hastily explained that the building was a German HQ. While Newman absorbed this, an Oerlikon mounted on a trawler in the Inner Basin opened up on them from only seventy yards away and he had to take cover rapidly.

Other quick-firing guns had already played havoc with the wooden MLs. Eric de la Torre was on the second launch on the starboard side of the column, also heading for the Old Entrance. The boat's portholes had been blacked out and they were all kept below during the run-in. But they had heard the guns target *Campbeltown*. 'Then as she got near the lock gates all Hell broke loose,' he remembered. 'The noise was tremendous.' The officer commanding his demolition party, Mark Woodcock, came down to them, carrying a stone jar. '"I think we should all have a tot of rum," he said. Everyone had one except Nosher Brown, which was extraordinary as he was always drunk! Maybe he thought he would think more clearly – looking back maybe he was right. We were all offered Benzedrine too, but no one took it. We all felt we were pretty alert.'

By now, so were the Germans. While one column of MLs headed for the Old Entrance, another six Fairmiles were due to land closer to the harbour entrance at the Old Mole, the planned site for the re-embarkation. Only one managed to do so. David Birney's launch was hit by flak and burst into flames. When it lodged on a sandbank, Birney gave the order to swim for it. That was the last time he was seen alive.

Bertie Hodgson was never to resume his diary. He was killed aboard another of the MLs in the port column, while that carrying Ronnie Swayne found the approaches to the Mole so choked with burning wreckage that the launch was unable to reach it and eventually withdrew downriver.

Micky Burn was in the lead craft in the starboard line. It was the first to be hit, and careered like a fireball across the path of the other boats, beaching south of the Mole. The survivors of his assault party threw themselves into the water but began to sink, weighed down by their grenades. A lance corporal, Arthur Young, grabbed Burn by the hair and slowly began to haul him towards the shore. However, Young was handicapped by a wound to his leg, and as the Germans were machine-gunning those in the water several times he had to pull them both under to avoid being hit again.

As they lay exhausted on the jetty, the orange light of the flames revealed a body floating lifelessly towards them. It was young Tom Peyton, who had been so excited by the prospect of the raid. '"Shall we pull him ashore?" said Young, and I said "It's a waste of time. He's dead." It was so heartless, it was extraordinary.' Numbed and horrified by what he had been through, Burn's fear now turned to an overpowering rage:

> As soon as I got up the jetty, I found a German who seemed to be lying down, facing away from the jetty, and I remember bashing him very, very hard and leaving him for dead, if he wasn't already, and thinking how cold-blooded I am. It was not the sort of thing I would normally do, even in a bad temper. I just went on and on, bashing him on the head with my revolver.

Of the other launches in the group, one had blown up, another had damaged its steering gear and turned back, and two more had overshot the Mole in the confusion. Only *ML 177* had managed to put its commandos ashore, but they were too few to do more than hold their ground at first.

Eric de la Torre was in one of the boats which had gone too far, and landed instead at the Old Entrance. Woodcock told him to bring up from below the rucksacks packed with explosives. Over his head he could hear the chatter of twin Lewis guns, and when he came on deck he could see them pouring bullets into a strongpoint. Woodcock jumped over the rail of the launch, and de la Torre followed him, carrying a crowbar to lever up the manhole covers on the swing bridge which they were to demolish. He sprinted ten yards towards a wooden fence but as he did so a stream of tracer went past his legs. The sergeant running beside him fell silently to the ground. De la Torre reached a gate, but as he went through it someone shouted, 'Get down!' He flung himself to the ground as an explosion erupted around them, and buried them in rubble.

At the Old Entrance, Newman was coming to realise that only a quarter of the ninety-odd men he had hoped to gather there had got ashore. Moss had been killed while towing survivors from his ML through the water on a Carley float. With the help of Sergeant Haines and his mortar group, Newman was able to silence the gun positions on the U-boat sheds and set up a defensive perimeter. But ranged against them were some two thousand troops in two anti-aircraft battalions, together with the port garrison and the crews of the ships and submarines in harbour.

Attacking the U-boat pens was out of the question, so the main responsibility now rested on those squads aboard the *Campbeltown* itself, whose target was the pumping station. When the ship had smashed into the lock gates, John Roderick had been surprised that the impact had not jarred more. He only had a few seconds to register the success of the ship's last voyage before a hail of fire began to beat on the steel slats behind which he was lying, wishing he was shorter. His Troop's mission was to destroy the gun positions amid the storage tanks to the right of the dock, but the bamboo ladder they were supposed to use to disembark had been broken. Clambering down a rope instead, Roderick and his men ran towards the first gun emplacement. Its crew was focused on the ship, caught in a lattice of searchlights. The next post had more warning, but with grenades, tommy-guns and Colts they were all killed as well. The commandos then came under attack themselves from further upriver. Roderick led them onto the lock gate itself, intending to fall back to the other side as planned, but *Campbeltown*'s bow blocked their way.

In the full glare of the white beams, they managed to haul themselves back up the ropes dangling from it, and then to shin down the other side, which they presumed by now would be safely held. As he dropped to the ground, Bren in hands, Roderick was hit in the back and sent sprawling. Forcing himself to keep going, he reached the perimeter established by Newman and gave the password: 'War Weapons Week'. The words had been chosen as ones that a German would have trouble pronouncing correctly.

Another covering party had tackled the guns on the roof of the pumping station. While the battle continued above his head, Stuart Chant used a four-ounce charge to blast open the building's heavy steel door. Then he and another officer ran down eight flights of stairs in darkness illuminated only by the torches clipped to their webbing. Forty feet underground they reached the impeller pumps.

Shrapnel cuts to Chant's hands made it awkward for him to handle the explosives, and it took him all of forty minutes to place them as planned on the most delicate parts of the five cast-iron pumps. He then pulled the two percussion igniters attached to the main fuses. Now he had just ninety seconds to get back up to the surface before they detonated. Breathing hard, his feet tripping on unseen steps, he reached the entrance and flung himself down in the open about twenty yards away. A few seconds later the windows of the building were blown out with such force that blocks of concrete – meant to protect against bombing raids – came hurtling past Chant.

He ran back to assess his handiwork, and almost fell forty feet into the chambers below. The explosion had collapsed the entire ground floor of the pumping station. For the next hour, Chant and the rest of his party smashed up the remaining transformers and control panels with sledgehammers.

Fourteen men should have landed with Micky Burn from his launch, but only five got off alive. Bill Gibson was not among them. Although no one managed to join him on the jetty, Burn was still determined to complete the group's mission of destroying the flak towers at the far end of the dock. Finding his way by the light of the burning buildings, he dodged from shadow to shadow, taking more than two hours to travel about a thousand yards. Until then, he had not had time to think about what was going on around him: 'I remember beginning to be frightened when I was crossing the dock,' he said later. Early on some enemy troops spotted and shot at him. 'I thought: "This is it!" They hit me twice – in my arm and near my groin, but not seriously.'

He pressed on, and soon heard some more Germans chattering near by:

> I thought really what I should do is to throw a grenade among them. But I thought this would be very unwise and call attention to myself, so I didn't. It wasn't very brave. I was very frightened then, particularly when I found I still had the grenade in my hand with the pin out. The tension in my hand was so great that it had kept the lever down.

He eventually threw the grenade into the water to get rid of it.

When he finally arrived at the two towers he found them deserted. Using a pile of uniforms to fuel the flames, Burn set them ablaze with incendiaries and then began to retrace his footsteps. As he approached the Old Mole, he passed through outlying groups of commandos and assumed that the area had been secured. So he was surprised to fall into the hands of three German sentries, and even more astonished to hear one ask the others: '*Sollen Wir ihm toten?*' – 'Should we kill him?'

It seemed so unreal that Burn felt as if he were on a training exercise. 'I said, in German: "You can't kill me. I'm a Very Important Prisoner." I gave them my compass and my watch – rather ingloriously – and I drew them on, chatting in German, to where I knew our troops were.' A challenge came, and his captors ran away. Burn's liberator was Sergeant Haines, who was holding Newman's defensive perimeter.

By now it had become apparent to the colonel that the chances of getting home by sea were fast vanishing. The time for re-embarking had arrived, but the only MLs that could be seen in the dock were on fire. Most of the raiders' goals had been accomplished – the MTB had even managed to torpedo the inner lock gates before being sunk – and there was little to be gained by remaining on the Mole any longer. Sixty per cent of the seventy or so survivors gathered around Newman were already wounded. 'I decided', he wrote afterwards, 'to break inland with the idea of making for Spain.'

Using the cover of railway trucks, parties of about twenty men formed up and set off from the bridgehead into the outer part of the port. 'Fires and smoke were everywhere, and small arms fire was coming from most of the buildings around us,' said Newman. His adjutant, Captain Stan Day, 'dealt with some screaming Germans up an alley between two buildings . . . Why do they scream so?'

They cleared the bridge leading from the Inner Basin and entered St Nazaire itself. The next half-hour was a non-stop series of frantic rushes – over walls in back gardens, through houses and dashing along side-streets in an effort to evade the Germans who were now pouring into the town. 'I remember going head first into a kitchen through somebody's window, there to see the breakfast or supper laid out on a check table cloth and thinking how odd it was,' Newman recalled.

For a while they held their own. A motorcycle and sidecar were shot up as they raced through a square towards them. But every cross-roads seemed to be covered by machine-guns, and their ammunition was running low. With movement becoming more and more difficult, Newman decided to let the men rest in the cellar of a house fitted out with mattresses for use as an air-raid shelter. There they would wait until the next evening before trying to get away again.

Leading the breakout had been Micky Burn. Accompanied by two men from his Troop, he got across the bridge and then decided to use his German to bluff his way past any opposition. He told the two soldiers to turn their jackets inside out and to throw away their weapons as they were obviously British. This they reluctantly did and Burn managed to get them through three sentry posts by pretending to be German and telling the guards that the battle at the dock was over. Further on they were challenged, however, and then fired at. 'I used to have nightmares afterwards in which I was running between rows of houses,' Burn said later.

By the time he got back to where he had started from, one of the men had disappeared, but an Irish commando, Trooper Paddy Bushe, was still with him. They decided to hide in the boiler room of a large merchant ship tied up in the dock. This was eventually searched, however, and they were rooted out at gunpoint. Fearing that they would be shot immediately, Burn threw himself across Bushe to protect him: 'I thought this is me being very public school and brave,' he reflected years later. 'It was really rather ridiculous.'

When Eric de la Torre picked himself out of the masonry which had fallen on him, he found himself alone except for Sergeant George Churcher. The others had continued on towards their target, and as it would be hard to find them amid all the havoc, Churcher told de la Torre to go and look for their ML. By the time he located it, some of his section had returned, including Captain Chris Smalley, who had been laying charges in the winding house.

De la Torre was sent below. 'There were two or three men lying across the table, dead or wounded. There was another one on the floor,' he remembered. 'Shells were coming through the wall – and out the other side. I thought: "I'm not staying here, it's safer on deck."' There he and Smalley tried to repair an Oerlikon which seemed to have jammed. With tracer flashing past them on all sides, Smalley got into the gun's webbing and brought the weapon to bear. De la Torre heard a loud bang beside him 'and then all I could see was a headless figure strapped into the frame'. The Oerlikon had exploded and decapitated Smalley, whose head rolled across the deck.

As de la Torre stood there appalled, he heard the coxswain yell: 'Skipper's orders – abandon ship!' The boat was burning fast. He grabbed a float and jumped over the side, plunging ten feet down because of the weight of the pistol he had in each pocket. His Mae West life-jacket brought him up to the surface but, 'just as I came up, a shell went through the middle of the Carley float. Fortunately it didn't explode – but I went down again.' When he got his head above water, he swam to a raft that was being carried along by the tide. Several others were already clinging to it, while Nosher Brown, who had been hit in the foot, was holding on to de la Torre himself.

Around them was a vision of Hell. Lakes of blazing fuel burned on the river, its surface puckered by shells and small-arms fire. Motor launches had been turned into funeral pyres from which black smoke streamed into the night sky. Corpses drifted with the living towards the sea. 'It was a scene of chaos,' recalled de la Torre. 'I thought no one could live through this.' Then through the confusion an extraordinary sound reached his ears. 'I could hear a voice singing. I'll never forget it. He sang one line of *God Our Help in Ages Past*. He just sang one line, then he started the second – and it went dead.'

Those who could not hang on to the raft any longer floated away into the dark. De la Torre saw a group of figures on the shore and, hoping that they were Frenchmen who might hide him, made his way towards them. When he got closer, he noticed they wore steel helmets, but he had already been spotted. 'They had a lorry waiting – they must have been tracking us. They were Marines. The officer sent his men into the water to drag us ashore. He spoke very good English, and got stretchers for the wounded . . . He saw the pistol sticking out of my pocket, however, so I handed that over. They were very good to us.'

Some of those involved in the operation had had more luck. Ryder had gone ashore to check that *Campbeltown* had indeed jammed the gates, but by 0250 he too had decided that it was time to leave. Miraculously, *MGB 314* had so far escaped serious damage, but as she turned out of the harbour she was hit repeatedly down the starboard side. All of her seamen were by now wounded, and some of the several dozen injured commandos that she was carrying were hit again.

'Our engines were untouched,' recalled her captain, Lieutenant Dunstan Curtis, 'so I put on full speed and rushed down the river at 24 knots under the beams of the searchlights . . . We had 6 Oerlikon shells through the petrol tank, but it was full and did not explode.' They made smoke over their stern in a bid to conceal their position, until the accurate shooting from both banks made it apparent that this tactic was actually giving it away.

By the time they reached the mouth of the Loire, all their own guns were out of action, and they could only take evasive action when raked by an armed yacht which nearly sunk them. Yet the engine held up, although it had to be repaired with a large piece of tin cut from the mechanic's helmet. Once out to sea, the MGB met up again with the destroyer escort and, despite a leaking hull and the attentions of German seaplanes, made it back to Falmouth the next afternoon. Only three of the other seventeen ships in the flotilla completed the voyage home.

Aboard *ML 306*, Ronnie Swayne had also got as far as the open water. His party's job had been to blow one of the sets of lock gates at the New Entrance to the port, but the combination of defensive fire and the burning wrecks of other boats had prevented them from landing at the Mole. The ship's captain, Ian Henderson, was reluctant to try further up the harbour without knowing what might be there, and there was much grumbling from the commandos when he put about and headed back down the Loire. They felt that all they had done was shoot out some searchlights. One of their few casualties had been Swayne, who had lost the skin on his palm when changing the red-hot barrel of a Bren.

Half an hour later, he was cutting up sandwiches for the men when Henderson told him to quieten them and handed him a pair of night glasses. 'There were the outlines of three German destroyers,' recalled Swayne. 'I was munching a sandwich and it turned to dust in my mouth. It was a very funny feeling because I didn't actually feel fear. It was a purely physical reaction. I suppose I was frightened but it didn't come into my brain, so to speak. It was very strange. And I had to spit the sandwich out.'

The ML was pinioned by a searchlight, surrounded by five larger enemy ships, and called on to surrender. The commandos replied with every weapon that they had. Stung to fury, one of the German vessels, the *Jaguar*, tried to run down the ML, but as nimbly as a matador, Henderson span her aside at the last moment. All the while, the soldiers continued to fire at the enemy, notably Swayne's young sergeant, Tom Durrant, whom he rated the best shot in the Commando. Although wounded in the run up the Loire, Durrant was manning the twin Lewis guns mounted on the upper works of the launch.

Then a four-inch shell exploded behind him on the bridge, killing Henderson and wounding all the other officers. 'I saw holes appearing in the sides of the ship,' said Swayne. 'It was rather hopeless really because they were very much higher than us . . . and they shot us up pretty badly.' Again *Jaguar* bore down on the ML, the decks of which were now covered in the dead and dying, and once more demanded she surrender. Again Durrant defied them and raked the bigger ship with fire.

For a few minutes more the uneven contest continued. Then *Jaguar* closed right in, and once more its captain, Fritz Paul, called on them to give up. 'I started parleying with them,' recalled Swayne, who had been hit in the legs by splinters, 'and I think it was at that point that Durrant gave the Germans another burst at the bridge.' This sent Paul diving for cover as shards of wood speared past his face.

'And they really let him have it,' remembered Swayne. Durrant had no protection where he was standing, and as every gun trained on him he was wounded numerous times, including in the head and the chest. 'But he went on shooting until he absolutely dropped on the floor . . . There was no point going on, and I threw in the ship.' Of the twenty-eight men on the launch, only eight had not been killed or wounded in the unequal battle. The German crew had also taken casualties.

As day broke, Swayne supervised the transfer to the destroyer of those who had been injured.

> The Germans were very good with the wounded – they gave Durrant some morphia. But I kept getting requests from the captain to go and see him. And I was very irritated and said so. Eventually, the ship's No. 1 came along – we spoke in French – and I said: 'I'm not going to be questioned by the captain of a ship.' And he said: 'No, he wants to give you a glass of brandy,' so I said: 'Well, that's different!'

That morning, the Germans began to interrogate their prisoners. Micky Burn was quizzed by Paul Schmidt, Hitler's own interpreter, whom he recognised from newsreels. During another interrogation, Schmidt asked a sergeant how Britain thought it could fight on when half the sea was dominated by the Germans and the other half by the Japanese. The sergeant earned Burn's admiration by quickly retorting: 'Yes, the bottom half.'

Stuart Chant was treated at a naval hospital, where he was visited by a party from the Red Cross and asked about his treatment. Only much later did he learn that his answers had been secretly recorded and used in a propaganda broadcast – and that his visitors' credentials had been bogus.

With twenty or thirty others, Eric de la Torre was brought back to the port and locked up in a cell by the docks. A wounded seaman was brought in to die there and for a time they thought they were the only survivors. A little later they saw Newman, who had chosen to hide in a cellar which was being used by the SS. It was directly across the road from a German HQ. De la Torre also saw Sam Beattie, *Campbeltown*'s commander.

The mood among the commandos was subdued rather than elated, and not only because they were now PoWs. For Beattie's presence was a reminder that, while the raiders had succeeded in ramming the lock gates, these had not been destroyed. It seemed the charges hidden in the *Campbeltown* had failed to explode. There had been two sets of fuses, the longer of which ran for eight and a half hours and had been started before the ship entered the Loire. More than nine hours had already gone by.

'We were very depressed,' confirmed de la Torre, 'because she should have gone up.' German troops were already swarming all over the ship, and by mid-morning it was attracting dozens of sight-seers, including a passing admiral. The sight of the destroyer slanted on top of the gates was certainly spectacular, and the Germans were impressed by the daring that had placed her there. But as they rounded up the last of the commandos they believed that the raid had failed.

How stupid could the English be, Sam Beattie was asked during his interrogation, that they thought they could block up the dock with an old ship? Within twenty-four hours it would be pulled out. But at just that moment the three tons of hidden explosives fired, obliterating the bow section and the caisson on which it rested. Sea water poured in over what remained.

'When it went up, we all gave a cheer because we knew the main job of the raid had been done,' said de la Torre. All the glass in the windows of the building in which he was being held was blown in by the blast. Huts and sheds around the dock were flattened, and debris scattered across the town. It included body parts of dozens of Germans who had been on *Campbeltown* at the time.

The explosion occurred just as *Jaguar* was tying up in port. 'We went running up on deck to see what had happened, and the

Campbeltown was coming down in pieces banging all around,' remembered Swayne.

The delayed detonation was probably due to the fuses being damaged in the impact with the lock. It led to panic in the German ranks, and there were scores of further casualties when their troops assumed it was a signal for another attack and fired wildly on both French dockworkers and labourers from their own Todt organisation. Garbled reports of this eventually emerged in the foreign press, but in the first days after the raid the Germans claimed instead that *Campbeltown* had blown up before she was able to ram the gates.

Indeed, for some time COHQ itself was unsure of the outcome of the raid. All those who had survived to see the destroyer explode had done so as prisoners, and without news of that there was little to balance the initial shock of the high cost of the operation. The first that the men of 2 Commando left behind at Ayr knew of their comrades' fate were reports in the papers which reflected what little the Navy then knew.

'Gloom over town,' stated the unit's daily war diary for 29 March. Even once more details started to emerge, there was little euphoria among those who had to send out to parents and widows the last letters written by their friends. 'Commando more or less stunned by the loss of so much that was fine,' the record continued. 'Unhappy days.'

Of the 265 commandos who had sailed for St Nazaire, more than 200 had been killed or captured. The sailors who had crewed their transport had suffered similarly. Only four out of the eighteen ships in the flotilla returned home, along with just over a third of the six hundred men who had entered the mouth of the Loire. Among their number, eventually, were five commandos who managed to evade capture and make their way back after weeks of wandering through France.

As the long lists of the dead and the missing came into COHQ, some officers were overwhelmed by grief. They broke down in corridors and map rooms and called aloud the names of those they would not see again.

Pride alleviated their sorrow a little when it was announced that eighty-three medals were to be awarded for deeds that night. They included five Victoria Crosses – the most for a single action in the entire war. The naval recipients were Beattie, Ryder and the pom-pom gunner aboard his MGB, William Savage, who was killed at his post. The Commandos' contribution was recognised by those for Newman and Durrant. Uniquely, the original recommendation that Durrant should be recognised came from an enemy officer, Fritz Paul of the *Jaguar*, who visited Newman in prison to tell him of the NCO's valiant last stand.

There were Military Crosses for many of the younger officers involved in the raid. One of the lessons of CHARIOT was that the Commandos' novel command structure worked. The decision to have very few senior officers placed more responsibility on their juniors, but the limited scope and duration of raids made this feasible and concentrated extra leadership where it would be most effective. Among those to win MCs at St Nazaire were Stuart Chant, Ronnie Swayne, John Roderick and Micky Burn.

Burn had continued the fight even after capture. 'There was a photograph of me, which the Germans used in their newsreel, with my fingers held up in the V sign to show the raid had been a success,' he explained. 'By then the destroyer had blown up. My future wife's cousin, Charles Haydon, was Mountbatten's military adviser and after the war I asked him if they had seen it and realised what it meant – and they had.'

The prisoners were held initially at Rennes, where for a time some were manacled. Ronnie Swayne remembered that it took him days after his shackles' removal before he regained control over his hands – at first, if he tried to brush his hair, he would miss his head altogether. Then the PoWs were sent to Bremen, where the padre was able to slip items of news about the war into church services. From there, Eric de la Torre wrote to his landlady in Scotland to tell her that there was a box of explosives under his bed and that she should ask the Commando to take them away.

Although many of his friends had been killed, de la Torre

believed that the results of the raid justified their loss. The *Normandie* dock was put out of action until after D-Day and the *Tirpitz* had been denied her harbour. 'If she had been able to come out of the fjords,' he reflected, 'if the dock had been available – and the *Bismarck* had also been making for St Nazaire when it was sunk – then just think of the casualties one of those ships could inflict on a convoy.'

His overwhelming memory of the operation was of everything happening in split seconds, of the noise of the guns, and of the faint glow of the blue lamps and the white webbing worn by the commandos for recognition. 'I can't say I did anything of real importance,' he said later, 'circumstances dictated what you did. If I'd been able to lay charges on the swing bridge . . . I'd have felt I'd done my job. But a lot of people weren't able to do their job.' It had, he thought, been a suicide mission for the men in the motor launches, but at least one that had succeeded.

The Germans agreed with that. 'It must be admitted that the enemy did achieve his principal aim,' they wrote in their own assessment of CHARIOT, although that was due not so much to the destruction of the lock gate as to the obliteration of the more complex pumping mechanism. Yet, while battleships could no longer use St Nazaire as a base, the raid had done no damage to the U-boat pens, which the Germans also believed to have been a key target.

As far as they were concerned, the British had not been sufficiently thorough. The attack had been well planned and executed with courage, but undermined by an 'unwillingness to sacrifice life even for a worthwhile cause'. Had the assault been made with eighteen hundred rather than six hundred men, and had there been a readiness by COHQ to accept greater losses, they thought the submarine base might have been put out of action, too.

Perhaps their analysis was right. In the short term, the operation was a success. But its strategic impact remains open to question. Certainly the *Tirpitz* stayed in Norway until she was sunk by the RAF in November 1944, but that vulnerability to air attack may well have ensured that she did not brave the North Sea even if St

Nazaire had been available to her. In any case, by mid-1942 the German campaign at sea depended far more on U-boats than on capital ships, and CHARIOT had done nothing to nullify that threat.

Yet the Commandos had accomplished all that was asked of them, despite the MLs' appalling vulnerability to incendiary bullets. Perhaps they had done too well, for the real importance of the operation was the lift it gave to Allied morale at a key period in the war. In the previous few months, Britain's belief in ultimate victory had been repeatedly battered by bad news: the entry of Japan into the war; the loss of Hong Kong and Singapore; Rommel's advances in North Africa; and the unhindered dash up the English Channel of the warships *Scharnhorst* and *Gneisenau*. CHARIOT broke that cycle of bad news. The fact that the Germans felt the British had been too cautious during it reflected not just a difference in mentality but also the balance of power at the time. The Germans believed that they still held the advantage, that they could afford to take risks, but after St Nazaire the British became more confident about going on the offensive.

From now on the pattern of the war in the West would consist of assaults by the Allies on positions defended by the Germans. The lesson drawn from St Nazaire was that these could be overcome. But that conclusion was wrong.

The Commandos had not defeated the port's garrison. They had merely made the most of the element of surprise, and even then *Campbeltown* had got through as much by luck as by daring. The real lesson of CHARIOT for COHQ should have been that if all went to plan, they might get away with it. The failure to grasp that was to have far-reaching and fatal consequences.

7

JUBILEE

Jim Spearman had never been on a raid before and he was not enjoying the experience. A couple of nights earlier, he had had a lucky escape when 4 Commando's first attempt to land near Boulogne had been thwarted and some men had drowned after their landing craft tipped over. To Jim's surprise, they had been sent back the same week. But as soon as he and his pal Joe Walsh got to the wire surrounding their objective 'all hell was let loose'.

'There was a slit trench in front of us from which suddenly a German with his helmet on stood up with his rifle and bayonet and lunged at me,' remembered Spearman, who was then only twenty.

> It was one of the easiest movements to fend off the bayonet by grabbing the butt of the rifle and tipping him over . . . I'd always wanted to do this, but when I lunged at the rifle, I missed.
>
> His bayonet went through my equipment – the webbing is quite thick, and the belt is doubly thick – but because of his momentum the bayonet went right through the explosives, right through the pouch and into me. And I thought: 'God, I've had it! This is the end of it!' And blood started coming through it all.
>
> Meanwhile, Joe had shot this fellow, I think with a Sten. And then after a few minutes I realised that I wasn't really hurt at all, I didn't feel anything . . . I've still got a scar where the

> bayonet went in. It must have gone in about an inch and a half. It didn't do any damage – but it made me feel a bit of a hero.

A Very light went up and Spearman and Walsh pulled back to the beach. Once on their LC, Spearman was transferred to an MTB accompanying the flotilla to have his wound dressed. There was still shooting going on and they were ushered below deck.

> So we settled down in this wardroom, and the radio office was adjoining it. Suddenly a shell came through, right through the side of the ship and exploded in this communications centre. And that was a most frightening experience – having got on a ship from a raid, thinking you were safe ... and I remember saying I was damn glad I'd left the Merchant Navy when the war started. Because that was terrifying.

Operation ABERCROMBIE, which took place in late April 1942, had had several aims. Its targets were installations around the coastal village of Hardelot, but the intention was also to make use of two resources which so far had had little opportunity to contribute to the war effort. The first of these was the Canadian Army, which its government had pledged to help Britain but which as yet had not been asked to do more than guard her coast against invasion. Accordingly, some of the detachments that sailed from Dover on the raid were Canadian soldiers from the Carleton and York Regiment.

Accompanying them were two Troops from 4 Commando, which as a unit had only taken part in the brief and largely unopposed attack on the Lofotens. While Nos. 2 and 3 had now seen action at St Nazaire and Vaagso, and three other Commandos had at least gone to the Mediterranean, more than half of the crack troops in the Special Service Brigade had spent nearly two years doing nothing but waiting.

After his stint training them in the Highlands, Shimi Lovat had transferred to the Commandos in the hope of taking a more active part in the war. He had duly been sent to No. 4 – but as their training officer. ABERCROMBIE was the first time he had led a raid and his first chance to put some of his theories into practice. It had gone awry almost from the off. The Germans had been too alert, the Canadians had got stuck on a sandbank, and Lovat had even had to reprimand one of his junior officers for forgetting his boots and landing in carpet slippers.

When he returned to England, it was to be greeted by pre-written stories in the newspapers acclaiming a successful raid on Boulogne by the Canadians. Rumours also began to circulate that the commandos had refused to go ashore because of heavy fire. Lovat was livid, but it was not long before No. 4 and the Canadians were ordered to prepare for another operation. It was to be by far COHQ's most ambitious yet.

The entry of America – and Russia – into the war on Britain's side in 1941 had brought both fresh hope and new problems. Not the least of the latter was agreeing on the best strategy for defeating Germany. The British wanted to consolidate their position in North Africa first, while the Americans pushed for an invasion of France as soon as possible. And from Moscow came increasing pressure to open a second front so as to divert Hitler from his thrust eastwards.

By the spring of 1942, the expectation was that there would be landings in Normandy the following year. Much still needed to be known about the logistics, but central to any plan would be the capture of a major port. Mountbatten was ordered to examine the feasibility of this, and COHQ was catapulted into the front line of the war. Until now its raids might have had a high profile but their effects were mainly short lived. Operation RUTTER, as it was to be called, would be nothing less than the dress rehearsal for D-Day itself. The port chosen for the attack was Dieppe.

Most of the main force of some six thousand troops would be provided by two Canadian brigades of infantry supported by their own armour. They would make a direct assault across the beach in front of the town, which was thought to be garrisoned by troops both few in number and low in quality. For Dieppe's principal protection was a pair of coastal batteries sited on the twin headlands between which it lay. These could pulverise the ships carrying any invaders long before they reached the shore.

Originally the plan was that these guns would be silenced by paratroopers, with the assault to take place at night in early July. A shambolic dry-run and bad weather caused it to be postponed, and by the time it was rescheduled for mid-August some important changes had been made. The attack would now be made at first light, and while there would be air cover it would not be preceded by an aerial bombardment. Surprise had to be preserved at all costs, and it was thought that it had been forfeited at St Nazaire because of the preliminary raid by the RAF. The parachutists, meanwhile, were to be substituted by commandos, who were believed to be less dependent on good weather.

Much of COHQ's role in what was now renamed JUBILEE had been to advise and to coordinate the attack, rather than to plan it. Nevertheless, Mountbatten had given it his approval, as had the general commanding south-east England, where most of the troops involved were based. Soon afterwards Bernard Montgomery departed for Cairo and the Eighth Army.

The two Commandos chosen to destroy the batteries at Berneval and Varengeville were No. 3, still led by John Durnford-Slater, and No. 4, which Lovat had taken over at the start of July. Higher up the chain of command, Charles Haydon had been succeeded as head of the Special Service Brigade by Bob Laycock, whose reputation had survived his North African misadventures. Now Lovat wrote to him, promising to make good the lack of leadership from which he felt No. 4 had suffered until now. 'You may depend on it that in three months' time we shall be ready to go anywhere and to give a good account of ourselves,' he assured Laycock. In the event, he would only have half that time to ready his men for JUBILEE, and he immediately set about practising on a mock-up of the battery built at Lulworth Cove, Dorset. As well as studying photographs and scale models, the men perfected their landing craft drill both by day and by night, and made eight assaults on the dummy guns.

Durnford-Slater's target was the Goebbels Battery on the high chalk cliffs at Berneval, four miles east of Dieppe. He quickly appreciated that it would be a very tough assignment. The plan called for his men to encircle the position by climbing two gullies which ran up from the beach below it, and he knew from photographs that these were blocked by barbed wire and probably covered by machine-guns. Yet he felt it would be bad for morale to make too much of this.

On the night of 18 August, 4 Commando boarded the ferry *Prince Albert* at Southampton. Mountbatten addressed them, emphasising how vital to the success of the whole operation their role was, and telling them that they must take their objective whatever the cost. Listening to him was Captain Pat Porteous, who all that evening had been watching the build-up of the 250-ship armada that would sail for Dieppe. 'We set off just before dark with an enormous convoy,' he recalled, 'hundreds of ships as far as we could see – landing craft, destroyers and minesweepers.'

Porteous was treated to an early breakfast of stew, but to the east 3 Commando were having to make do with tins of soup which they could not get to self-heat. They had sailed from Newhaven in twenty wooden landing craft called Eurekas, which reminded Durnford-Slater of ducklings as they straggled behind the gunboat in which he had his HQ.

He had just woken from a nap, with an hour to go to the beach, when from the deck he saw star shells bursting directly overhead. Less than half a mile away, five ships were bearing down on the little flotilla. Already the distance between them was filled with a bright stream of tracer and shellfire. Death seemed an instant away.

'It was by far the most unpleasant moment of my life,' wrote Peter Young afterwards. Hole after hole was ripped in the upper works of the Eureka in which he was crouching. For a few minutes its skipper tried to follow the gunboat, then finally accepted Young's advice and veered off into the darkness. The other LCs also scattered as best they could. They had had the misfortune to run into a coastal convoy out of Boulogne just when the commandos' escort –

a Polish destroyer – had contrived to lose touch with them. The German ships had been picked up on radar in Britain but a signal about them had failed to reach the raiding party.

Joe Smale was standing up front in another of the Eurekas as a German armed trawler loomed out of the night. Her first attempt to ram the LC failed when Smale's corporal smartly put the craft into reverse, but then Smale saw the larger boat closing on them again. 'It was going to hit us so we had to abandon ship,' he said later. 'I thought I'd have a jolly good try at swimming the seven miles to shore.'

Because of his experience at Guernsey, Smale knew that his boots would pull him down, so he tugged them off before jumping overboard. 'Have you got your boots off, Gerard?' he asked the corporal once they were swimming, but Gerard had forgotten and now found it impossible to untie the laces. 'I held him up as long as I could,' remembered Smale. 'Eventually, after several hours holding his head above the water, I found he had died in my arms. It was a terrible experience.'

Drifting with the current, Smale began to paddle slowly towards the distant coast, arms outstretched in front of him. 'It was cold, but I was very, very fit at the time,' he said later, although in fact he was still recovering from measles. Through the dawn mist he saw a rubber boat, only to discover that it belonged to a German air crew which had been shot down. 'Quite rightly, they thought that if I came aboard I would upset the boat, and I think I would have done the same in their position.' They disappeared back into the fog, and Smale swam on.

On the bridge of Durnford-Slater's gunboat, the bodies were piling up 'like a collapsed rugger scrum'. Half of the twenty men she was carrying had been hit. When daylight came, the colonel transferred to one of the few undamaged landing craft and headed for Dieppe itself. He spent the day there feeling thoroughly useless, and with no idea where the rest of the 420 men of his Commando were.

Often accounts of JUBILEE assume that the disaster which struck 3 Commando alerted the German coastal defences to an imminent attack and from that moment the main operation was doomed. But this was not the case. Neither the garrison at Dieppe nor the batteries were informed about the firefight because at that stage the German Navy assumed that they had simply fended off an attack on one of their convoys. The surprise on which JUBILEE depended so heavily had not been lost.

Nor had any of the Eurekas been sunk in the sea battle. While the commandos had suffered some casualties, what was more significant for the fate of FLODDEN – the attack on the Goebbels Battery – was that No. 3's LCs had been widely dispersed. Although half a dozen of them managed to regroup and head for land, when they beached below Petit Berneval they were half an hour behind schedule. In those thirty minutes, the cover of night had lifted and the enemy garrison had woken up.

In spite of these handicaps, and though numbering roughly half the expected force, the commandos pressed on. The senior officer was Lieutenant Dick Wills, the wit who had sent the telegram to Hitler from Vaagso. Two machine-gun nests in the dunes were dealt with at bayonet point as the raiders tried to fan out from the gully, but the other defenders had the advantage of height and cover. Wills was then shot through the neck, and thereafter the momentum of the assault faltered.

Also attached to the raid were some US Rangers. Lieutenant Edwin Loustalot led a party of them up a narrow lane behind the beach. There he died, the first American soldier of the war to be killed in Europe. Soon the survivors were pinned down by mortars and though one LC was able to get away with the beachmaster and a signals corporal, the rest were rounded up during the morning. The villagers had hidden as many as they could in cellars and attics but an Alsatian soon sniffed them all out.

Most of the other Eurekas which had fled also made it back across the Channel, but within a few hours 3 Commando had lost more than a hundred men, two-thirds of them as PoWs. Responsibility for silencing the battery – and preventing a massacre of the fleet steaming towards Dieppe – now rested with just twenty soldiers from the sole remaining launch, including Peter Young.

After evading the German attack, the LC's skipper, Lieutenant Henry Buckee, had been able to maintain his original course and at 0445 he put down Young's men at the second gully about a mile west of the battery. They were five minutes ahead of schedule. To their surprise, the defences on the beach were unoccupied. They quickly crossed the thin strip of sand and to their left saw a narrow cleft which was piled high with barbed wire and closed off by a ten-foot-high fence.

None of them had brought wire cutters, and when Young tried to scale the fence he fell backwards onto another officer, who suggested that it might be more sensible to return to the boat and go home. Between them they had ten rifles, six tommy-guns, a Bren, three pistols and a mortar. The battery was manned by some two hundred German troops. Young's only response was an aggravated growl, and he began to haul himself up the side of the cliff using the strands of wire as a rope.

Bracing his feet against the pegs used to secure it, and ignoring the barbs which dug into his palms, he reached the top in forty-five minutes. Further up the coast, he could see Wills's Eurekas running into their beach. He thought his men looked rather daunted by the prospect of taking on the guns, so he gave them a pep talk, telling them that it would be a story to pass on to their grandchildren one day. 'They looked a bit dubious,' he reflected, but through fields of ripened corn they began to push inland. Soon they had reached the outskirts of the village of Berneval, which straggled up the road behind the gun emplacement. A flight of Hurricanes came streaking in and strafed the battery while Young watched a woman placidly milking a cow under the apple trees. The commandos cut the telephone wires, and Young then decided that it would take too long to work their way forward through the gardens of the houses, so he opted to run straight up the main street. Ahead, he could hear the guns beginning to fire.

As the commandos drew level with the village church a

machine-gun opened up on them from a corner sixty yards ahead. The mortar crew promptly knocked it out and Young reformed his men in the churchyard. The sprint along the street and contact with the enemy had bucked them up, and he thought of placing a few in the church's belfry, from where they could snipe at the gunners in the battery. When he went inside to look for the entrance to the tower, however, he found that the steps to it began ten feet above the ground, and the ladder had been taken away by the sexton a few days earlier.

So, instead, the commandos tried to approach the battery under the cover of some orchards. But they were spotted and came under attack from sentry posts hidden in hedges. Bullets plucked the fruit from the branches and Young decided that they would all be safer in the cornfields beside the village. There he formed his troops into two long lines, kneeling down and well spread out so that the rear rank could aim through the gaps in front at the side of the battery two hundred yards away.

Taking the yellow flashes around the guns as their mark, they kept up a harassing fire for the next hour and a half. The German crews were largely protected by a low concrete wall but their reserve platoon had gone to deal with Wills's party so they had no one to send out to chase away Young's men. Proof that the constant whine of bullets overhead was making life uncomfortable in the battery came when a six-inch shell screamed past the commandos and landed in a valley a mile away.

The Germans had turned the nearest of the huge coastal guns on them, but it could not aim low enough to do any damage. Four rounds soared over Young before it once more swung round to face the sea. Nor did the other six guns in the battery seem to be having more success in getting the range of their principal targets. The huge cloud of smoke that covered the Channel off Dieppe prevented the artillery crews from seeing any of the ships there, and Young estimated that by 0800 – two and a half hours after the Canadians had landed – the battery had got off no more than twenty or thirty rounds. Usually it would have fired that many in a couple of minutes.

By then the commandos were running low on ammunition and Young was worried about the arrival of German reinforcements. He did not relish the prospect of confronting Panzers in the cornfield. Gradually he sent his men the half-mile back towards the beach, where Buckee had waited with the LC despite being shot at himself. Young covered the withdrawal from the clifftop and then waded out to the boat under a rain of fire from German rifles. There was no time for the Eureka to stop and pick him up, so he grabbed hold of a rope and was towed out to sea as she pulled away. Even then, shots hammered into the smoke canister in her stern, and a sailor close to Young was badly wounded in the leg.

By midday, Young was back in England and that afternoon he went up to London to report to Mountbatten, who was anxious for first-hand news. The reports coming back from Dieppe were universally gloomy. It was clear that the main attack was turning into a catastrophe. The only other bright spot had been 4 Commando's assault on the Hess Battery at Varengeville: Operation CAULDRON.

Like FLODDEN, CAULDRON had been designed by Lovat as a pincer movement. To get his way, however, he had to battle one of the planners at COHQ – Robert Henriques – who 'tried to do my thinking for me'. The qualities that Lovat valued in a soldier were not intellect but loyalty and commitment, albeit he himself had the casually confident manner of a boy who no longer has any use for school. His insistence on taking his own line frequently irritated his superiors, but as he showed the same contempt for the enemy many of his men also found him inspirational. And for all his air of nonchalance he was a meticulous planner.

Though 4 Commando saw the fireworks to the east when No. 3 bumped into the German convoy, they had a clear run towards their two beaches behind an MTB commanded by Peter Scott, the naturalist and son of the polar explorer. Three miles from the shore the Commando divided. While the majority were to land on Orange Beach II, a mile west of the battery, one and a half

Troops under Derek Mills-Roberts headed for the sand in front of it at Vasterival-sur-Mer.

Their landmark was a lighthouse and each time its beams swept over their boat, wrote Mills-Roberts, they felt 'like thieves in an alley when the policeman shines his torch'. Just as the beach came in sight, flak opened up on a squadron of aeroplanes roaring in low over the cliffs. Fearing that surprise had been lost, Mills-Roberts made a hurried landing at the foot of a promontory on either side of which were deep gullies. The one on the left was blocked by wire and chunks of chalk, so they turned their attention to that on the right. This seemed more passable, although it too was shut off by two banks of wire. A pair of Bangalore torpedoes soon blew holes in these and by 0540 the commandos had reached the holiday cottages at the top. Mills-Roberts's scouts returned with an elderly resident in a nightshirt, who complained about the damage they had done when passing through his hedge. Mills-Roberts noticed a pretty child on the house's veranda. 'Are you going to shoot Papa?' she asked philosophically.

Mills-Roberts could now relax a little. The plan was that at 0615 his section would distract the battery by mortaring it from the nearby woods, while fifteen minutes later Lovat's group would assault it from the rear. The main convoy should not be in sight of the guns until 0630. Mills-Roberts was therefore astounded when a shattering blast boomed over his head. The guns had commenced firing.

Indeed, from the beach came a radio message that the Allied fleet could already be seen approaching the coast. Somehow fifty minutes had been sliced from the operation's timetable and Mills-Roberts now had to improvise fast.

'We heard the battery fire six salvoes in close succession,' he later recalled. 'The noise was deafening.' Abandoning any notion of stealth, the commandos rushed through the undergrowth towards the seven guns, which were sited a thousand yards behind the cliff's edge. As they came over a little rise, they found themselves almost on top of the pits within which the crews were working and could clearly hear the words of command. Dropping onto his belly, Mills-Roberts worked his way through the scrub to get a better view. He then crawled back to the wood and ran to a barn which overlooked the battery buildings.

On the first floor, one of his snipers settled himself at a table. The guns were about 170 yards away and their artillerymen sheltered by a low parapet topped with sandbags. They looked extremely surprised when one of their comrades fell dead at their feet. 'It was rather like shooting a member of the church congregation from the organ loft,' thought Mills-Roberts.

It is difficult to pinpoint the origin of rifle fire when being shot at, and for a time the commandos' sniping prevented any movement at all in the pits. Then the Germans pulled themselves together. A revolving flak tower began to target the wood, sending splinters lancing into the scrub, while from beyond the battery mortars began to lob shells into the British positions. Tom McDonough had been lugging an anti-tank rifle with armour-piercing rounds specifically for the purpose of dealing with the flak tower if it gave trouble. He was glad to be able to use the weapon at last and soon put the tower out of action. The bursting mortar shells were more of a problem, though, and caused several casualties.

Jim Dunning had turned his back on life as a butcher's boy to seek adventure as a soldier in 1939. At the age of twenty-one, Lovat had made him a troop sergeant-major, perhaps the youngest in the Army. 'I was in charge of the 2-inch mortar,' he recalled, and this he now brought into play only two hundred yards from the guns. 'The first round went into the battery area, the second one went to the right a bit. The third hit the ammunition dump and that went up like a fireworks display.' He had hit the cordite stack.

'A blinding flash resulted, which silenced the guns at 0607,' wrote Mills-Roberts. 'I ordered the Bren gun in the scrub patch with me to fire bursts at the flames and I was sniping at figures around the main conflagration.' Despite the efforts of the Germans to extinguish it, the blaze grew and grew.

While Mills-Roberts had been coming ashore, the bulk of the Commando under Lovat had landed further west at the mouth of the River Saane. One section under Lieutenant Arthur Veasey scaled the precipitous cliffs and, achieving complete surprise, killed the sentries in a pillbox with grenades. The other sections had disembarked just three minutes later but they came under machine-gun fire from the cliffs to their left as they tried in the half-light to get across the wire that had been laid on the shelving shingle. Mortars then joined in and the first shell wiped out a whole sub-section of B Troop. This was led by Captain Gordon Webb, whose wrist was broken by the explosion.

Fortunately the mortars then concentrated on the LCs as they headed back out to sea and the rest of the Troop was able to get over the wire. Webb had been annoyed on the voyage out by a rather plump soldier who had complained about the standard of Navy cooking, so he now ordered him to lie on top of the coils while the others ran over him.

For a mile they jogged along the east riverbank at the double, knowing from the model they had studied that it was dead ground which would offer them cover. But the grass was lush and wet from flooding which made the going hard. At 0515 they reached a bend and turned eastwards. On reaching Blancmesnil Wood, B Troop forked towards the rear of the battery while F Troop began to work its way through the orchards and small enclosures on its flank. All the while the three-hundred-strong garrison was fully occupied with the diversion in front of it provided by Mills-Roberts.

From behind the guns, Webb's men began to creep slowly forward. Through a hedge they could see the flak tower, and watched in amazement as a German soldier in it toppled sixty feet to the ground after being picked off by a commando marksman. It seemed to them just like something from a film.

A small party led by a young officer, Donald Gilchrist, headed towards a machine-gun nest which guarded the rear of the site. 'Before us, not 70 yards away, was the battery position, German heads bobbing up and down. We began to stalk – we'd learned how – walking upright, our weapons at the ready. Suddenly, we froze.' Behind the battery ran a hedge, around which appeared a

German soldier carrying a box of grenades. Sensing something was wrong, he looked over his shoulder and stopped, open-mouthed, staring at the camouflaged faces of Gilchrist's men. Instead of raising his hands, he began to jump up and down like an angry baby, still cradling the grenades and shouting: '*Kommando, Kommando!*'

'I'll give him flippin' *Kommando*,' muttered one soldier, and shot him. The commandos ran to the hedge, waited a moment and then threw their own grenades over it and into the gun pit beyond. 'Every time a coconut!' said a Cockney voice approvingly, as the explosions were followed by loud cries of pain.

Veiled by smoke, F Troop had pushed on from the edge of the wood towards a farmyard. In command was Captain Roger Pettiward, a close friend of Peter Fleming and in peacetime an artist for magazines such as *Punch* and *Night and Day*. With him, acting as liaison officer between the two assault groups, was Pat Porteous.

'As we got into this area of the battery, which was typical country with masses of little hedges,' said Porteous later, 'we bumped into this truck of German soldiers who were just disembarking.' A platoon was forming up to counter-attack Mills-Roberts's men, but the Germans were facing away from the farmhouse around which F Troop now appeared, firing from the hip. 'We managed to knock them off before they got out of the truck: we killed virtually all of them with tommy-guns.'

The Troop's advance now disintegrated into a confused mêlée of individual battles. 'We started working our way through this very dense bit of country,' Porteous recalled. Around the edge of the battery were hedges and farm buildings from which the commandos came under fire. Pettiward fell while leading from the front. 'I think he must have got a bit separated because when we got in there he was well ahead of us and I found his body there with a bullet through his head,' said Porteous. 'And the other subaltern, John Macdonald, was killed by somebody who threw a stick grenade – the chap was hiding in the roof of one of the barns and threw it as he passed underneath.'

With their two officers dead, and a sergeant shot moments later, the Troop was in danger of losing the momentum necessary for the final assault. Ignoring the withering fire which flayed the open ground ahead of him, Porteous ran across a field to take command. He pushed on, but there was danger everywhere. 'I was going along a little lane towards the battery,' he remembered, 'and I suddenly saw a German popping up on the other side of the bank. I threw a Mills grenade at him and he threw a stick grenade at me. As soon as it went off I popped up but unfortunately he popped up a little bit quicker and he shot me – I had a rifle in my hand – through my left hand.' The bullet passed straight out of his palm and into his upper arm. Seeing that he had hit Porteous, the German assumed that he was no longer a threat and turned his aim on a commando sergeant. But Porteous had continued running towards his attacker and, despite his wound, knocked the German's gun aside before killing him with his own bayonet.

The Troop's sergeant-major, Bill Portman, had been a regular soldier in the Royal Engineers before the war and was trained in demolitions. He was carrying eighty pounds of explosives with which to blow up the guns and was meant to enter the battery only after it had been taken. But he had got mixed up with the main detachment and was wounded when a grenade exploded. A splinter went into his eye, another into his backside, while a fragment also passed through the charges in his pack – without setting them off. At first he had no idea where the missile had come from:

> Like a fool I was looking right – I could see some positions about 200 yards away. I should have known no man is going to throw a grenade 200 yards. I should have had a bit more common sense. I looked left and saw something moving and there was this Jerry looking out, so I pulled round and knocked him off, got him straight through the forehead.
>
> I thought I'd stick my bayonet on – I had an awful struggle to get it because it was hidden in my rucksack – walked forward and there was another guy in this slit trench. He didn't realise that his mate was dead as there was so much banging going on, so I managed to put a couple into him too.

Having recovered from being bayoneted at Hardelot, Jim Spearman was with B Troop in the woods behind the battery. Afterwards he stressed the part that its Bren gunners had played in covering the Troop's approach. 'Where you had open paths or areas to cross, the machine gunner's burst of fire would keep the enemy's head down, just for a moment while people were able to move . . . in little, short bursts it's a wonderful weapon.' But if used for too long, the barrel became red hot and could jam the gun, as happened now. 'The operator hadn't got a spare with him so he peed on it to cool it. And while he was doing this he burned himself quite badly. I don't know if he finished himself for life . . . of course, it's completely the wrong thing to do but he had no alternative.'

At 0628, a squadron of cannon-firing Spitfires swooped down to rake the battery, although they were tangled up with Focke-Wulfs and some of their shells hit the houses on the west flank from which A Troop were sniping. Jim Dunning then put down ten rounds of white smoke from the mortar 'and the Very light signal went up', he recalled, 'green over white over green. I can see it now. That was the signal for us to stop firing as they would go in with the bayonet to destroy the guns.'

'The Germans must have known that we were outside and waiting to come in,' believed Spearman. 'They must have been really terrified . . . Immediately the strafing finished we assaulted . . . and I must say all pandemonium let loose.'

Led by Porteous, the sixty men of F Troop rose as one and ran yelling towards the guns. 'It was a stupendous charge,' Lovat reported afterwards, 'in many cases across open ground swept by machine-gun fire, through a barbed-wire entanglement, overrunning strongpoints and finally ending on the gun sites themselves.'

'It seemed to be a hell of a long way,' recalled Porteous, 'but it couldn't have been more than 80 or 100 yards. The guns were fully occupied dealing with the chaps on the other side, and we got little opposition coming in.' He was being characteristically modest. In fact they had to run through a hail of fire, not least from snipers shooting from the windows of the battery office. The wound to his hand meant that he was unable to reload his pistol, which was soon empty, but he ran on regardless until hit again. 'I got another bullet through my thigh, which slowed me up . . . I felt it was rather like being in a rugger scrum. You got kicked about a bit, and the object was to get over the line, which was all that we did do in fact.' Weak from loss of blood, he helped to clear several pits of their crews and finally collapsed on top of a gun position. All around him, the commandos were bayoneting and bombing the battery into submission.

'It was total confusion,' said Spearman, 'because anybody you didn't recognise as a commando, you killed. People were running out of buildings, running into buildings. Some of them were quite brave, they were trying to put up a fight but they really didn't get a chance . . . Absolutely nobody escaped. They had nowhere to escape to.'

Bill Portman was with Porteous as they rushed the guns. 'I was so excited,' he remembered. 'I tossed a grenade into one position and all the cordite exploded. I jumped into it and there were two Jerries with all their clothes burned off.' Shortly afterwards, he was wounded by the second stick grenade to be thrown at him that morning. It blew the heel from his foot, but from a sitting position he continued to shoot down the enemy.

'Razor-sharp Sheffield steel tore the guts out of the Varengeville battery,' wrote Gilchrist later.

> Screams, smoke, the smell of burning cordite. Mad moments soon over . . . Laying in a yard was a wounded commando soldier. From the gloom of a barn emerged the German who had cut him down. He jumped up and crashed his boots on the prone face.
>
> Our weapons went up. A corporal raised his hand . . . The German clutched the pit of his stomach as if trying to claw the bullet out. He tried to scream but couldn't. Four pairs of eyes in faces blackened for action stared at his suffering. They were eyes of stone.

The battery had been taken in only a few minutes. Many of the defenders had been hiding in underground tunnels containing stores, in outbuildings, in the cookhouse, even under tables. Almost all were bayoneted or shot with tommy-guns. The battery commander was killed after being chased several times around his desk.

In spite of his own injuries, Portman ensured that Porteous was placed on a door – used as a makeshift stretcher – and carried towards the beach. Then he set about putting the beehive-shaped charges into the breech blocks of the guns, and fixing plastic explosive on the mountings. Exactly two hours after Cauldron Force had landed the battery was blown sky high.

Lovat inspected the results:

> The gun sites were in a remarkable state. Burnt and mangled bodies were piled high up behind two of the sandbag breastworks which surrounded the guns. The last survivors had fought it out with F Troop during their successful attack with the bayonet. Other bodies which had been sniped by Major Mills-Roberts and C Troop lay in heaps all round the area.

While the charges were being set, Lovat had ordered Spearman to reconnoitre a safe path back to the beach. The commandos would be encumbered by their wounded as they withdrew and he wanted to be sure they were not attacked. Spearman and his friend Percy Tombs zigzagged their way towards the sea. The fury of battle had worn off and they were now more anxious than ever to get home safely. 'When a raid is over, and you've gone through all that,' Spearman reflected, 'all you want to do is to get back. You don't want to be killed at the last minute.' He met a naval party coming up from the boats and, despite some German mortar and rifle fire, the withdrawal was soon completed. Only four prisoners had been taken and these were made to carry the injured troops.

By 0830, 4 Commando was heading back to Newhaven, where a crowd had gathered, knowing only that a major battle was being fought on the French coast. As the soldiers climbed wearily up the iron ladders of the harbour wall and assembled on the quayside for roll-call a shout went up: 'It's the Commandos, God bless 'em!'

The photographs which appeared in the press the next morning established the Commandos' image for ever. Rifles slung on their shoulders, clutching cups of tea and cigarettes, they posed for pictures that showed faces streaked with powder burns and heads wrapped in bandages. Many had on the woollen cap comforters that Lovat had ordered them to wear instead of steel helmets (though his own had been torn off when ducking under wire). The realism of the pictures presented the public with a strong contrast to the usual portraits of soldiers in immaculate order.

Yet undoubtedly these scruffs were warriors. Tired perhaps, but cheerful, and despite an appearance that desk-bound generals thought ill disciplined they had demonstrated their professionalism and sealed their reputation with the public. Gordon Webb, who had charged into the battery with his right arm dangling useless, was recognised from the photographs that evening in London and not allowed to catch his train until he was 'a little tight' after being plied with drinks by well-wishers.

Lovat had also made a particularly favourable impression. He was sometimes accused of taking too relaxed an approach to soldiering – the photographs show he wore uniform on the raid rather than the corduroys of legend, though he did take his own sporting rifle – but, when it had counted, his coolness under fire had inspired those around him.

Jim Spearman had followed his commander off the landing craft onto Orange Beach II. 'When machine-gun fire was coming in, your inclination was to dig yourself into the shingle to protect yourself,' he pointed out. 'But Lovat, with shells dropping and people being killed . . . stood up – I suppose he must have been 6ft 2ins – he stood bolt upright with his carbine under his arm to rally everybody. It took great courage to do that.'

Lovat was met at Newhaven by Laycock and Peter Fleming's brother Ian, who was in Naval Intelligence. They whisked him by staff car up to London, where long into the evening he was debriefed at the War Office. The only place that would let him in later that night, filthy as he was and carrying no money, was the

Guards Club. He fell asleep in the bath, dreaming uneasily of tracer fire and boots running too slowly over pebbles: 'with the false dawn came the realisation that I must break the news to the families of the men who died at Varengeville'.

In fact, 4 Commando's casualties had been lighter than expected. Only a dozen men had been killed and another thirty wounded from a total of 265 who had gone on the raid. The German losses were put as high as 150, though they may have been rather fewer. But despite the success of both Commando missions, the main operation had been a disaster.

The German defences had proved more alert and much stronger than anticipated, and in the absence of a heavy preliminary bombardment the inexperienced Canadian troops found it impossible to gain a foothold on the beach. The two flanking attacks made by them were repelled almost immediately, and as a result the invasion force was enfiladed by fire from both headlands as it tried to storm ashore. The sands of Dieppe became a killing ground.

Nearly two-thirds of the six thousand troops involved in JUBILEE failed to return. The Canadians suffered more than 900 dead and had 2000 soldiers taken prisoner. All 26 officers and 496 of 528 Other Ranks of the Royal Regiment of Canada were killed, wounded or captured. Almost thirty of the new Churchill tanks had to be abandoned, while the Navy lost a destroyer, many LCs and more than five hundred sailors. The RAF also endured one of its worst days of the war as one hundred of its aircraft were shot down over the port – twice the number lost by the Luftwaffe.

Everyone had their own theory as to what had gone wrong. For Charles Haydon at COHQ, the key mistake was to attempt a daylight landing. The change had been made to the original plan for RUTTER after the night-time rehearsal proved a fiasco. No doubt other lessons should have been learned then about the state of readiness for an operation on this scale, but the political pressure to proceed was overwhelming.

Mountbatten absolved himself as far as possible from blame. 'We at Combined Operations Headquarters were not responsible for detailed planning,' he wrote later, 'our role in this respect was an advisory one.' Yet, while the Chiefs of Staff had given JUBILEE's commanders in the field much latitude, Mountbatten now sat with them and his views on what was his main area of responsibility would have carried particular weight.

More valid was his judgement that Dieppe 'was the turning point in the technique of invasion'. It had been thought vital to capture a port both quickly and in a working state, but JUBILEE had shown that would be virtually impossible. The Allies would need to bring their own harbour with them. This insight led to the development of the Mulberry artificial ports that would be used on D-Day.

'What was equally important', Mountbatten continued, 'was that the Germans drew the wrong conclusions.' While Dieppe persuaded COHQ to abandon its blueprint for invasion, it convinced the Nazis that the Allies' principal objective would be a port such as Calais or Cherbourg. Therefore, they began to concentrate their strength in such places while leaving a thinner line to hold the coast between them.

In time, the new Atlantic Wall would cause the Commandos fresh problems. For now, however, they could reap the rewards due them. In his official dispatch, Vice-Admiral John Hughes-Hallett, the naval commander for JUBILEE, rated Peter Young's attack on the Goebbels Battery 'perhaps the most outstanding incident of the operation'. Whether the lack of damage done by the guns at Berneval was due more to the smoke covering the fleet than to Young's sniping is a moot point, but his courage in pressing on after the loss of the rest of 3 Commando is unquestionable and he was awarded the DSO for his efforts.

There were MCs for Mills-Roberts and Webb, a DSO for Lovat and a Victoria Cross for Porteous. Characteristically, the latter considered himself lucky to receive it, and later confessed to having been scared 'from the moment we started getting shot at, or before that – as soon as we realised we were going on an operation . . . I don't think there's a man on earth who is not frightened if he's going into an operation unless he's absolutely boneheaded.'

Among the letters of condolence that Durnford-Slater sent was one to Joe Smale's mother. To his surprise, back came a cheerful note assuring him that her son was a strong swimmer and that she fully expected him to turn up sooner or later. Her confidence proved justified a few weeks later when news came that Joe was a prisoner. He had been washed into Dieppe harbour after more than twelve hours in the sea, and passed out from exhaustion as he was being picked up by German sailors.

Smale was more fortunate than some other PoWs. After the raid, the Germans announced that they had found a dozen of their troops tied in such a way by the Canadians that they had choked to death. There were also rumours that 4 Commando had shot prisoners in cold blood on the beach as there was no room in the boats for them. Porteous vigorously denied the accusation in later years, but Spearman seemed to believe it, albeit without witnessing any of the alleged executions himself.

The Germans were never able to produce any evidence of such an atrocity, but what counted was that the allegation was given credence at the highest levels of the Reich (Goering referred to it during his trial at Nuremberg). The Commandos were clearly beginning to get under the enemy's skin.

Yet there was still much for them to do. Dieppe was supposed to be the run-through for the invasion of France: the beginning of the end. In fact, the Allies had reached only the mid-point of the long slog from Dunkirk to D-Day.

As they had run down the ramp of their landing craft at Dieppe, their bodies bent like 'half-shut knives' against the crackle of machine-gun fire, one private had turned to Donald Gilchrist and complained: 'Jesus Christ, sir, this is as bad as Achnacarry!'

The establishment in February 1942 of the ancient seat of the Cameron clan as the Commandos' main training ground had marked a major change for the brigade. Until then, each

Commando had been almost wholly the creation of its commanding officer. This had been largely effective in fostering the skills and spirit required to date, but now Haydon recognised that training ought to be centralised and standardised.

In part this was to ensure that all units learned the lessons of past raids and were properly prepared for the new challenges of mass landings that were soon to come. There was also the need for a guaranteed supply of replacements – St Nazaire and Dieppe had exacted a heavy toll on Nos. 2 and 3, in particular.

Yet, also in February, there had been another and more fundamental change to the Commandos' structure. Their increased success meant that they had become a key part of the Allied strategy for a second front, but the demands on them would require almost a doubling of their numbers. Stretched as it was by its commitments, and still riled by the measure of independence that the Commandos enjoyed, the War Office was highly reluctant to allow them to prise away thousands more recruits from the Army. So Mountbatten turned to another source of manpower already familiar with amphibious warfare: the Royal Marines.

The Marines had originally been earmarked for the roving role in the Norway campaign, but as they had not been ready in time the job had gone to the Independent Companies instead. Since then the Army had taken the lead in raiding, but to Churchill it seemed foolish to let an entire division continue to stand idle. The first Royal Marine Commando – No. 40 – was therefore raised at Deal, Kent, on Valentine's Day 1942. Another eight would follow over the next two years.

No. 40 was also the first into action, as part of the main assault force at Dieppe, but such was the concentration of fire brought to bear on its LCs that it proved impossible to land. Its first commanding officer, Colonel Joseph Picton Phillips, conspicuous in his white gloves, stood on top of his landing craft and motioned to the others to turn back. Many lives were saved at the cost of his own, but even so the new unit sustained heavy losses.

Nor was its formation welcomed by the Army Commandos. As

yet there was no suggestion that there would be any integration with the Marine units, but they still resented the newcomers. All those in the Commandos were proud of what they had accomplished, and particularly of their volunteer status. Much of the ill feeling that was to spring up between them and the Marines originated in the assumption that the latter were pressed rather than picked men – although, in fact, the troops of No. 40 were volunteers, too.

For their part, the Marines were often jealous of soldiers having usurped their traditional amphibious role. Like many in the military, they also felt that the Commandos were favoured too much by the press and by Downing Street at the expense of less glamorous units. In June 1942, Churchill had to deny in the House of Commons the common belief that the Commandos enjoyed special privileges such as extra leave and better pay.

The commandant of the new depot at Achnacarry therefore had important responsibilities. He not only had to process the large numbers of Royal Marine recruits quickly, but had to ensure that they met the standards set by the original Army Commandos. Only if training was equally tough for all, and only if passing out of Achnacarry became a badge of pride, would the Marines be accepted and tensions eased.

Laycock's choice for this key post was Lieutenant Colonel Charles Vaughan. A Cockney, he had served in the ranks of the Guards during the First World War and survived the retreat from Mons. After becoming regimental sergeant-major of the Buffs (the Royal East Kent Regiment), he had been commissioned and by 1942 was second-in-command of No. 4 Commando.

After Dieppe, Lovat had recommended that Jim Dunning undertake officer training, and as Vaughan knew him he was soon poached to be an instructor at Achnacarry. Dunning remembered the commandant as 'a guardsman out and out. He was a brilliant trainer who understood human nature and knew how to get the best out of trainees, even if he slaughtered the King's English with his accent. He was an awesome figure – an awesome figure.'

The battle training centre established by Vaughan at the Camerons' castle and estate near Fort William became not only the most famous of the war but also the model for similar bases all over the world from then on. More than 25,000 Allied soldiers passed through it, among them US Rangers and members of SOE as well as Polish, French and other exiles who now began to form their own Commandos. The great majority of its graduates, however, were British soldiers and marines who took a six-week course which retained the essentials taught at Lochailort but also added many refinements.

Bill Jenkins was just eighteen when he arrived at Achnacarry as a newly commissioned Marine officer. A few months earlier he had been studying geography at Oxford. He was the only officer on the draft and was told to keep an eye on two recruits with criminal records. At Glasgow, he patrolled the platform self-consciously as the troops teased him by whistling 'Pistol Packin' Mama'. His insecurities only increased when it emerged that the two men had got out of the other side of the train and escaped across the tracks.

He was the same age as Vic Ralph, an office boy from Bromley in Kent, who had enlisted in the Rifle Brigade at seventeen before joining 1 Commando. When his detachment arrived at Spean Bridge, the nearest station to Achnacarry, they found lorries waiting for them. 'We thought they were going to take us to the camp but all we were allowed to do was throw our kitbags in them. Then we were formed up and told to speed march to Achnacarry.' That was seven miles away, and uphill. Ralph and his friends found it hard going after their long train journey, not least because the marching pace of each recruit varied depending on their parent regiment. 'The column was bunching up and the Commando NCOs were blowing their cap badges,' he recalled.

There were no lorries to meet Jenkins, who had to cope with the added handicap of not having a kitbag (which he could have put on his shoulder) but a suitcase.

Once through the gates of the camp, the new arrivals' attention was caught by what seemed to be a line of graves. 'We got the fright of our lives to see an orderly row of crosses,' said Ralph. 'Each cross had a slogan on it – "This man forgot to take cover" and so on. It wasn't til much later that we learned that they weren't real graves. They were just put there to give us a real shaking.'

Next they were sent down to the loch and made to scrub, blanco and polish their kit. After an inspection Ralph and the rest of Laycock Troop were taken up into the hills for their first assault course. Ralph found himself jumping fifteen feet off a rock into two feet of mud: 'I'd hardly straightened my knees when someone landed behind me, gave me a push and I went head first into the mud.'

'Everything was that much tougher there,' agreed Jenkins, comparing it to his basic training with the Marines. 'Walls were not six but ten feet high. Previously we had done ten-mile speed marches, now we did fifteen. In Wales, the mountains were three thousand five hundred feet high, but at Achnacarry we had to go up Ben Nevis. It was that bit more rigorous.'

There were modifications to the training regime as the war progressed, taking account of the shift in the Commandos' role from raiding to assault troops. This necessitated learning to handle heavier weapons and to cooperate with other formations. Yet at its core remained the need to instil physical endurance and mental resilience. Officers were expected to surpass their men and to cope without their batmen, cooking their own food and cleaning their own uniforms.

'The object was to make sure we got the spirit, that we set out as a troop and came back as a troop,' said Ralph later. 'If someone was a bit weak on their legs the others would help him.' Central to this ethos was the system known as 'Me and My Pal'. 'The two of you watched out for each other,' explained Ralph. 'The basis of the success of the Commandos was that we were all taught to rely on each other – and we could rely on each other.'

Jenkins also had strong memories of the method:

> We tried to get chaps to link up together in pairs so whatever task they had they shared it. They shared cleaning weapons, they shared obstacle crossing, they shared living off the land – one would get firewood while the other built the bivouac or cooked.

> Once you got the spirit of cooperation going it was a great benefit. Military tactics work on the basis of fire and movement, so when you pepper-pot forward [take turns to dash across open ground] one would be giving covering fire as the other went ahead.

Recruits were taught how to abseil down the side of Achnacarry House, enter a window and herd a room's occupants to a pre-selected killing ground. They learned how to strip a Bren while blindfolded and how to make a meal from a hedgehog. The Tarzan slide twenty feet above the River Arkeig in spate daunted even the toughest. Jos Nicholl – an officer destined for 2 Commando – vividly recalled seeing a large policeman tackle it for the first time. Urged to hurry by the instructor, he threw his rope toggle over the wire but as he launched himself it got caught on a knot. Rifle slung around his neck, the man hung by his wrists until one slipped out and he fell, fortunately landing on the rope bridge underneath. Although he was as white as a sheet, the instructor made him attempt the crossing again.

> Panting for breath he sat on the same branch. Then with a tremendous effort, he threw the toggle rope over the wire a second time and threaded his wrists through it again. Then he pushed off and found himself hurtling across the stream. He hit the further bank with a hollow thump but he, and even the involuntary spectators, knew it had been worth it.

Another innovation was a form of all-out boxing between rival sections known as 'milling'. 'On the sound of the whistle the first two would get into the ring and slug it out,' remembered Ralph. 'There was no question of finesse or boxing capability. It was just to see if you had the spirit to keep on, whether even if you were being battered you would fight back . . . It was good for the confidence, that you didn't have to give in to anything . . . There was no surrender.'

Nicholl collected a pair of black eyes in his first bout, having never boxed at school and finding himself matched against a well-built policeman who was evidently no novice. He was then appalled to be told that his Troop had won their contest and was through to the next round.

Perhaps Vaughan's most important principle, however, was his insistence on the use of live firing. This had also taken place on exercises at Lochailort, but Vaughan adopted it more widely, most notably for the opposed night landing with which the course culminated.

Nicholl vividly recalled the moments before the start of this exercise, when he and half a dozen other men were crouched on the thwarts of a Goatley boat, a craft of uncertain buoyancy fitted with collapsible canvas sides. On the blast from a whistle they began to paddle frantically towards the loch shore a quarter of a mile away. Only their arms were allowed to be seen over the side: any more and they attracted extra bursts from Brens firing on fixed lines perilously near to them.

Bullets bounced from the water just feet from Nicholl and sometimes closer. 'It was fascinating feeling the tracer near enough to splash the paddles – sometimes even to splinter them or to knock them out of their owners' hands – and watching the ricochet whining away into the distance,' he wrote.

As the boat reached the shallows, grenades and smoke canisters exploded around them. The men at the bow leapt out and pulled the craft up onto the pebbles. While the others grabbed the rifles stowed in the bottom, the machine-gunners were already running ahead to set up their weapons and fire at targets on the hillside. When enough of the white metal discs had been hit, the signal was given for the rest to throw themselves flat in the mud and begin shooting. Another shout and they were up and bayoneting sacks stuffed with straw.

'In, out!' yelled the instructors. 'Hit 'em as though you mean it!'

Then a white Very light went off and there was a rush to get back to the boats. As they pulled away from the beach, the Brens opened up again and grenades raised spouts of water. Nicholl's sense of relief on reaching the boathouse drained away on hearing the order to go straight back across the loch again and beat the previous time: 'every thought was eliminated except the struggle to get that ungainly, wretched craft through the water at greater speed'.

Sometimes the bullets came too close. Nicholl remembered that the week after he had completed the exercise it claimed a man's life. The reports of casualties began to alarm Laycock and in June 1942 he wrote to Vaughan to ask for statistics on his 'battle inoculation' course. 'It is high time that junior officers and young soldiers are made to realise that they must not get excited and lose their heads when armed with lethal weapons,' he declared. 'We have had quite enough trouble already over shooting up our own side in operations, without repeating it in training.'

Vaughan's response was characteristically robust. In the four months since he had taken charge, 14 out of the 660 officers and men to pass through the camp had been hurt. That 2 per cent injury rate, he pointed out, was five times less than the equivalent figure at Lochailort. And Vaughan had a shrewd idea of the source of the rumours that had reached Laycock. 'The last 2 officers and 2 NCOs of the US Army sent to me for three days . . . put over a strong line that one was lucky to get out of the Commando Depot alive,' he wrote. 'They had been over the opposed landing once.'

For all his determination to make Commando training a realistic preparation for combat, Vaughan had no time for those who sought to make Achnacarry hellish for others. 'He couldn't stand bullying, wouldn't have any bullies among his instructors,' remembered one of them, Jim Dunning. 'And he couldn't abide the bloke who was tough after three pints of beer. Charlie used to say: "I can't stick these bloody 'oodlums. Three pints of beer and the smell of a barmaid's apron and they want to turn the town over. Get rid of them." They were RTUd, no messing, he couldn't stand any bullshitting.'

Everyone grumbled about the weather in the Highlands. 'It was always wet,' said Vic Ralph, 'I don't recall a day when it didn't rain. We were always soaking wet all day, either from crawling on the ground or going into the loch, which was icy cold.' Yet, like many others, once in the field he came to appreciate the value of what he had been through. If you could cope with Achnacarry, you could cope with anything.

'It's dirty and it's hard and it's wet and it's cold, but you didn't take any notice of it because you had done your training,' confirmed Charles 'Dinger' Bell. For all the jibes of their Army counterparts that they were not volunteers, Royal Marine commandos such as Bell were an elite. More than half of the thousand marines who normally made up a battalion had been rejected as potential commandos, and one of the benefits of Achnacarry was that there could be no arguments about those marines who passed the course not being up to Army standards. Their shared experiences at the castle may not have bonded the two groups together, but it did begin to breed a grudging mutual respect, albeit one that was yet to be tested by combat.

From the summer of 1942, soldiers and marines alike were presented with another innovation soon cherished by both: the green beret. Two years earlier, having seen the diversity of headgear sported by recruits, Roger Keyes had tried to secure approval for a common cap for the Commandos. Liking the black berets worn by the Tank Corps since their days in France in 1918, he had chosen those, only to be briskly rebuffed by the Army Council. It felt sure that 'these men . . . would certainly rather carry the badge and insignia of their own regiment than a newly invented headdress which appears to savour somewhat of the accoutrements of the Blackshirts'.

Under Roger Courtney, however, the SBS began informally to wear berets, and in 1942 two more offshoots of the Commandos – the SAS and the Parachute Regiment – also started to favour them as practical and distinctive; as did General Montgomery. Laycock decided to recommend them again to the Army Council, possibly after an approach from 1 Commando. The choice of colour may have owed less to the legends that have grown up around it than to wartime shortages and the berets' Scottish manufacturer having an abundance of green cloth.

Wearing them with pride from 1942 onwards, thousands of young men marched back down to Spean Bridge from Achnacarry as the newest members of the Commandos. As they passed him digging in his garden, an old admiral would give them a wave and a cheery reminder of their purpose: 'Kill the Huns. Kill 'em, old boy. And their wives and children.'

8

DRYAD

Gus March-Phillipps's act of piracy in African waters had given SOE just the lift that its chiefs had hoped for. But it had also created a problem. How should his talents be used next? The crew of *Maid Honor* were commandos, raiders better suited to smash-and-grab operations than to the clandestine work of the secret agent. Nor could there be any question of the team waiting in Nigeria until other targets presented themselves. POSTMASTER had made things too hot for them: despite the Foreign Office's denials of involvement, the wires from Madrid were still thrumming with affronted fury.

The solution was provided by Mountbatten. March-Phillipps's men had been lent to SOE because they lacked a cutting edge. As the Commandos began to become primarily assault troops for future invasions, Combined Operations now had fewer resources of its own to draw on for the pinprick raids and acts of sabotage that had been its original remit. Yet these still retained a value, especially for acquiring intelligence from prisoners. They also 'force the enemy to lock up in an almost passive role a large number of men . . . and equipment', according to the Chiefs of Staff, while COHQ thought they 'generally want to make the individual German long to go home'.

Such attacks would only require small numbers of troops, and kidnapping sentries should come naturally enough to anyone who had seized an entire ship. By March 1942, therefore, Maid Honor Force was back in England and in search of both more recruits and a permanent base. 'During Friday's house hunting we located an eminently suitable and magnificent house,' Geoffrey Appleyard soon told his parents, 'about seven miles from Wareham and ten from Poole. It is a large and very beautiful Elizabethan house and in every way ideal for our purpose.'

The nucleus of the new unit – renamed 62 Commando – gathered for the first time a few weeks later at March-Phillipps's wedding. His bride was an actress, Marjorie Stewart, who had given up her stage career to work at SOE and later became its first qualified woman parachutist. Among the guests was one of the founding instructors at Lochailort, Peter Kemp, who had been recommended to March-Phillipps after enduring a frustrating time with SOE in Spain preparing for missions which never happened.

Kemp was unusual in already having some experience of guerrilla activities, acquired a few years earlier during Spain's civil war. More rarely still, he had been one of the few Britons fighting not for the Republicans but for Franco. He was not so much a committed Fascist as a fervent anti-Communist. 'I don't regret it at all,' he wrote later of his choice. 'I've no doubt whatsoever that I fought on the right side.' For Kemp, the Nationalist victory had prevented Spain from becoming a client state run by the Soviet Union, and one which might have threatened Britain.

While the Republican cause had attracted more widespread support, his attitude was not uncommon among those of his background. An instinctive traditionalist and monarchist, Kemp was the son of the Chief Justice of Bombay and had not long left Cambridge when he was spurred to action by reports from Spain of leftist atrocities. He joined the Spanish Foreign Legion and was wounded several times in the bitter winter campaign of 1937–8 before a mortar shell shattered his jaw at Lerida. The surgeon operated on him without anaesthetic and did not expect him to survive. By the time he had recovered, back in London, the conflict was over. At twenty-six, his injuries had not dented his desire to test himself in battle, but when war was declared on Germany a medical board decided that he was not fit to be commissioned into the Army. As so often in the secret world, a chance meeting with an acquaintance – Douglas Dodds-Parker of SOE – led to his recruitment by that organisation instead.

By the time that he moved on to the Small-Scale Raiding Force (SSRF), as 62 Commando was also known, it numbered about thirty. As aboard the *Maid Honor*, almost half of its strength was officers, including the newly commissioned Anders Lassen. He and his French comrade André Desgranges welcomed other refugees from Nazi rule, too, among them Czechs, Poles and several Germans serving under British names.

The unit continued to be administered by SOE, but its raids were to be planned by COHQ and it fell under the authority of the Commandos for matters of day-to-day discipline. Yet, though its members were eventually issued with green berets, March-Phillipps was given a freer hand than other commanding officers in the brigade now enjoyed, and the relatively informal relations between ranks harked back to the early days of 'special service'.

The training at their new home, Anderson Manor, was also comparatively bespoke. Most of the force had already been through courses in the Highlands, but in bucolic Dorset March-Phillipps focused on perfecting two essentials of amphibious raiding. Surprise, and therefore the ability to move silently at night, was paramount. There was also much emphasis on boat work in all weathers. The Commando had been given the use of its own MTB, affectionately known as 'The Little Pisser'. This was stripped of most of its armament for speed and its torpedo tubes were replaced by dories, short wooden boats equipped with a motor and used to shuttle into beaches.

Appleyard kept up his prodigious physical fitness. Everyone was sent out at dawn for two hours of exercise before breakfast and once he and some of the others, including Graham Hayes, walked 120 miles in four days over rough ground carrying forty-five-pound packs. Jumping practice consisted of leaping over the manor house's deep moat, which by way of further incentive not to fail was filled with barbed wire.

There was also a pistol range in the grounds, and Lassen used every opportunity to improve his archery. When M.R.D. Foot went down from COHQ to brief them for a mission, he was greeted by an arrow thudding into the door-jamb beside his head. Afraid that Goebbels would make propaganda from it, Mountbatten forbade Lassen from taking his bow on operations.

For relaxation, they tended the house's formal gardens. 'We were a very happy unit,' recalled Kemp. By July, they were ready for action, but a frustrating few months was to follow. Raids were restricted both by the cycles of the moon – none could be made when it was too bright – and by the Channel being off-limits to other British vessels several nights each week as convoys passed up it. There were also the first hints of disputes to come between SOE and MI6 over choice of targets, and even when missions were authorised they often had to be abandoned as the MTB proved unseaworthy in more than moderate winds.

The strain of keying themselves up for raids told on the SSRF's nerves. At one point March-Phillipps and Appleyard became so worn down that they volunteered for an operation to attack the *Tirpitz* (still skulking in Norway) in a two-man submarine propelled by pedal power. Fortunately, perhaps, for them, this scheme was abandoned when the battleship shifted her position to another fjord where the current was too strong for the plan to be implemented.

It was mid-August 1942 before 62 Commando finally made its first successful strike, killing three and wounding six more of the garrison of an anti-aircraft post near Barfleur. Those who had taken part returned flushed with excitement, and Kemp eagerly awaited his own chance for action. It came on a blustery evening a fortnight later.

The target of DRYAD was the Casquets lighthouse and signal station. It lay six miles west of the Channel island of Alderney and was thought to be staffed by half a dozen German naval ratings. The operation was approved only a few days after the SSRF's initial raid and the dozen commandos who were to take part pored over a scale model of their objective in the conference room at the manor. Yet for the next week and a half they were bedevilled by poor weather and mechanical failure. Once they got within a few hundred yards of their goal only to be unable to find it in the thick fog.

The announcement on the morning of 2 September that they would try again that evening raised Kemp's spirits but he found the tension of the next few hours hard to bear. He had not slept well, having spent much of the previous night crawling about the grounds in the rain pretending to stalk sentries. By teatime he was decidedly jittery. 'Although we had the greatest confidence in our commanders and in each other, it was difficult not to contemplate the numerous possibilities of disaster,' he admitted.

A sing-song in the lorry carrying them to Portland cheered him up, and clad in a balaclava and felt-soled boots he lumbered up the ramp to the MTB. Despite carrying a tommy-gun, ammunition, grenades, fighting knife and explosives, the cumbersome inflatable life-jacket he also had to wear made him feel less than soldierly. March-Phillipps had no such doubts, and had topped off his array of weapons with an eighteen-inch carving knife.

Among the other officers aboard were Graham Hayes, the ginger-haired Captain John Burton, who had been with Kemp in Spain for SOE, and the half-Italian Captain Lord Howard of Penrith. Observing them from the bridge was *MTB 344*'s commander, Freddie Bourne. He had got to know March-Phillipps and Appleyard well. The latter, he recollected, 'was a university man, charming, brave', while 'MP . . . was slightly more aloof, tall, well-connected'. Yet, whereas 'MP had all the dash and flair, the outwards signs of the commando, Appleyard was much more the thinker, and gave much more detailed thought to what we were going to do.'

Buffeted by the wind, the small boat rocketed over the darkening sea. Kemp tried his best to take his mind off the dangers ahead by reading a thriller. Despite a recent complete overhaul, the engine again gave trouble, and it was not until almost 2300 that the ninety-foot-high rock of Casquets came into view. The moon had risen into a clear sky, and Kemp could see outlined against it the white needle of the lighthouse towering above the black bulk of the stone on which it stood.

Bourne manoeuvred his ship to within eight hundred yards of the island and anchored it with fifty fathoms of rope. Then a collapsible Goatley boat was lowered silently over the stern and the raiding party took their places in it. Shortly after midnight, they began to paddle through turbulent water towards a small bay, struggling against a flood tide that was running stronger than they had anticipated because of their late arrival. All the while Kemp was uncomfortably aware of how visible they must be to any lookout, and tried to console himself by thinking that they must make a small target.

Fearing that the obvious beaches might be mined or guarded, March-Phillipps had decided to try to land on a smooth slab directly beneath the tower's engine house. Hayes dropped a kedge anchor to hold the boat fast in the eddies that swirled between the rocks at the island's tip, but just as Appleyard gathered himself to leap from the bow, line in hand, the current began to drag the small craft backwards. The commandos dug their paddles deep into the water, striving as hard as they could to close the gap with the land, and when the swell bore the boat up, Appleyard jumped.

He landed hard on the wet surface of the rock. For a second, his arms flailed wildly as he recovered his balance, then he began to climb the eighty-foot cliff. Leaving Hayes and another man to mind the Goatley and stay in touch with the MTB through an infra-red receiver, the others followed him one by one up the rope. The only obstacle was a coil of barbed wire which was soon cut, and any noise they made was covered by the rumble of the surf and the heavy booming of the sea in the chasms below.

More tangles of wire blocked the main entrance to the walled complex of buildings at the top. Beckoning to the men to follow, March-Phillipps pulled himself over the coping and dropped unchallenged into the courtyard below. Nothing moved in the moonlight. A moment later the others were beside him. Everything was going to plan.

'Independent action!' he ordered. At once the commandos split into four parties and rushed the buildings around them. A quartet led by March-Phillipps attacked the garrison's living quarters, Appleyard and Company Sergeant-Major Tom Winter headed for the lighthouse, while two other men ran for the engine hut.

Kemp and Burton's target was the wireless room. Already they had seen that there was a light on inside it. The pair of them sprinted fifty yards across the cobbles, threw back the door at the foot of the tower and tore up the stairs to the first floor. The door to the transmitting room stood open. Revolver in hand, Burton was through it in a flash, closely followed by Kemp, finger on the trigger of his machine-gun. The room was empty. While Burton began to scoop up code books and signal pads that lay on the desk, Kemp stood guard. From below came a whistle, and he peeked cautiously over the balustrade. It was Appleyard, who told him that all seven Germans manning the post had been taken prisoner without a shot being fired. Surprise had been complete.

'I have never seen men look so amazed and terrified at the same time,' Appleyard told his father later. 'Three were in bed . . . two who had just come off watch were turning in, and the two on watch were doing odd jobs in the main buildings, filling up logs etc.' One of the sleepers had been wearing a hairnet, which for a moment had led March-Phillipps to mistake him for a woman.

The raiders' haul included two leading telegraphists, who might yield particularly valuable information about signals. Downcast and even teary, they were hustled back to the boat – greatcoats pulled on hastily over their pyjamas – while with an axe Burton smashed up the wireless sets. Kemp helped gather other documents and dumped in the sea the Germans' armaments, notably an Oerlikon cannon. Then he joined the others in making his way back down the cliff. It was one o'clock. The raiding party had been ashore for just half an hour.

Marshalled by Private Adam Orr – a German-speaking Pole whose original name was Abraham Opoczynzki – the prisoners were made to slide down the steep slab and then hauled into the boat as it rose on the swell. One mistake could turn a drop of five feet into twenty and sink them all.

With the prisoners secured, Orr jumped in holding his dagger and, landing awkwardly in the bow, stumbled against Kemp, who felt a sharp pain as the blade plunged into his thigh. There was no time to do anything about it, however, as March-Phillipps and Appleyard now came hurtling down into the boat as well, although the latter was also limping. After untethering the rope, he had shot down the rock on his back before the Goatley drifted away and his leg had doubled up beneath him.

The boat was made for ten people and, with almost twice that number aboard, it was now perilously low in the water, but they made it safely back to the MTB. The return voyage was bumpy and wet, but there were no more mishaps before they reached Dorset at dawn. The Germans were battened below deck and sat dejectedly in the fo'c'sle. On reaching England, they gave up useful information about codes as well as about the strength of defences at Cherbourg and other places where they had been stationed. One of them also revealed that he had worked on long-range rockets, confirming suspicions that the Nazis were developing a missile programme.

Kemp's wound had turned stiff by the time they entered port. He spent the next week in hospital recovering from an operation to remove clotting in his leg. Appleyard's injury was also more serious than it had first seemed: he had fractured his shinbone. Otherwise, though, DRYAD had been entirely successful. Mountbatten sent congratulations by telegram and, confident that the SSRF was starting to pay its way, March-Phillipps set to planning its next raid. Both Kemp and Appleyard were frustrated at being confined to the sidelines while they recuperated. But as it turned out, the accidents that they had suffered were to save them from worse.

On 12 September, Kemp invited two other members of the Commando to dinner at the cottage that he and his wife were renting a few miles from Anderson Manor. The evening was not a success. Only ten days after the Casquets raid, their friends were trying their luck again, and both Kemp and his guests were wrapped in their own thoughts as they watched the shadows steal over the fields beyond the house.

It was an unusually dark night and fog covered much of the Channel. Yet March-Phillipps was keen that the operation should go ahead, perhaps frustrated at having had to turn back the evening before in similar weather. M.R.D. Foot had briefed the party for AQUATINT, as it was codenamed, and observed its leader's aggressive nature at short range. 'At that time,' he later reflected, 'we stood on opposite sides of the gulf that divides the staff from fighting troops, and he made me well aware of it.'

The aim of the mission was again to take prisoners, this time by attacking houses occupied by the Germans in the seaside village of Sainte-Honorine des Pertes, north-west of Bayeux. As the operation came so soon after DRYAD, and indeed just three weeks after the Dieppe raid, enemy defences were likely to be on high alert. March-Phillipps accordingly took his best men with him. These included Appleyard, whose leg was still in plaster but who was acknowledged to be such a good navigator that Bourne allowed him to pilot the MTB.

To avoid the minefield that covered the Bay of the Seine, Appleyard steered a wide course from the Needles around Cape Barfleur. The fog was so dense that no trace could be seen of the French coast, and not until they closed within half a mile of the shore did the land loom up at them. Even then, although the raiders knew there were one-hundred-foot-high cliffs at Sainte-Honorine, they could not make them out. Nor could the commandos spot the cleft up which they planned to climb so as to approach their target from the rear. The only alternative was to land on the beach in front of the village itself.

'What do you think, chaps?' said March-Phillipps, looking around him at the tense faces in the boat. 'Shall we have a bash?'

Gazing at the long sweep of sand beyond, Bourne had misgivings. This was not their usual out-of-the-way landing point. But if anyone else shared his doubts, they kept quiet. 'Gus had that quality which made people follow him,' recalled Foot, and soon after midnight the eleven-strong raiding party was paddling through the surf. The lame Appleyard stayed on board the MTB with Bourne.

The first sign of trouble came thirty minutes later. Those on the boat heard tommy-gun and pistol fire at the foot of the cliffs, and this was rapidly followed by twenty flashes thought to be German stick grenades exploding. White, green and red flares went up from the shore and coastal guns opened up to the west. From the top of the heights, a searchlight began to probe seawards.

For the next half-hour, Bourne circled around, until at about 0120 the MTB was spotted and fired on. Two other machine-guns appeared to be shooting straight down from the cliffs onto the beach, as if the little force was trapped there. Appleyard could hear someone shouting, 'Come back!' and then Hayes calling to him. The voices were indistinct but seemed to be ordering him to escape as the landing party could not get away. Shells began to fall near the torpedo boat and reluctantly Bourne pushed both engines wide open, only to find that the transmission on one had been badly damaged by a bullet. He headed out to sea for two miles as rapidly as he could manage and then gradually throttled down so as to sound like a boat fast disappearing from earshot. No more shouts now came from the shore.

Appleyard's anguish is easy to imagine. His best friends, including his childhood playmate, Graham Hayes, were clearly in terrible trouble. They might still be trying to evade the Germans and relying on the MTB to rescue them. After about ten minutes, Bourne turned the boat about and began to drift silently back towards the coast. For the next three-quarters of an hour he anchored as close in as he dared. An infra-red light burned at the masthead but no one came.

Suddenly a shell whined overhead in the darkness. It pitched between the MTB and the shore. Another six followed, and then a dozen more from a different direction. The nearest landed just twenty feet to starboard and deluged Bourne and Appleyard with water. From further out to sea, two patrol boats were closing in on the British vessel. In a few moments her escape would be blocked.

Bourne ran east in the dark and then jinked north. After a mile or two he had shaken off the immediate threat. Yet with just one engine working he had little hope of outrunning any pursuers if he took the same course as before home. His only choice was to risk heading directly across the Channel minefield. This he did and, after passing through it without incident, docked in Portsmouth the next morning.

The news of AQUATINT's fate plunged the other members of the SSRF into despair. Peter Kemp had hung about his cottage all that day, his heart heavy with foreboding. Late in the evening he heard a lorry pull up outside. It was one of his guests from the night before, crying out: 'We've lost the lot!' Not for months to come would they discover exactly what had gone wrong.

In 1943, one of the survivors of the party was repatriated. Francis Howard had been wounded in his right leg and was allowed home to be operated on for gangrene. He had been left to guard the boat on the beach, however, so it was not until the end of the war that his account was rounded out by the newly liberated Tom Winter.

Winter revealed that, after posting Howard on watch, the others made a recce inland to establish their position. As they were returning to the beach, they heard a patrol of seven or eight men coming along the track at the top of the cliff and took cover. 'We would not have been discovered,' said Winter ruefully, 'had it not been for the dog which was with the patrol.' After it scented them, a firefight broke out. The commandos managed to scatter the opposition and ran for the boat, dragging with them a prisoner who complained loudly that he was not German but Czech. But more of the enemy soon arrived. Lieutenant Tony Hall was left for dead after being felled by a grenade, while the others, including the injured Howard, scrambled into the Goatley.

They had paddled about 100 yards from the shore when it was sunk and they had to swim for it. Winter believed that a bullet had hit the central strut of the Goatley and instantly collapsed it. It was impossible to find the MTB in the darkness, however, and with his strength failing he made for land. Lying exhausted on the sand, he was found by the Germans and dragged off to their headquarters. The first thing he saw was Howard prone on the floor. André

Desgranges had also been taken prisoner. A German officer informed the trio briskly that once they had been interrogated they would all be shot.

At least for the moment they were still alive. When morning came, Winter and Desgranges were made to drag three bodies out of the water as the Germans filmed them for propaganda. One of the dead men was the oldest member of their group. Private Richard Leonard, who was forty-two, had fought in the First World War as a teenager – for the Austrian Army. His real name was Lehniger and he had been born in Bohemia, then part of the Habsburg Empire. Being both Jewish and a Communist, he had fled to Britain from Czechoslovakia when the Nazis annexed the Sudetenland.

The second casualty was Sergeant Alan Williams, whose first operation this had been. The other fatality was Gus March-Phillipps. There was speculation later that he had drowned but Winter confirmed that he had died of his wounds. It was perhaps as he would have preferred. Whatever his flaws as a leader, there was no doubting his courage.

Tony Hall proved only to be wounded, although he had been so badly beaten that he would need months of medical treatment. Of the other four there was at first no word, until five days later Winter encountered three of them in prison at Rennes. John Burton, Adam Orr and Jan Helling, a Dutchman, had swum west and then made their way across country before falling foul of a parachute company on manoeuvres. Burton survived the war as a PoW; the precise fate of his two companions remains uncertain.

The Germans were well pleased with their night's work. Soon afterwards, an Alsatian could be seen padding along the hedgerows of Normandy with the Iron Cross dangling from its collar. Yet they seem not to have realised that one commando had got clean away.

Allowing himself to be carried by the tide, Graham Hayes had come ashore two miles further up the coast. There he sheltered in an abandoned building. The following evening, he entrusted himself to a friendly farmer, and for the next five weeks he was hidden in a safe house in Calvados. The Resistance planned to smuggle him over the border to neutral Spain, and in late October 1942 he travelled to Paris. From there he was passed along an escape line towards the Pyrenees. At the end of the month, accompanied by a trusted guide, he stepped across the frontier.

It was only when the Spanish police took him straight back to France, and the waiting Gestapo, that he realised he had been the bait in a trap. The Germans had long since penetrated the network which was helping him and, aided by the treacherous courier, had followed Hayes's every step in order to identify the remaining links in the chain.

The doctor and his wife who had cared for him in Normandy were deported to concentration camps, where they died. Others were arrested and, like Hayes, incarcerated in the infamous prison at Fresnes, outside of Paris. Quite probably Hayes was tortured, but he cannot have divulged any names as most of his other contacts were eventually released. Over the next few months he was able to pass on some details of his capture to an RAF officer in the neighbouring cell. They communicated by tapping in Morse code on the pipes, but on 13 July 1943 no answering signal came. Graham Hayes had been shot that afternoon by a firing squad.

The loss of so many men was a catastrophe for the SSRF, and the harder to bear because AQUATINT had not been a particularly important mission. There was little satisfaction to set against such a heavy blow. Yet it is now clear that the operation was even more of a tragedy than it seemed at the time, for its failure was at least partly self-inflicted. It was perhaps a mercy that the person responsible for the error seemingly remained oblivious to it.

As we have seen, March-Phillipps rated Appleyard so highly as a navigator that he asked him to guide the raiding party, despite his broken leg. In Appleyard's report, and in those of the other survivors, there is no indication that they thought they had landed anywhere other than at Sainte-Honorine. But German records, and the testimonies of local residents, reveal that the raiders were put ashore a full three miles west of where they should have been.

Unlike the small beach in sleepy Sainte-Honorine, the arc of sand below Saint-Laurent-sur-Mer is broad and smooth. Indeed, so inviting is it that the Americans chose to land there on D-Day, having codenamed it Omaha. And like the SSRF, they discovered that the Germans had appreciated its qualities as well and had fortified it heavily. Even in 1942, the cliffs above bristled with machine-gun nests sited to catch any attack from the sea in a lethal crossfire.

Appleyard's confusion of the two places is understandable. Weather conditions that night made identifying his location exceptionally difficult, and he may have thought that a river valley near Saint-Laurent was the cleft at Sainte-Honorine he was having trouble finding. Given those doubts, however, March-Phillipps should have turned for home instead of impetuously pressing on. Perhaps the two friends trusted each other too much. What followed was doubtless unforeseeable; but it was not just bad luck.

AQUATINT was not the end for 62 Commando. Naturally, the loss of its founder was keenly felt, not least by Mountbatten. In a letter of condolence to March-Phillipps's widow, who was pregnant, he paid an eloquent tribute to 'the fine spirit he had infused into the special Force he commanded . . . We can ill afford to lose someone of his character and ability. We shall miss him very much.' None the less, Appleyard was quickly appointed as temporary commander. Although he had lost two of his closest friends in a single night, he refused to bow to grief and set about raising the morale of those who were left. The best way to do that, he soon judged, was to lead another raid.

This time the objective was the small Channel island of Sark. A dozen commandos, including Appleyard himself and Lassen, spent several hours ashore there on 3 October gathering information from locals before surprising five Germans in their beds in a hotel. The prisoners were herded outside, into the cover of some trees, where Appleyard ordered their hands to be tied. This was to stop them from escaping while they were marched back to the boat. As this was being done, though, one of the Germans attacked his guard and began shouting to raise the alarm.

Accounts of what happened next vary. The only certainty is that four of the five Germans were quickly killed. Appleyard claimed in his official report on Operation BASALT that they had been shot while trying to get away, one accidentally. Yet, as he confessed afterwards to Foot, and as Kemp confirmed, at least some had been dispatched more quietly by Lassen's dagger.

Such ruthlessness no doubt seemed necessary at the time, even if it may have been tinged with vengeance for AQUATINT. Lassen's blood lust was, however, to have grave consequences for all commandos. Appleyard had had little option but to bind the Germans. 'As he said to me a few days after the raid,' recalled Foot, 'how else were you to move recalcitrant prisoners through gorse in a hurry? They had a tide to catch, in an area of ferocious tides.' Yet the discovery of the dead men with their hands tied behind their backs provoked a savage reaction from the German High Command.

Coming so soon after the choking of German captives at Dieppe, it reinforced the Nazis' belief that commandos were no better than bandits who operated outside of the laws of war. Accordingly, they reasoned, they should be denied those laws' protection. A fortnight after the raid, Hitler issued a secret order that in future any commando taken prisoner, whether in uniform or not, was to be handed over to the security services for summary execution. Of course, given his regime's scant regard for human life, such indignation was rank hypocrisy. At Nuremberg, in 1946, the directive formed a key part of the evidence used to convict the German Army's Chief of Staff, General Alfred Jodl, of war crimes. Yet, by then, it had led to the murder of scores of commandos and other special service troops, such as members of the SAS.

The British authorities evidently feared that the events on Sark might provoke a reprisal. In correspondence between Mountbatten and Churchill after later raids, Combined Operations assured the Prime Minister that prisoners were no longer bound. Overall, however, he was well pleased with No. 62's work that autumn. A week after BASALT, with satisfaction Churchill told an audience in Edinburgh that 'There comes out from the sea . . . a hand of steel which plucks the German sentries from their posts with growing efficiency.' With his backing, in mid-October it was decided to expand the Commando.

Four more houses near the south coast were commandeered as bases for groups of NCOs and officers who would be posted to No. 62 for short periods to gain practical experience of raiding. The first detachments were to come from 12 Commando. The enlarged No. 62, which would include those elements of the SBS quartered in Britain, was to be led by Bill Stirling. He knew Peter Kemp from their time at Lochailort, and soon after his arrival at Anderson Manor ordered him to train a batch of newcomers for an operation to be codenamed FAHRENHEIT.

The target was the semaphore station at Pointe de Plouezec, west of St Malo on the coast of Brittany. The garrison was thought to be a dozen strong, and Kemp was instructed to put together a landing party of about the same number. The aim was once more to take prisoners for interrogation, but Stirling emphasised to Kemp that he should not risk losing men in order to do so. Memories of AQUATINT were still raw.

It was the first time that Kemp had had his own command, and the responsibility weighed on him as *MTB 344* nosed out of the River Dart in fading light on the afternoon of 11 November. Although he had the comforting presence of Appleyard on board as navigator, most of the remainder of the group were soldiers from 12 Commando under Captain Oswald 'Mickey' Rooney. What Kemp had seen of them was promising, but they had all worked together for just a few days, and even the slightest misunderstanding might be fatal. So too might be their obvious eagerness to get at the enemy.

Shortly before midnight, Bourne switched off the boat's engines and anchored half a mile from France. It was a clear night, and the bulky silhouette of the semaphore station was easy to spot atop the headland which gave the point its name. Within a few minutes, the commandos were landing in a cove at the foot of the steep cliffs, which Kemp soon discovered ended in rocks instead of the pebble beach promised in his briefing. This forced an immediate change of plan, as one of the group would have to be left behind to keep the dory from being smashed by the tide.

Another problem revealed itself as soon as the rest of them scrambled ashore. The reconnaissance photographs that they had studied showed a track up from the water, yet in the dark this proved impossible to find. The only option was to begin hauling themselves hand over hand straight up the rock face. It was an ascent of no more than sixty feet but strenuous and dangerous. As he clung to the cliff, Kemp's feet scrabbled for purchase on slippery piles of shale. Gorse thorns pierced his face and fingers. After twenty long minutes he pulled himself over the crest, panting with exhaustion.

Ahead, he could see the path which led to the signals station and the guard house. The commandos ran forward quickly and took up an all-round defensive position about 150 yards from the buildings. Everything was quiet. Kemp was just congratulating himself on how well things were going when he saw Rooney examining two wooden noticeboards on either side of the track. On each was the same warning: '*Achtung! Minen*'. They had just passed right through a minefield; and would have to do so again on the way back.

Kemp hoped that the notices were a bluff, especially since Rooney reported that the road ahead was blocked by wire and patrolled by a pair of sentries. This meant that the party would have to traverse left through the suspected minefield in order to cross the wire elsewhere. Kemp told two more men to stay behind with a Bren to cover their retreat and the remaining seven started to follow him across the open ground. Bending low, he stared hard at the grass as he took each step. He had only gone a few paces when he almost trod on a mine.

They regrouped once more at the path. The only course now was to creep up on the sentries and eliminate them before trying to rush the remainder of the garrison. Feeling more apprehensive than ever, Kemp divided his force in three. Then, infinitely slowly, he began to stalk up the track. 'The night was uncannily still,' he wrote later, 'the very slightest sounds being audible.' Even at a hundred yards he could hear every word of the sentries' conversation, and behind him the noise of Sergeant Sam Brodison's breathing seemed as loud as a jack-hammer. The two Germans were alert and often stopped talking to listen for anything out of the ordinary. Each time they paused, so did Kemp. When he was thirty yards from them, he lay down flat and started to crawl ahead inch by inch, moving first one elbow and then the other. Out of the corner of his eye, he could see Rooney on the other side of the track, synchronising his progress with him. It required all his willpower not to go any faster, but he knew the slightest sound would give them away. Every few paces he rested and checked the sentries' positions. It took him almost two hours to cover just twenty yards.

Then, when he was only ten steps from the pair, he found himself blocked by a tripwire. Hoping that the guards might drift away, he lay there for a quarter of an hour, listening to them. Now and again they would break off and seem to stare right at him. Gradually, he could feel the tension building inside him until he was at breaking point. There was no way he could crawl back without being spotted. The Germans would have to be killed – but that could not be done silently since they were also the other side of the barbed wire.

Rooney had come to the same conclusion. A sharp click brought a sudden shout of alarm from one of the sentries and Kemp heard him snap back the bolt of his rifle. Then the still of the night was ripped apart by a shattering explosion and the blast from Rooney's grenade slammed into Kemp. From beyond the wire came the most agonising sounds that he had ever heard: shrieks of terror and pain, and again and again the words: '*Nicht gut! Nicht gut!*'

Even as he rose automatically to his feet, Kemp felt a thrill of horror at the transformation in the voices that he had heard chattering a few moments before. The grenade had been packed with plastic explosive for cutting the wire and it had burned the uniforms of the two men who were now writhing on the grass. One seemed little more than a boy, the other rather elderly. Less curious than Kemp, an NCO brushed past and finished both off with his tommy-gun.

From out of the guard hut scampered a small dog, yapping furiously. Rooney's men vaulted the wire and ran towards the courtyard in front of the semaphore station twenty-five yards away. As they did so, a German came tearing down the path towards them, firing a pistol. Shots from Kemp's and Rooney's Colts doubled him up, but he kept firing until hit by a machine-gun blast. As he fell, the door of the building behind opened, silhouetting another soldier. Two bursts sputtered from Brodison's Sten and the German pitched headlong down the steps.

Kemp's plan was to send half of his force to the rear of the post while he and three others attacked the front. But in the brief instants since they had opened fire, they had lost the benefit of surprise. The remaining defenders had organised themselves and were fighting back vigorously. There seemed more of them than anticipated, and Kemp thought there was little chance of crossing the wide courtyard without someone being hit. Stirling had told him to avoid casualties, and certainly there was no possibility of getting a wounded man down the cliff. Already they had killed four of the enemy and perhaps they should not push their luck. He gave the order to fall back.

Slithering and sliding, they dropped blindly through the gorse to the beach. When they were halfway down, two flares went up from the station, yet no pursuit came. The officer left with the dory had had to stand in the sea up to his waist for almost three hours to keep it off the rocks, but now he quickly brought the boat inshore. Fewer than ten minutes later they were all aboard the MTB. Kemp spent the return journey worrying if he should have pressed home the attack, and trying to blot out the sour memory of the two sentries' screams.

Waiting for them on the jetty at Dartmouth were Stirling and the Commando's intelligence officer. The latter's reaction to Kemp's report was to tell him to go back at once and get some prisoners, but Stirling was satisfied with what had been achieved. He had Kemp prepare two accounts of the raid – one for COHQ and a shorter summary for the Prime Minister. Appleyard later told him that, after reading his report, Churchill had simply remarked: 'Good!'

Nevertheless, FAHRENHEIT proved to be the SSRF's last operation of note. Several others were planned but cancelled before the turn of the year, when Mountbatten set out his future programme of pinprick raids to the Chiefs of Staff. Their response was an unexpected and, for him, rare setback.

MI6 (SIS) had become increasingly anxious that SSRF's attacks were making it harder for the service to carry out its own activities, such as landing agents on the French coast. Controlling, as it did, the priceless flow of information from its decoding centre at Bletchley Park, it had greater clout in Whitehall than SOE, under whose aegis technically the SSRF operated. In early January 1943, therefore, the Chiefs agreed that where 'the proposed activities of SOE and SIS and minor raids clashed in any area, SIS would be given priority'. Moreover, the Admiralty, rather than COHQ, was in future to oversee all clandestine seaborne operations to ensure this was the case.

Starved of action and out of favour, 62 Commando was reduced from a man-o'-war to a beached hulk. Bill Stirling saw this at once, and within a few weeks was headed for North Africa instead to raise a second SAS regiment for his brother. He meant to build it around the pick of the SSRF, so he took with him Appleyard (as his deputy) and Lassen.

In December, Appleyard had been awarded the DSO for his contribution to the SSRF's raids. 'What, you again?' said the King, as he invested him for the third time in a year with a medal for gallantry. With two young recipients of the Victoria Cross, he was then invited to spend a weekend at Chequers with the Churchills. Still only twenty-five, he was already a major, and with 2 SAS he was to enhance his reputation further. In May 1943, following the Axis defeat in North Africa, he was chosen personally by the theatre commander, General Sir Harold Alexander, to reconnoitre the Mediterranean island of Pantelleria. Its capture would represent the Allies' first step back into Europe.

Although Pantelleria is tiny, it was held by more than thirteen thousand Italian troops. Appleyard landed from a submarine on four nights to probe its defences. On the last, he climbed a cliff as the sentry above his head sang 'O Sole Mio', grabbed a prisoner and began dragging him back to the dinghy. When Italian reinforcements arrived, one of Appleyard's companions was killed but he and a sergeant accounted for six of the enemy before getting away successfully. The submarine rendezvoused with an MTB which was to rush him to Malta, from where he was to be flown to Tunis to brief Alexander. The MTB's captain had been told that he was picking up the most important man in Europe: he was disappointed to discover that his passenger was not Churchill.

On the night of 12 July, two teams from 2 SAS were dropped by parachute near Taormina to support the ongoing invasion of Sicily. CHESTNUT was the first airborne operation for the regiment and Appleyard accompanied the flight to observe it. After the men had jumped in brilliant moonlight, the Armstrong Whitworth Albemarle turned for home. It was never seen again. Almost certainly, it was shot down by anti-aircraft fire from the Allied shipping massed off the coast. A few hours later, Graham Hayes, Appleyard's boyhood friend and comrade on AQUATINT, was executed in Paris.

Stirling had not given Appleyard permission to supervise the drop, but the young major had got around that easily enough by not asking for it. His death was widely mourned. An obituary in *The Times* by another SAS officer declared that 'England has lost a leader of exceptional ability and courage,' while a friend from university told his parents that he had been 'the sort of man that men will follow anywhere'.

Fine leader though he was, the broader achievements of the SSRF are open to debate. In its six months of active existence it mounted eight operations of substance, killing or capturing some twenty German troops for the loss of half that number. It has been criticised for not doing more with its resources, but given the constraints of weather and transport, that is unfair. It was certainly not battle-shy. Whether there was a need for it to exist at all, and more particularly in the form that it did, is not so clear. For all March-Phillipps's dash, the SSRF was no more effective as a private army than as a regular unit, and perhaps less prudent.

Its real significance lies in its long-term legacy, much of which stems from Appleyard. For another pioneer of irregular warfare, the leader of 'Popski's Private Army', Vladimir Peniakoff, he 'was one of the few officers who developed the technique of the small scale raid'. To the fledgling SAS – its experience then confined largely to jeep-borne attacks – he brought his skills in clandestine infiltration. He was also one of the first soldiers to be equally adept in launching attacks by land, by sea or from the air. Short as was Appleyard's time with the regiment, and brief though the SSRF's life had been, both had shown not just what elite troops could do but to what they should aspire.

Several other veterans of the SSRF went on to have notable wartime careers behind enemy lines. Philip Pinckney, Patrick Dudgeon and Colin Ogden-Smith had all been on the Sark raid. The first two joined 2 SAS; both were shot after being taken prisoner on sabotage missions in Italy. Ogden-Smith was killed in Brittany in July 1944 when part of an SOE 'Jedburgh' team liaising with the Resistance. Peter Kemp also went on to serve with SOE, first in the wilds of Albania, later in Poland, and finally in South-East Asia.

Perhaps most heartening for his friends was the unexpected reappearance of another of the survivors of AQUATINT. In the summer of 1943, André Desgranges turned up in London, having escaped from his cell in a naval prison in Germany the previous winter. He had made his way across Holland and Belgium and, after living under a false identity in Paris for three months, had travelled through France and Spain to Casablanca.

At first the British security services were a little suspicious of Desgranges's story. He seemed to have got away too easily – unlike others on the run in rural areas, he did not mention having trouble with barking dogs – but after questioning by MI5 his account was accepted. His interrogator regarded him as 'about the slowest witted Frenchman that I have seen'.

SOE agreed that he was not especially intelligent, but thought him 'a nice, jolly tough ... with a strong, natural streak of that French peasant cunning we know so well'. They were delighted to have him back, even more so when he agreed to return to France as an agent for them. In November 1943, he was flown by Lysander to

Angoulême. From there he was sent south to run operations around Toulouse under the codename 'Maréchal'.

Scarcely a fortnight later he was arrested by the Gestapo. They had been watching the house where he arranged to meet contacts, and though he insisted that he was merely a black marketeer he was taken to Fresnes Prison. There Desgranges confided in a cellmate and asked him to organise the removal of two compromising suitcases from his flat. The man betrayed him, but to the Germans' fury they failed to find the cases when they searched the apartment. Another agent had got there first.

Desgranges was beaten and tortured, but he stuck to his cover story and after six weeks he was released. He resumed his work locally for SOE until April 1944, when the Gestapo again got onto his trail. He was therefore moved north, and until the liberation of France in August operated around the Marne and the Moselle.

A few months later he was awarded the Conspicuous Gallantry Medal by his grateful British allies. The recommendation was made personally by Colin Gubbins, the head of SOE, and praised the SSRF veteran's 'outstanding courage and resolution'. France decorated him with the Croix de Guerre avec Palme. From the swamps of West Africa to the hills of Lorraine, Desgranges had proved himself a true war hero.

Only now, however, has the release of his secret personnel records made it clear that this was not the whole story. For, in April 1946, a senior figure in SOE, Colonel Henry Thackthwaite, wrote to another old hand from POSTMASTER, Leslie Prout, with bad news: the French believed Desgranges was a traitor.

In the year since the war in Europe had ended, de Gaulle's men had been sifting through the mass of documents recovered from the Hotel Majestic, the Gestapo's HQ in Paris. Among them was a filing card bearing Desgranges's name, photograph and a note: 'Satisfactory'. There was also a receipt signed by him.

He had already admitted to the French investigators that he had lied about having escaped. He now claimed to have been picked up at the Dutch border, after which he had agreed to work for the

Germans if they let him go. Desgranges swore that he had never intended to keep this bargain and, wrote Thackthwaite, had said nothing about it to the British 'as he did not wish to give up his Commando work'.

'Needless to say I believe his story,' the colonel told Prout. Thackthwaite himself had spent much time in France undercover and felt sure that he and many other agents whom Desgranges knew would have been arrested had he been in German pay. With SOE continuing to vouch for him, Desgranges seems to have persuaded the French authorities not to try him for treason. He continued his military career until 1951, and then worked in a hospital until his retirement. He died in 1990.

Yet others who were close to him during the war remained unconvinced of his innocence. M.R.D. Foot, who went on to become the leading historian of SOE, tersely regretted having shaken Desgranges's hand when he briefed him and the other members of the SSRF. His suspicions stemmed largely from the evidence of Desgranges's female courier, then a student in Toulouse, who was certain that several times he had tried to get her caught, and that others had been less fortunate.

It is impossible to know whether his arrest so soon after returning to France was mere coincidence or proof of collusion. One can only speculate at the significance of the sinister assessment: 'Satisfactory'. Yet it is almost impossible as well to know the limits of what an individual can stand, and to appreciate the pressure that must have been brought to bear on Desgranges. Unlike most commandos, he was vulnerable in having a wife and family whose fate was directly under German control. Graham Hayes stood only to lose his own life. Gus March-Phillipps laid down his in the heat of battle. If Desgranges did become an active collaborator, his reasons for doing so are understandable. Nor would he have been the first SOE operative to have been turned. Many others, of course, were more resolute – or less lucky.

9

MUSKETOON

As he lay in bed recovering from the wounds he had suffered at Vaagso, Graeme Black was already planning his return to Norway. From his time with the Independent Companies, he knew the area around the strategically important town of Bodø, just inside the Arctic Circle. He now proposed to base himself in the region for two months with seventy men, some with local knowledge, and systematically to destroy all its infrastructure – bridges, ports and power plants. Once this was done, the force would make its way to neutral Sweden.

Nothing came of this scheme, and by the end of March 1942 Black was still not fit enough to sail for St Nazaire with 2 Commando. Its losses there only redoubled, however, the desire of those who came back to do more. When a modified version of Black's plan was approved in the summer, he had no trouble finding volunteers for Operation MUSKETOON.

South of Narvik, amid the mountains of northern Norway, lay the country's largest aluminium smelter. The plant at Haugvik produced about five thousand tons annually, but the demands on the German war machine were now so great that the factory's capacity was being expanded fivefold. Yet its output depended entirely on the electricity supplied from the power station a few miles away at Glomfjord.

SOE considered this too heavily defended for a conventional assault to succeed, and sited too close to local houses for it to be bombed without causing civilian casualties. Its machinery was water-driven, however, and aerial reconnaissance of the ridge above the plant had revealed two pipelines which connected it to the lakes beyond. If a group of saboteurs could reach these and sever them, a vast volume of water would flood unimpeded into the power house and, it was thought, put it out of action for up to a year.

Working closely with SOE and COHQ, Black spent several weeks planning his attack, which would require spending much more time in German-held territory than had been necessary for previous raids. He studied the local defences, the terrain and even how long snow stayed on the ground at different seasons, since this would affect speed across country. He was also able to examine the generators used at Glomfjord as they had been supplied by a Scottish company. By July, he was ready to choose the rest of his team.

Black's pre-war occupation of running a firm which made bespoke handbags for fashion houses such as Norman Hartnell might sound an improbable background for a commando, but he had grown up in the Canadian outdoors. At nineteen, he had been commissioned into a territorial regiment in Montreal; a decade later, in 1939, having settled in London, he had joined the British Army. He was known as 'Gay' to his friends, who thought him 'very jolly, great fun, very attractive – one with an eye for the girls'. His insistence on doing things his own way could irritate his superiors, but his dashing leadership at Vaagso had earned him promotion to captain and the MC.

His second-in-command for the mission would be Joe Houghton. At thirty-one, he was two years younger than Black, and like him the son of a soldier. He also shared his love of sport, especially golf and fishing. After leaving school at Marlborough, he had gone into the City to work for the African Manganese Company, but had loathed being in an office. So for several years he had managed their operations in Norway, where he learned to ski. He had come to 2 Commando from the Liverpool Scottish Battalion of the Queen's

Own Cameron Highlanders and had been wounded at St Nazaire. His sister Desirée, who was in the Voluntary Aid Detachment, was engaged to another officer in No. 2, Dick Broome.

They chose eight men from the Commando to go with them, including as NCOs a former policeman from Yorkshire, Company Sergeant-Major Miller 'Dusty' Smith, and Lance Sergeant Richard O'Brien, an Irishman who was an expert climber and also a veteran of CHARIOT. The party was rounded out by two Norwegian corporals, Sverre Granlund, who was going under the name Christiansen, and Erling Djupdraet, who called himself Høgvold when with his countrymen, and 'Edward Dawson' when among the British. Both had fought in the Norwegian campaign before sailing into exile. Djupdraet's father was in the Resistance in Bergen and, despite the risks, the pair kept in regular touch by wireless.

After a fortnight's training in Scotland, the twelve-man team embarked on the Free French submarine *Junon* in the Orkneys on 11 September (just as, far to the south, March-Phillipps was making final preparations for AQUATINT). The French craft had a similar profile to a U-boat, an asset on a mission such as this where she would have to come in close to shore to land the commandos.

The voyage took four days. Though it was uneventful, the weather was rough and they were all seasick, which tired them out. Conditions aboard were also very cramped and there was little to do but check and recheck equipment. Each man had only a knife and a revolver for protection, as they would each be carrying sixty pounds of gelignite for demolishing the pipes. They wore their uniforms, and to aid their escape afterwards had a compass sewn into the tab of each shirt collar.

Christiansen was familiar with the rugged countryside around their destination, and as they neared the coast he suggested to Black a change of plan. If, as intended, they landed from the sea at Ørnes, about eight miles north of the mouth of Glomfjord, they would have to pass many houses en route to their target. Instead, he advised heading right up the more isolated Bjerangfjord, which ran parallel and south of Glomfjord. Black agreed, and though its periscope was spotted by a fishing boat, *Junon* surfaced otherwise undetected on the night of the 15th.

The gear was carefully stowed in a large dinghy and, after paddling for about four miles, they came ashore at the north end of the fjord soon after midnight. The boat was deflated and hidden under some moss about two hundred yards up the mountainside. Then they began to walk as fast as they could up the valley ahead, so as to put some distance between themselves and their landing spot. No one seemed to be about, and Christiansen was relieved that no dogs barked when they crept past farmsteads. He had been away from Norway for so long that he was unaware that food was scarce and most farmers had been forced to get rid of their dogs.

They camped for several hours, and then at dawn on the 16th pushed on for a few more miles. While the others rested, Christiansen and Houghton went ahead to choose a route over the formidable Svartisen – or Black Glacier – which lay between them and Glomfjord. Although the Norwegian knew the area, he had never gone this way before, and it took the pair about four hours to find a feasible path onwards. Even so, it would be hard going and necessitate traversing several small crevasses.

All the next day they inched up the glacier. They roped themselves together with their toggles for safety, but only O'Brien, the Norwegians and one other soldier, Reg Makeham, had done this kind of climbing before. Nevertheless, Christiansen lost his pistol when reaching for a handhold. Houghton gave him his, since he alone also had a Sten.

At one point they had to slide round an almost vertical outcrop of rock. There was a precipitous drop below and they could only use their fingertips to cling on. With O'Brien's help, they each managed to negotiate it, but they were three thousand feet up and the effort exhausted them. Black called a halt and when Christiansen looked around he realised that someone was missing. Lance Bombardier Bill Chudley, a keen boxer and a large, heavy man, had become thirsty and wandered off towards a little pool surrounded by frozen water. When Christiansen looked in his direction again, he realised from a dark mark on the ice that Chudley must have fallen through. The Norwegian raced downhill, reaching Chudley just as his head popped up. He was clearly frightened by the experience but able to get out unaided.

As Chudley dried off in the warm sunshine, Black was thankful that at least so far they had met no one. But their progress had not gone unobserved. A German survey party was at work in the valley below, and through his field-glasses Leutnant Wilhelm Dehne had spotted a group of figures high up on the glacier. Later on, he also found the remnants of the commandos' camp, including some packets of Players cigarettes. Fortunately for them, he was busy and chose not to investigate further straight away.

By the end of the afternoon, the team had reached the northern edge of the ice. Black and Christiansen pushed on until in the distance they could see the lake and the pipelines behind the power station. On the following morning, Friday the 18th, Christiansen again reconnoitred the lie of the land ahead as far as their target. They were now a good way down the mountain and all further movement would have to be made by night. This would slow them down, but there was another reason for proceeding with caution. The slope that they were on was almost sheer, and it was vital to avoid giving themselves away by dislodging stones which might clatter down into the fjord. They could not afford to take any unnecessary chances.

For the next three days they camped in sight of their target, gradually moving closer and watching how it was guarded. They knew that the barracks held at least a hundred German troops. Black had originally decided to attack on the Saturday night, but as they headed down that evening they heard a boat coming up the fjord and the sound of singing. Black was unable to make out if they were German or Norwegian voices and hastily ordered the party to head uphill once more.

By the time dawn broke on Sunday they were still some way from cover and had no choice but to hunker down and wait again for dark. It soon began to pour with rain. Although this screened them from below, they now discovered that their sleeping bags were not watertight. All day they lay in puddles of water, and with nothing to eat. They were keeping their emergency rations for their escape and had finished their other food before setting off the previous evening. It was now five days since they had landed, longer than Black had planned. He knew that the longer he waited, the weaker they would become. They would have to go in that night.

Once more Black carefully went over every phase of the assault. The only decision left until now was which route to follow out towards Sweden, about forty miles away. Christiansen favoured climbing some steps that ran alongside the pipeline and then heading south again over the Middago Mountain. It was a more tiring option, since it involved a very steep ascent of 2500 feet, but they would leave no tracks. The alternative was longer but much easier, following as it did the road beside Lake Fykan above the power plant and then swinging north to scale the side of the Navervann. The path was soft and their footprints would be visible, but Black opted for this second route.

At 2245, they reached the bottom of the hill and split into two groups. O'Brien, Makeham and Djupdraet traced the two iron pipes up the mountain for nine hundred feet and started to lay the charges. Each of the tubes was about seven feet around and even though the gelignite had been shaped into collars it proved difficult to get them to lie snugly together. When O'Brien was finally satisfied, he fused the explosives with thirty-minute time pencils.

Meanwhile, Black told three men to act as lookout, while he and Private Fred Trigg went to cover the exit from the mile-long tunnel through the rock to Glomfjord village. Christiansen's role was to get into the power house itself. He knew that one end had been demolished in the ongoing expansion work, and with Houghton and two others he was able to slip into the building by pulling aside a temporary screen. He found himself in a brightly lit room which housed the five huge generators and the three turbines which sat between them. There was no one to be seen in there, but he caught a glimpse of a watchman on the floor above. Christiansen and

Houghton quickly nipped up the stairs and flung open the door in front of them. Three Norwegians sat there, amazed at the sight of men with guns in their hands.

'Are there any Germans in the power station?' Christiansen asked them. When they replied that there were not, he told them that it was about to be destroyed and that he would tie them up so that they could not be accused of taking part. They protested at this, so he waved his Colt menacingly and began to herd them downstairs. Meanwhile, Houghton, Dusty Smith and Guardsman John Fairclough placed their explosives on the casings of the generators.

As he was prodding the guards along the corridor at the foot of the stairs, Christiansen suddenly saw a German sentry dozing there. The soldier woke with a start, only for Christiansen to empty a full clip into him. He slumped to the floor as Christiansen rounded on the Norwegians: 'I asked them what the devil they meant by denying that there were Germans in the power station.'

Black had come running at the sound of the shots. The trio of Norwegians now admitted that there was one other soldier in the building, just as Houghton appeared and said that he had disturbed him at the entrance to the tunnel. The man had flung his rifle down and run off towards the village. They must now assume that the alarm would be raised at any moment.

Christiansen cursed his fellow countrymen as cowards for not telling the truth and Black and Trigg headed down the tunnel to set off smoke bombs. These should help to deter German reinforcements by convincing them that the plant was already ablaze. Christiansen began tying up his prisoners, at which point they asked if he knew that there were other civilians living above the control room. Black's meticulous plan was becoming more chaotic by the moment.

Leaving the Norwegians where they were, Christiansen ran back to the power house. He soon found the family who had been sleeping there. 'We told them what they had to do, and that they had better be quick about it,' he wrote afterwards, 'which they did.'

The commandos had already been in the electricity station for a quarter of an hour. It was time to go and Houghton fused the explosives for ten minutes' delay. The party had got a few hundred yards onto the hill when there was a tremendous roar behind them, soon followed by another. As they turned to watch, the whole building seemed to quiver and through its windows they could see a visible glow spreading. 'We saw flames start up and knew from that that the attack had been successful,' recalled Christiansen proudly. A resounding blow had been struck for a free Norway.

The wail of an air-raid siren reminded them abruptly of the danger they still faced. Christiansen and the remainder of the assault party now climbed over the ridgeline and down to the road skirting Lake Fykan. Black continued upwards to meet the pipeline team. They too had been watching for the blast below, which was their signal to snap the time pencils.

Black wanted to wait until MUSKETOON's work of destruction was assured, so it was not until thirty minutes after the first charges had gone off that the whole group was reunited. Just at that moment there was a colossal explosion which echoed around the fjord. Rocks were hurled so far into the air that the sparks they struck on landing could be seen two miles away. The ruptured pipes gaped open and millions of gallons of water cascaded down the mountain into the turbine room. It carried with it tens of thousands of tons of mud and gravel. Soon the delicate machinery was fifteen feet deep in silt and sand.

The attack had spread total confusion throughout the German garrison. When Leutnant Dehne reached the generators, where already a foot of water covered the floor, he was fired on with a machine-gun by a jumpy soldier at the far end of the room who mistook him for a commando.

Well pleased with their night's work, the real saboteurs were already a mile away.

Christiansen was more confident than the others over the rough terrain and he soon drew ahead. To his surprise, though, the road abruptly came to an end. He realised that in the dark he must have missed a turning over the broad stream which washed the foot of the Navervann. Although he and Black had scanned the mountainside from afar with binoculars, they had not seen the thirteen-hundred-step staircase which ran up from the track nor the narrow suspension bridge that led to it.

He knew that in a nearby hut there lived the men who worked the cable and hoist which connected the road to the dam above. As he entered it, he startled the young woman who acted as cook and who was too frightened by his sudden appearance to give him directions. He had no more luck with the two men in the next room. Despite pleading with them to draw him a map, they acted as if he were not there, perhaps fearing that he was a German trying to trap them into aiding the enemy.

Disgusted and frustrated, he strode back to the path and met Houghton and Djupdraet, who were looking for him. When they heard what had happened in the cottage, they went off to find it, leaving Christiansen wondering what he should do. Suddenly, from inside the hut, he heard shots.

Almost as soon as he had left it, two German soldiers had arrived. The Norwegians continued to say nothing and, seeing that there were no Englishmen about, the pair of Germans decided to have a smoke and to telephone headquarters. One went into a bedroom, and as Houghton and Djupdraet came in silently they saw only his comrade in the kitchen with his back to them. Unfortunately, one of the Norwegians was standing beside him, and when Houghton shouted at him to move so that he could shoot, the German turned and sprang: in civilian life he had been a famous goalkeeper. The two crashed to the floor with Houghton's Sten trapped between them. It went off, firing a burst through the wall of the girl's room, where she lay terrified in her bed.

In the other bedroom, the second German grabbed his rifle and aimed through the open door at Djupdraet. Only then did he remember that he had removed the magazine. Instead, he hurled the rifle like a spear and its bayonet went right through Djupdraet, slamming him to the floor.

Black ran up to the hut just as Djupdraet staggered out of the door. He had tugged the bayonet clear but was bleeding profusely from his stomach and back. Black flung himself onto the floor at the entrance and began shooting into the kitchen, where he could see Houghton wrestling with his huge opponent. As he did so, the second German fired at Black from his blind side.

All of their shots missed. Black rolled to his right and let fly into the bedroom, mistaking the Norwegian sitting there for the German who was now hiding behind the door. Two more shots failed to hit their mark, and realising that Black thought he had a gun, the Norwegian jabbed his finger towards their common foe. Black stepped over the threshold, turning and firing in the same motion. This time he aimed true and the soldier collapsed as if dead.

Houghton had also managed to win his struggle. He had never released his grip on his Sten, and by yanking it upwards was able to press the muzzle against his opponent's thigh and squeeze the trigger. The German flopped back and lay still.

'They're after us,' Black shouted to Christiansen outside the hut. 'Take the lads and go.' He, O'Brien, Fairclough, Trigg and Smith struck out along the stream, until Smith heard Houghton calling for the morphia in his rucksack. Djupdraet was in terrible pain and he turned back to help treat him.

There was no way that they could carry the wounded man, however, and they decided to leave him by the hut, where he was later found by Dehne. The German also came across the body of the soldier shot by Black. After coming round, he had gone outside to shoot at the retreating commandos, only to be hit again – this time fatally.

It is unclear if Black ordered the party to split up, but by now they had in effect done so. While Christiansen's group headed for the Navervann, on the other side of the watershed the two officers together with Rifleman Cyril Abram, Private Eric Curtis, Smith, Chudley and Makeham began to climb the lower slopes of the Middago. As dawn approached, they were spotted against the skyline by the pursuing Germans.

None of them had long-range weapons. Houghton stayed behind for a time to snipe with his Sten, but when he was hit in the forearm he decided to follow the others up the mountain. Occasionally they fired down into the valley to keep the Germans at bay, but soon they had exhausted their ammunition. Coming over the crest, they found themselves in a wide bowl where there was little cover. They had got halfway across it when field-grey uniforms began to line the rim on every side, having been brought up in lorries. Black crouched behind a rock, but when a couple of grenades were tossed towards the rest of the group he stepped out with his hands up. There was no escape.

While the seven prisoners were being marched back down to Glomfjord, Christiansen had found a place to ford the stream. He waded in as far as he could and then swam the rest. The current was evidently fast, however, and his three companions were reluctant to follow him. 'He was in much stronger form than we were,' recalled the British commandos, 'as agile as a goat and going strong when we last saw him.' He continued on alone on the other side, but he was on home ground and had little trouble finding help and shelter. At the end of the month he crossed into Sweden.

However, he had taken with him the only map that the little group had – and one of the two working compasses. John Fairclough had been a lorry driver in peacetime, and Fred Trigg a milkman. Despite their Commando training, they had never in their lives had to cope with a situation like this, so they looked to the more experienced Dick O'Brien to lead them. In the meantime, they were now so hungry that they sat down and ate all of their emergency rations in a few minutes.

They abandoned their haversacks, including their sleeping bags, and carrying only their side arms continued to walk beside the stream down the valley. From early morning onwards they could see aeroplanes hunting for them. In the evening they managed to get over the stream and walked all night. By Tuesday the 22nd, they were five thousand feet up into the mountains and marching straight into a blizzard.

O'Brien was able to get some bread and cheese from a farmhouse, but this stroke of fortune was countered by his discovering that he had lost the last prismatic compass. Those hidden in their collars had frozen, and by evening they realised that they had 'gone round in a circle, and we dropped with exhaustion'. O'Brien had spent six months as a climbing instructor in the Lake District, but for all his greater knowledge of the hills it was he who was weakening fastest. He had taken some Benzedrine tablets on an empty stomach and by Wednesday morning had such severe cramps that he feared staying with the other two would only handicap them. When they went to scout ahead, he wandered away and they did not see him again.

For the next four days, Trigg and Fairclough pressed on, relying on farmers for food and half-understood directions. The locals were ready to help, warning them of patrols and even letting them listen to the BBC news. But there were also rumours that Germans dressed as British soldiers were trying to catch out those who aided them, and the pair could not always find a bed for the night.

Their ordeal tested their powers of endurance to the limit but their spirits were lifted by even the smallest pieces of good fortune. Once they passed a woodman's hut and were able to fry some stale cheese and make doughnuts and coffee. At another point they saw the tracks of a commando's boots in the snow, but these petered out.

On the evening of Friday the 25th, they camped on a hill in six inches of snow, and the next morning scaled the high peak above. 'It was sheer rock and we were scared, sometimes the snow was up to our chests,' they said afterwards. But guided by some villagers, they crossed over the frontier that night. They had survived the Arctic, and successfully evaded the Germans, for a whole week.

After a few days, they were taken south to Stockholm for questioning. The police did not believe their story of having escaped from a PoW camp in Norway (since there were none) but nevertheless they were released and flew back to Scotland in early October. On arriving in London, both were interviewed by Mountbatten, who congratulated them and showed them photographs of the devastation at the power station.

O'Brien was to come much closer to being caught. He became

disorientated and delirious and could not later accurately recall all that had happened, but he was sure that he was sheltered by Norwegians on the first two nights after leaving the others. One night he spent in a large dog kennel, from where he saw two Germans a hundred yards away going from house to house looking for him. The next couple of days passed in a blur during which he waded across a river and became lost in a forest. Thereafter he was again passed on from one refuge to another.

Towards the end of the month, he was within ten miles of the border. Much later he remembered that that evening he had seemed to be in luck. He was enjoying a good supper in a farmhouse when he noticed that the woman who had taken him in had answered the telephone. He had not heard it ring. Something was wrong and he immediately ran out of the back door and began to climb the hill behind. Bullets cracked past him, and on the road below he could see three motorcycles with sidecars arriving with German troops. He had a head start, however, and they soon gave up chasing him.

For several more days he meandered on, staying in the huts of Laplanders, until on about 4 October he came across a Swedish constable. He realised that after thirteen exhausting days on the run he had made it. Soon afterwards he saw Christiansen in a holding camp, and was able to have a few words with him before both men were sent to Stockholm.

COHQ was naturally gladdened by the safe return of all four soldiers. But while MUSKETOON was hailed both during and after the war as an outstanding success, in private doubts and recriminations soon flourished.

The explosion which destroyed the pipeline had reaped an unexpected bonus. Automatic valves should have shut off the flow of water after fifteen minutes, but these were being serviced and were out of action. The plant had therefore been flooded to a greater depth than even Black had dreamed of. British hopes of taking it offline for the rest of the war, however, were not realised.

Intelligence reports soon revealed that one of the charges placed on a turbine had failed to go off, and although the turbine was damaged by the rocks which had buried the machinery, the generators were working at half-capacity again within three months. This did limit the planned output of the Haugvik smelter, but of more importance to aluminium production in Norway was a decision that Goering had already taken to end the expansion programme as it was too difficult to find qualified personnel.

The reports of the four returning commandos also prompted much internal bickering, as their superiors looked to apportion blame for the failure of the others to get away. O'Brien's belief that the team's exit would have been quicker if all were specialist climbers led Laycock to make a devastating assessment of the mission. Its success, he judged, had been impaired by the inability of the whole team to escape, and the fatigue which he thought had largely caused this was the responsibility of their commanding officers.

'This operation was the first of its kind,' agreed Mountbatten's staff, 'and we had an unduly high opinion of Black and Houghton's mountaineering and ability to train the force.' It seemed that they had spent a lot of time practising boat work rather than learning outdoor survival techniques. Seizing any chance to stifle COHQ's influence, the Admiralty's planning director also criticised the raid as being badly planned and retrieved only by good luck.

Certainly O'Brien, Trigg and Fairclough had needed some fortune to make their way out, given their lack of equipment and knowledge of their whereabouts in freezing conditions. That they did escape, however, was testament to both their natural determination and their endurance training. O'Brien may have been correct in thinking that Black had waited rather too long to get away after the first explosions, but given his lapses in memory too much reliance was placed on his evidence.

When all the accounts were in, it became clear that the main problem had been the unavoidable delay in finding the bridge, and that by splitting up Black had probably helped to draw the hunt away from Christiansen's party. Nevertheless, it was decided that a

Troop would be intensively trained in Arctic warfare and used for any future raids of this kind.

The only ones unable to give their verdict on the operation were those who had been taken prisoner. Reports had filtered through that Djupdraet had died in hospital after a few days, but the fate of the others was unknown. They had last been seen being manacled and driven to the docks at Oslo for transportation to Germany. A German sergeant, Josef Kubatzky, claimed later that he had refused to comply with the order to chain the commandos and had been threatened with imprisonment. Black had overheard this and told Kubatzky to proceed, before giving him a shilling and his home address and telling him to look him up after the war.

The next sighting of Black and Houghton was at Colditz in early October. They were brought out into the yard of the castle for exercise and were photographed with their kit. The following day they succeeded in overpowering a sentry, but were soon caught once they had got out of their cell. Even so, by leaving a letter there they managed to pass their names and details of the raid to some other prisoners, whose suspicions had been aroused because the guards tried to ensure that no one spoke to the pair.

Then they vanished. The only news of them for the next three years came from the Red Cross, who were told by the Germans that they had escaped from Colditz in February 1943. Houghton's mother sought in vain for more news from the War Office, as did the families of other missing special service troops with whom she was in touch. Sometimes they were not even the first to be given confirmation of their worst fears.

In November 1942, two months after MUSKETOON, airborne soldiers had mounted another operation in Norway. FRESHMAN's target was the Vemork Hydro, where heavy water was being made for the German atom bomb project. The gliders carrying the thirty-four men had crashed, however, and all the survivors had been executed in secret soon after by the Germans. The relatives, along with the other readers of the *Daily Express*, only discovered what had happened when the newspaper revealed the truth in May 1945.

'Our boys are sent on these suicide raids and we here at home naturally seek information from the War Office,' wrote Marjorie Pendlebury, the widow of one of the FRESHMAN team, a few days later. 'But all we get is sympathy, and I am afraid that doesn't help anyone very much.'

It was not until September 1945 that the MUSKETOON families heard for certain that their menfolk were dead. In conditions of extreme secrecy, all seven had been taken to the Sachsenhausen concentration camp, near Berlin, and shot in the neck on 22 October 1942. They were the first victims of Hitler's Commando Order.

This had been issued only four days before their deaths, and did not come into force in Norway until the 26th, more than a month after the raid itself. As a consequence, not content with pretending that the two officers had escaped, the Germans also falsified the date of their executions for their own records as having been 30 October.

This attempt to add a veneer of legitimacy to murder carried no weight in post-war trials for war crimes, and among those convicted of the commandos' deaths was the former commander of German troops in Norway, General Nikolaus von Falkenhorst. For his part, the High Command's Chief of Staff, Jodl, admitted that he thought the raid was a permissible military operation, but he had been unable to stand up to Hitler's anger at it.

The archive files on MUSKETOON contain one perplexing footnote. In early 1944, an officer of the Royal Horse Artillery, Tony Davies, wrote from a German PoW camp to an acquaintance in 2 Commando. In his letter, which was passed to the escape service MI9, he stated that he had 'just been speaking to some mutual friends of yours . . . Gay Black and Joe Horton [*sic*]. Both are well. I saw them a week ago.'

Davies had served with Houghton earlier in the war, so he could not have mistaken someone else for him, but since by the time of his letter the two men had been dead for fifteen months his intention is unclear. Perhaps the likeliest answer is that he had somehow got wind of their having been in danger at Colditz and through the misspelling was subtly trying to indicate that all was not as he wrote.

Even before their end was known, Black had been awarded the DSO and Houghton the MC for their gallant leadership of the attack. O'Brien received the Distinguished Conduct Medal (DCM), and Trigg, Fairclough and Christiansen the Military Medal. 'I have nothing but good to say about the men who composed the party,' stated the Norwegian in his mission report, 'especially Captain Black who organised everything splendidly well.'

He recalled, too, that as Erling Djupdraet had lain mortally wounded, he had said that he felt too young to die. But he had consoled himself with the thought that 'if a nation was to live some must be willing to die'. It was a sentiment that stood as a fitting epitaph for all those who failed to return from Glomfjord.

MUSKETOON was the first of a new kind of Commando operation. Those at St Nazaire and Dieppe had been made in greater strength, while the Small-Scale Raiding Force had only ever hit and run. Even their West African adventure had not required a lengthy approach march and exit through enemy territory. Perhaps the only precedent was the attack on Rommel's supposed HQ, which had been planned to take fewer days than it did, and which in any event failed in its aims.

Black had proved that a small group could go for days undetected where a larger one could not, yet still carry enough firepower to hurt the enemy. Less encouragingly, MUSKETOON had demonstrated as well that it was far more difficult to get away afterwards if there was no transport waiting.

Yet the risks, and so maybe even the losses, were worth it. Everyone whom Christiansen met on his epic trek to safety took renewed hope from what had been done at Glomfjord. 'They admired the way in which it was carried out,' he told those who had sent him, 'and said that they were real men who had done it.'

10

ANGLO

Graeme Black was not the only believer in the potential for small groups to cause disproportionate harm to the Axis. In North Africa, David Stirling's SAS had carried out a series of raids against German and Italian airfields in 1942 which, after a shaky start, had convinced Middle East Command to back his unorthodox ideas.

By the summer, with Rommel in the ascendancy, Stirling's reach was growing and soon came to embrace the SBS. Since the return of Jumbo Courtney to Britain at the start of the year to raise a second section, the three dozen canoeists based in Alexandria had been masterless. Attachment to the SAS at least offered them a degree of protection from interference by others, and the welcome prospect of action.

Stirling soon gave them that, expanding their role from beach reconnaissance and saboteurs of shipping to that of seaborne raiders on the lines of the jeep-borne SAS. This undoubtedly allowed them to engage the enemy more closely; but it also greatly increased the risks to a small unit which could ill afford heavy casualties.

Lieutenant David Sutherland of the SBS – 'Dinky' to his friends – had already experienced at first hand the hazards of Stirling's vision of warfare. After his narrow escape from the Rommel raid, when he had been swept off the casing of *Talisman* and failed to get ashore, he had joined an SAS attack on Benghazi in March 1942. Many of Stirling's men – notably his friend Jock Lewes, who had recently been killed – he already knew from their time together in 8 Commando.

The plan was for Sutherland to set off limpet mines in Benghazi harbour, but he never arrived there. While en route in a captured German staff car he ran over an Italian thermos bomb hidden in scrub and was severely wounded in his left arm. In April, after returning to duties with the SBS, he was sent with Tom Langton and two future writers, Eric Newby and Michael Alexander, to map the beaches of Syria and Lebanon. These might become of importance to the Allies if Rommel broke through to the Near East.

Yet Stirling had not given up on the notion of joint SAS–SBS raids, and in June they staged their first coordinated attacks in support of a vital convoy bound for beleaguered Malta. The SAS had so far concentrated their attentions on airfields in North Africa, but now Stirling wanted to use the SBS's amphibious skills to target those on islands in the Mediterranean as well. While his troops struck at four air bases in Libya, the SBS were simultaneously to hit three on Crete. A fourth was reserved for the SAS's French Squadron.

Sutherland's objective was the airfield at Tymbaki. Due to the limited space on the launch carrying them, he had only two men with him. One was Sergeant Willy Moss, who had shared his dinghy on FLIPPER, and the other John Brittlebank, the third survivor, with Laycock and Terry, of that catastrophe. As it was, when they got to Tymbaki they discovered that there were no aircraft there any longer. Elsewhere, the defences at Maleme proved far too formidable to penetrate, but the third SBS section did blow up eight planes at Kastelli.

At Heraklion, the four-strong French team did magnificently, accounting for twenty-one aircraft, but they were all killed or captured while getting away. Among the prisoners was the squadron's leader, Georges Bergé, whose rescue from the sands of Sables d'Olonne had won Geoff Appleyard his first MC. The only survivor of the raid was their liaison officer, George, Lord Jellicoe, another veteran of 8 Commando. The SBS had not been told of the French mission and Sutherland was taken aback to see Jellicoe sauntering jauntily down to the beach where they were waiting to be picked up.

Including the SAS's tally in Libya, almost fifty aircraft had been destroyed in a single night on the enemy's own ground. At a stroke the special forces had confirmed their worth. Yet such was the Axis power in the air that the convoy was still decimated. Only two out of seventeen ships made it to Malta. That was enough to stave off surrender for the time being, but there could be no let up in the efforts to supply the island.

Accordingly, more missions were mounted, often in a hurry, and in August the SBS suffered a major reverse when seven of its members, including Newby, were captured on Sicily. They had been attacking an airfield from which German bombers threatened one of the most famous convoys of the war, PEDESTAL. Later that month, Alexander was taken prisoner while raiding a forward aerodrome near Alamein. He was sent to Colditz when the Germans assumed incorrectly that he was related to his namesake, the newly appointed commander of British forces in the region.

That operation was part of attempts to disrupt the build-up for Rommel's next push towards Cairo. In July, he had been halted just one hundred and fifty miles from the city at the first battle of Alamein. By late August, he was ready to try again. The flow of munitions to both sides was becoming a critical factor in the campaign, and reducing the strength of the Luftwaffe and the Regia Aeronautica Italiana remained a priority for the British. Fears about Rommel's proximity had led the Mediterranean Fleet, including its submarines, to move its base from Alexandria to Beirut, and it was there that Sutherland was briefed for ANGLO. This time the target was to be Rhodes.

The island had lost none of its strategic importance in the months since it had been covertly reconnoitred by Courtney and Willmott. From Maritsa in the north and Calatos in the east, Junkers 88 and Savoia-Marchetti bombers dominated the waters of the eastern Mediterranean and the Aegean. Under the command of Captain Richard Allott, Sutherland and six other members of the SBS were to attack the two airfields simultaneously at midnight on 12 September. Also attached to the party were two Greek officers, as interpreters, and two local guides, formerly bus drivers on Rhodes.

The group would be landed by submarine and picked up a fortnight later, giving them time to get to their objectives and back. This timetable was fixed, since they would have no wireless with them and the submarines had immutable schedules of their own. There was very little intelligence available about Rhodes beyond the fact that it was garrisoned by thirty thousand Italian troops. Even the raiders' landing place had been selected from an aerial photograph in the hope, rather than the certainty, that it offered somewhere to hide their boats and stores.

The party left Beirut on the Greek submarine *Papanikolis* on the afternoon of 31 August. There had been a further blow to SBS morale earlier in the day when the officer bringing them their final briefing had been killed in a road accident, and the mood as they departed was more than usually pensive. With the extra men and equipment aboard, their home for the next five days was hot and crowded. Sutherland had a last lingering look from the deck at the sun setting on the mountains of Lebanon, wondering as he did so how remote their chance of success was.

Eighteen months earlier, he had been bound for Rhodes with Layforce before the attack was called off. He therefore caught his first glimpse of the island through *Papanikolis*'s periscope and was immediately struck by what he saw – a coastline of sunlit coves and beaches rising up to the heights of Mount Ilias. The submarine surfaced that night – 4 September – to a calm sea and a starlit sky. At 2200 the four boats floated off, accompanied by cries of 'Good luck!' in Greek.

After paddling for two hours, they landed on a beach five hundred yards west of their intended landing point near Stegna, but it proved ideal. Sutherland and Moss swept the sand clear of traces of their footprints with branches while the others hid the dinghies and food for their return. Then they began to climb.

The cliff was steeper and the going harder than they had anticipated. Every man was carrying around fifty pounds on his back, comprising ten days' food as well as ammunition and explosives. They wore khaki uniforms without badges or insignia, with camouflage nets around their necks and cap comforters to ward off mosquitoes. The troopers had .45-calibre machine-guns and the officers their Webley revolvers. Still shaking off the effects of having been in the submarine, Sutherland took half an hour to heft his load to the top, by when he was nearly worn out.

They spent that night and the next day resting in a cave, moving off in the cool of the late evening. Allott's aim was to get across the main road between Malona and Massari about two hours later, towards midnight, but the rugged hills they had to cross slowed them considerably. More worryingly, the two guides seemed unsure of their way, and by 0400 the group had covered no more than a mile. They found a grotto in which the party could hide up again the following day, but when the guides were sent to fill the water bottles they returned empty-handed, saying that they had seen the enemy near by. Although the team spent the next day in the shade, there was no relief from their thirst.

That evening's march repeated the same pattern as before. Rather than taking the road through the valley, the guides insisted on sticking to that along the steep flanks of a mountain. By first light, they were still short of Malona. Determined to get water, Sutherland sent two of his men into the valley with the guides with orders not to return until the bottles had been filled. When this had been done, the team laid up for the day on a hillside.

'Two valuable nights had thus been wasted by taking the mountain route,' recorded Sutherland. 'The guides at first said they knew the way, and latterly openly confessed that they were ignorant of their surroundings. One can hardly blame them since they volunteered to come on the operation at great risk to themselves. It is, however, advisable to ascertain how much a guide really knows about the country before entrusting him to lead a party. No guide is better than a bad one.'

The mission was now in trouble. Not only had the commandos been saddled with guides who were no use, but the two Greek officers were suffering from the unaccustomed physical hardship. Needing to make up for lost time, Allott and Sutherland decided to split into two parties. Allott would head north to Maritsa, about fifteen miles away, giving himself five nights to get there before he made his attack on the 12th. Sutherland would go south to Calatos, near Lindos and only about eight miles from their hiding-place.

All excess weight would be dumped where they were and guarded by the older of the Greek officers, Captain Tsoucas. The other, Sub-Lieutenant Calambakidis, would go with Sutherland, since the shorter march to Calatos would test his bad knee less. The rest of his group would consist of one of the guides, Nicholas Savvas, and Marines Duggan, Barrow and Harris. Corporal McKenzie and Private Blake would accompany Allott, as would Moss, since he and the second guide, George Kyrimichalis, could communicate in Italian. Kyrimichalis was just nineteen. Sutherland himself was only twenty-one.

The two officers agreed to meet again on 16 September where they had landed, and at 2030 on the 7th Allott's party set off north. It was the last that Sutherland saw of any of them.

For the next two nights, he moved steadily towards his target, covering short distances under the cloak of darkness and lying up by day in dry stream beds. By the evening of the 10th he was about two miles from the aerodrome and able to note the location of aircraft and hangars through his binoculars. A strong northerly wind had begun to blow, however, and even when they took refuge in a shepherd's cave the cold was so intense at night that they got little sleep.

On the evening of the 11th, the men who had gone out to fetch water came back with two shepherds who were friends of Savvas. They gave Calambakidis information about morale on the island, and produced a meal of bread, cheese and fruit which was gratefully devoured. As they tucked in, Sutherland made the final adjustments to his plan of attack.

The Italian aircraft were sited in two separate areas. A clutch of fourteen of them were parked close together on the north-east side of the landing ground, with more dispersed under nearby olive trees. They could be readily reached by anyone crossing the dry bed of the River Gaddura beyond. At least another seventeen bombers were gathered in the centre of the aerodrome, more widely spread out but also more heavily guarded. Sutherland and Duggan would take these, while Calambakidis and the other two marines would sabotage the first group. Sutherland hoped that, being fewer in number, he and Duggan would have a greater chance of avoiding detection where the defences were thickest, while Calambakidis needed the extra man as potentially he would have more targets. Their Bergen rucksacks and all other kit, except for the explosives, were given to Savvas, who was to rendezvous with them afterwards and lead them into the hills. Zero hour for placing the bombs was 2359.

As the rain teemed down, the entire party crossed into the Gaddura together and then separated in the river bed at 2315. Sutherland and Duggan stealthily made their way towards the aerodrome and by 2345 were within a hundred yards of their first target. The aircraft was guarded, but shortly before midnight the sentry walked away. They sneaked in and stuck bombs on it and two other Savoia-Marchetti 84s.

By 0020, they had got over barbed wire and an anti-tank ditch, and were walking down a path between huts towards the landing strip itself. 'This was our only way into the aerodrome, and the most direct route for the next attack,' wrote Sutherland later in defence of this daring decision, which backfired when they were challenged.

There was a sentry directly between them and the bomber they had identified as their next target, and although they retreated the way they had come he ran after them and began shouting. The lights were on in a building close by and, worried that if the alarm was raised it would also compromise the other group, they crossed back over the ditch in search of alternative places to plant their explosives. A fuel dump soon received its share but, finding no other targets, they placed the rest on the same three aircraft as before.

It was now at least 0130 and high time they left. There was no sign of Calambakidis's team in the river bed, so at 0200 Sutherland and Duggan pulled back towards the meeting point with Savvas. Ten minutes later their first bomb went off, soon followed by the other two. More explosions lit up the sky as the other section's charges began to go up and a red glow settled over the aerodrome. By the time that the pair had reached the rendezvous at 0330, they could see more than a dozen fires burning as fiercely as funeral pyres.

Calambakidis, Barrow and Harris were still missing, however, and it was clear that the Italians were not going to let anyone get away easily. Searchlights swept over the route that Sutherland was planning to follow into the hills, and Savvas became so anxious about the beams that he refused to go any further. Sutherland lost patience with him and, realising that Savvas would have no trouble hiding among the locals, decided to leave him behind while he and Duggan hastened to reach higher ground before the sun rose. Towards 0400 he heard what sounded like tommy-gun fire coming from the slopes beyond the airstrip and saw flashlights probing the ground. Then all fell quiet.

The pair spent the next day lying low and observing the result of their handiwork. Sutherland counted numerous charred carcasses of aircraft, but as they were often close together, having set each other alight, it was hard to make an exact reckoning.

When they came across Tsoucas, who had set up an observation post directly above where they were, he confirmed that as many as fifteen bombers had been destroyed. He also reported that a large plane had landed at the base the previous day. Sutherland began to wonder if it had come to carry away prisoners. A shepherd had found some abandoned water bottles, which suggested that at least the young guide Kyrimichalis had fallen into enemy hands.

Although this was a setback, Sutherland had no reason as yet to change his original plan, which was to meet up at the beach in two nights' time with the group returning from the airfield at Maritsa. Tsoucas had enough food for all three of them for a day, so the priority for now was to fill up with water. Sutherland had noticed a well behind the village of Caraci (now Haraki) close to the shore. Although it was surrounded by white-painted posts and he had seen no one close to it, he did not think it was mined, and in the cool of the evening he and Duggan slipped down from the hills.

As soon as Sutherland stepped over the fence around the area he felt his leg touch something. Across the path there stretched a thin wire. Tracing it carefully, he found that it led to a metal canister about ten inches high that resembled the Italian anti-personnel mines he had seen in the Western Desert. It would be madness to go on, so he gently backed away and decided to fill his bottle elsewhere.

The next morning they dozed in the heat. Nothing disturbed the silence except the distant clank of goat bells and the humming of insects. Then, towards 1500, they saw about thirty people advancing across the valley. Most were soldiers, guided by half a dozen civilians. When they were a thousand yards from where the three commandos were concealed, they split into two groups. One headed for the landing beach, the other directly for them.

Scooping up what they could carry, Sutherland, Duggan and Tsoucas ran pell-mell over the crest and into the bare ground above the cliffs, keeping as close as possible to the foot of the mountain. They had a head start and rested for a few moments in a small cave. Tsoucas was feeling the pace and did not want to go any further, but Sutherland hauled him to his feet. The cave was too obvious a hiding-place: they had to get higher. After scrambling frantically up through bushes and rocks, they found themselves on a small sloping ledge overlooking a shepherd's hut. There was no time to find a better place as just then several search parties came round the foot of the mountain from the other direction. By a whisker they had avoided being caught between the two pincers.

The troops spread out and the man hunt began. The commandos' only chance was to lie flat and hope that no one came up as high as they were. Although in shade, they were completely in the open. From below came the chatter of Italian, rising steadily closer, and the sound of the hillside being combed for traces of them. Soon the voices were just ten yards away, but at the last moment they began to fall and grow fainter. The soldiers seemed to have assumed that their quarry would not have had time to climb any higher, and started to sweep the ground further down.

It had been the narrowest of escapes, but a little while later the fugitives had another shock. Out to sea, an Italian torpedo boat began slowly to follow the coastline. Close to where they had landed, she shut off her engines and drifted under the cliffs and out of sight. When she reappeared, she was towing three black objects astern which were evidently the team's dinghies. Doubtless their stores had also been seized.

As dusk fell, Sutherland realised that in the space of a few hours the situation had changed entirely. They now had no food and no means of reaching the submarine. Moreover, the discovery of their cache suggested that someone had been forced to reveal it, presumably one of the guides, so the Italians would probably be waiting for the arrival of both Allott's group and the sub. Even though the beach would be guarded, Sutherland somehow had to warn them.

The next day was uncomfortably hot and, though no patrols came near them, they had nothing to drink for ten hours. When everything seemed quiet, at about 2000, the trio moved lower down and filled up their bottles from a stone water trough. Leaving Tsoucas with the remaining kit, Sutherland and Duggan then cautiously made their way towards the shore.

In a cave that had not been searched they found a signalling torch. The only way now to reach the submarine when it arrived the following night was to swim, so they also took with them three Mae West inflatable vests. A message for Allott was left tied to another torch: 'Boats captured, signalling and swimming from intended place.'

Shortly before midnight, they set off back up the mountain. As they did so, they heard shouts in Italian and saw flashlights moving about where they had left Tsoucas. It was obvious that a large force had come between them and him, presumably intending to ambush Allott's group as it returned. There was no way that Sutherland and Duggan could get through or round without being spotted. They would have to sit tight where they were.

At first light, they could see about thirty or forty men forming up about four hundred yards away. They were taking off their greatcoats and getting ready to move off. A few minutes later, half of them marched towards the beach. The others came right at them.

Sutherland had found a hollow under a large rock, and into this he and Duggan now slid. There was just enough room for the two of them, but it was cramped in the extreme. There was barely space for them to breathe, let alone stretch out. Nor did they have any food or water. Clearly they were in for an unpleasant ordeal, and the outlook soon became bleaker when yet another squad arrived from the direction of Calatos.

All morning the soldiers rooted around the mountainside, poking their rifles into every cleft and thicket. The two SBS men could see out under the rim of the boulder, and from time to time troops passed to and fro some way off, on top of the cliffs. Suddenly they heard a heart-stopping noise: footsteps right overhead. Someone had scrabbled onto the very rock beneath which they lay. For five long minutes he sat there, his boots dangling just a few feet above them. Then he was gone.

Their nerves were soon tested again. At about 1330, they saw two officers and a large detachment of troops heading down to Calatos. They were carrying full equipment, including machine-guns. Then, about half an hour later, four rifle shots rang out from the area of the cave where Sutherland had left the message. They were answered by what sounded like a revolver, accompanied by a lot of shouting, and at once all the soldiers near them headed at the double towards the shore.

Though Sutherland was not to know it, the source of the excitement was Calambakidis. Having evaded pursuit so far, he had got to the rendezvous only to find the warning note. It was too late. The Italians closed in, and a few minutes later he was taken.

The rest of the afternoon passed slowly but without any more alarms. Sutherland's plan was to head for the beach at nightfall, before the Italian patrol was in place, and there meet up with Tsoucas. They would signal to the British submarine *Traveller*, which was due at 2200, and then swim out to it. At 2000, he and Duggan were finally able to crawl out from under their rock and stretch their limbs.

There was no sign of Tsoucas down by the coast. (He too had been taken prisoner.) At 2130, Sutherland began to flash the recognition signal seawards – the letter 'K' in Morse code. Straight away Duggan thought he saw the reply, but Sutherland could not. In fact, it had been given through the submarine's periscope as it was still submerged.

Sutherland waited until 2200 and tried again. This time the response was clearly visible, although even with binoculars *Traveller* herself was not. Sutherland signalled one more time: 'Swimming; come in'. Then they shed their clothes and boots – Duggan's had already disintegrated – and entered the water. It was still but cold, and they had a long way to go.

Both men were barely into their twenties, and supremely fit, yet they had eaten nothing in the last three days – and only a tin of sardines in the two before that. Sutherland had lost more than a stone in weight in the fortnight he had been on Rhodes. 'Our physical condition for such a swim was hardly adequate,' he reported later, with heroic British understatement. Yet they were determined to reach the submarine, and urged each other on.

For more than an hour they swam towards where they had seen the recognition signal. Sutherland knew that *Traveller* had been told to switch her engines on to help them find her, and eventually they were cheered to hear the sound of them. But although Duggan flashed his torch from time to time, they still could not locate the sub. Then the noise of the motors grew fainter, and eventually vanished.

Despondent as they were at hearing what they thought was *Traveller* leaving them behind, they encouraged each other to keep swimming. They were now exhausted and starting to feel cold creep over them. If they did not find the submarine, they might not have the strength to make it back to the beach.

Five minutes later, *Traveller*'s captain was astonished to hear a stream of robust Anglo-Saxon abuse being shouted at him from the darkness. Michael St John had been watching for twelve paddlers in folbots, not the two shivering and emaciated men who at that moment were being helped over the foreplanes. They were escorted below and revived with large mugs of rum while the sailors tried to find clothes that would fit their skeletal frames. Then St John ordered a crash dive, just in time to survive the two depth-charge attacks which nevertheless rocked the hull. The engines that Sutherland and Duggan had heard had been those of an Italian torpedo boat looking for the submarine. St John had already turned

Traveller around so that her bows faced the open sea, ready for a fast escape. Now he set course for Beirut.

David Sutherland and John Duggan were the only members of the raiding party to escape from Rhodes. The remaining ten men were rounded up, including the whole of Allott's group, though not before they had destroyed at least twenty aircraft at Maritsa.

Sutherland was found to be suffering from malaria, but soon recovered and received the Military Cross. Duggan was awarded the Military Medal. The other commandos were sent to PoW camps, but a very different fate awaited their two guides. Nicholas Savvas was shot in early October. In consideration of his youth, George Kyrimichalis was sentenced to life imprisonment. He was released from solitary confinement in Siena in 1944 after the Italian armistice, but by then had contracted tuberculosis. He returned to his home village, where he died in 1949, aged twenty-six.

In dealing such a substantial blow to Italian arms and pride, the SBS had again proved the potential of amphibious raiding. Their legend was starting to be burnished. After the attack, the island's Italian governor, Admiral Campioni, wrote to Rome to explain what had gone wrong. Apparently a sentry had disturbed some of the saboteurs while they were planting their bombs, but when they had pointed a pistol at him and told him to keep quiet, he had fainted in fright.

Sutherland and Duggan had shown that it was possible to survive when things went wrong, but they had needed luck as well as cool thinking to do so. Had *Traveller* not waited as long as she did in hostile waters, the whole team would have been lost. There were risks inherent in any mission but the unit could not afford such an attrition rate. Aircraft were replaceable, yet so much unique skill and experience was in far shorter supply.

Desperate as the situation was in the Mediterranean, too much was being asked of the SBS; and if those who planned the section's operations continued to overplay their hand, the odds would continue to catch up with them. Even daredevils had their limitations. To imagine otherwise was romantic but wrongheaded.

11

AGREEMENT

The Afrika Korps lorry slowed to a halt. In the middle of the road, the driver could see a German soldier beckoning to him to stop. A rifle was slung on his shoulder, and the peak of his desert cap shielded his eyes from the headlights. Probably a checkpoint – there were plenty of them on the way up to the front line.

'How many are you carrying?' the soldier asked. It was a checkpoint.

'Just us two,' replied the driver, gesturing to the passenger next to him. He couldn't quite place the accent.

'Good,' said the soldier. 'Get your hands up!'

The doors of the cab were yanked open and the two Germans found themselves looking at two rather scruffy Englishmen holding pistols.

One of them, Lieutenant McKee, helped the soldier to tie and gag their two prisoners, who were dumped by the side of the road. A fourth man had appeared from the shadows and drove the truck off into the darkness. When it returned, there were half a dozen other Englishmen in the back, including an RAF flight sergeant and two officers from the Norfolk Yeomanry.

McKee had snatched a cap for himself from one of the Germans, and now he jumped in the front with the soldier, who also had on a British greatcoat. All night they drove, keeping to the back roads. By dawn, they had reached their own lines – and freedom – west of Tobruk.

Some days later, Captain Herbert Buck of the 1st Punjabis was told to report to Headquarters. The officer on the other side of the desk had been rather vague about his duties, but it seemed clear that Lieutenant Colonel Clarke worked in Intelligence. In particular, he wanted to hear all about Buck's recent escape from captivity – especially the part where he had passed himself off as a German.

Three weeks earlier, Buck had been a PoW in Benghazi. Taken prisoner near Derna at the start of February 1942, he had at once begun planning how to get away. When everyone else was being moved to Tripoli on the 5th, he feigned illness. Then he and McKee slipped into an empty shed near the perimeter of the camp. They had been timing the sentry's round, and once his back was turned they were through the wire in a couple of minutes.

For a week they walked east through the hills, before coming down to the main road again. Buck had studied German at Oxford before the war and spoke it fluently. Wearing a waterproof cape and a cap he had scavenged, he stopped the first vehicle which came along, a fifteen-hundredweight truck. While the Afrika Korps driver was busy looking for his papers Buck jammed a spanner into his ribs and told him it was a revolver.

He and McKee left the bound driver behind a bush and drove through the desert to Lamluda. There they ran out of luck, and were challenged while looking for petrol. Abandoning the lorry, they ran off into the scrub, pursued by pistol shots. For another week they wandered, picking up eight more stragglers and escapees as they went. On the evening of the 20th, Buck tried his ruse again on the Derna road, and this time he and his gang made it to safety.

Since leaving the Commandos behind, Dudley Clarke had been busy devising and running numerous deception schemes in North Africa. Buck's exploit was just the kind of trick which appealed to

Clarke – to such an extent that he recommended him for an MC – not least because he had a liking himself for dressing-up.

A few months earlier, after going to Madrid to meet MI6's head of station, he had been arrested by the Spanish police 'dressed down to a brassiere as a woman', as the Embassy told London. None of his explanations for his choice of wardrobe seemed very convincing to them.

Buck's success had depended on an anomaly of the war in the desert. Unlike in Europe, the British and German uniforms were almost indistinguishable. Both sides wore khaki shirts and shorts, and indeed often carried captured pieces of equipment. Moreover, the natural assumption of both lorry drivers had been that a German-speaking soldier, deep in their own territory, was no cause for concern. That had enabled Buck to escape. The question was: might it allow him to bluff his way back in again?

Within a few weeks, Buck was touring Army camps in Egypt in search of men who could pass as Germans. In an internal memorandum, Colonel Terence Airey, Director of Special Operations at Middle East Command, explained what Buck was up to: 'We are in the process of forming a Special German group as a sub-unit of the ME Commando,' he wrote in April, referring to the unloved successor to Layforce.

> It is intended that this sub-unit should be used for infiltration behind the German lines in the Western Desert under Eighth Army. The strength of the Special Group would be approximately that of a platoon. The personnel, a proportion of which are already selected, are fluent German linguists. They are mainly Palestinians of German origin. Many of them have had war experience with 51 Commando.
>
> They will frequently be dressed in German uniform and will operate under the command of a British officer who has already proved himself to be an expert in the German language . . . It is proposed to give them the cover name of the Special Interrogation Group [SIG].

The officer was Buck, then aged twenty-five, and the son of a career soldier in Britain's Indian Army.

By 'Palestinian', Airey meant Jewish émigrés from Germany and Central Europe to what had not yet become Israel. Many had particular reason to hate the Nazis, of course, but those who had joined No. 51 had only seen action against the Italians in East Africa before being rolled up into the Middle East Commando.

Buck soon found a dozen willing recruits. Among them was twenty-six-year-old Maurice Tiefenbrunner. His parents were originally from Poland, but they had moved to Wiesbaden, Germany, to open a kosher delicatessen. He had been born there, but since June 1939 had been a refugee in Palestine. 'My parents and a hundred other relatives were in dire straits in Poland,' he afterwards recalled. 'I had a dream that I could help them by joining the British Army and being parachuted into Poland.' Buck told him that his life would depend on his ability to pass as a member of the Afrika Korps, and an Aryan one at that. He would have to master their drill, their marching songs, even their slang. And Buck was frank about the risks involved. 'If your true identity is found out, there is no hope for you,' he told another volunteer, Ariyeh Shai.

Laycock had been rather dismissive of the abilities of the Palestinians when offered them for his Middle East Commando. Now they showed impressive dedication. Living and training apart from British troops, the SIG learned to behave at all times like German soldiers. They used German weapons, carried German pay books and cigarettes, and even goose-stepped to meals. In the middle of the night, they would be woken suddenly to see if they spoke in anything other than German. Their false identities were rounded out by love letters from and photos of bogus German girlfriends. In reality, British girls from the Auxiliary Territorial Service (ATS) in Cairo posed for the pictures.

Every detail was scrutinised by Buck's second-in-command, Lieutenant David Russell of Eton, Cambridge and the Scots Guards, who was reputed to speak half a dozen German dialects. Helping him were two decidedly less pukka soldiers. In fact, they were not British at all. Herbert Brückner and Walter Essner were two German infantrymen who had been taken prisoner near Tobruk in November. Both had served in the French Foreign Legion in the 1930s, but when war came they had been sent back to Germany and later conscripted. Having told their captors they were Communists who were opposed to Hitler, they agreed to spy on their fellow PoWs at the Combined Services Detailed Interrogation Centre (CSDIC) on the outskirts of Cairo. There they had 'provided Intelligence sources with very valuable information about German dispositions', wrote Buck, explaining why he had then asked them to join him. The link to the Interrogation Centre – which had also produced a captured German staff car for the SIG – probably explains Airey's choice of name for the new unit.

By the spring of 1942, the latest and smallest Commando formation was ready for its first tasks behind enemy lines. These were intelligence-gathering operations rather than sabotage missions. Dressed in German uniforms, the SIG set up roadblocks to gather information about transport and mingled with Rommel's troops to collect news. Tiefenbrunner even managed to draw pay from one unsuspecting Wehrmacht cashier.

Their first major test came in mid-June. As part of the SAS–SBS attacks on airfields in Libya and Crete in support of the HARPOON convoy, two detachments of the French SAS were to raid the bases at Derna and Martuba west of Tobruk. Stirling wanted them to be driven there by Buck's men in disguise while his pretended to be their prisoners.

Buck was given only three days to prepare. He briefed Essner, who acted as his sergeant, to make up the appropriate German identity discs and driving licences, but the rest of the party were only told the details of the plan when their three vehicles reached the Siwa Oasis. Soon after, the twelve SIG men – seven Palestinians, two Czechs, Buck and the two Germans – changed into their Afrika Korps uniforms and adopted their role as escort to the fifteen

Frenchmen. The Palestinians and Czechs were divided between two lorries, while the Germans, dressed as NCOs, rode in a command car driven by Buck, who was dressed as a private.

They had no trouble at the first checkpoint they encountered, the Italian fort at Gerari, and after eating that evening at a German roadside camp they spent the night near the airfields. The next afternoon, 12 June, Brückner drove one of the lorries past the landing grounds at Martuba, Derna and nearby Siret-el-Shreiba. Sat in the back, peering through the tarpaulin, were Buck and the leader of the French raiders, Lieutenant Augustin Jordan, Georges Bergé's second-in-command.

That evening, they divided into two groups. Brückner took Jordan and nine of his men, watched over by two of the SIG, to attack the two strips at Derna. Meanwhile, Buck and the rest of his team dropped the remaining section of five Frenchmen at Martuba. Essner posed as the convoy's commander and, noted Buck, his 'coolness and foresight' allowed them to pass through all the German control posts unchallenged.

In the small hours of the morning, Buck waited anxiously at the rendezvous for the parties' safe return. With him were the remaining members of the SIG, including Tiefenbrunner. 'I heard loud explosions, which meant they had succeeded in exploding some planes,' he recalled, but as time wore on and there was no sign of the others, 'I became very tense. Suddenly, I heard some shouts, and thinking at first that some real Germans had detected us, I took up my machine-gun to be ready.' But the figure who stumbled out of the darkness was Jordan – and he was alone. What he had to tell Buck came as a terrible shock: Brückner had betrayed them.

There are conflicting reports as to what exactly happened that night. It seems most likely that the lorry developed a mechanical problem as it neared the airfield, and on the pretext of asking for help Brückner got out and went into a guard post. The next thing that those in the back of the truck heard was a German voice shouting at them to surrender. According to a pilot captured a few weeks later who had been at Derna that night, Brückner told the guards that he was driving a party of Englishmen in German uniforms who had come to blow up the airfield. The German officer was suspicious at first, but Brückner pressed him to act quickly.

'The lorry was immediately surrounded and the occupants forced to get out,' the pilot heard. 'A few seconds after the last one had got out there was an explosion inside the lorry and it was completely destroyed. A mêlée then developed.' In the ensuing firefight, Jordan managed to get away, but the only other survivor was one of the pair from the SIG, who was caught masquerading as a genuine German soldier the next day when he tried to get his wounds seen to at Derna's hospital.

Stunned as he was by Jordan's news, Buck had no time to dwell on it. He had to assume that the enemy would know about the rendezvous or at least be searching for it. They could wait no longer for the other Frenchmen to get back from Martuba: they would have to be left to make their own way home through the desert. Tiefenbrunner remembered how they piled hastily into the lorry and steered a course far to the south to avoid any pursuit. Even so, they were attacked once by German aircraft until they laid a swastika out on the ground and convinced them that they were their own troops.

Tiefenbrunner kept a gun trained on Essner all the way. No one trusted him any longer. When they made it to base, he was handed over to the Military Police and, said Tiefenbrunner, shot dead a few minutes later while attempting to escape. By contrast, the British learned, Brückner had been awarded a medal by the Germans.

Although they had managed to get into Martuba, none of the remaining French troopers succeeded in escaping. Buck had therefore lost fourteen of the fifteen saboteurs the SAS had entrusted to him, not to mention three of his own men (including Brückner). Another French section had penetrated the landing ground at Barce the same night but found that every aeroplane had been given a double guard of two sentries.

While Buck believed that this extra vigilance was due to other Commando activities in the area, there were rumours that the

Germans had been forewarned about the raids. Certainly, that story had reached the ears of a second pilot from Derna taken prisoner in early July. He said a warning had been issued on the night of the attack that a raiding party would arrive 'consisting of British troops in German uniform, driving a German truck'. Buck's superiors preferred to conclude that Brückner's treachery had not been premeditated. But from now on, it was thought, it would be wiser 'not to tell Buck anything in advance'.

The officer who received the memo containing that advice was Lieutenant Colonel John Haselden, the Rommel raid's guide, whose own life often depended on the Bedouin disguise he wore while in German-held territory. His daring reconnaissance work had already been recognised by the award of two MCs. Yet the mission he was ordered to lead in early September 1942 would be far bolder than anything he had attempted before.

The desert war was essentially one of logistics. Although Rommel had now advanced as far as Alamein in Egypt, he was still dependent for the bulk of his supplies on the Libyan ports of Benghazi and Tobruk, hundreds of miles to the rear. Simply transporting fuel to the front consumed a large part of the same stock. With the Eighth Army's new commander, Lieutenant General Bernard Montgomery, preparing to take the offensive, the planners began to look at how to weaken the resistance he would face. If the enemy's harbour facilities could be destroyed, they reasoned, 'this may well lead to the rapid defeat of Rommel by land forces'.

Despite the failure of the SIG at Derna, the SAS's success elsewhere that same evening now led to the development of a highly ambitious plan along similar lines to its operations, but on a much larger scale. On the night of 13 September, several raids would be mounted simultaneously against Rommel's supply centres, including Barce and Benghazi. The main attack – codenamed AGREEMENT – would fall on Tobruk.

Two groups would approach the port from the sea. Force A comprised 11 Battalion of the Royal Marines, together with some gunners, aboard the destroyers *Sikh* and *Zulu*. Force C was made up of a company of Argyll & Sutherland Highlanders, plus a platoon of the Royal Northumberland Fusiliers, embarked on about twenty MTBs. Their joint objective was to destroy the port installations, especially the fuel storage tanks, after landing on beaches either side of the harbour. The southern landing point, the destination for Force C, would be first cleared of its defences by a third contingent, Force B.

The latter would be led by Haselden and consist of about eighty men from the former Middle East Commando, now renamed 1st Special Service Regiment. Since being reformed after the demise of Layforce, these troops had continued to languish largely unused. A review by a senior officer had concluded that 'Commando Battalions as such have hardly been of any value to us in the Middle East, and I do not think they will be in future.' It was hardly surprising that he had also concluded that the squadrons which remained in the theatre were becoming despondent.

AGREEMENT was their chance to regain a sense of purpose, but the plan called for them to make use of guile rather than just brute strength. Adopting the same stratagem as had been tried at Derna, the commandos would enter Tobruk in the guise of PoWs guarded by Buck and the rest of the SIG. Once they had put out of action the guns overlooking the inlet of Umm es Sciausc, they were to signal by lamp to Force C to land there. The briefing made it clear that 'the critical phase of the Operation is therefore the initial success of Force B and the immediate passing of this information to all other Forces'.

The officer entrusted with this responsibility, and with acting as Force B's adjutant, was Lieutenant Tommy Langton of the SBS. Just before the war, he had twice rowed for Cambridge in the Boat Race. Captaining the victorious Oxford crew in 1937 had been his friend Jock Lewes, later of the SAS, and it was rumoured that the two shades of blue in the winged insignia designed by the latter had been inspired by the oarsmen's loyalties to their universities. Commando training had further enhanced Langton's fourteen-stone physique, and there was little spare shoulder room once he took his place beside the driver of the last of the trucks bound for Tobruk. Painted on its side was the swastika-and-date-palm emblem of the Afrika Korps, while Langton wore a German forage cap on his head – which stuck out of the roof of the cab.

A few minutes earlier he had shaken hands with David Lloyd Owen, the commander of the Long Range Desert Group (LRDG) patrol which had escorted them as far as a small oasis south of Tobruk. The LRDG were due to attack radar and radio posts in the city during the operation, and to cover Force C's withdrawal. For now, however, Langton 'felt no fear at this stage, just excitement and a deep sense of inevitability of the whole thing, which had been growing on me since we left Cairo'.

Behind him, the commandos hid their weapons under blankets and tried to look like prisoners. Among the raiders was twenty-one-year-old Bill Taylor from Chertsey, Surrey. On the voyage out to Egypt, his ship had stopped at the Cape of Good Hope, and as a greengrocer he had been amazed to see pineapples on sale for just a penny each. He had originally been posted to the Buffs, but had joined the ME Commando to get into action.

Excited by the prospect of that, he and his mates had posed for photographs at the oasis, and had been surprised to see a section arrive dressed in German uniform. Buck's men had stayed out of shot. Now, in the back of the truck, Taylor checked and rechecked the Bren he was carrying. 'We were all confident of success,' he said later, 'we couldn't believe it could go wrong.'

But whereas previous raids deep behind enemy lines had been made mainly by small groups, a triple force of more than seven hundred troops was now converging on Tobruk, and it would be reinforced by air and sea power, too. Undoubtedly its size would allow it to do more damage, yet the increased coordination required meant that more could go awry. And as the operation was only one of four major attacks that night, there was more potential for word of them to have leaked out in the bars and bazaars of Cairo.

The latest intelligence assessment of Tobruk's garrison was that it consisted of a single brigade of low-grade Italian troops and a sprinkling of German technical personnel. If that should be wrong, it would be much harder for a larger force to get away than it was for a handful of saboteurs.

Behind Langton, someone was singing, 'If you go down to Tobruk tonight, you're sure of a big surprise …' He told them to pipe down and to look more downcast. Then the lorry clambered up the escarpment, and slithered down onto the Tobruk road.

The going was slow, and Langton soon realised that the convoy was already half an hour behind schedule. He did not speak German and, like an amateur actor thrust into the big time, began to fret that he was not behaving as a German would. As they started to pass rows of tents and huts on the outskirts of the city, he wondered if the men inside had any idea of his real identity, and tortured himself with visions of an ambush: 'I prayed that Russell and Buck and the other German speakers would have nerves of iron to bluff us all through.'

While he contemplated this, a motorcycle drew alongside them in the darkness and Langton could feel himself being scrutinised. The man beside him began to finger the butt of his tommy-gun, but the German soldier seemed satisfied and accelerated away. One of the 'prisoners' stood up and relieved himself over the side of the truck. Langton felt sure that a real guard would have shouted abuse at him, yet did not dare open his mouth. But there did not seem to be any roadblocks to negotiate, and soon they were driving down the hill to the harbour.

Langton began to gain faith in the operation, and when Russell returned from asking for directions, and whispered in English that they had missed a turning, he saluted him with a grin and a '*Jawohl, mein Kapitan!*'

'Shut up, you bloody fool,' came the terse response.

The wail of sirens and the crump of explosions signalled that the RAF's diversionary bombing raid had begun. White haloes of light briefly outlined the nearby anti-aircraft positions. 'I was surprised to see how close some of the guns were to us,' Langton wrote later, 'and then I realised that these were some of the targets we were about to attack. I was seized with a feeling of unreality. In the gun flashes, I could see the men of the gun crews. They were soon to get the shock of their lives, and for many of them it would be the last.'

Nevertheless, losing their way meant that the mission was now running late. They should have arrived at the cove of Umm es Sciausc by the time that the aerial attack began, and Haselden was now under pressure to do everything quicker than foreseen. There was another problem as well. On the journey, the officer in charge of the commandos, Major Colin Campbell, had developed severe dysentery. He had insisted on carrying on, but it was clear that he might struggle to lead an assault on the guns.

Haselden told Langton to act as Campbell's deputy. When Langton pointed out that it was his job to signal to the waiting marines, he was told to leave his Aldis lamp behind with Flight Officer Aubrey Scott, who was to signal from the other side of the bay, and to come back for it later. While Haselden went west with half the group, including the SIG, Langton reluctantly headed east, towards some stone sangars on the skyline.

Almost at once a rifle shot whipped past them and they threw themselves to the ground. In the dark it was hard to tell where it might have come from, and Langton sent Lieutenant Mike Roberts to investigate. His section found and killed two Italians in a trench, but on the way back the soldier who had relieved himself under Langton's irate gaze forgot the password and was wounded by the trooper sent to guide them to Campbell.

There was no time to do more than make him comfortable before the others pushed on up a valley towards the coastal guns. Ahead they could see a hut festooned with radio masts, and Roberts cautiously shone his torch inside. 'There was a stack of radio equipment,' recalled Langton, 'and the deep breathing of sleeping men.' Without hesitation, the commandos tossed grenades through the door and crouched outside, waiting for the explosions. Bill Taylor, still cradling his Bren, was among those who rushed in to finish the job a few moments later. 'They were all shouting and screaming "*Mamma mia!*",' he remembered. 'That stopped.'

Already more than an hour had passed since they had set out and Langton was acutely aware that it was now long after the time when he should have been signalling to the MTBs. At HQ in Cairo, they would be wondering anxiously what had happened. Away to the west, Haselden's party had sent up their success rocket, and Langton decided that it would be best to let Roberts carry on towards the guns while he tried to find Scott and his lamp. He began to head down the wadi, only to pull up short. He had completely lost his bearings. Across his path was a line of tents, and he could see men moving about inside them.

'I turned and clambered hard up the side of the wadi,' he recalled. 'At the top, I paused panting. I was not as fit as I ought to be. All those days in the truck with no exercise, and I'm alone, with enemies all around me. Suddenly, I realised I was frightened.'

Unable to find his way, he began to panic, and wandered blindly through the dark. The sight of Scott's lamp shining out from the western side of the bay came as an almost miraculous relief, but he knew that it would take him at least half an hour to get across there and return with the light. The best thing to do, he decided, would be to use his torch instead to signal to the MTBs. He remembered how glad he had been on the Rommel raid when he had seen Haselden's beam shining out from the beach to *Torbay*.

Leaving his haversack and tommy-gun on top of a low cliff which dropped sheer into the bay, he lowered himself down gradually to the water's edge. There he began to flash the agreed signal, synchronising it with Scott's lamp on the other side. The guns had fallen silent. The bombers seemed to have done their work, and Langton imagined MTBs crowded with troops appearing at any moment. But he could see and hear nothing. Then, to his horror, as if at a single command, all the searchlights in Tobruk seemed to come on at once. The Gulf of Bomba was flooded with light. Machine-guns and pom-poms erupted in a mad cacophony of sound. Out to sea, an MTB whirled in an aimless circle, while the white wake of another was cut by coloured streams of tracer.

Langton waved his torch frantically, shouting at the boats to come in. Two did run into the inlet, but no more followed. Suddenly he was illuminated in the full glare of a searchlight, and instinctively ducked. Then he realised that he could not be seen so far away. 'So I stared back at it and shouted "Bastards!" to relieve my feelings. And still the tracer made long, coloured lines in the darkness.'

He now had a dilemma. One of his other tasks was to guide inland those soldiers who had landed in the bay, but how could he do that and continue to signal? He decided to compromise by wedging the torch into a cleft in the rocks while he made his way to the shore. Breathing hard, he heaved himself back up to the top of the cliff, at which point he found that his pack and his machine-gun were no longer there.

Langton remembered having heard a scuffling sound in the area earlier, and as he began to cross the beach someone shouted in French, '*Qui va là?*' 'I lifted my pistol and fired deliberately in the direction of the voice. Once . . . twice . . . There was a whimper in the darkness, rather like the sob of a bewildered child.' He had no time to locate the source and hurried down to the water. One of the two MTBs had grounded, and the other was trying to tow it off. It soon gave up and crept out to sea again. The darkness was lifting and Langton felt weary.

No one else was in sight. From Tobruk came the occasional stammer of a Spandau and sporadic sounds of rifle fire. Langton started to make his way over to a hut where he was due to rendezvous with Haselden, but as he approached he saw a row of heads peering at him from it in the half-light. Bullets began to fly over his head and sent him running back to the beach where the MTB now lay abandoned. While he searched it for food and water, he was joined by Campbell's sergeant, Evans, who had been in 8 Commando with Langton.

Evans told him that when they had reached the gun emplacements, these had been so well defended by concrete and barbed wire that it had proved impossible to break in. Soon afterwards, they had been surrounded, but he had managed to shoot his way out. As he was recounting this, David Russell appeared, with some equally dispiriting news about the fate of Haselden's party.

At first, all had gone well. After Russell killed a sentry, they had no trouble in taking over a hut occupied by Italians which Haselden earmarked as his HQ. There they waited for the return of Campbell's section and those who had gone to destroy the guns to the west. But then, with growing frustration, they watched as the MTBs failed to find Umm Es Sciausc. Next, about an hour before dawn, they were attacked by two platoons of infantry. Unknown to the commandos, some Italians stationed near the hut had got away soon after their arrival and raised the alarm. For a quarter of an hour Haselden's men held their ground, and then he decided they should make a run for it.

Several wounded commandos had been brought in earlier after being accidentally shot by their comrades. Haselden ordered that they be loaded onto one of the Afrika Korps lorries, but as this was being done he came running back to say that there was an ambush ahead. Gathering the remnants of the SIG around him, he led a charge straight at the enemy. Buck and Russell were beside him, as was Private Charles Hillman. 'It was too dark to see the enemy but they were about 10 yards away from us and firing at us,' Hillman later wrote. Although some of this desperate little band were soon wounded, Haselden fought on, allowing the lorry to hurtle straight through the Italians' position. 'We continued to hold back the enemy for another ten minutes until we ran out of ammunition,' Hillman recalled.

In the meantime, the truck had halted further down the road and those in it brought a Lewis gun into play from the flank. Calling for support, Haselden ran ahead of the others towards the Italians. This time he was hit, and as he lay on the ground a grenade exploded beside his head. The last stand of the SIG was over. There was little choice for the survivors but to get away as best they could, and together Russell and Hillman made for the shore.

It was now clear to all that the main raid had been a failure. A mile out to sea, one of the destroyers could be seen towing its stricken twin, but both were well within range of the coastal defences and white plumes of water soon bracketed them.

The commandos' situation was no less precarious. No reinforcements would be landing to help them. Langton debated what to do with another officer, Bill Barlow, who had been driving the truck with the wounded: 'We discussed the situation; it was a pretty grim one. We were more than 300 miles from our own lines, with nothing but desert and the enemy in between . . . "What's more," said Barlow gloomily, "they'll shoot us if they find us, which they're sure to do."'

Eight men and the three officers – Langton, Barlow and Russell – lay up in a wadi all that day. When dusk came, they divided into three parties and struck out for the wire perimeter that ran around Tobruk. Soon afterwards, Langton was challenged by Italian troops as he made his way up the side of a valley. As shots began to ring out, he called out in German to hold fire, which bought them enough time to get over the ridgeline. There they met Barlow's group again, just as they bumped into another enemy post. There was a flash of grenades, and Barlow vanished.

Langton pushed on as fast as he could, only to fall into a deep ditch. It was a tank trap on the perimeter. Expecting at any moment to be mown down by machine-guns, his party helped each other through the wire, and as dawn was breaking found two small caves in which to hide. 'We wedged ourselves as best as we could into these,' Langton recalled, 'and prepared to pass another anxious, uncomfortable day.'

He spent the time taking stock of the others. Besides Evans and Hillman, there were four men from the Royal Northumberland Fusiliers who had landed from an MTB – Corporal 'Tug' Wilson, a Manchester grocer in peacetime, Private Macdonald, and a pair of twins, the Leslie brothers. These last two were short, stocky miners, with Geordie accents that were almost impenetrable to Langton.

He was more intrigued by Hillman, who was limping badly after tearing both his boot and his foot on the wire. Langton gave him his handkerchief to bind it. He had a strong dread of being taken prisoner, but in Hillman it seemed more powerful yet. There was good reason for that: he now told Langton that he was a Jew, born in Vienna, who had been imprisoned there for demonstrating against the Nazis before he had left for Palestine in 1939. He was still only nineteen, yet had already served in France with the Pioneer Corps and in Eritrea with 51 Commando before joining the SIG. He had also taken part in the disastrous raid at Derna, and was worried that Brückner had passed his identity to the Germans.

'We changed his name there and then to Kennedy,' wrote Langton, who ordered everyone else to address Hillman as that until they were safe. But they had a long way to go if they were to escape. The British lines were almost as distant as Glasgow is from London, and for rations they had between the seven of them a tin and a bar of chocolate, four biscuits, a few pieces of cheese and not quite four pints of water.

They finished the food on the second day. Those that followed blurred into one another. The nights were spent walking, and then they rested in what shade they could find. Their thoughts were dominated by the sun, and by a longing for water. When he was so tired that hunger did not keep him awake, Langton dreamed of swimming pools.

On the third evening they broke into a farmer's hut and found some flour, beans and a jerry can. Langton recalled:

> There was a little liquid in the bottom and we poured it out into each other's cupped hands and drank it. It tasted foul, but at least it was fresh water. It was only when we tipped it up to get the last drop that the dead rat slid through the opening and fell with a sickening squelch into the sand. Had I had anything in my stomach I should have been sick on the spot.

His plan was to make for Wadi Qattara, further up the coast, which had been designated a pick-up point. However, when RAF aircraft began to bomb Tobruk on the fourth night after the raid, he was shocked to see how close they still were to the city, and realised that they would never get to the rendezvous in time. 'I had to instil in my companions a hope and determination which I hardly felt myself,' he reflected. He had just decided that they must at all costs hijack a vehicle or otherwise surrender when he heard a dog barking. They had reached an Arab village. It was no more than a circle of tents, but their luck had changed.

Hillman spoke Arabic, and soon the Senussi were offering them tea and biscuits. 'We set upon it like animals, quite unashamedly, and could literally feel the strength returning to our bodies,' wrote Langton afterwards. For the next few days they were passed from encampment to encampment, and even though the locals were also short of food they would share eggs or bread with them.

They still had to be careful. Langton spent one morning hiding in the scrub while twenty-five yards away a party of German officers in a staff car argued over which direction to take. And when they finally reached Wadi Qattara, they found its beach patrolled by Italians. Langton knew, however, that Montgomery's offensive was to begin soon, and if they could avoid capture for long enough there was a chance that the British spearhead would reach them.

Yet the mental strain of their ordeal had begun to show, and the group had started to bicker and snap at each other. They were also hampered by Hillman's lameness. Langton needed to find somewhere they could stay for a while, and it was the Arabs who told them about two other soldiers who were hiding near by. One was a fellow commando, Ronald Watler, who told them he had become separated from Russell as they tried to get out of Tobruk. The other was a corporal in the Garwhal Rifles, Chattah Singh Rowat, who had already escaped from two PoW camps.

For the next month, the nine men lived in caves above a wadi that Singh Rowat had found. They were fed by the neighbouring Arabs. The only trouble occurred when Watler interrupted one of the locals while he was enjoying the affections of one of his wives, after which he was forbidden to return to the village. Hillman's foot soon healed, but as the rainy season began Evans and the Leslies fell ill with dysentery and had to be left by the main road for the

Germans to find. Meanwhile, Macdonald's continuous moaning had got them all down, and they were glad when he too disappeared, having decided to give himself up.

Langton became frustrated that the others seemed so dependent on him, but he felt responsible for Hillman in particular. At the end of October, unable to find out whether the Eighth Army was advancing, he decided it was time to leave. Drawing on all the resolve he had shown as an oarsman, he followed the stars southwards. In his wake, he dragged Hillman, Watler and Wilson, Singh Rowat having preferred to remain in the wadi. On 28 October, they crossed the wire into Egypt, and two weeks later finally came across British troops. The four men had marched for nineteen days, and hundreds of miles, on three tins of bully beef, a few scraps of goat meat and ten bottles of water.

As Langton recovered from his ordeal in a hospital bed, news of other survivors filtered through to him. David Russell had made an equally epic trek to safety, largely on his own. He had lost his compass getting out of Tobruk, and one night when the stars had been covered by cloud he had wandered off course. As dawn broke, he had found himself in the midst of two battalions of Italian troops, but as they were more interested in their battle drill than in him he was able to walk right through their ranks undetected. He too had had much help from the Arabs, and was eventually picked up by British armoured cars as they neared Benghazi in mid-November.

Montgomery's victory a few weeks earlier at El Alamein, and the subsequent German retreat, had come too late for the remainder of the Tobruk raiders. The other members of the SIG on the operation had been killed or taken prisoner, with Buck among the latter. At least one of his Jewish troopers was made to dig his own grave and subjected to a mock-execution.

Major Campbell, who had led the detachment from the Special Service Regiment, was badly wounded during the assault on the coastal guns. Bill Taylor, like most of the other commandos, was captured by a German patrol as he tried to get out of Tobruk. He would spend the rest of the war in a PoW camp.

Casualties during the main attack had been equally severe. Heavy seas had made it impossible for folboteers to mark the beach where Force A was due to land. As a result, they had come ashore much further west, where rocks had holed many of the marines' boats. Some had succeeded in getting inland, but there they had encountered much stiffer resistance than predicted. The Italian garrison had recently been strengthened by the addition of several thousand German troops as well as some formidable artillery batteries. Only 60 of the 360 marines deployed returned to Alexandria. The Royal Navy also lost several hundred of its men, together with *Sikh*, *Zulu* and the cruiser *Coventry*. All three warships were sunk by the Luftwaffe.

The other raids that night by the special forces had fared no better. The LRDG had got into Tobruk, but when Lloyd Owen received no word from Haselden he was forced to withdraw. Another of their patrols did destroy more than thirty aircraft at Barce, but an attempt to seize the Jalo Oasis was easily rebuffed. Meanwhile, at Benghazi, the SAS suffered one of their worst reverses of the war after being spotted en route, and then harassed mercilessly from the air as they tried to escape through the desert.

Although credible proof was never forthcoming, David Stirling suspected for years that the defenders had had advance warning of all four attacks. Certainly, security had been lax. 'Many too many were in on the operation from the start,' concluded one review of AGREEMENT, 'while certain officers who should have been told were not so informed.'

There had been more fundamental failings as well. Few of the lessons of Dieppe seemed to have been learned, notably the need to soften up defences with heavier air and naval bombardment than had taken place. Nor had the MTBs carrying Force C possessed any means of communicating by radio with Haselden's troops. Above all, the plan had been overly ambitious. Too many risks had been run for too little potential gain. It would have been almost impossible to have prevented the Germans from making use of Tobruk's harbour for a significant length of time and, as it proved, the inability to do so had had no adverse effect on the outcome of Alamein anyway.

That was perhaps little consolation to those who had taken part in the raid. Once more, too much had been asked of commandos, and the consequences prompted a major reorganisation of them by Cairo. The Special Service Regiment was disbanded and many of its personnel transferred to an expanded SAS. The handful of survivors from the SIG – including Tiefenbrunner and Hillman – went with them.

Following its heavy losses in Sicily and on ANGLO, Roger Courtney's Special Boat Section now lost its last vestiges of independent existence, at least in the Mediterranean, as it too was absorbed by the SAS. However, Stirling's capture by the Germans a few weeks later, at the start of 1943, prompted another redistribution of forces. His successor, Paddy Mayne, took the newly created Special Raiding Squadron west towards Tunis, while George Jellicoe based his Special Boat Squadron in the Lebanon.

Two of the three detachments of Jellicoe's unit would take their names from those of Courtney's veterans. David Sutherland commanded 'S' Detachment, while 'L' was put under Tommy Langton. The third – 'M' – would be led by Fitzroy Maclean. Yet, while the new SBS shared many of the characteristics, and much of the outlook, of its earlier namesake, its future lay in the wider amphibious raiding role envisaged by Stirling. The defeat of Rommel in North Africa had laid the Axis's southern flank open to invasion. The war was changing, and with it the task facing the commandos.

12

JV AND FRANKTON

The fading of Courtney's vision of the SBS as canoe-borne saboteurs was accompanied by twin ironies. The first was that, just as his ideas seemed to have been superseded, their viability was proved not once but twice in audacious operations. The second was that, instead of this being demonstrated by his men, it was done so by others.

For even in the Commandos, Courtney was not the only proponent of folbot raiding. Around the time he had established the SBS, a group of sappers in 6 Commando had set up a section on the same lines, known as 101 Troop. They, too, had seen the potential to attack shipping and carry out reconnaissance of coastal defences from the sea. Like Courtney, they spent months honing their techniques in the west of Scotland. But while his attachment to Layforce gave him an early chance of action, they languished in Britain.

Captain Gerald Montanaro, from a Maltese military family, had taken over the Troop in late 1940 after its original leader, John Woollett, was badly injured in a fall on a night exercise. Montanaro pushed them harder still, and was proud of their record time for a famous thirty-six-mile march over the hills first made by the Marquess of Montrose's army three hundred years before. But more significant opportunities to impress were rare. No. 101 was given a few beach recces to do, but in November 1941 Montanaro's second-in-command, Lieutenant Keith Smith, did not return from one such mission near Calais. Smith was a large man, whose bulk made it hard for him to launch canoes in surf, and Montanaro had agreed to his going against his better judgement.

Perhaps worried that the unit might now be disbanded unless it showed its worth, in early 1942 Montanaro proposed a new scheme directly to Mountbatten. When the wheels at COHQ failed to turn fast enough, he ignored protocol and urged his case on Vice-Admiral Bertram Ramsay, then in charge of operations at Dover. This earned him a ticking-off from Mountbatten, but such boldness was typical of the twenty-five-year-old Montanaro. His diaries chronicle not only an almost endless string of hangovers but also an enviable series of female conquests. He had originally planned to add to both tallies at a dance in Folkestone on the night of 11 April 1942, but a few days beforehand he was summoned to the Admiralty. Operation JV had been approved.

Its targets were to be two large tankers, thought to be filled with copper ore, which had been photographed lying in the outer harbour at Boulogne. Montanaro's plan of attack was straightforward but daring. A motor launch would drop a pair of canoes three miles out. These would enter the port at night, and then escape back into the Channel after fixing magnetic limpet mines to the ships. Part of the justification for the raid was to test the mines, which had been modified after proving highly unreliable in trials. From a batch of six given to the Troop, three had gone off at intervals of up to four hours' difference. The others had failed entirely.

'A great deal of the fun of the thing', Montanaro wrote later of JV, 'was the fact that I had the pleasure of designing and working up all the technical gear.' His Royal Engineers training proved invaluable in devising ingenious camouflage for both the boats and their crew. The former consisted of longitudinal flaps which could be rapidly flicked over, changing the canoe's colour from black to white for better concealment under lights. The paddlers themselves wore what he dubbed 'octopus suits', which could be turned inside out in five seconds to match the hull. Underneath, they had on down-filled jackets to keep them warm and provide buoyancy in case of capsizing.

While Montanaro attended a final briefing, his crewman, Trooper Fred Preece, boarded *ML 102* at Dover with the second team, Sergeant Weatherall and Guardsman Sidlow. Each canoe would carry eight limpets, and they carefully corrected the compasses to compensate for the metal's influence.

Then Montanaro returned, bearing bad news: it had been decided that it would be too risky to send in both boats. As Weatherall and Sidlow were stood down, the former swore angrily. Montanaro tried to reassure him that he had done nothing wrong. But now he and Preece were on their own.

It was a calm, bright night, and even several miles away enemy craft could be seen entering the harbour. Montanaro decided to delay their launch for a few minutes and used the time to remove the safety pins from the mines' fuses. Then they set off, the canoe rising and falling on the phosphorescent sea.

At first they found it hard going against the tide, despite the moderate winds, but by 0130 they were nearing Boulogne. Its approaches were guarded by a pair of forts, and they passed cautiously between the northernmost of these and an E-boat – the German equivalent of an MTB – in full view of each. The breeze had now begun to freshen, making progress more difficult since it carried the sound of their paddling further. Lying almost prone, they drifted past the second fort, hardly daring to make a stroke. Light was streaming from an open doorway and a party was clearly in full swing indoors. Then Montanaro's heart almost stopped. There was a splash next to the boat and freezing water shot over him. It took him a moment to realise that the cause was a drunken German lobbing beer bottles into the darkness. The night still enveloped them, however, and against the background of the breakwater they were almost invisible.

With a roar of their engines, three more E-boats emerged from the inner harbour on patrol. Their wakes rocked the canoe violently, but the commandos remained unseen and made for the shadow cast by the port wall. Still bent double, Montanaro scanned the berths with night glasses looking for the target, but suddenly the boat came to a shuddering stop.

Its bow had run up about five feet onto a concrete ledge covered by just a few inches of water. They were stuck fast. In frantic silence, they tried to bump backwards, but in doing so ricocheted off three rocks in succession. Aghast, Montanaro saw that the hull had been punctured and was beginning to leak. Thinking quickly, he told Preece to stuff his woollen cap into the hole. Meanwhile, he screwed down the fuses on the mines, so starting their chemical timers. Whatever happened, they were going in for the attack.

Easing out into the open, they paddled until they were under the tanker's stern. This was noticeably swept down and only offered them cover to port. On the starboard side they would be illuminated by the lighthouse on the breakwater just a few hundred feet away. And there was another problem. The mines were designed to be attached below the waterline with an extending rod, but the curvature of the hull made the latter useless. Montanaro would have to set them by hand.

While Preece kept the canoe in place, Montanaro scraped away as many barnacles as he could before fixing the first mine thirty inches under the waterline. Then they moved steadily along the ship, clamping on another three. Each would blow a hole six feet wide in the hull. Montanaro was conscious that the slightest noise might give them away, but twice the magnets took hold with a resounding clang. No watchmen seemed to be about, however, and on reaching the bow the pair began to slide astern down the starboard side – only to find themselves inside the hull itself. They had backed through a large tear in it which Montanaro assumed must have been caused by a torpedo.

As they paddled about in one of the ship's tanks for a few moments, Montanaro could not resist singing quietly to himself. He sneaked a glance under the canvas strip concealing his wristwatch. The luminous hands pointed to 0230. It was time to be going.

With delicate precision, he placed a mine against the side of the engine room, but as they moved away he heard it slide down the hull and feared it had fallen off. There was no time to check. Montanaro had spotted a flak ship close by and, all too aware how conspicuous they were on this side of the ship, decided that they had tempted fate for long enough. They flattened themselves over the canoe and, using just a single blade, once more followed the wall before striking out across the harbour.

Montanaro had intended to head for a gap by the southern fort, but when they got near it he could see that the surf was too strong for safety. There was no option but to go all the way past the northern fort again, even though this would put them still further behind schedule for their rendezvous with the launch. Yard by yard they crept towards the entrance, and then with the mole behind them began to paddle hard. Not only were they late, but there were now four inches of water in the boat.

They took turns at bailing it out with a cigarette tin, all the while swinging the canoe round to take up their original bearing from the southern fort. The craft began to yaw heavily, pushed by a following wind across the tide, and as the minutes passed it became more and more awkward to control. By 0320, they were back on track, but behind them they saw lights coming on and heard engines starting up. Fearing that they were about to be pursued, they redoubled their rhythm. The effort kept the creeping cold at bay a little better, but there was no avoiding the fact that they were sinking. Montanaro shifted their gear from bow to stern so as to bring the main weight of water into the rear of the canoe, where he soaked it up with their cap comforters. Between strokes, he squeezed out icy handfuls of water over the side.

At 0355, the noise of a motor reached them. Even though they were near the rendezvous, Montanaro had no way of knowing for sure if it was the launch. Yet their situation was now so desperate that he signalled in any case with his infra-red torch. No reply came, but the vessel continued to draw close. They stopped rowing and readied their weapons for a fight. Then, with relief, they saw that it was *ML 102*.

The two commandos were so tired and numbed that they had to be hoisted aboard. Montanaro estimated that in another fifteen minutes the canoe would have foundered. As it was, they had covered more than eighteen nautical miles without being detected. Although the charges did not explode until six hours later than planned, aerial reconnaissance the following day showed a patch of oil half a mile wide around the tanker, and her funnel blown off. The German war machine had been denied more than five thousand tons of copper.

Mountbatten was quick to congratulate Montanaro on his 'gallant efforts'. His earlier impudence forgiven, he was awarded the DSO. Preece received the DCM. The success of JV vindicated the supporters of such raids and, with Mountbatten declaring that others should follow, Montanaro had high hopes of 101 Troop seeing more action. Instead, within six months he would be sidelined.

Shortly after the Boulogne operation, Montanaro's section was merged with the newly formed 2 SBS. He became its chief instructor, and Courtney for a time thought of him as his natural successor. The regard was not, however, mutual. Montanaro viewed Jumbo as being 'very dithery and wild. He is a dangerously weak commander.' By June, he had sounded out SOE with a view to training saboteurs in Australia. Not long afterwards, he disappeared without warning from the SBS's base at Hillhead, on the Solent.

When he found out the reason for this, Courtney realised that he faced a larger problem yet. 'We have discovered what appears to be a planned attempt of certain elements in the Royal Navy to oust Commando personnel from any participation in Naval affairs,' he wrote to Laycock. There had, he complained, been a campaign against the SBS, and against him personally, for some time. This had culminated in all thirty-six of their folbots being taken from them. These, and Montanaro, had been handed instead to the newly established Combined Operations Pilotage Parties (COPP). This was the cover name for the beach reconnaissance teams which Courtney's companion from Rhodes, Nigel Willmott, had finally persuaded the planners were needed. The context for this was the coming invasion of Sicily, and it was galling for the SBS, who regarded beach reconnaissance as their specialism, to be told to train Willmott's officers to carry it out instead.

2 SBS would find a role in the Mediterranean in the autumn of 1942. Led by Courtney's younger brother Gruff, they would ferry the American general Mark Clark to secret meetings with senior Vichy French officers in Algeria before the TORCH landings in November. But the spat with the Navy had shown that others were more adept than Jumbo at military politics, and eventually his unwillingness to court his superiors would cost both him and his unit.

Long before then, Montanaro had moved on. Having seen that there was little prospect of realising his ambitions at Hillhead, the sapper captain had by the end of 1942 also been commissioned by the Navy as a lieutenant commander so that he could lead its Mobile Flotation Unit. He spent the rest of the war testing experimental amphibious craft, none of which got beyond the prototype stage.

The posting therefore proved to be a waste of his powers of aggressive leadership. There still remained scope, however, for someone else blessed with similar qualities to show what could be achieved by canoes – and what the cost might be.

Even as a boy, George Hasler would take tiny boats out to sea and disappear for days on end. He was still doing so when he had grown the vast moustache that led his fellow Royal Marine officers to call him 'Blondie'. In 1935, he sailed a twelve-foot dinghy single-handed from Plymouth to Portsmouth and back. Few others would have attempted such a voyage without a bigger ship and some crew. But Hasler's was a thoroughly original mind, and one not easily deflected from its purpose.

In 1941, he began to bombard the Admiralty with proposals for underwater attacks to be made by specially trained swimmers. These were rejected as outlandish, but Hasler knew that breathing apparatus was becoming more sophisticated, and following a series of successful operations by Italian frogmen against British warships in the Mediterranean he was invited to develop his ideas on naval warfare.

At first, he put his energies into creating an exploding motor boat which could be dropped by parachute. Courtney was aware of his work and thought him too obsessed by technology. Naturally, Hasler regarded folbots as too crude, but he changed his mind after Montanaro demonstrated their potential on JV.

He also grasped that those used by the SBS could be improved, not least to make them more portable by submarine. Working with Fred Goatley, designer of the eponymous collapsible boat, he perfected a more robust canoe which they named the Cockle. Its most notable feature was a hinged strut which folded to reduce the height of the boat's frame to just six inches, enabling it to be passed more easily through the hatch of a submarine.

Now he just needed some canoeists to prove how well it worked, and by mid-1942 Combined Operations had its third such unit. Its cover name – the Royal Marines Boom Patrol Detachment – implied that its role was harbour defence, but Hasler's criteria for selecting his men revealed his belligerent intent. The top two were 'eager to engage the enemy' and 'indifferent to their personal safety'; next to last was 'able to swim'.

One of his first recruits was a Cockney, Marine Bill Sparks. His father had been in the Navy before becoming a telephone engineer with the Post Office, and his grandfather had been in the Marines, too. Bill was apprenticed to a shoemaker on leaving school at sixteen, but when war broke out he signed up with the Corps for twelve years. He was aboard the battleship *Renown* during the hunt for the *Bismarck*, but what brought the conflict home to him was the death of his brother, the victim of a U-boat attack.

After returning late from leave because he had been drowning his sorrows, Bill was confined to barracks. While there, he saw Hasler's call for volunteers. 'Special service gave me the chance of revenge,' he later confided.

The Marines were by now beginning to come under the Commando umbrella, and when the detachment assembled at Southsea they were each told to find their own lodgings. Hasler's training methods also tested their initiative, but Sparks much preferred his system to normal soldiering. 'We used to do exercises where we were dropped from somewhere by lorry in the country and told to make our own way back,' he recalled. 'We had no money in our pockets, and we had to be sure to evade capture by the police.'

He took pride in his ability to get in and out of aerodromes unseen, but Hasler's ways of keeping them fit were less fun. 'He would run us up and down the beach, barefooted on the pebbles, and then finish with a swim in the sea. That didn't go down too well at all.' Even so, Sparks remembered, 'morale was terrific. The men worked very, very closely together.' No one wanted to be returned to their unit.

Hardly any of them had prior experience of boats, let alone canoes. Hasler's second-in-command, Jock Stewart, spoke later of how he was used as 'a guineapig': if he could learn how to do something, so could the others, reasoned Hasler. Soon they were proficient at navigating by compass, even in the dark. 'There's a terrific lot to be learned,' reminisced Sparks. 'You have to know the strength of the tide, the strength of the wind. All these can throw you off, and a few degrees out at sea can put you miles from your target.'

In mid-November 1942, Hasler staged the first major examination of their progress. The aim of Exercise BLANKET was for six two-man canoes to travel unobserved for seventy miles from Margate, on the north Kent coast, to the port of London. The authorities had been warned to patrol the banks of the Medway and the Thames, and they proved to be vigilant. Every canoe was challenged at least twice. One pair was even shot at by the Home Guard. Several times the formation lost touch overnight or during bad weather. Just a single crew made it to within two miles of the docks – Hasler and Sparks. All the others failed due to navigation errors or lack of stamina. The main lesson, noted Hasler, was that six canoes were too many for such an operation.

A week later, the same crews found themselves on the chilly waters of the Clyde, making dummy attacks with limpets against a Dutch minesweeper by day and night. 'The chaps didn't know what was going on,' Stewart recollected, 'they thought they were on advanced training.' But in fact Sparks and the others had realised that something was up: 'We were all convinced that we were going after the *Tirpitz*.' Hasler's actual plan was no less ambitious.

On the Sunday evening, there was a party. 'A Polish submarine had come in and they laced our drinks,' admitted Stewart. 'I passed out and had to be put to bed.' At breakfast he met Hasler, who was clearly feeling just as wretched. Still nursing their hangovers, the rest of the section embarked later that morning on the submarine *Tuna*. Only when they were aboard did Hasler tell them that, once he had briefed them, they would be sailing for France.

For some time, the Ministry of Economic Warfare – which oversaw SOE – had been growing anxious about Germany's success in securing key raw materials from the Far East. The flow of metals such as tin and tungsten, as well as animal and vegetable oils, was being maintained by a fleet of blockade runners, based at Bordeaux, which were also thought to be carrying weapons technology to Japan. In the year since July 1941, 25,000 tons of rubber had arrived at the French port – enough to meet the entire demands of the German military.

The Minister, Lord Selborne, explained to Combined Operations that the loss of just a little of that capacity might make a great difference. The Germans only had a small number of ships which could make the trip to the Orient without needing to refuel en route. If these were sunk, their replacements would have to bunker in Africa or South America, whose harbours increasingly were closed to them. Mines and submarines had failed to halt the trade, and aerial bombardment was too haphazard. Sabotage was now the only option.

The principal problem that confronted COHQ was Bordeaux's location. The city lies far up the River Garonne, more than seventy miles from the sea. Getting there would be difficult enough, getting away harder still. Yet Hasler was confident that his men could do so in their Cockles, and in mid-October Mountbatten approved his scheme, codenamed FRANKTON. The only change he made was to double the size of the mission to six canoes. He also forbade Hasler from taking part in it; his experience was too valuable to risk losing.

Hasler would have none of it. He argued that it would be hard for any commander to retain his men's respect if he did not participate in the unit's first operation. Moreover, FRANKTON would be unusually demanding. The plan called for the crews to hide by day and paddle up the river for four nights when the moon was dark. Navigation and seamanship would be crucial to their chances of success. Yet, Hasler pointed out, until a few months earlier none of the others had so much as rowed a boat. Having made his own name as a daring – even reckless – destroyer captain, Mountbatten admired those with a similar outlook. Hasler could go.

Lieutenant Richard Raikes, *Tuna*'s skipper, was contemplating the broad waters of the Gironde estuary. At least the sea was as calm as a millpond, whereas a storm the night before had forced the postponement of the operation by twenty-four hours. But this evening visibility was too clear for comfort. Urged on by Raikes, the deck hands began to pass up the Cockles from below.

The journey from the Clyde had taken a week and the passage had been rough. For the first three days, all of the marines had been seasick, until Hasler had told them that it was only a question of mind over matter and that the next man to succumb would lose his place on the mission. To Bill Sparks's surprise, the threat worked. The men found other ways to occupy their time, including celebrating young Bobby Ewart's twenty-first birthday.

A Glasgow boy, he had fallen for a girl from Southsea while stationed there. Heather Powell was only sixteen. They had all been instructed to leave letters for their loved ones in case they did not return, so Bobby wrote to her. 'You are young yet for this sort of thing,' he explained, 'but I had to do it, so please don't worry and upset yourself about me. With your picture in front of me, I feel confident that I shall pull through and get back to you some day ... I pray that God will spare me and save you from this misery, so hoping for a speedy reunion ... Chin up, Sweetheart.'

James Conway, who was twenty, wrote in similar terms to his mother and sister. 'I know it looks foolish to you that I had to do this but I've enjoyed it and I know that what we have done helps to end the mess we are in and make a decent and better world ... Don't think of this as a suicide note, but think of it just as I want you to.'

When Hasler told his team that the waiting was over, they were delighted. But not all of them would be going on the operation. One of the Cockles, *Cachalot*, was holed as it was being brought up from below decks. There was no way that its two canoeists could carry on. The other ten sat in their boats on *Tuna*'s casing as she prepared to submerge. His face and moustache obscured by camouflage paint, Hasler cheerily thanked Raikes for all that he had done. Then, as if for luck, he suggested that they should meet at the Savoy restaurant in four months' time, on 1 April.

At 2020 on 7 December, Raikes saluted 'a magnificent bunch of black-faced villains' as they melted like wraiths into the night. From now on, they would have to live every moment with the fear of being seen again.

Hasler's most valuable attribute was his confidence in himself. He had overcome the handicap of growing up without a father (his had gone down with a troopship in 1917) and had developed supreme powers of endurance. But sometimes a born leader can expect too much of those he hopes to inspire, and even before the Cockles reached the coast they ran into trouble.

As they approached the entrance to the estuary, the largest in France, Hasler received what he later described as 'an unpleasant surprise'. From ahead came the sound of broken water. He had seen no indication of this on the charts, but it could only be a tidal race – a huge wave which swept periodically down the river. None of the others had any experience of such a phenomenon. Calling them around his canoe, Hasler said that there was no avoiding the race, but if they kept the bows of the boat pointed ahead it would hold its course. 'Being with the Major,' Sparks recalled, 'we went through first, and I shall never forget those tidal races. They were terrific. The waves looked as if they were about 12 ft high, us being in canoes, and they tossed us all over the show. And then, just as quick as it started, we were through.' As soon as they had got clear, Hasler swung round to watch the rest emerge. One by one they did so, until it became apparent that the fifth Cockle was missing. Hasler turned back into the race to search for it, but of *Coalfish*, and Bobby Ewart, there was no sign.

The remaining canoes had still to enter the mouth of the river when they were struck by a second and still heavier wall of water. This time *Conger* capsized, tipping Marine David Moffatt and Corporal George Sheard into the icy Atlantic. It proved impossible to bale out the flooded boat and eventually the others used their knives to scuttle it.

While Moffatt clung to the stern of *Catfish*, Hasler and Sparks towed him through a third race, while Lieutenant John MacKinnon and Marine Conway did the same for Sheard. But then the tide began to turn. There was a real danger that all of them could be swept back into the ocean unless they reached the shelter of the river. The two swimmers would have to be abandoned. If they were carried any further, Hasler judged, everyone's life would be in jeopardy. The group was still one and a half miles offshore, but he hoped that the strong current would carry the pair inland.

As their fingers let go of the hulls and the men drifted away, he wished each of them luck. Each had on a life-jacket, and there was certainly a chance that they would make it. Yet, as Hasler afterwards admitted, he had noticed that they were already very cold and unable to swim properly. It had not been an easy decision to take, but in military terms it had been simple: the mission came first.

Moffatt and Sheard's predicament had brought the remaining three boats closer to shore than intended. As they entered the estuary, Hasler realised that the strength of the tide would force them to pass between the mole at Le Verdon and three patrol boats moored about three-quarters of a mile from it. These were sweeping the sea with searchlights, and to lessen the chances of being seen the canoes went one at a time through the gap.

For an instant, Sparks saw a sentry on the mole silhouetted in the beam, but he and Hasler waited until the light had wandered away before darting through. The crew of *Crayfish* followed them, yet there was no trace of MacKinnon and Conway in *Cuttlefish*. Hasler was mystified. The night air was so still that he would have heard any shouts of alarm. Just as during the exercise on the Thames, the formation had become separated in the darkness. A few hours ago, six Cockles had been preparing to go into action. Now there were only two left.

As daylight was breaking, the four men came ashore on a sandy promontory and hauled their boats into the scrub that flourished above the high water mark. They had covered more than twenty miles since leaving *Tuna*. It was soon clear, however, that they had chosen to hide in a spot where fishermen came to meet their families for breakfast. Some began to light a fire just a few feet away and the marines were spotted. Deciding that the best course was to reveal that they were British, Hasler appealed to the locals not to betray their presence.

'All that day, of course, we were on tenterhooks,' Sparks remembered, 'hoping that no one – even a child – would mention a word and the Germans would pick it up. But thankfully they kept quiet.' It was low water when they set off again shortly before midnight, forcing them to drag the canoes and their stores nearly three-quarters of a mile over sandy mud, but from then on they made good progress.

The river was almost five miles wide at this point, and there was little likelihood of their being seen solely by starlight. They spent the next day lying up, disturbed only as they launched their boats that evening by a Frenchman from a nearby farm. 'He was rather upset when we declined to go up to his house for a drink,' remarked Hasler afterwards.

Not long before daybreak on 10 December, they landed on a

small island which seemed a suitable place to camp. Hasler jumped out of his boat to make a quick reconnaissance first, only to come running back a minute later and hastily shove off. They had grounded yards from a German anti-aircraft position. It was now getting dangerously light, and they could not chance going much further. They pulled in at the other end of the islet, dragged the boats into a marshy field, and then lay under the camouflage nets they draped over them. Sparks recalled:

> We were so close to the ack-ack site that we could hear the Germans talking, laughing and singing. At one time, two Germans even walked past us. There was a herd of cows in the field, and as cows do they just stood in a big circle around us. When the Germans came along, they stopped and looked at the cows. We were dead sure this was going to be our lot.
>
> We were armed with silent Stens, and naturally these were pointed at the two Germans. Had they come too close, then we would have killed them. But, thankfully, they had a little laugh and walked away.

It rained all day, and Sparks was glad when night fell and they were finally able to get out of the canoe's cramped cockpit.

Hasler had meant to make the attack that evening, but they were still not close enough to Bordeaux for them to be able to withdraw afterwards in darkness. He therefore decided to push on again and rest up for the last time when within sight of their target. Accordingly, they spent the 11th hidden in some reeds, from where they could watch the traffic on the river – and see two large ships being unloaded directly across from them. During the day, they rearranged their equipment so that all their escape kit was to hand. At dusk, they fused the limpets.

By then, the strain was beginning to tell on their nerves. 'We were really thankful when darkness came again,' Sparks confessed, 'because this was going to be the night when it was all going to be over – one way or the other.' Hasler had hoped for rain or mist, but there was a clear sky and a flat calm on the water at twilight, and he waited until the moon had set at 2130 before setting off. *Catfish* would head along the western bank, while the crew of *Crayfish* – Corporal Bert Laver and Marine Bill Mills – would take the other. 'We shook hands with them, and wished them good luck,' remembered Sparks. 'When we parted company, I felt very, very lonely.'

It took them less than an hour to gain the main basin of the harbour. In the glare of the lights, they could see several large ships tied up, and decided to work their way backwards from the last so as to make their escape easier. They placed three limpets on a seven-thousand-ton cargo vessel, and then rowed down to a *Sperrbrecher*, a merchant ship which had been converted into a convoy minesweeper. While Hasler fixed another charge onto his telescopic rod, Sparks clamped a magnet to the hull to hold them in position. At that moment a torch lit him up like a burglar caught red-handed. 'Suddenly we were bathed in light. There was a sentry on the upper deck. We hadn't seen him, but he'd watched us come in.' Staying stock still, they let the current push them along the side of the ship. Seemingly unable to decide if the camouflaged canoe was simply a piece of driftwood, the watchman followed them with his torch until they floated under the bows and disappeared from view. For the next five minutes they waited there as the sentry paced the deck in his hobnailed boots. Finally, they heard him turn and slowly walk away. 'He must have thought that we were flotsam,' believed Sparks, 'because he never challenged us.'

With their hearts still racing, they resumed their course downstream. The next target was another cargo ship, besides which was anchored a small tanker. To save time, they decided to pass between the two vessels. It was almost a fatal error. The current began to push the ships together and the Cockle was held fast. 'We found we were trapped. We could hear the plywood top of the canoe creaking and groaning,' recalled Sparks. 'I thought: "My God, I'm going to be crushed!" Thankfully, the tide turned and the ships opened enough for us to push ourselves out.'

Having set their three remaining limpets, it was time to be off.

They headed again for the river, paddling as hard as they could for the next quarter of an hour. When they paused for breath, they heard splashing ahead and saw it was Laver and Mills in *Crayfish*. They had also got as far as the docks, but after finding no suitable targets they had come back to attack the two large ships which had moored opposite their hiding-place during the day.

Carried by the ebb tide, both crews strove to get as far away as possible from Bordeaux. Not long before dawn, they arrived at an island off Blaye, about twenty miles away, and parted once more. Hasler and Sparks slit *Catfish*'s buoyancy bag and pushed her under water. To Sparks's dismay, Hasler also made him bury the Sten, although he allowed him to keep his Colt and knife.

They had travelled more than ninety miles unseen. Now all they had to do was get across much of southern France, and then over the Pyrenees.

Hasler's planning of the operation had been meticulous. By contrast, that for the escape seemed to leave everything to chance. The marines were still in uniform, so they would have to obtain a change of clothes. Then they would need help to reach Ruffec, more than a hundred miles away, from where they had been told they could be smuggled into Spain. Of the four, only Hasler spoke French. They were entirely in the hands of the Resistance – if they could find them.

At first light, Hasler went into a farmhouse and returned with dungarees, jackets and berets for himself and Sparks. For the next week they walked north-eastwards, scavenging food and shelter as they could. Once they tried to sleep in a cowshed, but were seen by the farmer. He invited them in, only to learn that someone else had tipped off the Germans that they were there. The two men left hastily through a window. Seeing half a dozen policemen coming along the track behind the shed, they spent the night hiding under a hedge in the biting December rain.

When they got to Ruffec, they searched for the address where the Resistance were to contact them – the Café de Paris. Unable to find this, however, and worried that the German troops on the streets would notice that he and Sparks were strangers, Hasler went into another café. There he attracted attention at once by being unable to produce the necessary coupon for the meal he ordered: no one had briefed them that rationing was now in force in France. In the end, he had to resort to writing a note to the waitress admitting that they were commandos, and asking her to pass it to the Resistance.

After making contact, the Resistance brought them to a safe house in Lyon. For the next few weeks, they were looked after by an Englishwoman, Mary Lindell, who was married to a French aristocrat. As well as insisting that Hasler shave off his prized moustache, she also revealed why he had been turned away so often when he had asked the country people for help: he spoke French with what sounded like a German accent.

Yet, though the Gestapo was actively hunting her, Lindell was blasé about her own security. 'She was terrible – she had no thoughts of fear at all,' declared Sparks. Given that her own network had been betrayed, Lindell decided to entrust the pair to another escape line. The three of them travelled to the rendezvous by tram. 'It was well packed,' Sparks recalled, 'and I was jostled up one end and I thought to myself, me not speaking French, "Well, I've got to watch her to see where we get off." But I needn't have worried. When it came to getting off, she shouted down the tram in plain English – "*I say Bill, we get off here!*" I tried to shrink in the corner because everybody looked round.'

From Marseille, Hasler and Sparks crossed the Pyrenees on foot with the help of Basque guides. After three months on the run, they arrived in Barcelona in the back of a lorry laden with lavatory seats. By early April, Hasler had returned to London. He met Raikes at the Savoy just a few days later than planned.

Not being an officer, Sparks had a harder time of it. While Hasler was sent home from Madrid by air, he was formally put under arrest in Gibraltar since he had no identity papers. When his ship docked at Liverpool, he was interrogated on board by MI5, and then sent south under military escort. But he gave his guards the slip at Euston Station and went to the East End to let his father know that he was alive. When he reported to the Admiralty two days later, he was again threatened with arrest, but one officer with a sense of perspective sneaked him out of a back door and sent him across Whitehall to Combined Operations. There he was greeted with surprise which soon turned to joy. He was awarded the Distinguished Service Medal (DSM) while Hasler, who was recommended for the VC, received the DSO. 'Few decorations have been more deserved,' thought Mountbatten.

Their bravery has never been in doubt, but what is questionable is how much FRANKTON accomplished. Churchill is reported to have said that the operation shortened the war by six months. It is doubtful if it did so by six minutes. Three of the four ships attacked by *Catfish* sank, but only in shallow water, and they were soon refloated and repaired. *Crayfish*'s targets suffered similar damage. It has also been claimed that the raid boosted morale at a time when the Germans still appeared to have the upper hand, but in Britain, at least, news of it remained secret until after victory had been won.

And it was not until then that the full cost of the mission was revealed. Of the ten men who entered the Gironde, all but Hasler and Sparks perished. Bobby Ewart was never to see Heather again. He and Sergeant Sam Wallace – the pair who failed to make it through the first tidal race – gave themselves up after beaching on the coast later that night. George Sheard also made it to land but, exhausted by his long swim, died of exposure. The body of David Moffatt was washed ashore several days afterwards. The crew of *Cuttlefish*, John MacKinnon and James Conway, who lost touch with the others when passing the mole, carried on towards Bordeaux, only to be wrecked on an underwater obstacle. They sought treatment in a hospital but were betrayed to the Germans. The last to be caught were *Crayfish*'s Bert Laver and Bill Mills, taken prisoner soon after setting out for Spain. All six of the captured men were shot in accordance with the Commando Order.

Their deaths were not confirmed until October 1945, and led to war crimes trials at which Sparks refuted claims that they had landed in disguise and so could legitimately be executed as spies. It also emerged later that SOE had had agents in Bordeaux at exactly the same time as FRANKTON – and working on precisely the same mission. The embarrassment this caused led to better coordination between it and COHQ. Had that rivalry been set aside earlier, however, the marines might have had help with their escape from the harbourside onwards.

That failure, and SOE's exaggerated assessment of the importance of the target, was not Hasler's fault. Against extraordinary odds, he succeeded in the mission he was given. Even the Germans could scarcely believe what he had done. But did those under his command ever have a fighting chance? Did he ask himself whether he was demanding too much of men with far less experience of the water than he, and who were ill equipped to evade capture in France? Above all, why did he not ask Mountbatten to delay the operation when the dress rehearsal on the Thames plainly showed that the section was not yet ready?

Certainly, by comparison with Sparks's description of the raid, Hasler's official report appears to play down the hazards that they encountered. Even accounting for gentlemanly reserve, there was no reason for him not to mention the German soldiers who saw the cows standing around the canoes, nor being crushed between the two ships.

Sparks's memory may have grown more vivid, of course. Or it may be that Hasler began to reproach himself for exposing the others to such risks and preferred to gloss over how dangerous – even reckless – the mission had been. For Mountbatten, no other raid carried out by Combined Operations was more courageous or imaginative. But sometimes it requires more courage and imagination for a leader to turn back.

13

TARBRUSH

Of all the secret weapons in the Allies' armoury, perhaps the most improbable was an Edwardian photograph of a lady in her bloomers. It seemed an innocuous snapshot, but by 1943 Robert Henriques and his fellow planners at COHQ were studying it intently. Their interest lay not in underwear of days gone by, but in where the picture had been taken. The woman and a small boy had been out shrimping on the French coast and she had tucked up her skirts to walk across the beach at low tide. From the depth of the footprints the pair had left in the wet sand, Henriques was able to gauge that it would not bear the weight of heavy vehicles.

The success of the Normandy landings would depend on the collection of thousands of pieces of information like this. The defeat of the Axis forces in North Africa had lent new urgency to the plans for D-Day which Combined Ops had been working on for some time, and Montgomery's insistence that he would need five divisions for the invasion, rather than the three originally envisaged, meant that even more research now needed to be done.

For instance, by early 1943 it was known that, because of their deep draught forward, many of the large Landing Ships Tanks (LST) had difficulty in disembarking their loads if the angle of the beach was not sufficiently steep. The gently sloping sands of Europe were a problem not foreseen by the vessels' American designers, and at one point it seemed as if two-thirds of all the vehicles needed for OVERLORD would be unable to land on flat beaches.

The problem was how to measure the gradient of prospective sites when they were closely guarded by the Germans. One solution was an appeal by the Admiralty to the public for their pre-war holiday snaps of France. The most useful were those which showed groups of people – especially children, whose height varied less – paddling, wading and sailing model yachts on the foreshore. From these it was possible to deduce the relative depth of the water, and hence the slope of the sand.

But some details could only be gathered on the spot. Therefore, while far fewer cross-Channel raids were staged in the eighteen months before the invasion, so as not to prompt the Germans to reinforce their defences further, small groups of commandos were used to carry out reconnaissance and intelligence-gathering. Sentries were snatched for interrogation, potential landing zones probed for mines, obstacles covertly drawn or photographed.

As late as the start of 1944, the entire D-Day plan was threatened by the discovery of a line of dark shadows in aerial images of the Bay of the Seine which it was feared might be peat bogs. Several perilous missions had to be mounted by COPP swimmers from mini-submarines to obtain samples of rock and shale; these showed that there were no swamps into which tanks and troops might sink.

Besides such scouting expeditions, the Commandos were also involved in a second and more subtle aspect of COHQ's preparations. The main danger to the invasion was of its failing to establish a bridgehead on the first day, and it was clear to the planners that it would face less concentrated resistance if the Germans could be deceived beforehand as to its location. This was to be done in part by feeding them false reports from spies that they thought they controlled – the famous 'Double Cross' system. Yet this scheme was not the whole picture.

In April 1943, the invasion's planning staff, known as COSSAC, ordered that a series of raids be made on the stretch of French coast between the Seine and the border with Belgium. Those leading the operations were to be told that their aim was to take prisoners for questioning. However, a secret memorandum set out the real objective: 'to convince the enemy that a large-scale landing in the Pas de Calais area is imminent'.

This inference would dovetail with the bogus information that the Germans were receiving from Double Cross, and was intended to divert their attention from the Allies' real destination – Normandy. To ensure that their presence was noted, the raiding parties were to leave behind black-and-white beach markers, as if they had been making a survey of the place.

About a dozen missions were to be staged in the dark periods of the moon between July and September. COHQ was given the task of organising them. It assigned some two hundred men to FORFAR, as the plan became known, mostly from 12 Commando. Among them was the unit's twenty-two-year-old intelligence officer, Lieutenant Ian Smith.

While Smith had already seen much of the Commandos, they had yet to see the best of him. Perhaps this was because he seemed to evade easy categorisation, a characteristic which sometimes had not helped his progress in the Army. Although his great height, moustache and glasses at first glance suggested scholarly diffidence, in reality he was naturally aggressive and had played rugby for Harlequins. His background, as the son of the manager of the giant Wills tobacco factory in Bristol, also implied that his sympathies lay with the officer class, whereas in fact he had found many of the other cadets at Sandhurst absurdly snobbish.

He had been at the college when war broke out, and was originally commissioned into the RASC. He joined the Commandos in 1940 after spotting the application form on his way to the mess in search of a stiff drink: he had just seen one of the two Belgian soldiers who were helping him to examine a haul of foreign weapons shoot dead the other while demonstrating how to twirl pistols like a cowboy.

Smith was posted to 2 Commando and, when they were converted into the first British parachute unit, made the second ever jump by a member of the new airborne forces. He later fell out with his commanding officer, however, and was transferred to the staff at Achnacarry. Returning from an inspection round there one day, he felt as much as heard a colossal explosion as the ammunition store went up behind him. The jolly sergeant who ran it turned out to have been selling arms to political extremists, and when Special Branch closed in he committed suicide by setting off a box of grenades. It was something of a relief for Smith to be sent soon afterwards to 12 Commando, part of which had been training in the far north of Scotland under Major Ted Fynn to become the winter warfare specialists that Mountbatten had called for after MUSKETOON.

Fynn was now leading one of the three groups taking part in the Pas de Calais raids. Among the last of these to be mounted was FORFAR BEER, staged on the night of 1 September 1943 at Elétot, near Fécamp. There had been three previous attempts to carry out this operation, but twice the sea had proved too rough, and on the third occasion, though the team had landed, they had been unable to find a way up the cliff.

This time Fynn and Smith, together with seven other men, started scaling the cliff face shortly after midnight. But after two hours' climbing, when they were close to the top, they found their way barred by a large overhang. Refusing to abandon the mission again, Fynn decided to tell the MTB that was waiting for them to return in forty-eight hours' time instead. While the rest of the party set about stashing their kit at the base of the cliff, Smith and a French commando, Corporal Laurent Casalonga, walked up the shingle as far as St Pierre-en-Port. They returned before dawn after spotting a sentry post near the town's casino.

After resting up, the raiders spent the afternoon trying unsuccessfully to find a way up from the beach. Eventually, Fynn thought it worth taking the risk of attracting the attention of a fisherman who had come down to see to his nets. He was a little suspicious at first, but Casalonga's presence was sufficiently reassuring for him to indicate the whereabouts of a path into town which he said was not patrolled at night.

That evening, Fynn and the others again probed one or two

promising-looking gullies, while Smith, Casalonga and Sergeant-Major Sam Brodison followed the fisherman's directions towards St Pierre. Just as they had hoped, they found the promised gap in the barbed wire strung across the beach, but when they approached the town centre they heard a sentry moving about ahead of them. They waited for an hour, but were unable to get any closer as the white pebbles underfoot offered no cover at all.

Smith felt that there was no point in remaining where they were, so he began to crawl back. As he did so, a challenge rang out in German. The three men waited for a few moments, and began to inch forward. At once they were challenged again, and then fired on, first by a rifle and then from the cliff top by a light machine-gun. 'The shooting was wild to start with, but the third burst from the machine-gun was very accurate,' recorded Smith later. Alarmed, he leapt to his feet. 'I could see no point in loitering and made a dash for the sea. I plunged in and swam as much as I could under water. Their aim improved, and I was treated to an underwater firework display as the tracer bullets entered the water and glowed for a few seconds, but luckily they avoided me.' It was high tide, and he floated for some distance down the coast before cautiously making his way ashore. There he ran into Brodison, who had crept round the cliffs when the shooting began, and at length Casalonga also reported back to Fynn. Smith was soaked through, and glad when the sun came up and he was able to dry off.

Having learned that it was possible to get into St Pierre, Fynn resolved to take another look that evening. This would mean postponing their rendezvous with the MTB again. They had two carrier pigeons with them, and he attached a note to each asking that the boat come back the following night. No sooner had the pair started their journey homewards, however, than five peregrine falcons swooped down from the cliffs and pounced on them. The pigeons took refuge on a ledge, but when one fluttered gamely upwards it was swiftly seized by the waiting talons. The other bird was lost from sight, but none of the commandos had any illusions about its fate.

As the raiders absorbed this setback, another followed. The

fisherman to whom they had spoken the previous day had agreed to meet them again in the morning, but he failed to show up at the allotted time. When he did finally arrive, he explained that he had been questioned by the Germans, who had told him that the British had made a landing during the night. He was upset to hear from Casalonga that his assurance that there was no sentry on duty near the wire had led them to be shot at, and as if to make up for it asked if postcards of St Pierre would be any use to them. When told that they would, he arranged for a friend of his to meet them on the beach that afternoon. In his pocket, the man had some views of the seafront, on which he pointed out the German positions. 'He was at pains to explain to us where the Boche machine-guns were,' reported Casalonga, 'where they had their guns, mines, billets and headquarters – in fact he gave us every scrap of information he could.' This was just the sort of thing that Fynn was after.

The first fisherman then returned with his brother, and revealed that morale was low in the forty-strong garrison, many of whom had recently arrived from the Russian front. Just that morning, one of the soldiers, who had been to Berlin on leave, had told them: '*Deutschland ist kaput!*' The Frenchmen were also able to give the commandos the news that the Allies had landed in Italy, which they had heard on the BBC.

At 2300, Fynn took five of the team down the beach once more, walking as silently as they could on the shingle. The group soon got tangled up in the wire, however, and although they exploded a charge under it, and fired some shots with silenced weapons at the sentry post, nothing could persuade the Germans to come out. Time was slipping away, and Fynn accepted that he was not going to get his prisoner. After living on their nerves for three days, the commandos were exhausted, and wading neck-high through the waves to the waiting dory took every ounce of their remaining strength. By morning, they were breakfasting in England.

FORFAR BEER was not a spectacular raid, but it was representative of many others being undertaken at the time. Unlike the earlier attacks by the SSRF, there were few tangible results to show for the effort expended, but collectively the operations did succeed in keeping the Germans guessing as to the real location of the invasion that all knew must come soon.

In the autumn of 1943, 12 Commando was disbanded. Ian Smith had managed to catch Bob Laycock's eye at a conference of intelligence officers (also attended by Evelyn Waugh, conspicuous in a fez and using an ear trumpet), and he was among the troops subsequently transferred to No. 10, the Inter-Allied Commando, based at Eastbourne and led by Laycock's brother, Peter.

During the winter, 10 Commando continued the work begun by FORFAR in a series of raids codenamed HARDTACK. Smith took charge of the first one, at the end of November, which reconnoitred a gully at Creil-sur-Mer. One of his tasks was to try out a new rocket-powered grapnel, known as Agincourt. This had been designed by Nevil Shute, the author of such novels as *On the Beach*, who had a parallel career as an engineer and spent the war developing weapons for the Navy. With Barnes Wallis, Shute had done much of the work on one of the technological marvels of the age, the *R100* airship, but Agincourt failed to function properly on this occasion and Smith had to abandon it. (It was deployed with more success at Omaha Beach on D-Day.)

Smith returned to the Dieppe area a month later, just after Christmas. Two of his eight men scaled the cliffs near Creil and let down ropes for the others to follow. But just as the first of these was reaching the top, a light was seen coming towards them over the fields. Behind it were fifteen German soldiers, and the commandos rapidly shinned back down to the shore. There they waited anxiously as the patrol passed along the path above them.

It was hard to make out the Germans' footsteps, so hand-over-hand Smith pulled himself slowly back up the rope, and hung there in the darkness until he was sure that there was no one lurking at the cliff edge. The coast proved to be clear, but not long afterwards their MTB was seen and fired at, and when they headed out to it in the dory they narrowly avoided being intercepted by E-boats.

Smith may have got away with it, but several of the HARDTACK raids suffered casualties. Two nights earlier, an officer from 2 SBS, Captain Philip Ayton, had been killed after stepping on a mine on Jersey; and on 28 December two French commandos died in the same way on Sark. For, unlike FORFAR, not all of the missions were confined to the Pas de Calais. Indeed, at the exact moment when Ian Smith was dangling in mid-air, another team was surveying what would become – in six months' time – Utah Beach.

Although this group brought back measurements of a new kind of anti-tank obstacle, dubbed 'Element C', which the planners had been eager to have, COSSAC was now beginning to believe that such operations were counter-productive. 'The more I think about it,' wrote Montgomery's Chief of Staff, Major General Freddie de Guingand, in late January, 'the more I come to the conclusion that a policy of raiding *anywhere* on the Belgian/French coast is wrong.' The best way to fox the Germans as to where the invasion would come, he felt, was to stop the raids altogether.

Although Bob Laycock thought that they still offered valuable experience to his commandos, COSSAC's view prevailed, and from February 1944 Smith found himself idle. One consolation was the award of the MC for his part in the winter's work, while another was more frequent trips up to London with Peter Laycock for lunch at White's, the gentlemen's club. Given the constraints of wartime, Smith was astonished by the excellence of the food, and by the members' casual approach to security. He had not told even his fiancée what his work involved; yet, as the port was passed around, details of operations were discussed openly. To Smith, it seemed as if the ruling elite thought that rules about secrecy did not apply to them.

For several weeks, he tried to stave off boredom by staying fit and keeping his eye in: he became so proficient with a Sten that he could hit a tin can rolling down a slope, blasting it into the air, and with subsequent bursts stop it from hitting the ground again. Then, in early May, he was abruptly summoned to COHQ.

A month earlier, a bombing raid on coastal defences near Deauville had set off a string of detonations all along the beach.

Combined Operations' scientific adviser, the physicist J.D. Bernal, thought that these might indicate that the Germans had fixed a new type of mine to the obstacles sited there below the waterline. It was known that ordinary pressure mines were sometimes attached to these so as to explode if touched by a landing craft. Countermeasures against them had been created, but Bernal suspected from the chain reaction seen at Deauville that the mines there might be electrically or acoustically activated. It could take months to devise a defence against such a mechanism, and D-Day was only three weeks away. If it was not discovered at once how the mines were triggered, the entire invasion might have to be called off.

At Montgomery's request, 10 Commando was ordered at just twenty-four hours' notice to examine the obstacles in several places on the French coast. To avoid drawing attention to the proposed landings in Normandy, however, the missions were to be mounted around Calais and Boulogne. Four small teams were rapidly assembled for TARBRUSH. Each consisted of half a dozen commandos and a sapper officer who was an expert on mines. Because of his raiding experience, Ian Smith was chosen to lead TARBRUSH 3, so he was among those briefed by Bernal.

When someone asked him if the noise of the dory's engine might set off the mystery charge, Bernal's less-than-comforting answer was: 'Wait and see.' More certain were the risks that the expeditions faced from the Germans, who were expecting an invasion and would be on full alert. Privately, Combined Ops believed that most of the raiders would not return.

TARBRUSH 3 left Dover on the moonless night of 16 May, bound for Bray-Dunes, just over the Belgian border. Smith was hurriedly introduced to the Royal Engineers officer who was to identify the mine, Lieutenant John Groom. The dory was dropped a mile offshore, and when they were a hundred yards from the beach the survey party transferred to the dinghy and paddled in. Smith had had to change course several times in the Channel to avoid enemy trawlers, but such was his seamanship that when they landed at about 0115 they were within a yard of the spot he had chosen on the map.

Only Groom, a sapper sergeant and a signalman were supposed to go ashore, but Smith decided to accompany them, as his Sten would offer extra firepower if needed. No sooner had they started to haul the dinghy clear of the surf than they smelled cigarette smoke. Just at that moment, there was a flash of light about 150 yards away, illuminating a man sitting on the sand. 'We correctly assumed that it was coming from a sentry illicitly having a puff whilst on guard duty,' Smith later wrote. 'Then we heard a long conversation in German: clearly they were changing the guard.'

The sergeant began to walk the other way along the beach, carrying a mine detector, followed by Groom and the signalman, who was paying out a tape that would lead them back to the dinghy. They moved as silently as they could, but the small shells underfoot seemed to crunch louder and louder with each step they took. Soon they came across a small forest of timber stakes planted at the water's edge. On top of each was a mine which Groom quickly confirmed was of the standard, pressure-activated type. It was securely fastened and any attempts to remove it might alert the relief sentry, who just then lit up his own cigarette.

The commandos had got all the information that they had come for, so they decided to head for home while they could. Picking up the tracing tape brought them back to the dinghy, and then they reached the dory by hauling on a line. 'We slid quietly over the side and then paddled as far as possible from the beach before starting our engine,' recalled Smith. 'Somewhere out there was an MTB.' The boat was equipped with an early homing device called an S-set, but it was not responding. As they fiddled with it, Smith looked up to see an armed trawler bearing down fast on them.

'It turned on a searchlight scanning the sea ahead. How it did not see us, I don't know.' They lay flat in the bottom of the dory, as if playing a lethal version of hide and seek. They felt as much as heard the ship slide by them. 'The trawler passed us by a few yards,' Smith remembered, 'and then the searchlight went out.' It seemed as if his phenomenal luck had held yet again. Then, just as the S-set began to make contact with the MTB, the trawler turned around. The light snapped back on, and shells started to smash into the water ahead of them.

Only a few hundred yards separated the two vessels. Closer and closer the trawler came, although it had still not picked up the dory in its beam, and Smith assumed that its fire was being directed by radar ashore. The commandos' only protection was the dark, but Smith feared that would be stripped away at any moment.

Then there was a sudden ringing of bells and the sound of orders being shouted. The trawler started to slow down and then stopped altogether. Smith realised it must have grounded on a sandbank as his own craft continued to pull away. 'I remember putting my paddle down,' he wrote, 'and we only had just enough water for the dory.' A few minutes later, they were aboard the MTB and speeding towards Dover.

Smith's was not the only miraculous escape during TARBRUSH. The night before, another team had gone to Quend Plage. Intelligently, Lieutenant John Stone, the sapper officer in the party, had brought with him a stepladder to make it easier to examine the obstacles. He soon found that the beach was studded with rows of wooden posts, about six yards apart and some eight feet high. Stone climbed up his ladder to check the mine on one of these, but when he reached the top he lost his balance. The ladder toppled over, and Stone was left hanging from the mine, which was bearing his whole weight. After he had been clinging to it for a few seconds, he decided that it was probably not booby-trapped.

When Robert Laycock got to hear of this incident, he paid Stone the compliment of saying that it had been the type of raid to which Commando skills were especially suited. The ability to hold one's nerve presumably extended as well to sappers. The team repeated the raid the following night, but were discovered after twenty minutes and only got away after a firefight.

Most of the commandos who took part in TARBRUSH came from one of the more remarkable units in the British Army. Each Troop in

10 Commando, which was formed in 1942, was drawn from a country occupied by the Nazis, such as Norway, Belgium, Holland and France. However, No. 3 – or X Troop – was largely composed of men who were technically enemy aliens. Most were Germans and Austrians; others were from Romania or the Sudetenland. There were also a handful of Hungarians, several Poles and a Russian. Almost all of them were Jewish refugees, some were political exiles, and a few were both. At least two had already spent time in the concentration camp at Dachau. The majority were recruited from the Pioneer Corps, which had absorbed those of fighting age originally interned on the outbreak of war. Others came from SOE. All had been promised British citizenship in return for volunteering for the Troop, and all had exchanged their names for more English ones. Nathan became Howarth, Hajós was now Harris, and Sauer Sayers (after Dorothy, the writer of detective stories).

The Troop's principal role was liaison and interpretation. Rather than fighting as a unit, its men were usually attached in small groups to other Commandos to help with intelligence-gathering. A few of its number had been in the SSRF, while several others took part in the Dieppe raid, and later in the invasion of Sicily. But for most, the FORFAR and HARDTACK operations represented their first taste of action. Over the next eighteen months, almost a third of X Troop would be killed or wounded – an exceptionally high casualty rate.

Each of them knew that they could expect no mercy from the enemy if their real identities were discovered. Despite running such additional risks, however, and even though most were highly able men in civilian life, by D-Day only one had been made an officer. He was the leader of the final TARBRUSH raid, which was to result in one of the most extraordinary encounters of the war.

Lieutenant George Lane had been born Dyuri Lányi in northern Hungary in 1915. Four years later, he and his landowning family had found themselves near-exiles in Budapest after the area in which their estates lay was assigned to Czechoslovakia after the First World War. Yet though he grew up with little money, Lane – who was Jewish – knew how to make the most of his intelligence and his charm. By 1939, he was studying at university in London and making friends in high society. When the Home Office tried to deport him as a security risk after war had been declared, he was able to persuade Anthony Eden, soon to be Secretary of State for War, to vouch for his character.

Lane joined SOE, but was obliged to leave it after refusing to be parachuted back into Hungary. Laycock then agreed to take him in the Commandos. This was a less straightforward decision than Lane knew. Through a family friendship with the Dean of Windsor, he had for several years lived at the castle itself. But some of his other acquaintances were less wholesome, among them an Austro-Hungarian count who vanished, leaving behind vast debts which Lane had to settle as best he could.

This episode seems to have reached the ears of another inhabitant of the castle: George VI. When it was suggested in 1940 that Lane become an officer in the Grenadiers, the King let it be known – Laycock now learned from Mountbatten – that he did not think him 'a proper person to be given a commission in the Brigade of Guards'. There was no objection, however, to his commanding other foreigners in X Troop.

Perhaps the most vivid record of the unit was left by Lane's wife. Miriam Rothschild, who was herself half-Hungarian, was a member of the most prominent, and richest, Jewish family in Britain. When she and Lane married, they had to do so almost clandestinely in the City of London, so as not to draw attention to either Miriam or X Troop. She had left a suitcase at the family bank to establish residence, sweet-talked the registrar into hiding the announcement on the noticeboard, and used a taxi driver and a passer-by as witnesses. Since the wedding made her an alien as well, and so subject to a curfew and forbidden from having a radio, she arranged to be naturalised as British again the next day.

By the autumn of 1942, she and Lane were living in the seaside village of Aberdovey, on the edge of Snowdonia, where the Troop was training. She was immediately struck by the unit's unusual mix of personalities. Many came from countries where she had relatives, and as most were Jews and refugees, she sympathised with their problems and mindset. 'They were an intellectual group,' she remembered, 'so different from an ordinary Army section. You don't expect six privates to be talking about Schopenhauer.'

Miriam was a world-class scientist and quite able to hold her own in any discussion of German philosophy. She worked for a time on codes at Bletchley Park and while in Wales studied pests in pigeons for the Ministry of Agriculture. Because she kept the coops for these beside her bed, she was soon denounced as a spy, and the local police arrested her and the 'carrier' pigeons. Fortunately her brother, Victor, Lord Rothschild, was in MI5 and able to get her (and the birds) released.

Sometimes the Troop's foreign ways worked in its favour, however: the housewives of Harlech had been reluctant to have them as lodgers, until they learned they were not English.

The unit's commanding officer was also Welsh. Captain Bryan Hilton Jones, who had studied German at Cambridge before the war, was as tough as the mountains he loved to climb, and he drove the Troop hard in his quest to make it one of the best in the Army. Miriam recalled one night exercise on Snowdon from which Hilton Jones had returned to the bar of the village hotel where they were living with not a hair out of place. When she went upstairs, she found Lane and a corporal named Latimer lying comatose on their beds, 'apparently corpses, except they were breathing'. Pulling off her husband's boots, she found they were full of blood and his feet had been flayed raw. He and Latimer were the only ones who had finished the march, with Lane having carried another man's rifle as well as his own to stop him from being court-martialled for throwing it away. His motivation for pushing himself so hard was his desire to defeat Nazism, although he did not expect to be there for the celebrations when that finally happened. 'I really believed that eventually I should be killed,' he said later. 'What was important was to do what was possible before the end.'

It was with this in mind that he approached the enemy coast on the night of 17 May 1944. TARBRUSH 10 had been launched on the

15th, when the party had got ashore and examined the obstacles. (The following night, they had been unable to land because of bad weather.) Their report confirmed the impression that there was no new type of mine, and that those set off at Deauville had probably become unusually sensitive through seawater corroding their firing pins. None the less, Lane was sent back just to make sure. He was also to photograph the obstructions known as Element C with an infra-red camera.

The night was pitch black, pierced only by a single searchlight which swept the sea rather than the beach at Ornival that was their target. Passing through a phalanx of hewn timber posts that extended along the shore as far as they could see, the team landed shortly before 0100. With Lane was Lieutenant Roy Wooldridge, a sapper who had already won an MC for clearing mines at El Alamein, his sergeant Eric Bluff, and a signalman from the Marines, Corporal King.

'Naturally one was very scared,' Lane said of the TARBRUSH missions later, 'but we thought it was worthwhile because of the information we were bringing back.' There was no one about on the beach, however, and they were able to inspect the four lines of obstacles meant to wreak havoc on any invasion, and to note their construction. Although Bluff scaled two or three of them, none had mines fitted. Nor did they see any Element C.

However, Lane knew from aerial photographs that there were some of these to the south-west, near Ault. At 0140, he and Wooldridge set off in that direction, having sent the NCOs back to the dinghy so that, if there was any trouble, they would be able to get away with the notes they had already made. The two officers said that they would be away for about an hour, but when they had been gone for only a few minutes, Bluff saw a bright red flash about three hundred yards off. As it died away, a shout came in German – and then a scream, as if someone were being knifed.

Three shots followed. At once star shells rocketed skywards, lighting up the MTB offshore as if it were daylight. While the two NCOs were wondering what to do, they saw a patrol heading for the water's edge and then lighting a row of flares. These stopped the pair from making a run for the dory, and soon afterwards it became clear that they had been spotted where they were hiding near the dinghy.

Bluff and King ran inland, but were then fired on by another patrol from only twenty-five yards away. More star shells went up, and Bluff readied himself to shoot back, but King convinced him that they stood more chance of getting away if they did not draw further attention to themselves. When the flares had died down, they doubled back to the shoreline and swam out to the dory. All this time, Bluff had been lugging a mine detector, which he was reluctant to leave behind as it would indicate what the commandos had been doing. It was simply too heavy to swim with, however, so once he had passed the low tide mark he dropped it in six feet of water.

Hilton Jones, who had been waiting aboard the MTB, was relieved to see them, but naturally anxious to know what had happened to Wooldridge and Lane. If they had been captured, not only did they face an uncertain fate, but the presence of the camera would betray the mission's purpose.

It was now about 0330, and the MTB's captain was keen to be off, but he allowed Hilton Jones to go back to the beach in the dory to see if there was any sign of the missing men. He cruised up and down the shore for five minutes, but saw no one. There seemed little doubt that – at best – the two officers were now in German hands.

But this was not so. For about forty-five minutes, they had walked towards Ault in teeming rain, and after failing to find any Element C had turned around. They had got near the dinghy's location when a volley of shots erupted overhead. Two of the patrols searching for Bluff and King had probably mistaken each other for them, but it compelled the other pair to lie low for a time. They eventually reached the dinghy, only to discover that the NCOs had disappeared. (Neither of them seems to have noticed the terrible scream heard by Bluff.)

There was only an hour of darkness until dawn and their options were decidedly limited. Assuming that the others had been captured, and receiving no answer to the signals they flashed out to sea, they resolved to set off in the dinghy themselves. They tried to keep up each other's morale with talk of a flying boat coming to rescue them, but when the sun rose they had only covered about a mile. Their chances of escape seemed very remote, and so except for their pistols they threw all their equipment over the side, including the tell-tale camera.

Soon afterwards, they saw a boatful of German soldiers approaching. Lane, who was a natural optimist, started to hatch a plan to overpower them, but thought better of it once he had three Schmeissers pointing at him. 'With a rather theatrical gesture, we put our hands up,' he later admitted. As they were marched into a guard post on the seashore, they were greeted with the no less theatrical remark 'For you, the war is over.'

The sea had been choppy and the two men were wet through. This lent credibility to their story that they had been on a boat involved in a battle, but when Wooldridge gave his rank and number, his interrogator looked in a directory and announced that he must be in the Engineers. Now that they were presumed to have been on a commando mission, the future appeared bleak. 'They told us that we were going to be shot since it was obvious we were saboteurs,' recalled Lane.

For several days they were moved from place to place and kept apart. Lane picked the lock of his cell on the first night, but ran straight into a sentry who told him to get back into it. They were repeatedly questioned by men with Gestapo armbands, whom Wooldridge later realised were ordinary soldiers in disguise, but stuck to their story. Then, one morning, the pair were blindfolded and driven for hours through the Normandy countryside. By leaning back in his seat, Lane found that he could see out under the bandage, and just before the car stopped he saw a signpost for La Roche Guyon. When the blindfolds were removed, they saw that they were in front of a chateau. Once more they were separated, and Lane was shown into a room where an impeccably dressed officer offered him coffee and sandwiches.

In perfect English, he was told that he was about to meet a very important person. The officer then handed him a nail file with which to remove the worst of the dirt from his fingers. A door was opened by another immaculate aide, and Lane was escorted into a very large room furnished with books, tapestries and a marble fireplace. At the far end was someone seated behind a desk: it was Rommel himself.

Surprised as he was to see the field marshal, Lane was more impressed by his getting up and coming over to greet him. 'So you are one of these gangster commandos?' he said disarmingly in German. What must be one of the most peculiar interviews of the war then followed. On one side was Hitler's greatest general, now in charge of repelling the imminent Allied invasion. On the other was a Jewish refugee pretending to be a Welsh soldier so as to hide his Hungarian accent. Lane also concealed the fact that he spoke German, talking through an interpreter to give himself longer to think.

'You realise that you're in a very tricky situation?' said Rommel. 'Everyone thinks you're a saboteur.'

'Well,' replied Lane to the interpreter, 'if the field marshal thought I was a saboteur, then I wouldn't have been invited here.'

Rommel smiled at such a charming and spirited response, and the atmosphere became even more relaxed. Lane was allowed to ask questions, and when Rommel wanted to know how Montgomery was getting on with his invasion plans, the Hungarian told him that he would soon be able to ask him in person. The conversation ended with the general giving his word that Lane would be well looked after.

Wooldridge was also taken in to meet Rommel, but was dismissed after refusing to confirm that he was a sapper. Both men were then taken to Fresnes Prison, but instead of being executed there like many other commandos, they were sent on to PoW camps. Rommel had kept his promise. From a book in his camp's library, Lane was able to identify the chateau, and the information was smuggled back to Britain.

Not long afterwards, Rommel was severely wounded when his staff car was strafed by fighters near Caen. Lane naturally hoped that his tip-off lay behind the attack, which removed Rommel from the front line until his enforced suicide several months later following the attempt on Hitler's life. Yet, as the vehicle was hit more than fifty miles from the field marshal's HQ at La Roche Guyon, any direct connection seems unlikely.

Perhaps the first person to realise that Lane had been taken prisoner was his wife. A Dutch member of the Commando told her the next day that while listening to radio traffic he had heard German messages about two Englishmen being captured on a beach. The past few weeks had been a nerve-racking time for her, as she had never known when there might be a knock on the door, summoning George from their bed and on to a mission. When she confronted Peter Laycock with the news, he said it might well be true, but was at least a sign that Lane might be alive. Even so, she had no idea when she might see her husband again; she would have to endure pregnancy alone.

A comfort of a kind was the award to Lane of the MC. Eight were given for TARBRUSH, as were five MMs, with the other recipients including Wooldridge, Hilton Jones, Ian Smith and John Stone. The recommendations for them paid tribute to the unusually high risks which had been run to obtain information 'vital to our impending campaign'. The months of work spent collecting samples and reconnoitring beaches had paid off. Thanks to the Commandos, D-Day was still on track.

Some months later, after Paris had been liberated, J.D. Bernal visited a friend of his who was a professor of geology at the Sorbonne. At once the professor asked Bernal if the data he had sent had been of help. Anticipating that any invasion must come from the sea, in the early years of the war he had collected everything he could about the sands, tides and gradients on France's shores, and, at great danger to himself and others, had arranged for it to be smuggled to London.

Bernal found it all on his return to England from Paris, neatly labelled, recorded and filed away in a cabinet. It seemed that no one had ever bothered to look at it again.

14

FLOUNCED

'Bravo!' The shout was loud, and accompanied by a slap on his back hearty enough to make the shepherd break off the tune he had been furiously whistling. Beneath the layers of mud and stubble that caked his face, he was alarmed, fearful that the German sentries they had just passed would wonder what his companion was celebrating. But they saw nothing amiss, just two Yugoslavs driving their flock into town at sundown.

Soon the pair came to a barn and slipped inside. Two more men were waiting there nervously. A mule stood patiently to one side, and the whistling shepherd began to rummage in the bundle of brushwood it bore on its back. He pulled out a magazine, a silencer and a Sten gun, and expertly assembled them. Then he took off his smock, revealing the uniform of a Commando officer. In a few moments, he would take on a new role: that of assassin.

Lieutenant John Barton had only joined the Commandos two months earlier, and for the past three weeks had been in the Adriatic as part of a force supporting Marshal Tito's hard-pressed partisans. On 13 February 1944, he was sent from their base on the Dalmatian island of Vis to raid its neighbour, Brac. Known for its stone, which had been used to build the White House in Washington, it was occupied by 450 mountain troops from 118 Jäger Division.

Almost as soon as Barton and his ten-strong party landed on Brac, they found themselves hunted. Under torture, a partisan had given the Germans the location of the cove where the British schooners put in and the whereabouts of the local partisans' HQ. 'We moved camp immediately,' wrote Barton afterwards, 'and only just in time.' Once the search had been evaded, the commandos reconnoitred German positions on the island. Snow lay on the ground, and they endured long night marches, bitter winds, and days without food.

The partisans proved to be impressively tough and mobile allies, but lacking in discipline. 'When it came to the actual ambush they were hopeless,' Barton noted, 'for the moment they see a German they fire everything, whether the target is within range or not.' For several days he had been hatching a plan to show the Yugoslavs how it should be done, and now told them that he intended to kill the garrison commandant, Hauptmann Kunstler.

Even in the context of the ruthless war waged in the Balkans, Barton's proposal was controversial. Some of his fellow officers would later disapprove of the operation as being unworthy of a soldier, but the attempt to kill Rommel showed that it was not without precedent. Indeed, only a fortnight before, other troops from Barton's unit had tried to kidnap the German commander of another nearby island, Hvar, but the officer leading the raid had been fatally wounded in the attempt.

It has been suggested that Barton was driven by a desire to avenge the Germans' torture of the partisan or their reprisals against civilians, but there is no evidence of this. He himself never revealed his motives. Certainly, the fact that he was raised a devout Methodist would seem to indicate that he was not simply a cold-blooded killer. What appears more likely is that he possessed an unusually strong sense of duty, taking responsibility for what needed to be done. The year before, when still with the Reconnaissance Corps, he had won an MC in North Africa for continuing a patrol through a minefield – and back again – after all but one of his men had been wounded crossing it. He was then aged twenty-two.

Just after 1900 on 20 February, Barton crept up to the door of Kunstler's billet in Nerežišća, in the centre of the island. A curfew had been in place in its darkened streets for an hour already, and the servant who answered the knock was startled to see him. Barton had been gathering intelligence for days and knew that there was no sentry on duty. Expecting to find soldiers working in the kitchen, however, he left one partisan to watch the street while he and another ran straight through the house. Stens at the ready, they barged through the kitchen door, but all those inside were civilians. The sight of the two armed men sent a maidservant into shrieking hysterics and the partisan made the remainder hold her down and keep her quiet. Another woman spoke in French to Barton, who told her that he was a British officer and would do them no harm: he just wanted the commandant. Unexpectedly, she replied that he was dining out, but said that one of the men would show him where.

Although this change of plan made the operation riskier still, Barton agreed. First, though, he went to search Kunstler's bedroom. He pocketed a compass, binoculars and an automatic pistol, but as he was looking for an identity card he heard a noise from the adjoining dining room. He rushed back out to the corridor, then, with the partisan covering him, charged inside. To his surprise, the room appeared to be empty. There was just a candle flickering on the table. Then, amid the shadows in the far corner, something glinted. It was an Iron Cross. 'I gave it a burst of about eight rounds and as the body fell to the floor, another burst through the head. He was a big man of about 180 lbs and well over 6ft tall; he was definitely dead.'

Despite the silencer, the phut-phut echo of the Sten had reached the kitchen and triggered a new bout of screaming. A dog began to bark, and the village to rouse itself. Barton had no time to check the man's papers or rank, for the partisan was pulling him from the room. As they reached the lane outside, they saw Germans running towards them. Barton calmly pointed them on down the road, then vaulted a garden wall and sprinted for the open countryside.

Barton's exploit gave an immediate lift to partisan morale, and a wave of ambushes and killings of collaborators followed over the next few days. However, when he reported back what he had done, he was ordered to return to Vis at once. There his claims were treated with some scepticism by his superiors as he had no independent proof of them. So the following week he landed on Brac again, this time in search of prisoners who could confirm his story.

He had already been planning to raid the fishing village of Pučišća, where eight Germans were quartered, and was pleased to find that despite his previous attack they had not changed their routine. In a single night, he and ten partisans marched twenty miles across the hills, and the next evening prepared to surround the house on the seafront where the soldiers were sleeping. Barton's hope was that he could bluff them into surrender by pretending his force was larger than it was.

He had brought two other commandos with him from Vis. Fritz Hausmann (now calling himself 'Fred Houseman') was the son of a German Army officer and a Jewish mother. He had managed to escape to Palestine when both his parents were sent to concentration camps. Although a university lecturer in civilian life, his hatred of the Nazis had turned him into a formidably aggressive soldier. By contrast, John Morris had left school at fourteen and then worked as an errand boy for a Cardiff grocer. He had spent the first two years of the war installing telephone lines with the Royal Corps of Signals, and had volunteered for the Commandos to escape from a posting on the remote Scottish island of Benbecula.

'I hadn't realised that Barton had shot this German,' Morris later reflected, 'and that there was a price on his head. If we had been captured . . . Hitler's Commando Order was in operation by then.' Other dangers lay closer to hand. After the tiring approach march to Pučišća, Barton told Morris to get some rest in the cave where they were sheltering. 'It was pretty dark, but I managed to push myself in between these two partisans and sleep,' recalled Morris. 'When I could see, I realised that I was sleeping between two partisan women. What shocked me more than anything was they had their grenades buttoned to their battle-dress blouses through the pin!'

In the early hours of 3 March, Barton divided the partisans into two groups to cover the rear and front of the Germans' house from the end nearest the sea. In the meantime, the three commandos and a guide worked round the side of a burned-out ruin until they were just ten yards from the door of the billet. Two sentries patrolled the street outside.

So far the quartet had gone unseen, but no sooner did the guide begin to whisper to Barton than one of the guards advanced towards their hiding-place. He had got to within fifteen feet of them when he seemed to change his mind and turned away. Then, without warning, he whipped round and fired at Barton from point-blank range.

'We were just tucked behind this corner,' remembered Morris. 'I was crouching down, Barton was behind me, looking round it. He was lucky because the bullet hit the corner and just skipped the top of his helmet.' Barton himself had been about to shoot, but his aim was shaken and his return fire only knocked off the German's own hat. The sentry had lost his nerve, however, and ran back towards the house.

'I could see two silhouettes by the door,' Morris recalled, 'so I got out a hand grenade, pulled out the pin, threw it and took these two Germans out.' The man who had shot at Barton was knocked unconscious and the other guard killed instantly. 'This was the signal for everything to start up,' recorded Barton, as the partisans now opened fire. 'Unfortunately the danger to us was far greater than to the Germans in the house.' The commandos found themselves pinned down in an exposed position by a Schmeisser poking through an upper window. 'I decided to crawl round the flank,' wrote Barton, 'but before I had done this, Private Hausmann . . . dashed forward under very heavy fire.' Kicking open the front door, he hurled a grenade inside, then ran in wielding his tommy-gun and calling on the occupants in German to surrender to the British.

The blast had killed one soldier and wounded another two in the room, and the sudden ferocity inflicted on his men stunned their officer into submission. 'There is no doubt at all that had it not been for Hausmann's bravery and initiative, the position would have been very difficult for me to take,' reported Barton, 'and the Germans, believing us to be partisans, would have fought to the last man.' As it was, only with difficulty did he stop his allies from finishing off the injured and the other prisoners on the return march.

Hausmann was awarded the DCM while Barton – now that the death of Kunstler could be substantiated by the prisoners – received the DSO in July. This led to more controversy as, despite an Army order to the contrary, Barton's name and the fact that he had concealed his uniform were widely reported when the story was picked up by the press. Eventually he was pulled out of Yugoslavia for his own safety since he would have been in too much danger if captured.

Nevertheless, the missions he had commanded, and others mounted from Vis, including piratical attacks against shipping along the Croatian coastline, did succeed in unnerving the German garrisons in the islands. Forcing them to hold down territory also prevented them from joining together to capture Vis itself. Yet, while such operations appeared aggressive, in reality raids of this sort were a defensive strategy. They were the bullfighter's cape and lance, feints and pinpricks which could irritate and distract, but not finish off, a more powerful foe.

Swift jabs of this sort were precisely what Winston Churchill had in mind for the Commandos when they were formed in 1940. Four years on, however, the nature of the conflict had changed. Now the Allies were on the offensive, but to deliver the knockout they needed to fight toe-to-toe with the Germans in what would be a brutal slugging match. 'We knew we couldn't do much on Vis,' acknowledged John Morris, 'but at the time we were the only Commandos doing what we were trained for – raiding. In the middle of the war, the Commandos were mainly treated as glorified infantry. Anything tough, they were sent in.'

The first confirmation that the momentum of the war in the West had shifted in favour of the Allies was the success of the North

Africa landings in November 1942. The months which followed transformed the standing of the Commandos within the Army as a whole, but they also exposed their limitations and led to fundamental changes in their organisation.

The mauling that Layforce had taken in Crete in 1941 had proved that commandos lacked the punching power for sustained bouts of combat. It had also confirmed their own belief that the Army Staff – unlike COHQ – had little understanding of how to use the advantages they did possess in terms of stealth and mobility.

The dislike was mutual, however, and the strength of feeling on both sides was reinforced by the campaign to take Madagascar from the Vichy French in the spring of 1942. In the first such extension of their role, 5 Commando was deployed not just to secure the beachhead – as had been done at Litani – but also during the fighting that ensued inland. Opposition turned out to be relatively light, yet, despite securing their objectives, the Commando incurred the displeasure of the commander-in-chief of the East Africa theatre, Lieutenant General Sir William Platt. 'Having one administrative officer, with no other administrative personnel, and no transport, they become a parasite on other units,' he complained to the new Chief of the Imperial General Staff, Sir Alan Brooke.

> In operations such as these ... a Commando is an expensive luxury. I would rather have had an ordinary well-trained battalion on even a reduced establishment. The discipline and example of a Commando is not up to the standard of an average battalion ... the press give them advertisement at the expense of other units, and out of proportion to their contribution to the common cause.

Platt's grievances may have been those of the conventionally minded, but his impression of the Commandos was widely shared by the rest of the Field Army. In the case of No. 5, there were some unique issues which stemmed from a failure of leadership: its colonel was removed after the medical officer diagnosed him as an alcoholic, while the choice of his successor divided the unit into factions. And most of Platt's more general criticisms were entirely accepted by the Commandos. What rankled was the feeling that these were not their fault. 'It's very surprising how prejudiced against us everyone seems to be,' wrote one officer to Laycock in early 1943, in a letter which detailed how hampered the Commandos were by a lack of a proper staff. The impression that they were expected to do too much with too little only deepened as they began to advance into Tunisia after TORCH.

A conference of the Commandos' leaders had accepted that 'raiding for the sake of raiding was unlikely to be undertaken' and that they must be prepared for 'a role as specialised and highly trained infantry, possibly for protracted operations'. Yet, without the heavy weaponry and the supply of replacements for casualties which would make this viable, the units at the sharp end in North Africa suffered.

No. 6 took especially heavy losses in repeated assaults against dug-in German positions at Green Hill in late November 1942. More than eighty men were killed or wounded. Forty others had died or been injured when the unit had been strafed a few days earlier. Its leader, Lieutenant Colonel Iain MacAlpine, was assessed by Laycock's liaison officer as being 'full of self-pity for himself and the men under his command', and when he fell ill Laycock appointed the more obviously pugnacious Derek Mills-Roberts in his stead. None the less, by April 1943, No. 6 had been reduced by almost two-thirds to just 150 men, and it had to be withdrawn to Britain. By contrast, No. 1 – which was led by cousins Tom and Ken Trevor – was felt to have 'done nothing but good for the reputation of the Commandos'.

Despite their very different fates, however, both units succeeded in tempering much of the ill will harboured towards them by soldiers in less elite, and so less publicised, regiments. Now that the Commandos had shared in the boredom and discomfort of campaigning, 'that feeling – in North Africa at any rate – no longer exists', their Corps commander, Lieutenant General Charles Allfrey, informed Laycock.

Even so, if their task was to be standing and fighting rather than hitting and running, it was clear that they would need greater firepower. In the late summer of 1943, every Commando was increased by a Heavy Weapons Troop equipped with two three-inch mortars and two .303-calibre Vickers machine-guns. Each sub-section also acquired a portable two-inch mortar, and the number of Brens in each Troop was raised from four to six. For the first time, they were also given their own dedicated transport, to carry the extra ordnance.

By then, it was apparent that more wide-ranging changes would have to be made to the structure of the Special Service Brigade. Given the proposed scale of the Commandos' involvement as assault troops in the coming invasions, the most pressing need was simply to boost their numbers. As early as the summer of 1942, ministers had begun to suggest that the additional manpower should come not from the Army, but from the Royal Marines (RM).

The first marines to be converted into commandos retained their own administrative arrangements, but before long it was proposed that they should be integrated into Laycock's brigade. Both he and Mountbatten resisted this, believing that the principle of volunteering and selection was central to the Commando spirit. They would 'lose their individuality, their esprit de corps and their inspiration' if merged with the Marine Division, wrote Laycock in August 1943, faced with a plan to have two Army and two RM Commando brigades in a single Special Service Group. He wanted them to run in parallel but remain separate, not least, perhaps, because in the projected set-up Laycock would only be deputy to the Marines' commanding officer, Sir Robert Sturges.

'The situation, quite bluntly, is that whether we like it or not the re-organisation is going ahead,' he was told by COHQ later that month. 'The battle has been lost and the Marines have gained possession of the field.' But the suggestion that this development had been driven solely by the Marines, and that they were all enthusiastic at the prospect of becoming Commandos, is wrong. The order of the day which conveyed the news to the division makes it clear that its troops also regarded the reorganisation as a disappointment, and one that threatened their own traditions. None the less, by 1944, nine RM battalions had been turned into Commandos, with all but the first two undergoing the centralised training course at Achnacarry. The new Special Service Group eventually comprised four brigades, each consisting of both Army and RM units, in an effort to prevent potential rivalries.

At the same time as the amalgamation with the Marines was confirmed, there was a further shock for Combined Ops to absorb: Mountbatten was leaving. In October 1943, he was made head of South-East Asia Command, taking charge of Allied operations against the Japanese. The identity of his successor at COHQ came as a jolt even to him.

'The news of Bob's appointment was a great surprise,' he told Charles Haydon, on whose military expertise he had leaned for two years, and who might fairly have thought to have been his natural replacement as Chief of Combined Operations (CCO). There seems to have been a perception that Haydon was tired and in need of a new challenge, so in early 1944 he was given command of the 1st Guards Brigade in Italy. Other leading candidates, Mountbatten heard, had turned down the post, and so it was that Churchill turned to Laycock.

Mountbatten had given Combined Ops the clout in Whitehall that it had lacked under Keyes. In exchange, he had made it his empire, with fifty thousand men under his command. Laycock would not have that magnitude of power. There were no raids to mount any longer and the D-Day assaults would be largely directed by commanders in the field. The Admiralty had already taken back control of most of the shipping to be involved.

Laycock's role as CCO would therefore be more advisory and supervisory. For all that his critics disliked his evident ambitions for his professional and social standing, his drive and connections fitted him for the task. He had also thought – and perhaps cared – more deeply than anyone else about the best way to use the Commandos; and if his emollient manner could be self-serving, it would surely help to obtain the resources they needed. For instance, two weeks before his appointment, he was interviewed on Churchill's instructions by Lieutenant Colonel Ian Jacob, one of the Prime Minister's chief assistants. Until then, Laycock had vigorously opposed the entry of the Marines into the Commandos. But now, Jacob reported, he declared that his doubts were resolved and he was content with the reorganisation. Laycock knew that there was nothing to be gained from fighting the prevailing wind, and had trimmed accordingly. And while he had a line to Churchill via Jacob, he used it to ask for something the Commandos really needed: that the War Office give a high priority to finding them more recruits.

All that summer of 1943, Laycock had seen for himself the challenges confronting the Commandos in their new incarnation. In July, he had led them in the invasion of Sicily. Then he had commanded the newly formed 2nd Special Service Brigade, consisting of two Army and two RM Commandos, in the landings on the Italian mainland. These had taken place simultaneously at Reggio di Calabria and Salerno.

The Allies' aim was to drive north from the latter to capture Naples, but the countryside behind the beaches on which they disembarked was easily defended, overlooked by hills and cut by wooded valleys. As Laycock was crossing from Sicily on 8 September, Randolph Churchill translated the extraordinary news he could hear on the local radio stations: Italy was seeking an armistice and its forces had surrendered. This raised hopes that the invasion would be unopposed, but soon the troops found German armour waiting for them instead.

In the week of ferocious fighting that followed, 2 Commando suffered 50 per cent losses. Of 23 officers, 7 were killed and another 4 wounded, while 147 of the 315 Other Ranks also became casualties. Among the dead was the 6th Duke of Wellington, who fell while attempting a flanking attack as his men were pinned down by crossfire.

No. 2 was soon exhausted and hurting badly. One young officer, Jos Nicholl, traced his future career as a priest back to the experience of burying so many friends. Yet the survivors continued to attack and then to hold the ground they had taken. It was an achievement that owed much to the inspirational example of their commanding officer, Jack Churchill.

Mad Jack had been given the job of rebuilding No. 2 after its losses at St Nazaire. His style was to lead from the front, where, as he displayed during the raid on Vaagso, he invariably cut a distinctive figure. In another man, flamboyant touches such as the brushed-up moustache and the insistence on dousing everything he ate in chilli sauce might have seemed affectations. In Churchill, they were simply indications of a disregard for convention and the opinions of others. These characteristics could infuriate the higher ranks, but they were evidence of a single-mindedness and self-confidence invaluable in a commanding officer. Churchill once arrived late for a conference with Montgomery, who was a stickler for correct form. Eventually his jeep swirled to a halt in a cloud of dust only feet from where the general sat at a table in the open air. Churchill hopped out, raked over his hair while looking in the wing mirror, casually saluted and sauntered over to his chair. Montgomery was lost for words.

'One of the great things in war', Churchill maintained, 'is first to prevent your kit from being stolen. The second is to avoid being shot by your own side. Once you have established these two good points you can set about the enemy.' This he proceeded to do at Salerno, personally leading an attack on a German battery soon after landing and then organising counter-charges against enemy infiltration of the unit's positions. Explaining why he acted more as a troop leader than as the colonel of the Commando, he said: 'I demoted myself . . . because I was much better at fighting than any of these people were, I knew far more about it, and had done a great deal more.'

On the evening of 15 September, No. 2 made a joint attack with 41 Commando (RM) on three hills just to the east of the port from which the Germans threatened the beachhead. While the marines advanced up the main valley, Churchill's men were to clear any opposition in the adjacent defile and then capture the village of Piegolelle. This sat atop a steep ridge terraced with vines, up which

Churchill clambered, sword in hand. Behind him came his soldiers, shouting 'Commando!' as loudly as they could every few minutes, as he had ordered. This allowed them to keep in touch with each other while they swarmed over the rough terrain. The sound of their cries echoing off the rocks so frightened the defenders that most capitulated as soon as the British emerged from the gloom. Within a few hours, they had captured nearly 140 prisoners and were told to return to their start line. Only then did Churchill learn that there had been a mix-up, and that instead of Piegolelle being taken over by other troops, it had been reoccupied by the Germans. They would have to turn round and assault it again.

When they reached the outskirts of the village for the second time, a brilliant moon had risen in the night sky. The commandos could also hear the clink of spades as the Germans dug in. Having halted the Troop accompanying him, Churchill walked on ahead up a footpath, accompanied only by Corporal Ruffell. The glow of a cigarette gave away two sentries' position beneath an archway; the sight of Churchill's gleaming claymore rapidly convinced them to surrender. Next, he awoke a group of ten men slumbering around a mortar. Then, again at swordpoint, he made one of his prisoners do the rounds of the other sentries, surprising each in turn. Forty-two soldiers, their hands raised high, were eventually shepherded back to the waiting commandos on the edge of the village.

Once captured, Piegolelle was held by Nos. 2 and 41 for the next few days, despite heavy bombardment and determined counter-attacks. Their stubborn resistance helped the Allies to consolidate the landings and then to break out of the Salerno pocket. On 20 September, Fifth Army entered Naples.

'It is beyond doubt that Lt-Col Churchill's gallantry tilted the scales of battle on more than one occasion,' read the citation for the DSO he was subsequently awarded. 'His powers of endurance and the cool and unflinching manner in which he exposed himself to danger . . . rank with the highest traditions of the British Army.' At night, Churchill had strode up and down the streets of Piegolelle, playing his bagpipes to encourage his tired men to fight on.

When the Commando was finally pulled back to rest, the Corps commander, General Sir Richard McCreery, came to congratulate Churchill. He told him that the example set by the Commandos had lifted the morale of the other forces in the bridgehead. At last, it seemed as if they were beginning to be appreciated, but such praise came at too high a price to win round Churchill. 'The tendency was for generals to use Commandos as attacking troops,' he complained in later years. 'I thought this was entirely wrong. Infantry battalions ought to be doing their own damn attacks. We weren't storm troops to be doing attacks for the infantry in inland battles. We were formed as Commandos to do raids on the coast.'

He soon got his wish, when he and some one hundred men from No. 2 were sent to the pine-fringed hills of Vis to aid the partisans. Over the coming months, most of the other units making up the 2nd Special Service Brigade – now commanded by Mad Jack's brother Tom, following Laycock's promotion – would spend time on the island as well.

Life with Tito's men had all the excitement and unpredictability of the exotic. The advance party was fired on as its landing craft entered the harbour because the partisans had mistaken it for a German attack. After that, though, the commandos received a warm welcome, and were impressed by their allies' commitment to the war effort. 'The Communist Party running the affairs of the island appears to be ruthlessly efficient,' noted No. 2's war diary. 'Everything appears subjugated to the war effort.'

This included love, and the Bofors gunners who had accompanied the force were understandably shocked when they witnessed two women being executed by a firing squad for the 'crime' of falling pregnant. Indeed, the partisans' attitude to the sanctity of life was very different to that of the British. On raids, one man would be sent on ahead to check for – and often set off – tripwires, and enemy positions were usually carried by sheer weight of numbers in a headlong charge. Prisoners were often killed, especially if they were Ustaše, members of the Croatian Fascist militia. Jos Nicholl found such brutality easier to understand after seeing some photographs which showed a group of Germans and Ustaše together. 'They were standing behind a pile of some 15 or 20 bodies. Some of the bodies were mangled, but some were of women and youths . . . The shooting party, just as though they had come back from a grouse moor, were leaning on their rifles or shot guns and were grinning proudly.'

Politics would increasingly become a complicating factor in relations with the partisans. Among the earliest indications of this were problems arising from the presence on Vis of the Yugoslav Troop of 10 Commando. Their native country had seemed the ideal posting for them, but many of the officers were monarchists loyal to King Peter, whom the Communists did not recognise. Equally, most of the rank and file in the Troop were tempted to throw their lot in with the partisans. Eventually it had to be withdrawn to Italy, and then disbanded when the ideological divisions grew so violent that its commanding officer had to seek sanctuary in a church from some of his own men.

Another import by the British to Vis fared rather better. A display match of rugby was played in February and greeted with wild enthusiasm by the locals. The war diary recorded, however, that 'the Medical Officer is anticipating a flock of non-battle casualties from the Partisans, as he states he definitely observed some of them studying the hand-offs and looking puzzled as to why the flat hand and not the fist is used. He considers the rules will be amended by them accordingly.'

'It is about time the selfish British Public were reminded that they have got an Army overseas and it is the Army in the end that will have to finish and win this war,' grumbled one commando in a letter home, but in general morale on the island was high. 'I know you are wondering why I joined this band,' wrote another trooper to his father. 'Well, somebody has to do these jobs . . . If you only knew where I am. The job is so interesting, always something new . . . now I am a Commando and proud of it.' A third told his mother, 'The officers are a good lot and live up to Commando reputation, but they also are human beings and understand their men . . . Somebody has to do this job and we're all volunteers because we wanted excitement and real soldiering.'

Spirits were also lifted by the improbable but indomitable presence of the oldest member of the Commandos – then aged seventy-three. Admiral Sir Walter Cowan, who as long ago as 1898 had taken part in the expedition sent to avenge the death of General Gordon at Khartoum, was a friend of Roger Keyes, who had made him his liaison officer. 'I'm very anxious to see a little action before I die,' Cowan had confided, and in North Africa he had rapidly endeared himself to the commandos. Standing only a little over five feet, he refused to take cover from enemy fire, and would ask young soldiers discomforted by their first taste of this if there was anything wrong.

At Tobruk, he had been taken prisoner after the armoured personnel carrier in which he was travelling was hit by an Italian tank. The driver had run off as the tank closed in, but Cowan stood his ground until his pistol had run out of ammunition. 'They ordered me to put my hands up,' he informed the First Sea Lord in a letter from captivity, 'but this I could not do. They overpowered me. I hope you do not think the worse of me.'

When Cowan was released in an exchange of prisoners, Laycock suggested to Mountbatten that he should be permitted to take up his post again. 'I can't hope to be of any great value,' the admiral told Laycock, 'I need a certain amount of refitting in the way of teeth.' Yet, according to Nicholl, he was to prove 'an inspiration quite out of all proportion to his value'.

Clad in his naval cap and khaki shorts that came well below the knee, he clambered nimbly over the hills of the Adriatic, showing himself fitter than soldiers fifty years his junior. Between raids, he paced the quay outside No. 2's base at Komiza as if he were back on the quarter-deck, 'mentioning incidents in the Zulu War as if they had happened yesterday'.

Cowan was the second man into Grohote, the target of Jack Churchill's most successful Yugoslavian raid. Soon after midnight on 18 March 1944, four Troops from 2 Commando prepared to beach

Joe Houghton (left) and Graeme Black led Operation Musketoon, which proved the viability of raids by small groups. Both were executed in accordance with Hitler's Commando Order. (Mrs Desiree Roderick MBE and Commando Veterans Association)

One that got away: Dick O'Brien in civilian clothing after his escape to Sweden. (IWM)

The Glomfjord power plant, Norway, was put out of action by blowing the high-pressure water pipes on the mountainside above to flood it. (National Archives)

Oasis of calm: members of Force B pose before the raid on Tobruk in 1942 in which commandos disguised themselves as German soldiers. (IWM)

SBS officer Tommy Langton (right) rowed in the Boat Race in 1938. After the attack on Tobruk failed, he walked hundreds of miles to safety. (Getty Images)

Gerald Montanaro showed that shipping was vulnerable to seaborne raids by sinking a tanker in Boulogne harbour, even though his canoe had been holed. (Liddell Hart Centre, King's College London)

Cockleshell Hero: 'Blondie' Hasler (right) penetrated far upriver to strike at targets in Bordeaux in one of the boldest – and costliest – missions of the war. (Royal Marines Museum Collection)

First of the Commandos: John Durnford-Slater (left), who led some of the earliest raids, reports to Generals Montgomery and Allfrey in Italy, 1943. (IWM)

Born warrior: Anders Lassen VC (right) enjoys a smoke. He fought with the Commandos, the SAS and the SBS to free Denmark from Nazi occupation. (IWM)

Dressed as a shepherd, John Barton infiltrated enemy erritory in Yugoslavia to kill a German officer, and then worked behind the lines in Italy. (Barton Family)

Captured on a D-Day reconnaissance mission, George Lane was interviewed in person by Rommel. He convinced him he was Welsh rather than Hungarian – and Jewish. (Lane Family)

6 June 1944: Royal Marine commandos move inland from Sword Beach. The shared experience of battle in Normandy helped stem rivalries with their Army counterparts. (IWM)

French troops of 10 (Inter-Allied) Commando march through the streets of Flushing during the hard-fought operation to clear the approaches to the port of Antwerp. (National Archives)

3 Commando Brigade take it easy before embarking for the Myebon Peninsula, Burma, in 1945. The swamps and jungles of the Arakan were formidable obstacles to victory. (IWM)

Firing a mortar from his hip at close range, George Knowland broke up an attack by 300 Japanese troops. He was awarded a posthumous VC. (IWM)

Patrick Dalzel-Job in Germany, 1945. Said to be the model for James Bond, he served in 30 AU, a unit set up by Ian Fleming. (Liddell Ha Centre, King's College London)

To give and not to coun the cost: the Command Memorial is dedicated b the Queen Mother at Spea Bridge, near Achnacarry, i 1952. (Popperfoto/Getty Image

on the island of Solta, which faces the port of Split on the mainland. As their landing craft entered Tatijak Cove, the loudest sound was of the engines ticking over as the vessels drifted towards the shore.

The raiders' numbers were swelled by 155 American troops of Greek and Yugoslav extraction, and by Commando heavy weapons teams, equipped with mortars and Vickers machine-guns. There were also three pieces of Italian field artillery. All the weapons and extra ammunition had to be manhandled up the steep escarpment which rose from the shingle. As the troops laboured along the zigzag path to the top, they dislodged tiny flakes of flint which tinkled as they fell, 'like cow-bells in a pasture'.

There had been a serious setback shortly before the landings when a party sent to reconnoitre the island had been attacked by a German patrol. After the survivors regrouped, it became clear that the group's leader, Captain Ianto Jenkins, had been severely wounded and probably taken prisoner. He had been making notes about the German positions and Churchill feared that these might have been found on him, so alerting the enemy. In fact, surprise was achieved and by 0530 Churchill's five-hundred-strong force, reinforced by partisans, was in place.

'We all got into our positions behind these vineyard walls, waiting for Kittyhawk divebombers to come in,' remembered John Morris, the veteran of Barton's raid. 'About 6am they came in, took out all the defences, they were marvellous.' Thirty-six aircraft swooped low over the town, reducing much of it to rubble. 'Jack Churchill got on the megaphone,' Morris recalled. 'We had a number of German Jews in the unit and they shouted to the Germans to surrender. The German commander didn't come out so the bombers went in again, and then we did.'

'It was the first time that anyone in the assaulting ground forces had seen the RAF attacking an objective that was of any real interest to them,' commented Churchill sardonically. None the less, at Grohote the theory of combined operations worked perfectly, and no sooner had the bombs fallen on the town than the commandos were on their feet and into the ruins.

'There was a lot of street-fighting, which is horrendous,' said Morris later.

> Your stomach is all knotted up. Looking back I'm surprised that I could do this sort of thing. We only suffered two casualties. I always remember one. The Germans started to surrender and there was a Spandau post in front of us. There was a young chap named Cox, he was from the police intake. We were always taught that if you see a white flag you don't get up at once. Silly devil, he did and got a full belt in the stomach. Down he went. Anyway, we went in, we were so angry that no-one came out of that alive . . . I can picture it now, this chap lying on the stretcher with all his insides spewed out. He died a couple of days later.

The 150 soldiers in the garrison were quickly overwhelmed and more than 100 prisoners taken for the loss of that pair of Allied casualties. By nightfall, Churchill's force was back on Vis. The next contingent of German troops sent to hold Solta was three times the size.

The raid had succeeded because it had been mounted on Churchill's terms, but also because nothing had gone wrong. As the scale of operations became larger, they became more dependent on close cooperation not simply between the various Commando formations but also with the partisans. Ten weeks later, Mad Jack's luck would run out.

At the end of May, German parachutists launched an attack on Tito's HQ in Bosnia. He managed to evade capture, but asked the Allies to stage a large-scale diversionary attack in Dalmatia to relieve the pressure on his forces. A plan was quickly put together for the soldiers on Vis to land on Brac in such numbers that the Germans would think their positions on the mainland coast opposite were threatened. The hope was that this would draw off some of the troops hunting the partisans inland.

Jack Churchill had his doubts about this operation – codenamed FLOUNCED – from the start. A few days earlier, he had become acting commander of the brigade when his brother returned to Britain to prepare for D-Day. He wanted to send his own men from No. 2 to Brac, but they had just finished their fortnightly rota of raids and all of their officers had been sent to a parachute school in Italy. When Churchill asked for them to be flown back, he was told that to do so would annoy the RAF, who had organised the course. Instead, it was suggested that he should use one of the RM Commando units on Vis – No. 43 – but this he was reluctant to do. 'They never get any prisoners and they're no good,' he told his superiors. This adverse opinion may have resulted from the failure the previous week of a raid by them on the island of Mljet, although in all fairness they had been hampered by particularly arduous terrain and inaccurate intelligence from partisans as to the enemy's location. Churchill, however, had 'precious little confidence' in No. 43's commanding officer, Lieutenant Colonel R.W.B. 'Bonzo' Simonds. Despite having organised several successful raids, Simonds had apparently told Tom Churchill that leading commandos was not for him, a sentiment with which the brigadier did not disagree.

None the less, on the night of 1 June a motley fleet of some forty vessels of all sizes ferried 43 Commando (RM) to three beaches on Brac. They were supported by the Heavy Weapons Troop of No. 40, field artillery and some two and a half thousand partisans. The German garrison, which numbered about two thousand, was divided between three areas, the key positions being those on three hills in the centre of the island, near Nerežišća. The commandos were to assault these, while the majority of the partisans attacked the strongholds to the north and east, so as to prevent their contingents from sending reinforcements.

It soon became apparent that the German defences were formidable. An observation post linked to coastal guns overlooked the climb of fifteen hundred feet up which the marines had to heft their mortars and Bangalore torpedoes. Beyond lay miles of bare hillside commanded by machine-guns sited in concrete bunkers. These posts were protected by wire and minefields, and proved invulnerable even to a rocket strike by Hurricanes.

Several attacks were mounted on two of the three hills, but all were repulsed. By late afternoon, the marines were exhausted, while the partisans had lost heart and at the last minute refused to take part in the final sortie of the day. This was broken up by heavy Spandau and mortar fire, and when the commandos withdrew they were strafed by the RAF for the second time in as many hours. The only comfort was that the partisans had largely succeeded in their operations against the other towns occupied by 118 Jäger.

German reinforcements were expected overnight, so Churchill summoned three hundred more partisans from Vis and the rest of 40 Commando (RM). Its commanding officer was Lieutenant Colonel James Manners, known as 'Pops', even though he was only twenty-eight years old. For five hours on the morning of the 3rd, Churchill reconnoitred the enemy positions, eventually deciding that they would fall if the dome-shaped central hill, known from its height in metres as Point 622, was taken.

After much wrangling with the partisans, it was arranged that they would fire on (if not attack) the two hills either side of Point 622 that evening, while No. 43 made the main assault with support from No. 40. This plan was radioed to the two Commandos, but the hilly landscape made wireless communications unreliable. Therefore, at 1430, Churchill sent his planning officer, Captain Roger Wakefield, to give a copy of the orders to Manners, who was about a thousand yards away.

The attack was due to go in under a creeping barrage from 2030. About twenty minutes beforehand, Churchill walked down to the start line, expecting to see both Commandos preparing to set off. 'To my astonishment,' he recalled, 'I ran into Manners walking towards me.' He told Churchill that he had received no orders, and his men were currently having their evening meal.

Manners sprinted back to his positions to get his troops moving, but No. 43 had already begun their advance alone. The partisans had failed to quell the posts on the other two hills and the

Commando was swept by crossfire from the flanks as it reached the wire below Point 622. All the officers and six of the sergeants in the two leading Troops became casualties as they charged across open ground towards the pillboxes on the crest. These were cleared and by 2150 the Commando was in possession of its objective.

However, by now ammunition was running low. The beach was six miles away, and the four mules bringing up reserves had collapsed that afternoon under the broiling sun. At 2215, a strong German counter-attack came in, and the marines were driven back to the lower slopes of the hill.

Far below them, Jack Churchill was picking his way through burning gorse which had been set alight by mortar fire. No. 40 had set off an hour late, led by Churchill himself and Manners. When they had got to the start line, they had come across Wakefield, who had been led all over the island by the guide after he had lost his way. Although he was tired, Wakefield asked to come with them as he was a gunner and had never participated in an infantry attack.

From what he could hear, Churchill assumed that there was little fighting left to be done, so he was surprised to run into B Troop of No. 43, which had become separated from the rest of the Commando. An officer told him that they had been held up by barbed wire and mines, an explanation that rendered Churchill indignant. 'I said: "Barbed wire and mines? How many men have been killed?" And he said no one exactly has been killed. And nobody has been wounded. So I said: "How the hell have you been held up by wire and mines?"'

The officer replied that he had seen posts marking a minefield.

'I said to Manners: "Now, look here, we're going straight across this ... There may be some mines here but in any case this is an enormous hill and if there are any mines they will be few and far between."'

Churchill told the commandos to lift their feet up high as they walked, to reduce the risk from tripwires, and played his bagpipes to encourage them. 'I didn't hear a single mine go up, and I don't think anyone had any losses.' His leadership had again rallied troops as they faltered, although official records show that they did suffer several casualties that evening. Moreover, despite Churchill's reservations about No. 43, B Troop did then pour fire into the German positions as Manners's men charged line abreast up the ridge. Point 622 was captured for the second time, a feat signalled by Churchill with a salvo of Very lights.

He had been expecting, however, to find the remainder of 43 Commando near by. Manners and Wakefield set off to search for them in the moonlight, but 'Manners had only gone about 20 yards when he shouted "I've been hit!"' As Churchill helped to dress the wound in the colonel's chest, Wakefield was also gravely injured. A marine began to bind him up, only to be shot through the head and collapse on top of the injured officer. The lines of tracer coursing through the air showed that another counter-attack had begun.

'I thought that the time had come to play a pipe tune,' recalled Churchill. 'I rolled on my back and played the pipes lying down on the ground. The tune was *Will Ye No Come Back Again?*' It was heard, and its meaning understood, by Walter Cowan down at Brigade HQ, but there were no reserves to send to Churchill's aid. He continued to resist with his carbine – and Manners with his revolver until he was mortally wounded – but in a very short while only three of the dozen men on top of the hill remained unhurt. 'Then the next thing that happened was that a mortar fragment hit me on my steel helmet and knocked me out.' When he came to, Churchill found that the Germans had once again reoccupied Point 622. He surrendered to them in the traditional manner, offering them the hilt of his claymore over his forearm.

He was taken to Divisional Headquarters at Mostar and then flown to Berlin for further interrogation, as his surname had led his captors to hope he might be related to Britain's leader. When Churchill was left on his own for a few moments in a Fiesler Storch at Tempelhof aerodrome, he used matches and newspapers to set the aircraft on fire. Even in captivity, Mad Jack was still at war.

Simonds took over command of the weary troops on Brac and evacuated them the following day, 4 June. More than fifty British soldiers had been killed in the operation, and twice as many wounded. Partisan losses had also been heavy, while estimates of the German dead rose as high as 350, although this was probably an exaggeration.

There was no doubting the spirit and determination that both 43 and 40 Commandos had shown in adversity. Yet the uncomfortable truth was that the attack had failed. 'The bald facts are that a strong Allied force landed on a Dalmatian island, did not overrun it and withdrew with casualties,' declared a report on FLOUNCED. Nor was it thought that the raid had succeeded in drawing off any of the German troops engaged in Bosnia.

This was ultimately to prove of little consequence, but the difficulties endured by the Commandos in overcoming fortified positions was an unpleasant taste of the obstacles that barred the road to Berlin. Far to the north, Allied troops were already embarking for the Normandy beaches, and only a few weeks later the brigade began to pull out of Vis. The Germans were preparing to leave Yugoslavia and this had emboldened the partisans' ideologues to become less tolerant than ever of the British imperialist presence.

Even so, Tito reviewed No. 2 on Vis before its departure, addressing it from the middle of the hollow square they formed around him. A little later the same day, Walter Cowan also left the island. After inspecting a guard of honour, he stood on a bollard to make a farewell speech, but was overcome with emotion after uttering only the words: 'My dear friends'. As the MGB carrying him to Italy drew away, three tremendous cheers rang around the harbour.

'It was the most stirring event most of us have ever witnessed,' recorded the unit's war diary. 'It was with very great regret that the Commando saw their greatest admirer depart.' Two months later, and half a century after he had first won the DSO, Cowan was awarded a Bar to it for his rescue under fire of a wounded Commando colonel in Italy and for his bravery on Solta. There can be few other septuagenarians who have received medals for acts of gallantry on active service.

'His determination to be where the battle was fiercest, combined with his encouragement and cheerfulness . . . has been a very real contribution to the fighting spirit of the brigade,' ran Cowan's citation. He had not been alone in regarding his time in Yugoslavia as good sport. 'I believe it was his sincere desire to end his life with his teeth in the throat of a German soldier,' thought Laycock.

Others would continue the raiding tradition established by the Commandos, notably Jellicoe's Special Boat Squadron on the Greek islands, but Vis was the last hurrah for its original creators. Grimmer battles lay ahead.

15

OVERLORD

On a summer afternoon, late in May 1944, James Kelly was sitting in the back yard of his billet in Hastings. Spread out before him and his mate was a groundsheet covered in ammunition. Methodically they cleaned and polished each cartridge before slotting them into magazines. Something made Kelly look up, and at the window he saw the kindly face of their landlady. It was wet with tears.

'She was looking down at two young kids loading all this regalia of war,' he reflected later, 'and she knew in her heart that very soon we would be going away and using it to kill someone. Or to be killed by someone else.'

For a year and a half, the Commandos had been readying themselves for the invasion of France. D-Day would be the acid test of how well they had adapted to their role as light infantry. They would land two brigades in Normandy, yet neither had much experience of their new remit.

The 1st Special Service Brigade, under Shimi Lovat, was to come ashore on the extreme eastern flank of the offensive, codenamed OVERLORD. It comprised 6 Commando, led by Derek Mills-Roberts, which had not seen action since North Africa; 3 Commando, headed by Peter Young, which had last fought in Sicily a year before; 4 Commando, now led by Lieutenant Colonel Robert Dawson, which had not participated in a raid since Dieppe in 1942; and finally the untested 45 Commando, made up of marines.

The brigade would be in the second wave of landings. Its job was not to knock out the beach defences as this would already have been done by county regiments, such as the Suffolks and the South Lancashires. Instead, it was to push inland and link up with the 6th Airborne Division at the bridges over the Caen Canal and the River Orne.

By contrast, the 4th Special Service Brigade was to be stretched across the centre of the Allied line. Spreading between the country west of the Orne and the Americans on Omaha Beach, it was to clear the small coastal villages either side of Arromanches, where a Mulberry artificial harbour would later be sited. Led by Brigadier Bernard 'Jumbo' Leicester, the brigade consisted entirely of Royal Marine Commandos. No. 41 – with which James Kelly was serving – had already taken part in operations in Sicily and at Salerno, but for Nos. 46, 47 and 48, D-Day would be their introduction to combat.

These tasks were important, but they were not ones which made particular use of the commandos' specialised training. Certainly, their mobility would help Lovat's men to reach the bridges quickly. Yet it seems perverse that, given their expertise in amphibious warfare, those Commando units which had previously experienced enemy fire were not asked to play a more prominent part in subduing the first line of defence. If this were not done quickly, the entire invasion might fail.

The planners' reasoning was that the assault could be executed just as well by conventional infantry and armour, units of which had also been specially trained and equipped to breach the Atlantic Wall. It was an argument which perhaps owed a little to the Field Army's lingering resentment of the Commandos' higher profile, as well as to an understandable pride in its own abilities. That self-belief would be largely justified on D-Day. But, for many, pride would be no substitute for knowing how to stay alive on a hostile beach.

Growing up in Liverpool during the Depression had been no cakewalk for James Kelly. His parents' home had a single cold-water tap and in hard times the family lived on bread and jam. The Marines offered three meals a day and hot showers, and he had had no hesitation in signing up in 1941, at the age of eighteen, despite the recruiting sergeant's pitch for the Irish Guards. This had been accompanied by the reassurance that he would unfailingly receive the last rites before being sent into battle.

In July 1943, he had volunteered with others from the 8th Battalion RM for hazardous duties, and after passing the selection process had found himself one of sixty-five men in A Troop of the new 41 Commando. There had been another brief period of training in Sicily before they were thrown into the cauldron of Salerno.

Now the preparations for a still more daunting test were over. Kelly packed up his kit, said farewell to his landlady, and assembled with the Commando at Littlehampton. There his bolt-cutters came in handy for cutting the wire around the temporary barracks when sneaking out in search of a drink; he put other skills to use in evading the Military Police on the way back in.

Great swaths of southern England had been turned into an armed camp. Lovat had established his Brigade HQ in the Rising Sun pub on the River Hamble. 4 Commando was marshalled on Southampton Common, where they were briefed on their D-Day objectives. Although the names of villages and towns had been replaced by false ones in the aerial photographs that they were shown, the French troops from 10 Commando attached to the unit recognised the area at once. One man had even operated the lock gates on the Caen–Ouistreham Canal. As a result, all were confined to camp until they sailed.

For several days, foul weather delayed embarkation. 'It was at tea time on June 5th, when I saw the minesweepers beginning to creep out, that I realised the show was on,' remembered No. 4's medical officer, Joe Patterson, in civilian life a GP from Windermere.

'It was a lovely evening,' reminisced Lovat's personal piper, Bill Millin. 'We sailed down the river towards the Isle of Wight, where there were thousands and thousands of ships. Lovat had me up at the front of the landing craft, playing the pipes. As we drew level with these ships, a terrific roar went up because they had put me over the loudhailer – admirals were throwing their hats in the air.'

'Going across the Channel, the enormity of everything began to become apparent,' agreed Jim Spearman, one of No. 4's veterans of the Varengeville battery raid. 'Because no matter where you looked, you found ships of all shapes and sizes, war ships and merchant ships in every direction, as far as the eye could see.' More than six thousand vessels were involved in NEPTUNE, as the seaborne phase of OVERLORD was codenamed. Two-thirds of these were landing craft of various sizes, including those that were carrying the 1st Brigade to France. Aboard his, Kelly was cramped and seasick. The crossing was rough and the thought of making himself a tin of self-heating soup repelled him. He was more tempted to down the full pint of rum with which he had been issued, 'but I was terrified in case I got drunk and did the wrong thing and got killed.'

Conditions were more comfortable for Patterson aboard the converted Belgian ferry *Princess Astrid*. In the days before, he had been bedding down on its deck in a sleeping bag borrowed from one of No. 4's officers, David Haig-Thomas, who would be dropping with the 6th Airborne as their link to the Commandos. But by the time that Patterson was stirring on 6 June, not long before dawn, No. 4 had already suffered its first casualty: Haig-Thomas had been killed just a few hours after landing.

The early morning air was cold and grey with mist. As the men struggled into bandoliers and rucksacks, there was a loud explosion away to their left. A Norwegian destroyer escorting them had struck a mine. It broke in two, each half rearing skywards before succumbing to the sea.

'Everything seemed to stand out in Technicolor,' thought Warwick Nield-Siddall, a Mancunian in 41 Commando. 'Everything was brighter than normal.' Above the excited chatter of the soldiers rose the bellow of battleships already bombarding the low strip of coast on the horizon. An endless cavalcade of aircraft streamed towards France. 'And it was us, and we were going,' realised Nield-Siddall. 'And we wanted to go – most of us. It was something that had to be done ... I don't remember talking to anyone who was frightened. We were all so eager ... it had been coming so long.'

The *Astrid*'s anchor went down with a clatter and the commandos began to board the smaller assault craft. There was a heavy swell, and the boats rode freely on the waves. Their white, grey and blue camouflage made the squat vessels hard to pick out against the sea, but ahead Patterson could see the first ranks already going in to Sword Beach. At 0730, the amphibious tanks of the 13th/18th Hussars splashed up through the surf, followed shortly afterwards by the 8th Infantry Brigade. The doctor recalled:

> The East Yorks were to go in at H hour to clear the beach defences and to make gaps in the wire and minefields for us. We were to go in 30 minutes later, pass through the East Yorks, dump our rucksacks and crash into Ouistreham, taking the beach defences up to the canal mouth from the rear, and clearing up the strong point round the Casino and the six-gun battery at the eastern end of the town. The rest of the Brigade – Nos. 3, 6 and 45 Commandos – had no assault task and were to come in at H plus 3 hours and make their way straight to the bridges over the Orne canal ... and hold the bridgehead thus established against all attacks.

All along the shore there rose flashes of orange from bursting shells, answered by coastal artillery. A thick pall of smoke hung over the beaches. Behind the flotilla of LCs, a sheaf of light erupted from a rocket ship. In front, a crescendo of noise grew and grew as the land drew closer.

Patterson's hand was numb and his teeth chattered with cold and fright. His batman, Fred Smith, looked terrible but gave him a grin.

> I took a look around the boat. Private Hindmarch beside me, looking surprisingly pink. Lieutenant Kennedy – I always remember him as a sergeant in No. 5 – looking rather grim but enjoying his rum. Just as well, too, as he was never seen again after leaving the boat. Little Mullen, the artist, grey as a corpse . . . Gordon Webb and Peter Beckett in the bows were peering forward, alert and tense . . . I could hear snatches of song from the other boats. Hutch Burt's boat went in singing *Jerusalem*. We didn't sing in our boat. My mouth was bone dry and I was shaking all over.

Sword was obscured by smoke. But as the rattle of small-arms fire began to be heard above the roar of the naval guns, Patterson knew they were getting near. A plume of spray broke over them as a shell came down beside the LC. Away to starboard, something exploded in a cascade of oil and flame. Bullets began to thud against the side of the craft and splinters whined over the top.

'Ready on the ramp! Going in to land! We touched, bumped and slewed round. This was no true landing, we could feel.' Patterson and his medical team were at the stern of the LC and the last to leave. He passed the limp body of a commando whose letter to his wife he had censored earlier in the week. 'I am no hero,' the man had written, 'I did not volunteer for this lot.' Now his forebodings had been realised.

Patterson grabbed two stretchers and jumped from the bow into the water:

> It came up to mid-thigh as the craft had grounded on some softish obstacle, probably a body . . . I have no idea how long it was from when I left the boat till when I reached the wire . . . I noticed after a few paces that there were many bodies in the water . . . As I got nearer the shore I saw wounded men among the dead, pinned down by the weight of their equipment.

Brian Mullen, the Commando's official artist, was among the casualties:

> He was submerged to his chin and quite helpless. Somehow I got my scissors out and with my numb hands, which felt weak and useless, I began to cut away his rucksack and equipment. Hindmarch appeared beside me and got working on the other side. He was a bit rattled but soon steadied when I spoke to him. As I was bending over I felt a smack across my bottom as if someone had hit me with a big stick. It was a shell splinter, as appeared later on, but it hit nothing important and I just carried on.

The horror of the scene struck Jim Spearman moments after landing:

> I was shocked by the number of bodies, dead bodies, living bodies and all the blood in the water, giving the appearance they were drowning in their own blood for the want of moving. The whole place was littered with it. There were great, monstrous fortifications on the beach like tremendous cubes, or criss-crossed steel, girders to stop gliders landing, to stop ships coming in. There were girders penetrating into the beach, sticking up to stop boats coming in. The whole beach area was supposed to be, and in fact was, covered by flame-throwers. It was a desperate situation.

In that sector of Sword, the East Yorks had run into trouble. Lashed by a storm of bullets from enfilading pillboxes, their natural reaction had been to stop and seek cover where they were. Spearman knew that it was a fatal mistake:

> It's only a person who's been through it a number of times that can know you've either got to stay and die – or get off and live. I know, because I once lay down, that if you get down with a pack on your back, you can't get up again. And if you elongate yourself on a beach, you're a much easier target to hit. We were all fit and thin, and standing up you present less of a target . . . We had one object in mind: to get off the bloody beach. Having

seen all the bodies doubled our determination. No matter what happened, we had to get off the beach. Once you're off the beach, you're out of fire.

But it's a very hard lesson to learn. We were, of course, transfixed with fright. But we had the certain knowledge that you either stopped and died – or you got off and got away.

Two hundred yards ahead, a line of wire and concrete emplacements blocked the approaches to Ouistreham. The only way off the sand lay through their interlaced fields of fire. 'We'd never really been on a beach that was so heavily defended,' Spearman reckoned. Forty commandos were soon casualties, yet the constant thump of mortars encouraged the rest to keep moving.

First to the wire was the officer in command of the Machine-gun Troop, Knyvet Carr. Scrambling up the mound supporting a pillbox, out of sight of the apertures cut in either side, he managed to lob a grenade into the sandbags behind it from where a Spandau was firing at troops to his right. With this threat eliminated, they ran through into the dunes beyond and took the post from the rear. Soon the entire Commando was moving in a human wave past the German defences.

Not everyone had been able to get out of the danger zone yet, though. Patterson had had to stay at the water's edge, tending to an injured soldier, Donald Glass. 'As I was doing so, I became conscious of a machine gun enfilading us from the left. In a minute, I was knocked over by a smack in the right knee and fell on Donald, who protested violently. I cautiously tried my leg and found it still worked, though not very well.' He and Hindmarch put Glass on a stretcher and carried him through the wire to No. 4's assembly area. There the doctor took a swig of rum and had a look at his own wound. He discovered that the bullet had passed through the tendons and muscles behind the knee, narrowly missing the artery. This was also when he learned that a piece of shrapnel had lodged in his buttock.

Lame as he was, Patterson hurried along the main road into Ouistreham, which was under heavy mortar fire. At the corner of a copse, he came across a group of six dead, among them Lance Corporal Joseph Pasquale, one of the two Cockney Italian orderlies in his medical section. It was unwise to linger in the gaps between houses, so he kept moving.

> About 200 yards further on we passed two more of our chaps, one dead and the other almost gone with his head smashed in. I pushed my helmet over his face and went on. Another 100 yards on we found my L/Cpl Farnese, quite dead. The same mortar bomb had killed another man, an old Frenchman who had come out to welcome us, and severely wounded another man in the shoulder.

That shell had narrowly missed Sergeant-Major Bill Portman, another veteran of the Varengeville raid. The Germans had started to get their range a mile up the road from the beach. The Frenchman had come out of his house to tell the Allied troops that his brother had been hurt. Portman had told Farnese to go and have a look, and at that moment had heard the noise of a *Minenwerfer* light mortar. 'It used to sound like a donkey, you could hear it in the distance and knew they were coming . . . As we were talking, down came a "mini". It killed Farnese, it killed this Frenchman and it blew me on my face. And I never got a scratch. I was the luckiest man alive.'

The British and French contingents of the Commando had different targets in Ouistreham. While the latter worked round to the casino, which had been converted into a blockhouse facing the sea, the former headed for two batteries which covered the entrance to the canal up to Caen.

'We were under constant sniper fire the whole way,' remembered Spearman of that mad dash through the town's streets. 'By the time you heard the crack it was too late. There was no point in stopping, you had to go on.' Mortar rounds skimmed over the roofs of houses and dropped all around them. 'You did have to stop for that. If you didn't throw yourself to the ground you could get killed by shrapnel.' On one occasion, Spearman and a friend took evasive action at almost exactly the same time. 'He was just a fraction later than me going down, and when I got up, he never did. I turned him over and he had got shrapnel in his head. Killed outright.'

The batteries were protected by a fourteen-foot-wide anti-tank ditch. During their training on Pevensey Marshes, Portman had decided that the simplest method of crossing such an obstacle was via a lightweight footbridge in two sections, so he made sure his section took one to Normandy. However, 'I lost three men from my troop on D-Day carrying that bridge,' he later remarked. 'And blow me down, when we got there we found that Jerry had been sneaking out of his barracks at night across a couple of planks nailed together.' Moreover, when they got over the ditch, the commandos discovered that the battery contained only dummy guns made of wood.

The Germans in the high white flak tower were real, however. Many men were soon wounded, including a Bren gunner in Portman's section who was hit in the stomach. The bullet passed through a phosphorus grenade and began to burn his skin until doused with a water bottle.

There was clearly nothing to be gained by hanging around and taking more casualties, so they pulled back to the main junction, where Patterson had set up an aid post. Among the injured was 4 Commando's CO, Robert Dawson, who had a split temple and shell fragments in his leg but refused to be evacuated. 'We had suffered heavily,' wrote Patterson, 'about 150 all ranks' – almost a third of the unit – 'being killed or wounded.' But by 1100, the French had taken the casino and the battle in the town had died away. Those who were still on their feet formed up to push inland and on to the bridges over the Orne.

Away to the west, 41 Commando (RM) had landed at the other edge of Sword Beach, on the far side of Ouistreham. James Kelly had been carrying a Bren gun, hunched down in a line of six across the deck of his LC. He could see the shambles ahead on the beach and wondered how he would survive it.

The landing craft headed straight for its marker, a house with a gabled roof at Hermanville-sur-Mer. When the ramp came down, however, the boat's momentum caused it to veer round. As he prepared to step off, Kelly found himself looking down at waist-deep water. 'The next thing I remember is a terrible blinding flash and a terrible bloody smell of cordite.' Charlie Hall, a Geordie who was number two in his Bren section, was lying down with blood pumping from his neck, but a voice told Kelly not to stop and help.

In the thin morning light, everything looked black or grey. Shells threw up great spouts of dirt, and dust-coloured smoke poured from the turrets of burning tanks. But the flails had beaten a path through the mines and wire, and within five minutes of getting ashore at 0840, Kelly's troop commander, Captain Nicolas Powell, had got them clear of the beach. In the confusion, however, other sections had come ashore in the wrong part of the landing zone. There resistance was heavier and there had been many casualties. These included the unit's second-in-command, the signals officer and the regimental sergeant-major.

No. 41's aim was to move westwards along the coast road through Lion-sur-Mer and join up with their fellow marines of 48 Commando at Petit Enfer. Powell soon received reports from the South Lancs, who had landed first, saying that they were now being held up by German armour. Kelly was sent to find HQ and report this. He did not relish going back down the narrow lane up which they had just come. And he liked even less the prospect of returning to Powell a little later with a message to hold on.

At one point a burst of fire hit the brickwork a few feet above his head and he dived into a hedge. Then another fusillade sent him bounding into what proved to be an air-raid shelter occupied by civilians. After accepting a drink of wine, he set off once more and eventually found his Bren section holed up in a large house. The courtyard was littered with the dead and wounded. The body of a signaller, his wireless on his back, was still twitching. Angrily, Kelly let off several clips at a hedgerow where Germans could be seen moving about, but it was not long before they began to mortar the Troop's position.

Powell – who was a student at Cambridge when war broke out but had already won the DSO in Italy – had once stood on Kelly's back during training to encourage him to get closer to the ground. Now he seemed just as calm as he had been then, walking about and telling the men what to do – until he was shot through the mouth. 'There,' thought Kelly, 'that's shut him up for a bit.'

At 1330, A Troop began to fall back. Kelly and Powell were the last to pull out and together they ran through an orchard towards a high wall. As he reached it, Kelly turned round to see that Powell had fallen about fifteen feet behind him and was groaning in pain. His leg had been broken by a bullet and he told Kelly to go on without him. By way of reply, Kelly began to drag the captain through the grass towards the wall. But Powell was exceptionally tall and the effort exhausted Kelly. Moreover, the wall was ten feet high, so there was no chance of either of them getting over it unaided. 'Who thinks straight in a situation like that except John Wayne?' said Kelly afterwards. He found a ladder and hoisted the wounded officer over his shoulder. As he began to climb, the third rung collapsed under their combined weight. Both men fell to the ground, swearing.

Just then, two marines appeared at the top of the wall. Kelly managed to prop Powell up against it as the others hauled him up by his wrists. Hastily, Kelly threw the Bren over and took a running jump at what was left of the ladder. All the while, he was aware of German soldiers watching from the edge of the orchard, and the fact that they were holding their fire.

When he dropped down on the far side of the wall, he found Powell lying in a ditch. The pair who had pulled him over had not realised that the captain had been wounded. Kelly scouted around and came across a wheelbarrow. Into this he bundled the officer, before wheeling him up the back steps of a house, through several rooms and out the front door to the street beyond. There he flagged down a Jeep that was acting as an ambulance. 'When that Jeep drove away, the loneliness that I felt standing there . . . a bedraggled young marine, standing in this street, clutching an empty Bren gun and watching his Troop commander being driven away, bereft.'

When he finally caught up with the rest of the unit, Kelly was sent to take up a defensive post in a house which had a thick front door covered in studs. By now he was so overwhelmed by events that his automatic response was to pull out his pistol:

> I fired one shot at the lock. There was a tap on my shoulder, and when I turned round there was a priest in his robes. His head was shaking, he reached forward, turned the handle and opened the door. I slunk inside, went up to the bedroom and cried my eyes out. I thought I'd made a complete and utter mess of the whole thing ... I realised how immature I must be, green, what I was doing there God only knew.
>
> When I'd recovered a little bit, I filled the magazines and then the training took over – don't break the windows, leave the curtains where they are, don't put the gun up by the window but keep it well back. I suppose I started to function like a soldier again then. It started to get dark then. That was my D-Day.

Piper Millin had been an instructor at Achnacarry and until summoned by Lovat he had not expected to go to Normandy. Yet his girlfriend, Rebecca, who was from the Western Isles of Scotland, had a premonition that he would play a part in the invasion. She believed that Millin would come through it unscathed, but 'the tall man' would be severely wounded a week after landing.

Lovat had been forbidden from taking a piper with him, but he briskly told Millin that since they were both Scots, what the English War Office said did not apply to them. His Brigade HQ landed on Sword, under heavy fire, with the second wave at 0840. Clad in a Cameron kilt, and the green beret that Lovat had insisted all his men wear instead of helmets, Millin began to play as soon as he waded off the ramp into the water. Lovat turned round, smiled and walked on.

When Millin reached the beach, his first instinct was to dash for the exit. Then he saw some of the wounded lying in the path of a flail tank and went back to find Lovat, who was just hearing from the brigade major that the Airborne had taken the bridges over the

Orne. Lovat turned to Millin and told him to give them another tune. Given the situation, at first the piper thought the suggestion was 'ridiculous':

> There was shellfire and all kinds of things going on. It was mad enough we three standing there, we should have been lying down. And I thought I may as well be ridiculous too, so I asked him which tune I should play. And he said: 'Play *The Road to the Isles*.'
>
> And I said: 'Would you like me to march up and down?'
>
> 'Yes, yes, march up and down, that would be lovely.'
>
> The whole thing was ridiculous. The bodies down by the water were wafting up and down on the tide. The next thing I felt was a hand on my shoulder, and it was a sergeant I recognised. 'What are you playing at, you mad bastard? Every German in France knows we're here now!' Anyhow, I walked on, and there were people up at the wall cheering!
>
> Everything was happening so quickly and so suddenly – the noise and the action, some wounded and some dead, their heads blown off – I don't think I was frightened at all. The fear was later on, some hours after I came ashore.

Naturally, Lovat himself had no intention of showing that the Germans were to be feared. 'There he stood in highly polished brogues,' said the watching George Saunders, 'and every time there was a burst of machine-gun fire, he nonchalantly flicked the sand off his shoes ... As each unit came ashore he said "Good morning, gentlemen." He just ran it like a grouse shoot on his own moor. It was fantastic.'

But for his Jewish blood, Saunders might have been among those trying to kill Lovat. As a boy, he had even been in the Hitler Youth, albeit in a Troop led by the Jesuits who ran the school in the Black Forest that he attended. Born in Munich as Georg Saloschin, he and his aristocratic parents – who were already refugees from the Russian Revolution – had left Germany for Scotland in the late 1930s. His father had been at school with Kurt Hahn, the founder of Gordonstoun, who took him on there as a teacher, and his two teenage sons as pupils. When war came, Georg was denied a commission in the British Army because of his nationality. Instead, he joined X Troop of 10 Commando, changing his name in the process. Later, he commented:

> War, to the uninitiated, is like a Marx Bros film. Everything is a balls-up. This young naval officer thought we had already touched the beach but we had merely run across some barbed wire defences underwater and temporarily came to a halt. This timid young officer lowered the ramp, and the intelligence officer revved his bike and dived over the side into the deep water. That was the last we saw of him.
>
> This naval lieutenant went back and had another go and beached us in quite shallow water. It came up to about our waists. You mustn't forget that on that day we were loaded up like mules, packs fore and aft, little pack behind, munitions, tommy gun . . . that is where I saw His Lordship with his piper, a sight I will never forget.

On D-Day, Saunders and the other German-speaking members of X Troop were attached to various Commandos as interrogators and intelligence gatherers. Soon after landing, Saunders was wounded by a grenade in an attack on a farmhouse. Its cellar provided consolation by way of bottles of Château d'Yquem and row upon row of Camembert, treats he had not seen for years – 'so that was my lunch'.

Later that afternoon, he found a bicycle and set off to find the British lines. As the sun was setting behind him, he came to a junction around which stood a group of soldiers. Thinking they were Allied troops, he waved at them, only to hear one say, '*Das ist ein Engländer!*' He leaped from the saddle into a ditch just as they began shooting.

> They hunted me for over an hour. My advantage was that I spoke German. I heard this officer saying: '*Aren't you ashamed, it's only one Englishman.*' And I heard one of the ORs saying:

> '*Why don't you go, Leutnant?*' Then I knew they were demoralised and shit scared. I must have killed five or six.
>
> I had the standard Type 36 grenades, a tommy-gun and phosphorus grenades – you're not supposed to use them for anti-personnel work but they're very effective. They hunted me up and down the ditch. Every time I heard someone nearby, I got up and threw a grenade.

In the corner of the field into which he crawled there was a small stagnant pond. He slithered into it and pulled his camouflage net over himself. Only after he had been there for a while, shivering with cold, did he realise that a German soldier was staring at him from just five yards away.

Saunders heard the German officer shout, 'Can you see him?'

'No,' the soldier said, and turned away.

That evening, Saunders met up with the British forces, and after being taken to see Lovat at his HQ he volunteered to lead a patrol back into the area where he had been hunted. It ran into opposition and, handicapped by his earlier wound, Saunders was taken prisoner. Fortunately, he managed to conceal his real identity from his captors, who assumed that he was British. 'If they had discovered I was German, I would have been shot like a mad dog. Not only that, I was a deserter, I had a *stellungsbefehl* – call-up papers – under my name, Saloschin. I had already been told which unit to report to in case of war.' By the early hours of D-Day+1, like many other German-born soldiers, he was bound for a Wehrmacht field hospital.

Carrying up to 140 pounds per man, the three other Commandos in the 1st Brigade – Nos. 3, 6 and 45 – began a forced march of eight miles as soon as they were off the beach. Lovat followed them, with Millin playing his pipes to let the Airborne know they were coming. As they neared the village of Bénouville, he was at the head of the column and spotted a sniper in one of the tall poplars which lined the dusty white road. 'I was so close I could see the rifle, then the flash and the sound of the shot. I looked round. The Commandos were lying prone, but Lovat was on one knee.' The sniper struggled down from his perch and fled into a cornfield as the brigadier fired at him with his Garand rifle. Half a dozen men ran forward and found the body. Lovat told Millin to start playing again.

On the outskirts of the village, they came across Derek Mills-Roberts and 6 Commando. As soldiers were sent in to clear the streets and deal with snipers in the church belfry, Millin continued to pipe as he jogged down the road to what became known as Pegasus Bridge. It was now approaching 1300.

Twelve hours earlier, a glider-borne company of the Oxfordshire and Buckinghamshire Light Infantry, led by Major John Howard, had seized the crossings. They had soon been reinforced by paratroops under Lieutenant Colonel Geoffrey Pine-Coffin, and together they had held off a series of German counter-attacks. Nevertheless, they were beginning to despair of help arriving.

Then the first notes of a Highland tune reached them. Around the corner came Lovat, at an easy pace, his rifle over his shoulder and a walking stick in his hand. The owner of the local café dashed out with a celebratory glass of champagne, but was waved away. Instead, Lovat went to greet Howard and Pine-Coffin – and to apologise for arriving two minutes behind schedule.

In truth, the Commandos were probably later than Lovat always maintained afterwards, but the Airborne were so pleased to see him that they hugged each other with joy. Pine-Coffin warned Lovat, however, that the bridge was under fire. He was astonished to see him motion Millin forward, with orders to keep playing no matter what happened. Halfway over the bridge, Millin turned round to look at Lovat: 'It was as if he was out for a walk on his estate – he was neither up nor down.' Yet, as the commandos ran across the bridge, and then over the narrower one at Ranville a few hundred yards on, they were shot at by snipers and suffered a dozen casualties. Many of those hit were shot through the head, and Lovat was later criticised for rashly refusing to let his men wear helmets. 'We had to move very fast,' he said, explaining his decision, 'and we didn't like being cluttered up with heavy equipment. I always say that wearing a tin hat on your head is rather like walking about with a piano on it. You can't think, you certainly can't move ... If you're shot through the head by a sniper then a tin hat isn't protection anyway.'

Perhaps such reasoning owed more to a Roman Catholic's fatalistic view of life than to Lovat's sense of his own superiority. And he did have wider responsibilities to consider than the fate of individual soldiers. But he did consistently strike others as aloof and haughty, with even the bumptious Laycock deploring his 'pointless bad manners' towards those he considered inferiors. 'My dear Shimi,' Laycock wrote in 1942, 'When will you learn some tact? I know that it is uphill work dealing with officers who, to put it very snobbishly, do not come from the same social status as those with whom you were used to deal in peacetime ... yet nevertheless you *must* learn to bear with them.'

Yet that same disdain which the 25th Chief of Clan Fraser had for those below the salt extended to his enemies, and his contempt for the Germans rubbed off on his men. 'Lord Lovat was the perfect leader,' believed Millin. 'He brought up to date the warfare which the British were famous for – Drake and so on. The British, especially the Scottish, were always good at raiding, burning and looting. Lovat was typical of that kind of leader. He believed in hard training and hard fighting and then get out. He was a master at that ... He inspired us.'

'We were like a machine,' agreed Jim Spearman, 'nothing was going to stop us, we could tackle anything.' Nevertheless, when Spearman's Troop of 4 Commando reached the bridges in turn, they decided to ford the water rather than expose themselves to fire. The only casualty was Lieutenant Peter Mercer-Wilson. At the time he was thought to have been shot by a sniper, but Spearman later confirmed that the officer was killed when his rifle went off as he handed it to someone to pull him up the bank.

As the Commando began to fan out towards the high ground beyond the Orne, Spearman gazed at the mangled wreckage of the Ox and Bucks's Horsa gliders. He was mystified as to how anyone could have survived such a brutal landing.

That evening, Joe Patterson watched from the beach as more gliders cast off and circled down to the eastern salient, where the

Commandos were already digging in. From his foxhole, Millin saw the same aircraft coming over and decided to stretch his legs since all seemed quiet. Just as he returned, two mortar bombs suddenly dropped out of the dusk, sending shrapnel thudding into the gable end of the farmhouse behind him. He was sharing his trench with a corporal, a fellow Scotsman, and heard him running back. 'He was a big, beefy man, and he fell into the trench feet first,' Millin remembered. Overcome by fatigue, the piper then slept for an hour. When he awoke, he realised that his companion was not breathing. He reached out his hand, and brought it back covered in blood. Shrapnel had taken away the back of the corporal's head. 'I remember lying there, staring out towards the coast,' said Millin. 'Now and again a gun would fire, shelling the bridges. I was thinking: "They've got to take him away – he and those other chaps yesterday evening were supping pints in the canteen at Southampton. Now they're lying dead in a ditch with soil thrown over them."'

Four years to the day since Dudley Clarke had brought them into being, the Commandos had played an important part in securing the Allies' return to France. Yet they had perhaps done no more than live up to expectations. For all that some of the units lacked combat experience, their tasks had been within their capabilities, and on D-Day they had had the advantages of surprise and numbers over the opposition they had faced. What was far more impressive was the brigades' resilience in the months that followed.

'We thought we'd be ashore for about three days,' Lovat observed, 'be treated as shock troops who would bust and knock out the opposition, and then be withdrawn.' In fact, they would be in the line for eighty-three days without relief and their casualties would mount relentlessly towards 50 per cent – a rate closer to that of the First than the Second World War.

'It was not really our kind of war,' reflected Spearman. 'The invasion was over: now it was a question of stopping the Germans coming through.' 4 Commando hurried to dig in around the chateau at Hauger and prepared to hang on.

Forming a crescent on the left flank of the Allied bridgehead, the 1st Brigade held a ridge fringed by woods and hedgerows which allowed the Germans easy approach under cover. There were nightly infiltrations of their positions, and by day they were subjected to strafing and shelling. For both sides, Normandy became a campaign of grinding attrition.

'It was not a role for which we were equipped,' said Bill Portman, referring to their lack of artillery and reserves, 'but we never lost a foot of ground. They tried everything they could to blast us out . . . I'd landed with 68 men in my troop, and on D+4 we only had 18. We had a pretty tough time – but never gave an inch.' He was wounded four times. The last of these was the most serious – a bomb splinter which pierced his foot – but he refused to be evacuated to Britain, signed himself out of a hospital near the beach, and returned to his post in a Jeep he had liberated from the Airborne.

The constant threat from mortars tested even the bravest. Millin recalled seeing one commando being dragged out from under a truck where he had tried to hide, as his officer threatened to shoot him. 'I don't care what kind of special troops you have,' the piper declared, 'everyone has their breaking point.'

Casualties were especially high during the early attacks in which the brigades attempted to complete their initial objectives. On 12 June, Millin was at Breville when told that Lovat wanted to see him. He found him standing in a knot of Airborne officers, one of whom told him to push off. 'So I gave a smart salute and pushed off.' At that moment, a shell burst – probably a stray British round – throwing him forward on his face. He patted himself down and found that he was unhurt, apart from a bloody nose. The explosion had killed or injured several of the group, however, including Lovat. Grievously wounded, he was taken to a farmhouse.

'There he was, lying on a stretcher,' recalled Millin. 'His face was all grey and he had a hole in his back from shrapnel in which you could get a fist – two fists. I said to myself: "You've got no chance" and shouted to someone to get a priest to give him the last rites.' Lovat was bundled onto a Jeep and sent back to the beaches. He would survive, but would never see active service again. Rebecca's prophecy had come true.

Lovat's role was taken on by Mills-Roberts. The 1st Brigade's four Commandos had already lost two commanding officers in the first two days, among them Robert Dawson of No. 4, who was evacuated back to Britain with the unit's medic, Joe Patterson. So great was the flood of casualties from Normandy that Patterson had to remain on a ship in Portsmouth harbour for two days before he could disembark. There followed a stint on a hospital train before a bed was found for him in Birmingham, eight days after he had been wounded.

The 4th Brigade had also gradually mopped up their remaining tasks. The last of these had been the capture of the radar station at Douvres, which was eventually taken by No. 41 on 17 June. All of the Brigade's Commandos were then sent into the line to consolidate the gains made. James Kelly found himself at Salenelles, a low-lying village between the marshy coast and the depleted remnants of No. 4 at Hauger. 'The aim was to dominate no-man's land, to understand what the enemy was doing and deny them knowledge of our own dispositions,' he recalled. Kelly had been made corporal, although he had been reluctant to accept the promotion. This was partly because being seen to give orders attracted snipers, but also because he preferred not to have to tell others to do something which might endanger them.

None the less, Kelly had a busy rota of patrols to organise. Either these were from dusk until dawn, or the men went out just before first light and stayed out all day. Then they would have to lie up hidden, unable to eat, drink or even urinate because any movement would give away their position. The mental strain was considerable and there was little chance to rest, even at night. Aware that the Commandos were under strength, the Germans attacked regularly. 'The most sleep you could get once you were back in your trench would be two hours before you had to stand-to again,' Kelly recalled.

Out on reconnaissance one evening, it began to rain heavily, and he took the chance to hunker down and close his eyes. 'When it started getting light I found I had a companion. It was a dead German. He was in a shallow grave and the water had washed it all away. I was lying across his chest.'

'The whole of Normandy smelled of death,' concurred Jim Spearman. 'The air was pervaded everywhere I went on my patrols by the smell of death.' He often came across bodies of British paratroopers who had been killed a fortnight earlier. 'You would smell rotting flesh first, then the whole body would be nothing but maggots, just crawling . . . It was terrible to see.'

Spearman was a sniper, and the small fields and high earthen banks of the Norman *bocage* became a prime hunting ground. 'The Germans often knew where you were,' he recollected, noting that they sometimes left booby-traps in his favourite spots.

> But if you waited long enough, someone would come along and he'd have a mirror or something and start combing their hair, something you would know you would be doing yourself. I didn't like doing it a lot of times, but they were the sort of people I shot. You knew if you'd hit your target because they dropped. They'd disappear anyway if you shot, but they'd drop in a different way if you'd shot them.

He found accompanying patrols at night much more frightening than this game of hide and seek. 'It was never bloody easy . . . everybody was on edge. We did a lot of fighting patrols. Nobody really relished them. Everybody began to hope that they weren't on the list for a fighting patrol.'

At first, most of Spearman's comrades were keen to volunteer, but as the months passed without any sign of relief the atmosphere in camp became tenser.

> On one occasion, I was taking an intelligence officer and some of his people out with the object of getting a prisoner. Prisoners

could give you a lot of information that you couldn't get from observation.

We were on one side of the hedge and there were Germans on the other. We thought we'd achieved our objective – we just needed to grab one silently and get home ... Then they opened fire suddenly on us as if we'd walked into an ambush, and the crescendo of fire from such a close range was bloody terrifying, especially as a couple of people dropped straight away.

As we were running away, they started mortaring just where we were. This fellow who was on a stretcher got up and ran like hell, and he was quite badly wounded! It just shows you what fright can do to you.

Stalemate prevailed in Normandy until late August, when the Germans began to withdraw towards the Seine. The Commandos joined in the steady pursuit until the remaining German forces in the region were trapped at Falaise at the end of the month. Paris was liberated two days later.

Bill Millin and the survivors of the 1st Brigade returned to Britain in early September, having added a lasting reputation for bloody-minded tenacity to that already established for dash. Of the 2500 men who had landed with the Brigade three months earlier, 978 had been killed, wounded or were missing. No. 4 was down to about a third of its strength, and elsewhere very few veterans remained from those first raids at Lofoten, Vaagso and Dieppe. But there would be replacements to come from Achnacarry.

Millin had told Rebecca that he would go up there to see her when the campaign was over. She had warned him that, when he came, he would find that she had died the week before. At the time, he had laughed this off. Yet when he got to her croft near Fort William, the hearth was cold and the house was deserted. Rebecca had died ten days earlier.

16

INFATUATE

If Operation MARKET GARDEN had succeeded, Montgomery hoped that the war would be over by Christmas 1944. In fact, the failure in mid-September to seize the bridge spanning the Rhine at Arnhem, and so to thrust open a door into Germany, provoked the most serious dispute between the Allies' military commanders since the breakout from Normandy.

The inability of reinforcements to reach the Dutch town before the Airborne troops who had captured it were overwhelmed starkly revealed the major weakness of the Allies' rapid advance. In North Africa earlier in the war, Rommel's push towards Cairo had been hamstrung by his long supply lines. Now Montgomery faced the same problem.

The time taken to overcome the German garrisons in Channel ports such as Calais and Dieppe meant that, even as the Allies drove deep into Holland, they were still dependent on supplies being landed in and transported from Normandy, hundreds of miles away. Even once the nearer French harbours had been liberated, by the start of October, it would still be months before their docks were fit to use again.

As early as 4 September, however, the second-largest port in Europe had been taken by the British, and in the wake of MARKET

GARDEN Montgomery was chastised by his naval counterpart, Admiral Ramsay, for failing to make more of the advantages offered by Antwerp. It was time for a rethink.

Montgomery had not neglected Antwerp just because he was focused on more dazzling opportunities. Opening it to Allied shipping would also mean grasping the very prickly nettles of its extended defences. For the city sits at the head of the estuary of the River Scheldt, some sixty miles from the open sea, and while the southern banks of the waterway were now in Allied hands, its northern and western reaches were still in those of the Germans. In particular, its mouth was dominated by the batteries on the Dutch island of Walcheren, which Hitler had ordered be turned into a fortress. The only approach by land was from the west via the low-lying peninsula of South Beveland. The Canadians had been given the task of clearing this, but as it was linked to Walcheren by just a single causeway surrounded by almost impassable marsh and mud, any attack from that direction would be fraught with difficulty.

Accordingly, Ramsay's staff began to plan to take the island by an amphibious assault. This would be launched across the Scheldt from the south, as well as from the North Sea itself, and would be spear-headed by the Commandos of the 4th Special Service Brigade.

The first that 4 Commando knew of their coming involvement in this were movement orders to return to the Continent. They had had a fortnight's leave after Normandy, and then been sent for jungle training. The assumption was that they would soon be heading for the Far East. Instead, they found themselves in Belgium. Almost as unpalatable as the unfamiliar beer was the discovery that they had been transferred from the 1st Brigade to the 4th in place of No. 46 (RM), and that they were now the lone Army Commando in what was otherwise an all-Marine formation.

For all the lip service paid to integration between the two types of commandos, and indeed despite a grudging recognition by the Army units that the Marines had done their fair share in Normandy, there was still a feeling among many of the former that the latter were interlopers. 'When they became Commandos,' complained Jim

Spearman, 'they just gave them green berets. We always felt uncomfortable with someone becoming a Commando without having done our sort of training.' Although this resentment was increasingly without foundation, it was reinforced when No. 4 saw the role planned for them in the forthcoming operation, INFATUATE.

Walcheren is about ten miles long and eight wide – about half the size of the Isle of Wight – and is shaped like a crater. Much of the centre of the island lies below the level of the sea and is protected from its incursions by a rim formed of dykes and dunes which top seventy feet in parts. In four separate raids in October, the RAF breached this wall repeatedly, allowing the tide to pour in and submerge large areas of land under several feet of water. At the cost of the lives of two hundred civilians, this succeeded in its aim of concentrating the German defenders in the coastal batteries and the main towns, and in isolating these detachments from one another.

Under cover of an aerial, naval and field artillery bombardment, the three Royal Marine Commandos in the Brigade – Nos. 41, 47 and 48 – would land either side of the largest of these breaches, which was not in the batteries' field of fire and lay just south of the fishing village of Westkapelle. Once this had been captured, No. 41 would turn north and work its way along the crest of the sand dunes, clearing defensive emplacements as it went. Meanwhile, the other two units would perform the same task as they headed in the opposite direction, eventually meeting up with 4 Commando, whose initial objective would be the historic port of Vlissingen, known in English as Flushing. Other infantry and armour would follow in behind it.

To the experienced eye of Bill Portman, this looked like a tough job. It would be the first time since the catastrophe at Dieppe that a frontal assault had been attempted against a defended harbour, and during the briefing he was teased about this forbidding prospect by the marines. 'It was clear from the aerial pictures that we would have to land smack on top of pillboxes,' he reminisced. The other units' landing looked to be more straightforward. 'But', he noted, 'it was they who got the dirty end of the stick.'

In reality, few of the planners were under any illusions as to the potential pitfalls that awaited the Commandos. Walcheren was as heavily fortified as any stretch of coastline in Europe, and while not all of its garrison of some ten thousand soldiers were high-quality troops, they were well dug-in and outnumbered the assault force. For the moment the advantage lay with them, and should INFATUATE be repulsed, it would have grave consequences for the Allied armies' logistics. Their success in recent months had depended on maintaining a high tempo that gave the enemy little respite. Without Antwerp, the pace of the advance must slacken, giving Hitler time to think and manoeuvre.

For several weeks, the commandos trained in the sand and shattered streetscapes of the Belgian seaside, familiarising themselves with the tracked amphibious vehicles that they would be using on Walcheren – the Weasel and the larger Buffalo. When James Kelly of No. 41 was billeted in a hotel at De Haan, it was the first time since D-Day that he had not slept on the ground. Unlike the 1st Brigade, the 4th had not had any home leave after Normandy, being pushed instead straight into the Low Countries.

In the very early hours of 1 November, 4 Commando boarded their landing craft in the town of Breskens, three miles across the Scheldt from Flushing. They were accompanied by two of the French Troops from No. 10. It was cold and wet, and a thick curtain of mist meant that the planned bombardment by the RAF had been cancelled, aside from strafing runs by Mosquitoes. Yet as they set out across the dark channel almost three hundred guns opened up behind them, pulverising the harbour front and providing a protective screen for the LCs as they ran in.

Attempts at reconnaissance had been made by small teams operating from dinghies and dories – operations again codenamed TARBRUSH – but most of these had been spotted and little had been learned. Accordingly, the choice of landing area, towards the east of the beachfront, near the Orange windmill, had been largely based on the local knowledge of a policeman who until recently had lived in the town.

The Commando's orders were to establish a bridgehead and then secure as wide a perimeter as possible, leaving individual strong-points to be mopped up by the infantry arriving in the succeeding waves. There were thought to be three thousand Germans in Flushing – odds of six to one against No. 4, many of whose recent recruits had no experience of such an action. Much would depend on surprise being achieved.

The TARBRUSH teams touched land at 0545. Before long, a report on the operation recorded afterwards, there were '20 or 30 badly scared Germans kneeling in the mud near one of the pillboxes with their hands clasped over their heads'. They had been found cowering on the floor of the emplacement.

Next in was the first full Troop of Commandos, including Jim Spearman. 'Just before the shelling stopped, we rushed ashore,' he recalled. 'There wasn't a shot fired.' They felt their way along the mole in the murky light, marking a path for those to come with white tape. Then they began to fan out through the wreckage of buildings strewn across the cobbled streets.

The other Troops waited their turn offshore. The assault craft lay low in the water, making their silhouettes hard to see at night, although the white spray from their bows gave away their presence. None the less, most of what fire there was from the land passed harmlessly overhead. The defenders still seemed confused by the suddenness of the attack, and as each detachment disembarked it met little opposition.

Bill Portman remembered:

> We landed on a jetty and went through a boat yard. There were three pillboxes there. My troop took the first one. The Commando then pushed on into Flushing and we took the right flank . . . I used my smoke mortar and blanked out this pillbox.
>
> We chucked a few grenades in and these Jerries came out like rabbits . . . Within a few minutes we had 120. And there were just

three of us – me, my Bren gunner and my mortar man . . . I think they'd had enough because we plastered them before we landed.

Surprise had been complete, revealed the unit's war diary:

To anybody on the British side, it seemed that the enemy must have been expecting an attack at the time and place we had chosen, but the Flushing garrison commander was later to confess that the preliminary artillery bombardment was the first real indication that the town was to be assaulted, and that by then it was too late to take any special measures.

No. 4's main tactical objectives were two bottlenecks which separated the older, residential part of Flushing from the docks. Dubbed 'Dover' and 'Bexhill', they lay on the western outskirts of the town, and the sections heading for them soon met pockets of resistance.

'You were constantly under fire from across the street, or from upstairs – it was dreadful,' felt Spearman. 'It was a different kind of warfare. It was all street fighting.' This was house-to-house combat. 'You mousehole from one building to another . . . throwing grenades and giving bursts of fire to people as we came into rooms. It was horrific really. You get used to it after a couple of days.'

Spearman recalled sniping at two targets from the vantage point of a window overlooking a crossroads strongpoint. Then he was seen and a heavy-calibre gun was trained on him. 'A spatter of bullets hit the building and I got blown into the room. I felt a pain in my leg and thought: "Christ! I've had it!" In fact it was just a splinter from the window – it still sends my leg numb from time to time after all these years.'

Much of the port was under British control by mid-morning, as reinforcements from the King's Own Scottish Borderers swept in to consolidate the landing. While they were crossing the estuary, however, they suffered losses from heavier mortar and artillery fire as news of the attack reached outlying batteries, and one entire platoon of twenty-six men was killed when their LC sunk. Sharp skirmishes and winkling-out operations would continue in Flushing itself for several more days.

Accounts of the action have usually depicted the German troops there as having low morale. Many were from 70 Infanterie, nicknamed the 'White Bread Division' as its ranks included those with gastric disorders, and certainly at least one prisoner begged not to be parted from his stomach powders. Another wanted to take his hair restorer into captivity. Yet some of the other defenders were tougher, even brutal.

On the morning after the landings, as the commandos assembled near 'Dover', it was discovered that the Germans had reoccupied a house slept in that night by a member of 6 Troop. Finding British equipment lying around, they had taken the entire family who lived there outside and shot them in cold blood.

4 Commando also suffered casualties of its own. Lieutenant Nick Barrass, the officer who had replaced Peter Mercer-Wilson, killed on the banks of the Orne, was shot through a window by a sniper while crouching at a bend in the stairs of the house across the street. And forty-year-old Private Henry Donkin, the oldest man in the unit and the father of ten children, was killed as he mowed down a dozen Germans with his tommy-gun. He missed a man on his left as he swung right, and a bullet took him in the throat. He was avenged by his pal within seconds.

In the main, however, noted the war diary, 'the weakness of the tremendous German defensive system was proved to be the men inside'. Having appreciated the mistake of the French in trusting to the impregnability of their Maginot Line, Hitler was now making a similar error. 'We found the lay-out and construction of these strongpoints formidable in the extreme . . . only the will to fight was lacking.' But while that may have allowed No. 4 an easy landing at Flushing, those involved in INFATUATE II at Westkapelle received a very different reception.

Standing on the seat of his Buffalo, Kaspar Gudmundseth had a grandstand view of the two hundred craft spread around him like steel daisies in the wateriest of meadows. Unlike the Army commandos, the marines were attacking in broad daylight – at 0900, as the tide turned – and relying on force to bludgeon their way in.

In the absence of the RAF, and with the artillery barrage from Breskens largely ineffective this time, the main protection for the force came from the Navy. Fifteen-inch guns were among the few weapons which could penetrate the ten feet of concrete which shielded the German batteries, and from a dozen miles out into the North Sea, the vintage battleship *Warspite* pounded the shore defences. So did the monitors *Erebus* and *Roberts*, smaller vessels fitted with outsized armaments. (One of the guns from *Roberts* is now sited outside the Imperial War Museum, London.)

Most of their suppressing fire did little damage, however, which was to have grave consequences for the other naval contingent now steaming towards Walcheren. This comprised the twenty-seven ships of the Support Squadron (Eastern Flank), a group of landing craft modified to carry heavy weaponry and designed to engage coastal artillery at close range. But unlike at Flushing, the two main batteries either side of Westkapelle – designated W13 and W15 by the RAF – were alert and motivated.

A former Army NCO, Gudmundseth was now a twenty-four-year-old lieutenant in the Norwegian Troop of 10 Commando, which, with its Dutch and Belgian counterparts, was to land with the marines. Their LC was steering right for the four-hundred-yard gap in the dyke which had been carved out by the Lancasters' bombs, and about thirty minutes out from the shore Gudmundseth heard *Warspite*'s bombardment begin.

'You could see the explosions on the seafront, so that must have done a fantastic amount of damage,' he thought. 'Then we saw the first group of landing craft with rockets. The first four came in, broadside to the shore and fired their rockets. Then they disappeared from the sea – direct hits from the land.' Shocked, he watched as the slaughter continued. 'Then the next four came in, and three of those disappeared. The last one ran onto the land, out of control. The last ones came in – these carried guns – and two of those also exploded.'

James Kelly of 41 Commando, the Normandy veteran, was perched on the back end of a Buffalo parked on the rain-swept open deck of an LC. His Troop had sailed from Ostend the previous evening, an arduous journey inside the cramped confines of the vehicle, and now he wanted a good view of their destination:

> It was the first time I'd ever watched an approach right the way through until the time I landed. I saw these craft sinking, and on fire, and I thought: 'Good Lord, we're going to have a tough time of this!' They seemed to be sinking them quite easily. Then when the rockets fired, one of our own tank landing craft was immersed in the explosion. They fired them short and the sea boiled in front of us. The rockets were useless, firing at that small strip of ground.

Ten of the Support Squadron's vessels were destroyed in short order. Only a fortuitous hit by *Roberts* on W15, and W13 running out of ammunition, averted even more losses. With great gallantry, one of the adapted craft got right up onto the beach and traded blows with a pillbox for forty minutes, but even at close range its twin seventeen-pounders could not penetrate the bunker's cement shell. It sank soon after being forced to withdraw. Most of its complement was saved, but almost a third of the thousand men in the squadron were killed or wounded in a single lethal hour.

Another member of No. 41, Warwick Nield-Siddall, would celebrate his twenty-second birthday the next day. Afterwards he remembered seeing twinkling lights greeting him from Walcheren, and realising that they were German guns firing at the commandos. Yet the devastation wreaked on the Support Squadron largely spared the waves of marines arriving behind them. At about 1000, the leading troops of No. 41 began to scramble over the slimy mud at the foot of the northern shoulder of the breach in the dyke.

But not everyone was so lucky. The detachments from 10 Commando, led by Peter Laycock, were due to land a few minutes later, and Gudmundseth was watching the progress of the first sections when a shell exploded on the bow of their LC. It killed the crew and jammed the doors shut. 'Then we got one in the side and we decided that there was no other option but we had to jump.' They were still about eighty yards out from the shore, and the Norwegian was weighed down with eight or nine extra grenades, not thinking that he would have to swim. He touched the bottom as he fell into the freezing water, then began striking out for land as best he could. The sea was full of bodies from the support craft, and one of them seemed to clutch at his arm. 'I wasn't quite sure what was going on ... I was looking to see if my boys were going to come on, so maybe I drew my arm away, I don't know. I have dreamt many times about this, that maybe he was alive.'

Gudmundseth stumbled over rocks towards the Troop's rendezvous, only to find there that fourteen of his eighteen men appeared already to have perished. With the remaining four, he set off for the battery that was their target, but though that could not train its guns on the foreshore, the beach was still a killing zone. Behind a boulder he came across a ditch filled with dead German soldiers. None the less, this gave them protection from the machine-gun fire raking the dunes where they had landed, and allowed them to work north towards their target, W15.

At the western edge of its defences, they met up with P and Y Troops from No. 41, led by its colonel, Eric Palmer. The attack began with grenades lobbed into the battery's ventilators, and soon after midday resistance from it ceased. Many of the German prisoners were shocked to see their captors wearing green berets, and assumed from the propaganda they had read that they would be executed at once. The Norwegians made the main bunker their HQ, while the two No. 41 Troops headed north along the coastal road.

Nield-Siddall, once a cabin boy on Cunard liners, had had a cushier time of it. Within moments of exiting his LC straight onto dry land, he was inside one of the German pillboxes. 'They were having breakfast, would you believe? So we came flying in – "*Hände hoch!*" – and three or four minutes after coming ashore we were having coffee.'

But the going had been harder for James Kelly and A Troop. 'When we landed . . . the place was boiling with fire, the Germans had concentrated all their guns on it,' he remembered. Even so, they managed to get aground without taking any casualties, lumbering down the LC's ramp in their Buffalo. However, they had only gone a few yards when it became apparent that there was no way off the beach for it, and they all had to get out. Other Buffalos and Weasels then began to pile up behind them. Ignoring the jam, they headed up a flooded road under grey skies towards Westkapelle's main landmark, the six-storey lighthouse at the eastern edge of the village.

'Out of the top window I thought I saw a movement,' said Kelly later. 'I shouted and fired at the same time.' An answering burst of fire came from the tower, hitting the mortar officer at the back of the column. The Troop ran for the houses through the water on either side of the road, leaving Kelly and Captain Paddy Stevens standing in the middle, reluctant to get their feet wet. When Kelly turned around, he thought at first that several of the men had dived into the water in search of cover, but then realised that in their haste they had fallen over garden fences concealed beneath the flood.

Meanwhile, Stevens approached the lighthouse and called on the occupants to surrender. The doorway was filled with barbed wire, preventing anyone from climbing the stairs, and the nearest window was twelve feet off the ground. A direct assault was not an option. Instead, Stevens ordered that the tower be attacked with a Piat, the Troop's anti-tank weapon, but it proved impossible to elevate it high enough to aim at the top window. The problem was solved when a Sherman tank from 79th Armoured rumbled into view. Its first shot set the roof of the lighthouse on fire, and the smoke and falling timbers soon forced the defenders out with their hands up.

By early evening, No. 41 had advanced several miles across the soft dunes to the village of Domburg, penning most of its garrison in the woods beyond. Snipers still remained behind, however, and over the next few days 10 Commando helped to eliminate them. Gudmundseth and the others operated in four-man groups, leapfrogging and mouseholing from house to house, clearing one street at a time. 'We would go into the ground floor, throw grenades first, with lots of noise and lots of firing,' he explained. 'Those on the higher floors didn't know what to do.'

Support provided by two Shermans from the 1st Lothians proved vital, as did an unexpectedly ruthless policy towards prisoners. 'At first we shot anyone who moved, including those who wanted to surrender – about eight of them,' confessed Gudmundseth. When they saw this, another twenty-seven snipers rapidly gave up the fight. The rough justice meted out to the first group 'put so much fright into the others that they gave in', the Norwegian felt. 'It saved a lot of people on our side.' Nevertheless, that evening, when the platoon were bedding down in the church that was their temporary billet, he had second thoughts about those peremptory executions earlier in the day. One man knew how to play the organ, and as the men sang hymns, the tears flowed.

To the south, the other two RM Commandos – Nos. 47 and 48 – had encountered trouble as they tried to take two key batteries, W13 and W11. Caught between the flooded polders to the left and the sea to their right, they could only advance on a narrow front. The high dunes blocked wireless communication and the sand played havoc with rifle bolts and machine-gun parts. Despite strikes by rocket-firing Typhoons, stiff German resistance inflicted numerous casualties, including all five Troop leaders and several NCOs of No. 47 during an attack on W11 at dusk. Sixty Other Ranks were killed or wounded before the battery finally fell on the afternoon of 3 November, and the Commandos were able to link up with No. 4 near Flushing.

Kelly and No. 41 (RM) had been sent to help in these assaults, but when the batteries surrendered before they could be deployed, they marched north again. By 6 November, they were taking turns with 10 Commando at pushing along on either side of the road. Their objectives were the last two remaining emplacements, W18 and W19.

Their tactics reminded Kelly of trench warfare. Because of the limitations of the terrain, there was no room to fire and move, so each Troop would run from dune to dune in an extended line. Kelly and Stevens were on the right-hand side of their section, with the latter carrying the Schmeisser he favoured rather than a British weapon. Then they came under attack, as Kelly recalled:

> Whatever hit him [Stevens] hit his smoke grenade. They were filled with phosphorus . . . they were miniature flame throwers, because if you got hit by the phosphorus you couldn't get it off. And they hit it. I said: 'There's smoke coming out of your pouch.' He looked down, calmly unbuckled it and threw it to one side. Now that thing could have exploded at any moment . . . he would have disappeared in a cloud of white smoke. He was a very, very cool customer.

Kelly himself was exhilarated by the old-fashioned nature of combat required on Walcheren. 'It was much better than crawling along to attack somebody – I felt it was better to run in and charge like that,' he reasoned.

That day, however, they ran into a minefield. Among the wounded was Sergeant Milligan, who had been promoted in preference to Kelly when they were at De Haan. Step by step, Kelly walked back into the minefield to rescue him. Milligan had been hit by shrapnel in the back of the head, and was lying prone. 'When I lifted him up . . . out of the ground popped an S-mine. It just lay between the middle of his back and my chest. I thought: "God almighty – four seconds to live!" But it didn't go off. I lifted him up, avoided it, dragged him to one side and got him out.' Kelly's miraculous escape convinced him that he would come to no harm there. 'I didn't bother anymore in that minefield . . . I thought: "There's no way I'm going to be killed in this minefield." I just walked back in my own footsteps and I picked them all up and brought them all out. I think it was four fellows in the end.'

Kelly remembered spending that night sleeping on top of a pillbox, knowing that there were Germans inside who had refused to come out. They did so the next morning, and A Troop moved off across the dunes once more towards W19. By 1500, they were clambering across an anti-tank ditch when they were met by heavy enfilading fire from a wood to the south, where most of the battery's garrison had hidden themselves.

Typhoons were called down to plaster the area, while the Troop tried to find a way through a minefield that lay in their path. Stevens led them across a vast, saucer-shaped mass of soft sand, followed by Kelly and his Bren group. All at once mortars began to drop onto them. 'I remember getting slammed, a very violent push down my side,' said Kelly later. 'I got smacked into the sand, which came as a great surprise . . . I stood up and I felt a bit groggy, and all warm and wet on one side. But I still didn't realise what had happened.' One man had been killed instantly, and another eleven wounded, including Kelly. It took more than three hours to extricate the casualties, who were eventually loaded into Weasels and ferried back to the beach.

Kelly was taken to hospital in Antwerp, suffering from shock and multiple shrapnel wounds, and then invalided back to Britain. Once recovered, he would spend the rest of the war in a Holding Commando.

The remaining German troops on Walcheren capitulated on 9 November. In eight days of fighting, the 4th Brigade had lost more than a hundred men killed, while another three hundred had been wounded – almost a fifth of its fighting strength. The Allies' total casualties for the operation, including those who had died or been injured supporting the landings, exceeded fourteen hundred. Set against that, they had taken more than ten thousand prisoners.

At least one enemy commander wept, and even lost control of his bladder, when obliged to surrender. Control of the German forces had been divided between the Wehrmacht and their naval comrades in the Kriegsmarine, and each proved eager to blame the other for the failure to defend the island to the last.

Where the fault lay was of little interest to its inhabitants. At the hamlet of Vrouwenpolder, the final place on the coast to be liberated, there was much surprise when a British officer was seen approaching on the bonnet of a German staff car. 'The locals were at first in some doubt whether or not it was advisable to wave and cheer,' noted 4 Commando's war diary. But 'The beaming smile on the Intelligence Officer's face did not leave them long in doubt.' There was soon much waving and signalling of thumbs-up, while from every balcony and lamp-post fluttered orange flags and Dutch tricolours which had been hidden for four long years.

The Commandos' achievements that week were recognised by the commander of the Canadian forces in North-West Europe, General Harry Crerar. 'You and your fellows put up a magnificent show right throughout the piece,' he wrote to the 4th Brigade's commanding officer, Jumbo Leicester. 'The assault landing and capture of Walcheren was a further example of gallantry, determination and military ability which your Command has consistently demonstrated.'

This was more than conventional politeness. Although a rather forgotten campaign, Walcheren demonstrated beyond doubt that the Commandos – Army and Royal Marines alike – had not only adapted to their new role, but matured into a formidable weapon that could be used with confidence, by land or by sea, against the toughest of obstacles. Few other formations now offered the Commandos' blend of rapidity, flexibility and firepower, and if a little élan had been lost as it became a more conventional unit, much had been gained along the way.

Moreover, the opening up of the Scheldt to shipping, which began to dock in Antwerp within the month, was to prove of much greater significance than commonly recognised. It enabled supplies for both the Allied land and air forces to be delivered far closer to the front line, allowing them to maintain the pressure on the German armies and exploit any cracks that appeared. There would be no repeat of the MARKET GARDEN debacle.

Hitler would make the port the target of his offensive in the Ardennes, and later of more than twelve hundred V1 and V2 rockets, the greatest number launched against any city other than London. But the thousands of tons of fuel, ammunition and spare parts that were unloaded there every day helped to defeat both assaults. By May, almost two-thirds of the *matériel* needed by the

Allies for the final reckoning in Germany was flowing through Antwerp, and it was feeding the liberated populations of Northern Europe as well.

The 1st Commando Brigade (as it became in December 1944, when the hated Special Service – or 'SS' – denomination was replaced) would take part in operations up to the crossing of the Elbe in April 1945, but the 4th would see out the war in Holland itself. The success of INFATUATE II had, for the marines at least, justified their place in the Commandos. Some even saw it as an overdue reclamation of the amphibious role that had been theirs since they manned Nelson's bomb ketches. Their understandable desire to receive credit for the operation only served, however, to underscore the lingering tensions between them and the Army commandos.

Bob Laycock was already embroiled in a spat with the Admiralty about its poor coordination of signals with land forces during the mission, and in December he stoked the flames by claiming that naval press releases about Walcheren implied that only Royal Marine Commandos had taken part in its capture. This the Admiralty denied, but the row rumbled on for several months.

That festering rivalry was also reflected lower down the chain of command, but while Walcheren had confirmed the resentments some held against the marines, it had also generated a reluctant acceptance of their courage and their right to wear the green beret. Jim Spearman, of 4 Commando, was not alone in holding both sets of opinions:

> From our point of view, we were the one Army Commando in a Marine Commando Brigade and they gave us what appeared to be the toughest job – a heavily defended port, do a frontal assault on it. We were always taken aback by that.
>
> But in the event we did our job and had few casualties, we were lucky. Westkapelle was the most heavily defended beach and the Marines ran into all sorts of trouble. They really proved their worth there.

17

TALON

War against the Japanese, many commandos found, was not so much a more brutal experience than that in Europe as more brutalising. As Charles 'Dinger' Bell explained:

> I know all about the Geneva Convention, but that's made by people who aren't in that situation. We had phosphorus grenades, and to be quite honest we threw them in their faces – dozens of screams as they're burning their eyes out – and delighted in it. Because you're in a situation where you're so furious now, because you've lost so many people, and you know that these people are going to fight because they're like rats in a corner, and you've got to kill them.

The Commandos came late to the conflict in Asia. The distances and terrain would have made deployment of them in their original raiding role impracticable, while operations behind the lines became the province of Orde Wingate's Chindits, some of whom were trained by commandos.

A handful of veterans of Layforce were among the first British troops to confront the Japanese, even before the two nations were at war, when they were sent secretly to instruct the Chinese armies in guerrilla tactics. Many of these men subsequently took part in the defence of Burma in 1942, and had to make an arduous retreat by foot over the mountains towards Kunming.

However, it was not until the arrival of Mountbatten as Supreme Commander in the theatre in late 1943 that amphibious operations began to be contemplated there. The 3rd Special Service Brigade was sent out to India at the end of the year, but a shortage of landing craft, most of which had already been earmarked for OVERLORD, restricted them at first to more conventional jungle warfare. In March 1944, though, Nos. 5 and 44 (RM) were set down in the rear of the Japanese at Alethangyaw as part of the attempt to clear the road from Maungdaw to Buthidaung.

By the end of that year, following the victories at Imphal and Kohima, conditions were riper still for the Brigade to make use of its maritime capabilities. As the Japanese Twenty-eighth Army withdrew deeper into Burma along the Irrawaddy Valley in the face of the Fourteenth Army's decisive offensive, XV Indian Corps began racing down the Arakan coast to the west with the intention of cutting across its lines of retreat. This was Operation TALON. At the beginning of January 1945, the island port of Akyab was occupied bloodlessly by the Brigade, whose gaze then turned south-east to the Myebon Peninsula. If this could be taken, it would deny Lieutenant General Shigesaburo Miyazaki control of two important waterways along which he could move his forces. It would also open up a route into the high, razor-edged hills through which part of his 54th Division was planning to escape.

Since the invasion of France, there had been little work for the Commandos' canoeists to do in Europe but, reporting to Blondie Hasler, 2 SBS and the COPPs had carried out dozens of reconnaissance operations along Burma's coastline. COPP 4 now gathered data on the tides at Myebon, while on the night of 11 January three canoes from COPP 3 were ordered to destroy a line of defensive stakes beneath the waterline there. Each of these proved to be made of teak a foot thick, requiring collars of explosives with time-fuses to be fitted to them. (On discovering this, the leader of the

COPP team, Lieutenant Alex Hughes, was glad that he had ignored the original suggestion that he deal with the timber with a saw.) The only moment of anxiety came when the canoes grounded as they were making their survey and had to be dragged for a distance, but fortunately the sentries heard nothing. Although not all the charges detonated properly, twenty-three of the stakes were severed, creating a gap large enough to let Hughes pilot in the first wave of landing craft soon after dawn the next morning.

A flotilla of almost fifty elderly ships of every kind had been pressed into service to carry the Brigade. Despite the efforts of a flight of Mitchell bombers, some of the beach's defenders survived to oppose 42 (RM) and 1 Commandos as they came ashore, but they were soon dealt with. However, by the time that the Brigade's two remaining units – Nos. 5 and 44 (RM) – were ready to disembark, the tide was going out. This potential problem had been foreseen, but a mix-up had led to them being wrongly guided into the same beach as used by the others. Four hundred yards from the shore, the boats began to touch bottom, leaving their passengers to wade to land through a mixture of mud and brine that in places was chin high.

Twenty-four-year-old Harry Winch from Walthamstow was an NCO in one of No. 1's Mortar Troops. Posted to the Green Howards after being called up from Plessey, the munitions firm where he had worked since the age of fourteen, he had been packed off to the Commandos as a way of getting shot of a disruptive influence. Arriving at Achnacarry close to midnight, he had immediately fallen foul of a staff sergeant and been put straight onto guard duty.

Burma's climate may have been more clement than that of Scotland, but its attractions were lost on Winch as he struggled over the foreshore at Myebon, slipping and tripping on the mangrove roots hidden underfoot. 'So I finally got ashore, smothered in mud, I've got two rifles – I don't know where I got two from – and I'm washing the rifle in a stream, and all of a sudden I pull the bolt back and a round fell on the floor. A voice from behind me says: "You'll need that." I look back, and it's Peter Young – and he's immaculate!' The leader of the raid on the Berneval battery was now second-in-command of the 3rd Brigade. 'I said: "How?" and he said: "You don't think I'm going through that lot!" He was a brave man. He'd taken his boat round, and walked through the Jap lines and come back to us.'

44 Commando had just as hard a time of it, as Sergeant Jack Johnson – who had been a physical training instructor in Liverpool's boys' clubs – recalled:

> There was as much mud as there was water. We were all in denim uniform. We all had 50 rounds of ammunition strung round your neck or your waist. You had your rifle or your TMG or your Bren or your Boyes anti-tank weapon, and you had your boots on. I was very fortunate. I was probably the strongest swimmer in the Commando and I was able to get ashore in something like 2 hours – and we were supposed to be commandos doing an assault landing!

Dinger Bell and the regimental sergeant-major, Jack Stokes, put their heads together: 'We worked out a plan that if we lifted each other out of the mud a foot, and then he lifted you a foot and so on . . . Everybody started doing that, this was where "Me and My Pal" came in, we operated that same system, working in pairs. It took us four hours to get ashore.'

When he got to dry land, Johnson found some ropes and began to throw them out to the troops still stuck in the mud. 'These were hardened commandos, young men, fit, who were crying as they came ashore, on their bellies and they could hardly get up . . . Whoever was responsible for it should have been shot . . . If the Japs had stayed where they were we would have been wiped out.' As it was, when Johnson investigated the enemy's coconut-log bunkers, he found that they were empty, although the blankets and rice left behind were still warm.

Air support proved vital in clearing the remaining opposition from the slopes behind the beach the following day. This opened up larger possibilities for XV Corps' commander, Lieutenant General

Sir Philip Christison. The capture of the peninsula meant that the only line of retreat now open to the Japanese in the Arakan was along the road to Tamandu. This entered the Chin Hills at Kangaw, several miles inland from Myebon. If that was held by the British, Miyazaki would be likely to send his elite Matsu detachment of five thousand soldiers to retake the junction. Should they prove unable to do so, not only would Miyazaki's division be trapped on three sides, but the commander of the Japanese 55th Division, which lay in the path of the advancing Fourteenth Army, would probably have to weaken his forces by sending reinforcements to Kangaw. Victory there might well be crucial to the entire Arakan campaign, and the 3rd Commando Brigade – as it had become – was entrusted with paving the way.

The rugged country between Myebon and Kangaw was scored by several rivers whose main crossing points were dominated by Japanese artillery. It was therefore decided to see if it might be possible to approach Kangaw obliquely by way of a tortuous journey up a winding channel, the Daingbon *Chaung*. This was only thirty yards wide in places, thick with the stumps of mangrove trees and said to be infested with crocodiles. Hughes was again ordered to lead the recce and set off on the night of 18 January, accompanied by the Brigade's commanding officer, Campbell Hardy of the Royal Marines, who had won two DSOs in Normandy.

The COPP party left camp at 1700 in an assault landing craft, moving slowly as they had no depth charts to follow. At about 2230, when darkness had fallen, they made out the shape of another boat approaching and pulled in to shore. The other vessel only saw them when it was about thirty yards away and despite putting its helm over rammed the LC sharply on the bow. An angry volley of Japanese curses was directed at Hughes, but he had previously ordered the group to fire only if they were attacked first so as not to compromise the mission. He recorded in his diary:

> The armoured sampan heeled over then carried on down the *chaung* [stream] with the visible crew of four screaming their

> heads off. One can only guess what they thought but I should think they assumed us to be an ordinary river craft – we had a low silhouette – or we were a raiding craft too well armed for them. The former I think as we made no sound and didn't fire.

The COPPs then unshipped their canoes, and probed up the waterway as it grew narrower still. There was thick jungle on both sides and, aside from the usual noises, Hughes heard the sound of someone walking – 'presumably Burmese, but alarming'. Another hazard was snakes which slid onto the bows of the canoes and had to be hastily brushed off with a paddle.

By 0330, several viable beaches for a landing had been found, and the recce party turned for home, although the motor launch escorting them was left high and dry near the mouth of the *chaung* by the outgoing tide. 'I don't think he will go on another COPP operation,' Hughes wrote of Hardy. 'But I do like him – he is approachable, easy to talk to, understanding and doesn't interfere in any way. I admire him for going with us too.'

The Brigade duly followed Hughes's route and landed two miles south-west of Kangaw at 1300 on 22 January. There was no enemy in sight to hinder 1 Commando as it scrambled up the clay banks of the *chaung*, and the troops began to tramp across flooded rice fields towards the pair of hills four hundred yards away that were their objectives. The second of these, codenamed 'Brighton', was also known as Hill 170 – a seven-hundred-yard-long, steep and wooded rise that was the most prominent feature on the horizon. A small pocket of Japanese troops was lodged on its northern tip, and the Commando moved to attack.

Among them was Vic Ralph, who as a recruit at Achnacarry had been so shocked by the bogus gravestones. As he advanced through the long grass, he saw a sight that would continue to haunt him for many years:

> Half-way up the hill, there was a young Burmese girl, maybe 17 or 18, with her baby, only months old, and they were lying in

> a pool of blood, she with her stomach torn open. And the thought occurred to me – was it our shelling of the hill that did that, or when the Japs had mortared us? Then it occurred to me that it didn't matter very much: she was in her homeland and here were two foreign powers fighting each other, and she and her baby had died because of that.

During the night, the Japanese troops on Hill 170 put in a fierce counter-attack, but this was driven off and the position was cleared early the next morning. While 5 Commando remained near by in support, and No. 42 secured the area by the beachhead, No. 44 was sent forward to a 150-foot-high tree-covered knoll which had been codenamed 'Pinner'. The marines had been told that they would only be resting on it a short while before moving down to the village of Kangaw, but by 2100 they were still there and Dinger Bell could hear tracked vehicles moving down below.

Some of the men had tried to make foxholes with their entrenching tools, but had met rock six inches down and given up. 'I was lucky,' reflected the Northumberland-born Bell, 'because being from a coalmining area I knew how to dig – I'd been digging all my life.' He had soon made a pit for himself on the brow of the hill.

Sergeant John Webber had grown up near Yeovil, in Somerset, and worked as a gardener on the Cricket St Thomas estate (later the setting for the sitcom *To the Manor Born*). He remembered that there was a beautiful moon over 'Pinner' that night and he had the feeling that something was about to happen. 'No sooner had we heard the explosion of the firing than the shell exploded in amongst us on the hill,' he recalled. 'It was tree-covered and they just plastered us with this bombardment. It was tearing through the trees, shredding them into sharp splinters which came down on us.'

'When the shell hit the trees,' explained Johnson, 'it fragmented and anybody below got wounded or killed.' The casualties included BBC pianist Peter Kirby, who died after both of his hands had been severed by shrapnel as he rested them on top of his trench.

'I had a lance-corporal with me, my orderly,' said Bell. 'I suddenly found in a bit of a lull that he wasn't with me. I got up and went looking for him, and found him about five yards behind the weapon pit with a great hole in his back. Why he got out I'll never know.'

One of John Webber's corporals, 'Ack-Ack' Marshall, was also hurt:

> I remember lifting him out of his slit trench and taking him down the back of the hill. Getting hold of his shoulder was like catching hold of pulp because he'd been hit by all this wood. He kept shouting 'Come on, No. 1 Section, at 'em!' which was bad really because it was pinpointing our position. He subsequently died during the night. Fleming was killed, Tiger was killed, they were all members of my section. Nothing miraculously came near me . . . it was a very long night.

The shelling was followed by frontal attacks. 'It's when the lull comes you get on the alert,' Bell had learned.

> When the Japs came crawling in, they had sandbags on their heads . . . It gives you terrific camouflage cover because it's shapeless. You've got to try to break shape up. That's why we wore berets instead of steel helmets. It definitely gave us head casualties, but it increased our efficiency by 20%. Wearing a steel helmet in the jungle was useless. A beret's got no outline, it's ideal. When I was in HQ, I always knew where the padre was because you could see his peaked hat against the skyline.

Wave after wave of assaults were launched, seemingly without regard for casualties. Bell was astonished by the enemy's methods: 'The thing we found out about the Japanese when they were attacking is that when a British officer is probing a place and finds it's strongly defended, he'll move to the side and try again, and find a weak spot and go in. But the Japanese wouldn't. Once they started attacking, it's just attack, attack, attack.'

The Commando had soon exhausted its supply of conventional

grenades, although a sergeant who worked in the canteen brought up phosphorus grenades throughout the night. 'It was very frightening, very frightening indeed,' Bell confessed. 'This was ferocious hand-to-hand fighting. I'm talking about throwing things at a bloke who's five yards away, you're killing them at that range. When you're in personal combat with a bloke, you leave it as late as you possibly can, when you know you can kill him. Otherwise he's going to kill you.' Remembering his training, Bell used a Colt revolver rather than a rifle at such short distances. The lower muzzle velocity meant that the bullet was less likely to go through its target, and the shock was greater.

When the fighting died down for a few minutes, Jack Johnson thought that he deserved a cup of tea. As the shooting started up again, he was lying next to an officer who was also enjoying a brew. 'If you think about it, it's stupid to have a white mug out among greenery, and the next thing which happened is that a bullet goes right through his mug and hits my heel and takes a piece out of my boot. So we realised then we were in the firing line.' He rapidly shifted his position twenty yards so that he was on the reverse slope of the hill. The shells continued to pass overhead.

> I must admit I was beginning to get a bit frightened. I said to my pal: 'I tell you what, Tom, the way things look at the moment we're not likely to be here very long.' He said: 'Why, do you think we're getting off the hill?' And I said: 'No, you're going to be dead the way things are' . . . So we sat down and got our photographs out and we had a little chat and we said cheerio to everybody, because we thought honestly that we were in for it.

Dinger Bell had the mournful task the next morning of counting the survivors. 'We lost 27 killed that night,' he revealed, 'and nearly 100 wounded, some of whom had arms or legs blown off. We had gone into action well below strength, at about 320 of us. When I did my muster that morning there were about 180 left to fight out of a Commando of 450.' He organised the funerals that same day, burning the names of the dead onto makeshift crosses with a nail.

The British troops had not been the only ones to suffer. Fourteen Indian stretcher bearers had stayed at their post lower down the hill. 'The Japanese got round behind us and we could hear them kicking these Indians' heads in,' said Bell. 'They were screaming "No, sahib, no sahib!" When we saw them the next morning they had all had their heads smashed up. The Japs are a very cruel race.'

But savagery infected both sides. 'The first thing we did at six o'clock in the morning – by then things had cooled down – we sent patrols out, and if any of the Japs were wounded they were seen off so that they didn't have another chance to fight,' admitted Johnson.

A sergeant on one of these expeditions saw a pair of legs in the undergrowth and automatically gave them a burst with his tommy-gun. They proved to belong to a commando who had gone missing during the battle after previously being refused home leave following the death of one of his children. He lost the use of both legs.

This was not the only example of such an accident. Even within the Marine Commandos, there was tension between the regular, pre-war troops and those who had been conscripted. Johnson felt that the former looked down on him: 'They thought that hostilities-only men weren't as good as them. They'll deny it but they did. They thought their training was better than ours – which it was – but their fighting wasn't any better.' As proof, he cited an incident in which a Marine sergeant had drifted off his flank into the centre of an attack. Seeing two men coming up behind him where he wasn't expecting them, he shot them. They were both from Johnson's Troop: 'They got it, and they screamed all night, and they died.'

Brigadier Hardy came over to 'Pinner' on the morning of the 24th, and expressed surprise that No. 44 was still holding it. They were relieved by two companies of the Hyderabad Regiment and withdrew to another hill, behind 170. Over the next week, the 51st Indian Infantry Brigade moved up into Kangaw and flushed the ranges beyond, while ambushes were set for stragglers on the main road by the Commandos.

For several days, Hill 170 was subjected to heavy enemy artillery bombardment, with 182 shells landing on it in the space of half an hour on the 25th. Harry Winch was with the Mortar Troop in the centre of No. 1's position, trying to make himself comfortable in a mosquito-infested foxhole. 'You're in the jungle,' he reasoned, 'you can't expect an armchair.'

At night, the Japanese sent out 'jitter parties', who shouted in English, threw fireworks and preyed on the Commando's morale. 'If anyone had been indisciplined, they would have opened fire, and of course they're watching for where the flash comes from and then you've had it,' Winch recalled. In turn, he left booby-traps for the enemy patrols. 'You get a tin of 50 Players cigarettes and tie it to a tree. You put a grenade in and pull the pin out so that the lever is still held in place. Then you tie it with a bit of string or wire to another tree so that directly they pull it the bomb goes off,' he explained.

Winch offered an officer newly posted to No. 1 some of the tins he had managed to acquire. 'As he walked away, he turned round with a half smile and said: "Can I ask you where you got them?" And I said: "If you do, put them back," for the simple reason that being an officer he wasn't allowed to do that – to connive at pilfering.' As it was, despite his fresh-faced appearance, twenty-two-year-old Lieutenant George Knowland had a shrewd idea of their source, having worked his way up through the ranks of 3 Commando before being commissioned a few months earlier. A bank clerk in London in civilian life, he had only joined No. 1 at Myebon.

By 31 January, the area appeared to be firmly under control. The artillery bombardment of Hill 170 had diminished markedly and there were no signs of vehicles having used the road through Kangaw for four days. It was merely the prelude to the storm, however. No. 1 was in the process of arranging to hand over their positions to the 2nd Punjabis when it broke on them. 'One of the Indian regiments was coming to relieve us,' recalled Vic Ralph. 'And lo and behold, on that morning the shelling was much thicker and heavier and longer than it had been. An awful lot was laid down. And all of a sudden, the Japanese put in their main attack to try and dislodge us from Hill 170. And it was virtually hand-to-hand fighting all day.'

At dawn, a battalion of Miyazaki's 154th Infantry Regiment launched a surprise assault on the front of the hill. The general had given his troops fearsome orders for the coming battle: 'Every man will kill no less than three enemy. Kill, kill, kill.' In the first wave was a suicide party of engineers bent on destroying the three Sherman tanks laagered near Harry Winch's post. 'All at once we see – I'm told there were 60 of them – come rushing at a tank. First they blew up its ammunition truck, then they were rushing this tank which was firing at them. They got on top of it and blew themselves up on it.' Two of the three Shermans, and their crews, began to burn. Ten dead Japanese lay in a ring about them.

The brunt of the attack fell, however, on the sections of 4 Troop which held the far tip of the hill. More than three hundred Japanese soldiers were ranged against the twenty-four men of Knowland's platoon, fourteen of whom almost immediately became casualties of the heavy mortaring and machine-gun fire which preceded the first charge. Knowland moved from trench to trench, distributing ammunition and encouraging those who still could to resist. One advantage of being equipped with the semi-automatic American Garrand rifle was that his sections could get rounds off more quickly than if working the bolt of a Lee Enfield.

Despite the danger to himself, Knowland stood up to fire his rifle and throw grenades, and when one of his Bren crews was wounded he ran forward to man it himself. While waiting for a fresh crew to arrive, he stood on top of a trench to get a better shot at the advancing Japanese, firing from the hip and keeping them at bay until a second team of replacements arrived, the first having been wounded on the way up.

With the Troop's number so reduced, the only thing holding back the Japanese was the weight of firepower that could be concentrated on the narrow wedge of slope beneath Knowland's position. When another attack began, he picked up a two-inch mortar whose crew had been sent to man a trench and began to fire it from the hip, letting a tree stump absorb the recoil. His first bomb killed six of the enemy. Once he had used up all the ammunition, he ran back through heavy mortar and grenade fire to fetch some more, and when that was finished he continued to fire down the hill with his rifle while standing in plain view of the Japanese.

Vic Ralph watched the young lieutenant's actions in awe:

> I don't know whether he was just mad. Men in the Bren pit were being wiped out but he was walking about in the open with a mortar, firing a Bren, anything he could lay his hands on . . . Men behave in that fashion for two reasons. Either they are very stupid, or very, very brave. To put that in perspective, there was a private who previous to us going into action was bragging that he was going to win the VC. But when it came to action, he stuck himself behind a tree and wouldn't move.

The situation was now desperate at the northern end of the hill. Six of Knowland's trenches had been overrun, and if the enemy were able to wipe out 4 Troop they could spread out across Hill 170. Once that fell, the beachhead would be threatened, and the entire 51st Infantry Brigade inland cut off from its supplies. All TALON's gains would be undone.

Without time to refill his rifle magazine, Knowland snatched up a tommy-gun and sprayed the Japanese ranks as they closed in on him. Ten fell dead or injured no more than ten yards from him before he himself was mortally wounded. The rest of the Troop, however, continued to hold on.

At 0930, three hours after the attack had begun, they started to receive support from other detachments in the Commando as well as from some of No. 42. Under the hot sky, the battle raged all day with pitiless intensity. Ralph remembered a Japanese warrant officer charging alone with his sword, drawing the fire of every man on the hill. He also saw a wounded soldier pull out a grenade and set it off under his stomach rather than be taken prisoner by the British.

'It was hand-to-hand fighting,' said Winch. 'I know that one of our chaps, as they ran at him he grabbed hold of the bayonet with his right hand, and they pulled the trigger and the bullet shot all the way up his arm. As he was falling down, he put his hand round this Jap's throat and strangled him with one hand. He was a farmer's boy.'

For hours, neither side gained an advantage. When No. 1's 6 Troop attempted a counter-attack at 1400, they lost half their men within thirty yards and had to pull back. Ralph compared it to being at Rorke's Drift. At times, enemy soldiers were within twenty yards of him, the overgrown vegetation making it hard to see their approach. 'It wasn't frightening at all at the time,' he said. 'It was frightening afterwards. You were too busy to be frightened. I don't think any of us expected to come out of it. You had too much to do to be afraid.'

The arrival of 5 Commando from 'Pinner' helped to turn the tide, as did that later of the Punjabis, and though the Japanese launched several attacks during the night, by the morning of 1 February they had started to withdraw. More than 340 Japanese lay dead 'like a carpet' in an area of no more than a hundred square yards. The Brigade's casualties in the action were forty-five men killed and twice that number injured. Harry Winch had taken a bullet in the forearm that would force him to spend the next year in and out of hospital.

The long and bloody battle for Hill 170 – and in particular 4 Troop's blunting of the initial attack – proved to be decisive in the Arakan campaign. The Japanese 54th Division was now trapped, and more than a thousand of its soldiers were killed during the next ten days as they tried to flee the forces bearing down on them from the north. The Twenty-eighth Army fell back still further into Burma to avoid being caught up in the rout.

1 Commando was commanded in Burma by Ken Trevor, who had taken over the colonelcy from his cousin Tom. When they had been in North Africa together in 1942, Laycock had had doubts about him: 'Much as I like Ken, I have never thought that he has either the personality or the drive for Commanding Officer. I will

not recommend him for Command . . . Of course, there is just a chance that he will prove himself a brilliant leader in action, but I should be very surprised if this is so.' At Kangaw, Ken Trevor's astute handling of his forces, the heroism he managed to wring from them and his own obdurate refusal to yield amply confounded Laycock's assessment of him, and he received the DSO.

Campbell Hardy won a second Bar to his DSO, while George Knowland was awarded a posthumous Victoria Cross. The latter's father displayed the VC at his pub, the Spreadeagle in Finsbury, north London, until it was stolen in 1958. It has never been recovered.

Rangoon was captured in May 1945 and, following the final destruction of the Twenty-eighth Army in July, the whole of Burma fell to the Allies. The 3rd Commando Brigade then prepared to take part in the invasion of Malaya, but the dropping of the atomic bombs resulted in Japan's surrender before this became necessary.

The Commandos carried home with them the proud memory of their stand at Kangaw. In his Order of the Day of 17 February, Christison had saluted 'your courage and determination in assault and attack, your tenacity and aggressiveness in defence and counter attack . . . You have gained a reputation throughout the Corps for indifference to personal danger, for ruthless pursuit in success, for resourceful determination in adversity which has been a source of inspiration to your comrades in arms.'

George Knowland and the lone Troop of commandos who stood with him merited no less a tribute to their fighting spirit.

18

ROAST

The SBS patrol crept forward. Sound travelled in the still night air and there was little cover to be had on this narrow road above the flood. Somewhere up ahead in the dark was the town of Comacchio, and there were bound to be guard posts near by. Major Anders Lassen motioned to two scouts to push on cautiously. It felt good to be raiding again.

Almost immediately a challenge stopped them short. The language was Italian but the accent was not. Nor German. Probably Turkoman – a recruit from the Caucasus. '*Siamo i pescatori di San Alberto!*' shouted the commandos, in an intonation that was not Italian either, 'We are fishermen from San Alberto!' The sputtering chatter of a Spandau showed that the sentry was not fooled.

The patrol unleashed their own fire and Lassen instinctively ran forward, throwing grenades as he went. Two Turkomans were killed and two more taken prisoner as the dugout was stormed. But by now two blockhouses further on had opened up as well. Ignoring the bullets sweeping the road, Lassen charged towards the nearer of them as his men covered him. Again the enemy position was silenced with grenades and overrun. The survivors came out with their hands up.

Yet by this time the SBS had also taken casualties and their own firepower had been almost halved. They continued to be raked by machine-guns from the third bunker, and Lassen rallied his troops for a final effort. Enveloped by a heavy cone of fire, he again led from the front. A barrage of grenades brought cries for mercy from inside the post, and he walked up to it to take the surrender.

By March 1945, the situation in Italy had been transformed since the Commandos had landed at Salerno eighteen months earlier. After the fall of Rome in June 1944, Kesselring's forces had been driven steadily northwards, until by the end of the year they had fallen back on the line of the River Po. Stalemate had set in during the winter, but with the coming of the thaw the Allies gathered themselves for the final assault.

The Supreme Commander, Field Marshal Sir Harold Alexander, intended to break into the Po Valley, and then on to Bologna and Venice, through the so-called Argenta Gap. This was a corridor of low-lying land between Ferrara and Lake Comacchio, a vast lagoon that abuts the Adriatic north of the *pineta*, the pine groves beyond Ravenna where Byron once rode.

This hundred-square-mile expanse of brackish water was now to become the focus of an elaborate scheme of deception. Alexander hoped to convince the new German commander in Italy, General Heinrich von Vietinghoff, that he would open his campaign with a full-scale landing in the Po's delta, north of Comacchio. If the plan worked, it should draw off troops from west of the lake, where Alexander meant to make his main thrust.

The diversionary attack would need to take account of Comacchio's awkward geography. The local garrison of about twelve hundred soldiers, both German regulars and Turkomans, was concentrated on a narrow spit of coastal sand. On one side they were protected by the sea and on the other by the wetlands, which were shallow and navigable only with great difficulty. In places, the water was just two feet deep, and a man burdened with equipment would sink up to his ankles in the soft mud below.

The plan envisaged simultaneous assaults on the spit by land and across the lagoon. It was a bold amphibious strategy that seemed tailor made for the 2nd Commando Brigade. Now under Ronnie Tod, who had led the early raids on Guernsey and the French coast, it was formed of Nos. 2, 9, 40 (RM) and 43 (RM) Commandos. They had seen plenty of action separately in Italy, but had not yet fought as a brigade. Attached to them was 'M' Detachment of the SBS, commanded by Lassen, and several COPP teams. Both of these now took to their folbots to reconnoitre suitable routes for Operation ROAST.

Each sortie was long and tiring. Not only was their work of charting the lake necessarily slow, but the flatness of the landscape and the lack of conspicuous landmarks, except for a few islands and houses, most of which were in enemy hands, made it easy to lose one's bearings. The COPPs began using a fisherman's punt to get about as they took soundings and searched for channels deep enough for the Commandos' boats.

Meanwhile, the units who were to make the attacks familiarised themselves with the assortment of craft and tracked vehicles which they were to use. Already it was evident that the approach across the lake would be anything but plain sailing. Most of the men would be carried in stormboats, which had a shallow draught, but they would have to push or paddle these at least two thousand yards over the mud before the water became deep enough to start their outboard motors. And once started, the engines had no neutral gear, so the problem of coordinating the movements of eighty of them would be considerable.

Simply getting the boats to their assembly area required a titanic effort. Each needed thirty-five men to lift it and the equipment it held, all of which had to be heaved – in secret – across the River Reno at the southern end of the swamps during the two nights before the landings were to be made.

The assault itself was to consist of seven phases. 2 Commando was to follow a northerly track across the lake and land on the far side of the Bellocchio Canal, which divided the spit in half. They would seize the bridges over it, if these were still intact, as 9 Commando, who were to take a more southerly route, cleared the enemy from his positions below the canal. The major obstacle for both units during the crossing would be the Argine. This was a dyke made of mud, sand and stakes which formed a wall almost four feet high across the lagoon and over which their boats and amphibious vehicles could only pass in three places.

As the Army Commandos swung their surprise left hook over the water, the Royal Marine units in the Brigade were to begin methodically working their way up the spit itself. All the German positions had been given biblical names in the plan, so No. 43 was to eliminate 'Joshua' on a tongue of land that ran beside the Reno's estuary before crossing the river and dealing with 'Acts'. No. 40 would make a feint to draw enemy fire as the main assault went in. Then they would attack the emplacements on the far bank of the Reno. Eventually, all the Commando units were to meet and push up towards the small harbour of Porto Garibaldi on the northern rim of the lake.

At last light on 1 April, COPP parties and crews from the SBS set out in their canoes to illuminate beacons across the swamp for the assault craft to follow. Behind them, Wagner's 'Ride of the Valkyries' blasted from dozens of loudspeakers in an attempt to drown out the noise of the boats forming up. The first Fantails – lightly armoured troop carriers – plunged into the murky water, sending up clouds of mosquitoes, but a spell of dry weather during the preceding weeks had turned the lake into a quagmire. The carriers soon became bogged down in the mud a few yards from the shore and all efforts to shift them proved in vain.

Abandoning the Fantails, the soldiers tried to push and drag their boats through the shallows, but by midnight the orderly attack had been reduced to complete confusion. 9 Commando was bunched up behind No. 2, units were trying in the dark to find their leaders and sub-leaders, and everyone was tired and angry. 'It was', according to the Brigade's war diary, 'the end of the Henley Regatta transferred to a setting of mud, slime and a few inches of stinking water.'

The COs of the two Commandos appealed to Tod to call off the operation, but as the artillery bombardment had begun he decided that surprise had been lost in any case, and told them to press on. So, yard by yard, and boat by boat, they continued to struggle towards the far shore.

Captain Jos Nicholl and 5 Troop of No. 2 finally got going at about 0330. He was acutely aware that he was behind schedule, but no sooner had the flywheel sparked his transport's motor into life than they hit a sandbank. Three other boats stopped to try and help them shove off it, but in the end Nicholl had to tell the men to jump overboard and push. Once afloat, he scanned the horizon for the pilot lights that were flashing at points 'Able' and 'Baker'. Neither was visible. But the shells bursting on the skyline provided the only compass he needed.

Then the motor packed up. After what seemed like an eternity of paddling, they reached the Argine as dawn broke at about 0600. The Troop was already exhausted, yet they would now need to empty the boat of all of their kit, tug it up and over the dyke, and then row another six hundred yards to their landing zone. Weighed down by seventy pounds of equipment, Nicholl clambered over the bows and began to help lift the craft up, hoping that its canvas frame would not tear on the stakes.

5 Troop's progress in the distant moonlight had been watched by those commandos who had had an easier crossing of it. Many were wireless operators and batmen, who were not supposed to be in the assault party that was to storm the bridgehead. But with daylight coming on, it became clear that the attack would have to be made with whichever troops were available.

As soon as the barrage lifted, they began to paddle for the beach, only to stick in the mud two hundred yards short of it. They eagerly leapt out of the boats, and sank up to their waists in soft ooze. But so well had the artillery done their work that not a shot came their way as the men floundered ashore. Soon prisoners were being rounded up.

5 Troop had to watch from the Argine as white phosphorus shells landed on the positions that had been their target. They finally

reached the spit at 0700 and were immediately given a new objective some eight hundred yards away – 'Amos', the bridge over the Bellocchio Canal. Thick drifts of white mist still clung to the small copses and clumps of reeds amid the dunes, and Nicholl could see no more than twenty yards ahead. His sections started to fan out and move up through a plantation of saplings. Speed was vital if the defenders were to be surprised before they could destroy the bridge. Yet that only increased the chances of blundering into their defences, none of whose locations Nicholl had time to reconnoitre.

A shot rang out from a high mound of sand in the distance. It was answered by a Bren, betraying the presence of British soldiers on the spit. Now it was as if he were in a race from a nightmare, sprinting through the fog, tripping over the scrub, as German troops popped up on all sides from unseen weapon pits. Nicholl destroyed several of these himself, as well as a Spandau post, but before he reached the mound there was a huge explosion behind it. 'A solid slab of concrete seemed to lift itself up and then drop out of sight,' he wrote later. The bridge had been blown.

While Nicholl was getting his breath back, another veteran of the Brigade's time in Dalmatia was trying to see the funny side of being shot at.

Once the two lead Troops of No. 43 had cleared Joshua and reached the end of the tongue, Lieutenant Bill Jenkins and E Troop boarded a Fantail to cross the Reno. Jenkins stood on the rear tailgate to get a better view, but as the vehicle entered the water, the driver's inexperience told. He locked up the gears and it circumscribed a slow circle in the middle of the river as every machine-gun on the far side seemed to take aim at it.

The Fantail's sides were thinly armoured so as to give it more buoyancy, but fortunately the Spandaus were too far off for their bullets to penetrate its shell. At last the carrier made it to the riverbank, where the commandos – heavily laden with ammunition – faced an uphill trudge through waist-deep silt. They made it, but the tanks that had been supposed to support them did not. The Troop would now have to advance, exposed and alone, across eight hundred yards of flat hinterland towards the higher ground where lay their objective – Acts.

The ace that they were able to play was the forward observation officer accompanying them, who radioed for gunnery support. 'The Artillery was magnificent,' acknowledged Jenkins. 'As we went across this flood plain, we had this curtain of shells in front of us. We'd never seen anything like this in Yugoslavia – not a shot was fired at us. That was just as well, as we had to cross drainage ditches, and each time we had to go in thigh deep.'

They reached Acts when it was still blanketed in smoke, swept over the German positions and then took them from the rear. With the commandos pouring grenades and bullets through the entrances to their dugouts, the defenders stood no chance. Many were still in shock from the preliminary bombardment. Eighty prisoners were soon in the bag. Jenkins saw a man lying on the ground whose shoulder was now a mess of blood and white bone. Four other German soldiers passed him carrying a blanket from which seeped groans of pain.

The survivors would have to look after themselves as best they could. E Troop was already moving on to its next target – 'Hosea I and II'. Jenkins had seen their campfires at night from the other side of the Reno. As he headed towards them, he saw movement from behind a hedgerow ahead, and sent a Bren group on to distract attention while he took the rest of the Troop around the flank.

Running rapidly across a large field, they came up behind half a dozen German riflemen facing the other way and, as Jenkins intended, wholly focused on the other section. They were taken completely by surprise when the commandos burst from cover and surrendered without a fight. But there was more work for the Troop to do. 9 Commando had been held up by mortar fire at 'Leviticus', so No. 43 were ordered to take 'Matthew I and II', at the base of the spit. These were strongly protected by minefields and machine-gun nests, but they turned out to be manned by Turkomans who saw little point in dying for them. Then it was on to 'Mark', above the northern bank of the Reno, which had so far resisted the efforts of

No. 40 to suppress it. 'We slogged back,' said Jenkins, 'and were able to see the routes through the minefields and again took them in the rear. Then we had a long march through the night to get up to the bridges.'

It had been a long and very tiring day. They spent the night by the canal, and the next afternoon prepared to complete the sweep of the spit north to Porto Garibaldi. Artillery and armour had swatted aside most resistance, but sited among the Turkomans were units of German mountain troops with greater self-belief.

The Valletta Canal formed the boundary of the northern edge of the lake. All cover for six hundred yards south of it had been removed so as to make it a killing zone. C Troop of No. 43 was on point in the advance towards it and was soon pinned down by exceptionally heavy machine-gun and mortar fire. Among the injured was the Troop's commander.

Twenty-one-year-old Corporal Tom Hunter, in civilian life a stationer in Edinburgh, spotted that some of the enemy were ensconced in houses on the near bank, about two hundred yards away. He stood up and charged forward alone, firing his Bren from the hip. Three Spandaus opened up on him, soon joined by six more from across the canal. Somehow reaching the houses unscathed, he ran through them, changing magazines as he went. The trio of machine-guns was silenced. Half a dozen Germans surrendered, and others pulled back over a bridge. To give the rest of the Troop time to reach the cover of the houses, Hunter then made himself a target, taking up an exposed position on a heap of rubble and pouring fire into the concrete pillboxes opposite. He was still calling for fresh magazines when he was killed by the concentrated fire of several Spandaus.

It was clear that a more powerfully equipped force would be needed to storm the canal, and the Commandos were ordered to hold their ground until they could be relieved late on 4 April by the 24th Guards Brigade. Yet ROAST had been both a tactical and a strategic success. At a cost of 25 dead and 110 wounded, the Commandos had annihilated at least three battalions of enemy infantry, and taken almost 950 prisoners.

But more importantly for the Allied plan, the Germans had moved five of their battalions eastwards, towards Comacchio, and recalled an entire division from north of the Po. Even as these troops prepared to meet the non-existent threat in the delta, Alexander's tanks were accelerating towards the gap opening up at Argenta.

Since the reorganisation of the SBS by Jellicoe following its losses on Rhodes, it had become an even more effective raiding force. Better support, more firepower and operating in larger groups had all contributed to this, as had the waning of German strength in the Mediterranean, but another reason for its success had been the recruitment from the SAS of Anders Lassen.

The Dane had made an immediate impression on joining David Sutherland's 'S' Detachment in Lebanon, though not always for the obvious reasons. Jellicoe recalled:

> My most vivid memory of him was not his efficiency on exercise but going on a night out with him in Tel Aviv. We had a certain amount to drink, not excessive. Then we were having a chat in a nightclub with him, a friendly chat I thought, and I must have said something which didn't appeal to him.
>
> The first thing I knew was getting up after being knocked down – I had been knocked out for a bit – and trying to work out what had happened. I'd seen what this young man was worth and decided to drop any case against him.

In almost any other unit, assaulting one's commanding officer would have resulted in a court martial, but those like Jellicoe and Sutherland who had served in the Commandos had less orthodox views about the respect due to rank.

Moreover, there was something about Lassen – a transparency to his character – that made it impossible to hold anything against him. 'He was irresistible,' said Sutherland, 'absolutely irresistible. He had that Viking charm.' He was also inspirational.

In July 1943, the SBS had again raided the airstrip at Kastelli on Crete. Lassen led one of the parties, and bluffed his way into the base by pretending to be a German officer. He passed three groups of sentries, but had to shoot a fourth when he became suspicious.

The alarm was raised but Lassen and his companion, Gunner Ray Jones, were able to withdraw safely to the airfield's perimeter. Half an hour later they tried again. However, the guard had been trebled, and Lassen was again forced to kill a sentry. He and Jones were then herded by enemy search parties towards the centre of the base, where they were caught in the glare of searchlights and shot at from three sides. In spite of this, they again managed to escape, and with the help of the remainder of the unit were also able to set fire to several aircraft. As Jones pointed out, Lassen got the credit for a diversion which had in fact gone badly awry, but that was typical of him. He was awarded a Bar to his MC for the operation, and won another in the Aegean in the autumn. Soon his men would follow him anywhere.

Amalgamated as Raiding Forces, the various special service units mounted more than 375 separate attacks on 70 different islands in 1943 and 1944 as the Germans were harried from Greek waters. The Commandos themselves might now have a different role, but they had left a legacy which would be perfected by others. One of the lessons that the SBS had learned from them was the need for adaptability, and the greater ease of that in small units. So it was that, on the day that ROAST ended, Lassen's squadron switched from waterborne reconnaissance to more aggressive duties.

Operating with sixty former partisans as 'Fryforce', they seized four small tussocky islands amid the rushes near the town of Comacchio, and used them as a base to harass German lines of communication on the northern side of the lagoon. One of their early coups was to take some prisoners whose identity provided the first proof that ROAST had indeed diverted enemy forces away from the Argenta area.

'The SBS mess at that time seemed to be split,' noted Ian Smith, the veteran of the TARBRUSH operations before D-Day who had joined the force late in 1944. 'There were those who wanted to have one last go, and those that took the view that they had been at very considerable risk for the last four years and . . . why risk it all on one more operation which could not possibly be essential for victory?' Smith was newly married and understandably disinclined to try his luck further. Lassen could never have his fill of adventure.

It was towards midnight on 8 April that a seventeen-man patrol under Lassen landed on the coastal road and was attacked as it advanced towards Comacchio. As he went to take the surrender of the third blockhouse that he had subdued, a machine-gun opened up at point-blank range and he was fatally wounded in the stomach. Knowing that he was dying, he waved away attempts to help him, ordering the survivors to do their best to evacuate the other injured members of the party. Eight of them had been killed or wounded.

The news of Lassen's death came as an overwhelming shock to the SBS. Many who heard the news could barely believe it. The action in which he had lost his life might have been more reckless than strictly necessary, but he had taken such risks before with barely a scratch to show for them. Lassen had been such a talisman to the unit that the thought of him not being a part of it seemed impossible.

As David Sutherland – now the SBS's commanding officer – tried to piece together what had happened he formed the idea of permanently honouring Lassen's memory. He drove down to Rimini to see Brigadier Tod and asked him to recommend Lassen for the Victoria Cross. But Tod shook his head, saying that he thought the skirmish would have merited the DSO if Lassen had lived. Overwrought, and conscious of how much the Dane had meant to his men, Sutherland stormed off without saluting.

A little later, he learned that Tod's refusal to support him was in part due to military politics. Tom Hunter had already been recommended for a posthumous VC for his courage at Comacchio, and there was an informal rule that not more than one of the medals could be awarded to the same formation for the same action. Moreover, the Royal Marines had yet to win a VC during the war.

There seemed little likelihood that Lassen's bravery would be recognised. Then Sutherland remembered that a friend of his from Eton, Tony Crankshaw, was the military assistant to the Commander-in-Chief of the Eighth Army, Lieutenant General Sir Richard McCreery, in which the Brigade was serving. By this time, McCreery's headquarters were in Austria, and Sutherland drove there non-stop to put his case to Crankshaw.

The old school tie has its uses: in December 1945, Lassen's parents were presented with his Victoria Cross. They had had almost no news of their son for six years, and only learned of his death the week after VE Day.

In the years after the war in Denmark he became seen as a leading figure in the resistance to the Nazis. However, remarkably, he was not alone in his family in having that status: his first cousin, the German soldier Axel von dem Bussche, was among the chief architects of the plan to assassinate Hitler. Lassen's VC remains to this day the only one to have been awarded to a member of the SBS or the SAS. He was not the perfect soldier, being too ready to take risks for their own sake, but few others have rivalled him as a born warrior.

Within a week of Lassen's death, the Allies stood poised to begin the last major offensive of the Italian campaign. While the British 78th Infantry Division, supported by armour, attacked Argenta from the east, from its other side the 10th Indian Division would loop north of Bologna. Once out into the flat country of the Lombardy Plain, there would be no stopping them.

In order to impede their advance, the Germans had flooded the fields west of Argenta for about ten miles. To prevent the 78th being enfiladed from this direction, the area would have to be cleared of any remaining opposition, but the only way through it was along a series of high floodbanks. These protected the edge of the town and then followed the River Reno westwards. Running along the entire four-mile length of each was a narrow backbone which varied in width from forty to twenty-five yards, and on which there was not a stitch of cover.

By 17 April, 2 Commando had taken the bridges over the canal that ran between the dykes, but enemy troops were still dug in on top of them. Very early the next morning, No. 43 started to move up from the front line towards two objectives they had been given – a group of fortified houses and a pumping station about a mile north-west of Argenta. They were to receive fire support from a Troop of Churchill tanks, but no sooner had the first of these trundled towards the embankment than it hit a mine, cast a track, and slewed round so that it blocked the road for those behind. 'It was a very inauspicious start,' thought Bill Jenkins. He and E Troop proceeded on foot, accompanied by D Troop on the left side of the canal, while A and B Troops advanced on the right.

The narrowness of the path beside the dyke meant that they had to move in single file, and in the darkness Jenkins was unsure of what lay ahead. He decided to push on by himself, but he had gone no more than twenty yards before he was challenged. Two riflemen were dug in behind a fence, and a Spandau section was embedded in the side of the embankment. Jenkins realised that if he could get on top of this, he might be able to outflank them, and began to scramble up its side.

Uncomfortably aware of how visible his silhouette was on the skyline, he started to feel his way slowly forward. To his surprise, a pair of ornamental gates, set between tall brick pillars, came into view. They were ajar, so he walked cautiously through them, searching for tripwires. Nothing happened and, deducing that he had gone beyond the German positions in the bank below, he turned back to fetch support. As he did so, the night was torn apart.

> Just as I was rounding the gate, there was a muzzle flash about six or seven feet below me on the eastern side of the embankment. There was a searing pain in my neck. So I spun round, and then there was another muzzle flash and I was absolutely lifted off my feet by a kick like a mule and I went face down on the central embankment.

Jenkins's first thought was that he must be dying and that the shock had obliterated the pain. He wondered briefly if he was going to Heaven or to Hell. Then he found that his arms and legs still worked, so he took out a grenade and threw it at the foxhole from where the shots had come. It exploded, and he heard a man running away, followed soon after by another.

A few moments later, he heard a rustling noise much closer to him. He reached out with his hand and felt the edge of a slit trench: there had been a position on top of the embankment after all. 'I reached in my holster for my .45, cocked it and shot into the front part of the trench. Then something shot up from under my nose.' A disjointed puppet began to dance before him, shouting: 'Don't shoot! I'm Austrian!' The frightened soldier had been crouched in the back of the trench all the while.

Jenkins took him prisoner, and five others soon surrendered, including those manning the Spandau in the side of the dyke. When he later examined his wounds, he discovered that he had splinters in his neck from where the first bullet had clipped the gate beside him. From six feet away, the second had thudded into his backpack and gone through his camera, his wash bag and his mess tin. But it had been unable to penetrate his biscuit ration.

There still remained, however, E Troop's original objective. They now resumed their march towards the pumping station. Then, as they crossed a railway line about a hundred yards from it, they came under attack at almost point-blank range from two Spandaus belonging to a German platoon grouped around the nearest houses. Jenkins was in the lead and realised the danger posed to those still outlined on the floodbank. With his tommy-gun at the hip, he charged straight at the first Spandau, whose crew was so unnerved that they immediately surrendered. The rest of the Troop quickly mopped up the other posts in the nearby gardens and houses, taking more than twenty prisoners and leaving many dead, although Jenkins himself was wounded again.

While the PoWs were being taken off, Jenkins wandered back on his own to the ornamental gates. It was starting to get lighter, and he was startled to see a file of seven Germans approaching along the bank. They were clearly the relief for those in the trenches, and equally clearly oblivious to Jenkins's presence. There was no cover so all he could do was squat down and wait until he was sure that they had all arrived. It was important that none got away to raise the alarm, or E Troop might find themselves surrounded. For several minutes he watched as the squad chatted among themselves, rifles over their shoulders. Finally two stragglers joined the group.

> I stood up and marched forward and bellowed out: '*Hände Hoch!*' They were absolutely dumbfounded. The trouble was that they didn't put their hands up. I walked right up to a couple of yards from them, and swung my tommy-gun round and said '*Hände Hoch!*' again. They just looked at me. The ghastly thought went through my mind that I might have to mow them down.

At last, their sergeant-major reached for his rifle and handed it to Jenkins.

The surprises continued. More than forty minutes later, white handkerchiefs began to be waved from another slit trench that no one had spotted. 'If they had been a bit braver, they could have shot us all from their position,' Jenkins observed later.

Their luck put him in a generous mood when a lone figure appeared unexpectedly on the dyke on the other side of the canal. 'A tall chap on the embankment to the east of us got up and started clapping his hands and stamping his feet.' From his coat it was obvious that he was a German soldier. Evidently he was unaware that the marines had taken over the post opposite his. 'The Bren gunner eagerly asked if he could shoot him . . . The truth of the matter is that I just did not feel like shooting a man in cold blood.'

Twenty minutes later, though, Spandau fire began to rake the poplars above Jenkins's head. The tall German was aiming for ricochets into the base of the embankment where the commandos were sheltering. The Bren gunner moved gently up the slope. 'He was just about to shoot when he gave a gasp and slid down wounded into my arms – the Spandau had beaten him to it.' Jenkins had been made to pay heavily for his gesture of humanity.

Over the next few days, the Allied armour began to spread out behind the German lines. As No. 43 moved up towards Ferrara, they encountered weary columns of prisoners heading south. A patrol from 2 Commando took off their trousers to wade across the canal to the village of Marmorta, and found themselves marching semi-naked in a victory parade as the local girls thrust bunches of lilac into their arms. The Brigade was pulled out of the line on 21 April, and a fortnight later the German forces in Italy surrendered.

Bill Jenkins spent VE Day guarding PoWs on the Adriatic coast. He had only just celebrated his twentieth birthday, and his display of leadership on top of the dykes would make him the youngest marine to win the DSO during the war. Of the other five officer cadets in his intake, two had been killed and one had lost a leg.

The 2nd Commando Brigade had also suffered heavily in their Mediterranean campaign. In eighteen months of near-continuous fighting, three hundred men had been killed and another twelve hundred wounded. Their comrades who had survived would carry painful memories with them for the rest of their lives. But for now they would enjoy the spring sunshine, the prospect of a few days' leave in Florence, and the news that those taken prisoner at St Nazaire were being repatriated. They were all going home.

19

ECLIPSE

Wartime train journeys in Britain tested the patience even of the saintly. As late as 1944, there were long, unexplained delays to endure while troop movements were given priority or a V1 rocket devastated the line ahead. Many signposts remained painted out – a hangover from invasion fever – so passengers were even denied the small comfort of learning that they were stuck at Adlestrop. In such circumstances, people did something unthinkable: they talked to strangers.

So it was that Eve Fleming fell into conversation with the good-looking officer seated in her compartment. Like her son Ian, he was in the Navy, and by chance it turned out that he worked for him. Everyone was beginning to think what life might be like after the war, and Eve confided that Ian wanted to become an author. She rather had her doubts, however, as to whether he would sell any books. Surprised as she was to be by the success of James Bond, she might have been more astonished still to discover that she was speaking to his real-life inspiration.

According to one of his comrades, Patrick Dalzel-Job 'had a cast-iron constitution and was seemingly without a nerve in his body'. He was a qualified parachutist and diver, an experienced skier and yachtsman, and had done intelligence work behind enemy lines in Norway. Like Bond, he had finished his education in Switzerland, where he had grown up following the death of his father – like Fleming's – on the Western Front during the First World War. And now he had joined the most secret of all Commando units, set up and supervised by Fleming himself.

Perhaps surprisingly, its roots were German. In the invasion of Yugoslavia, a specialised force – the *Abwehrkommando* – had been sent ahead of the leading troops to seize codes, technology and documents before they could be destroyed. It was an idea that caught the imagination of Fleming, who was working at the Admiralty as assistant to the Director of Naval Intelligence. At his urging, in late 1942 it was agreed that a small group of 'authorised looters' should be formed 'to capture enemy material ... of special importance'. This organisation would undergo several changes of name, among them the Special Intelligence Unit and 30 RN Commando, but from the end of 1943 it was known as 30 Assault Unit.

30 AU has always been treated by historians as a Commando, and to an extent it was. It was administered by, though was only notionally under the control of, the Chief of Combined Operations. Its personnel wore green berets, and included marines. But its name was misleading. 'It was selected with a view to security,' noted one high-ranking officer. 'Intelligence Assault Unit is rather too self-evident a title.'

Although initially commanded by Robert Ryder VC, the hero of St Nazaire, it was always intended to be an intelligence-gathering rather than a combat formation. The confusion as to its role extended even to some of those who served in it, and inevitably led outsiders to assume that its main task was to fight. 'Half of the trouble and mutual mistrust was caused by the unit being called 30 Assault Unit, and as such, disliking being told to do a bit of assaulting,' reflected Robert Sturges, the head of the Commandos, in the autumn of 1944.

'It must be accepted that 30 AU is a private army,' concurred one of its members, pointing out that it had other priorities than those of most soldiers.

Its early troubles stemmed, however, mainly from its internal organisation. It was not staffed solely, or even largely, by commandos but instead was created as a tri-service unit. Although the RAF declined to become involved, one Army and one Navy Troop were formed. There was also a Royal Marine Troop, meant originally to serve as a bodyguard to the naval contingent, most of whom were engineers and technicians. While speed of action would be essential, these were not trained raiders.

There was at first little integration between the two wings. They took their orders from their parent services, which led to a wide variation in the support they received and how they went about their work. The friction this caused was exposed during their first operations in North Africa and then in Italy. Hampered by poor logistics, they tended to arrive in the wake rather than in advance of other troops, though they did have some triumphs, such as the capture of an Enigma machine in Sicily and discovering that the Italians had penetrated the British convoy code. 'It always felt like it was an unwelcome child,' thought Ryder's successor, the polar explorer Quintin Riley, 'owing to its three-dimensional status and many masters.'

Fleming was also unhappy with 30 AU's performance in the Mediterranean, where he accused them of lacking in discipline and behaving 'like Red Indians'. By D-Day, the unit had been reorganised and given specific lists of targets contained in so-called Black Books. Among these were the concealed launching sites for the V1, some of which were found, although little use seems to have been made of the intelligence recovered.

However, as 30 AU advanced across North-West Europe, with Lieutenant Commander Dalzel-Job in the lead Jeep directing traffic with a sword, it finally began to realise Fleming's vision. With the front line so fluid, and with senior commanders now aware of the unit's purpose, it could for the first time get to its objectives before plans and weapons were destroyed or looted. Under these conditions it was forced, as well, to behave more like a Commando, fusing the boldness required of raiders to the power needed by a spearhead.

This process reached its culmination during ECLIPSE, an

Anglo-American operation to ensure that strategically important territory, technology and individuals were under their control, rather than that of the Soviets, when the war ended. Dalzel-Job's Team 4 had as its objective the dockyards of Bremen, and on 26 April 1945 it detached itself from the Army's line of advance and raced towards the city centre.

The streets were in ruins, and the main square deserted except for a lone policeman. He approached Dalzel-Job with a request: would he be interested in taking Bremen's surrender? Inside the Town Hall, the mayor was waiting in a top hat, and Dalzel-Job did his best to assure him of British help in keeping essential services running in return for civic cooperation. All the while, however, he was conscious of the need to get to the Deschimag shipyard, not least before it was shelled by the Allies themselves.

Deciding that nothing would be gained by exposing the whole force to any die-hards that might be about, he decided to go on ahead with a driver in a scout car. They stopped at each corner, looked about them, and then sped across the junction to the next. Then, just as they arrived at the dock gates, the engine died. It was out of petrol.

Unable to summon the rest of his group by wireless because of signals interference, Dalzel-Job borrowed a bicycle from a workman and began to pedal back slowly towards the centre. It seemed to him only a matter of time before a lone British officer proved too tempting a target for a sniper. His men thought so as well, and as he rounded the corner to where they were waiting, he was dragged onto a scout car as it roared towards the water.

Beyond the gates, the bombed dockyard was 'a mess of drunken bits of U-boat, twisted girders, smoke-blackened sheds', thought one marine. The rest of the squad began to round up the company's technical experts and its directors. They had arrived just in time to prevent the destruction of the next generation of German weaponry. On the slips sat two destroyers and sixteen submarines of the latest type. Dalzel-Job was not quite sure what to say when the next day a staff officer demanded that he provide a receipt for them.

The unit's other coups in Germany included the seizure of more secret U-boat technology in Hamburg and at Kiel, where they were among the first Allied troops into the city, and the discovery of the entire German naval archives at the castle of Tambach, near Coburg. These contained one of the fullest political, as well as military, records of the history of the Third Reich.

30 AU was not a Commando as such, but the use it made of the Commando approach to operations – versatile, decisive, self-reliant and unorthodox – showed how far that mentality had spread in five years, even among those without Commando training. It had also shown how much could be accomplished by a small group, or even just one man, equipped with the right skills and attitude. 'Initiative and resourcefulness are essential,' wrote Riley, adding that the ideal officer ought in the future to be intelligence trained and able to parachute, blow safes, live off the land, speak languages and fly aeroplanes. It might have been the template for Bond.

Dalzel-Job never read any of Fleming's books, but the author told him that he had been one of the models for his hero. All that, however, lay in the future. For now, he just wanted to find the Norwegian girl he loved and take her back to Scotland. He had had enough of war.

'With the disbandment of the Commando Group (a formation second to none in the fighting forces of Great Britain), the Green Beret will be worn no more,' Bob Laycock told his veterans in October 1945. 'It is a thing of war but not of peace . . . To you, the wearers of that Beret who have made it a symbol of honour and of bravery unsurpassed, I send the unbounded gratitude of those whom you have served. Your country is justly proud of you – your spirit and valour will live for ever in the annals of our Nation.'

The revelation the previous month that the Commandos were to be stood down came as a shock to them. The news, meanwhile, that three of the Royal Marine Commandos were to remain in being as the sole heirs to the wartime legacy of the formation was regarded with anger by many of those who had come to it from the Army. Yet the War Office was adamant that with much-reduced forces, in an age of austerity, there was no justification for retaining such a large specialised body of troops.

It is a judgement which it is hard to dispute. High as their reputation stood with the public at the end of the war, the Commandos had been created in response to a state of siege which, in the short term at least, was unlikely to recur. Laycock warned that future conflicts needed to be prepared for but, contrary to what might be thought, there was no general acceptance within Whitehall that the Commandos' skills needed to be retained. It would be difficult to argue, for instance, that their role as storm troops could not be carried out instead by conventional infantry given some additional training. The taking of Walcheren and the assault at Comacchio had been triumphs for the Commandos, but Pegasus Bridge, after all, had been seized by detachments from the Ox and Bucks who had prepared just for that operation.

Nor, when examined soberly, did the results of the Commandos' earlier missions suggest that raiding should be central to military thinking in the years ahead. There had been a lengthy and bloody list of failures, among them the attacks on Bardia, Tobruk and Rommel's HQ. Often their outcomes had not been the Commandos' fault, nor had they materially altered the course of the war – but neither could that be said of their successes. The attack on Vaagso in 1941 had shown the Germans that they would not have it all their own way, but the Norwegians would still endure another four years of occupation. St Nazaire had been a dramatic coup, but would have had real significance only if it had stopped U-boats operating from there. One measure of the strategic impact of such raids is that the Germans did not seek to emulate them (although during their early campaigns in Europe and Russia their Brandenburg commandos did operate behind the lines as saboteurs and shock troops, often in disguise). For all the effort invested in the Commandos' missions, and for all the courage they required, none had been essential to victory. The Commandos captured the headlines but, once it had the right commanders in place, it was the Field Army that won the key battles.

Moreover, there were many in that Army who felt that they would have won the war sooner had the Commandos not creamed off the best of their men. 'Every platoon can be analysed as follows,' concluded a War Office report on the fighting in Sicily in 1943, 'six gutful men who will go anywhere and do anything, twelve "sheep" who will follow a short distance behind if well led, and from four to six ineffective men who have not got what it takes in them ever to be really effective soldiers.' Most British troops were conscripts, civilians rather than professional soldiers, and for all their training few at first were willing to risk their lives. In that context, the difference made by strong leadership could be vital. 'A few strong toughies influenced a lot of others,' believed Geoffrey Picot, an officer who served with the Hampshires in Normandy. 'The formation of airborne forces and the Commandos took a great many strong toughies away from the infantry of the line, who were thereby weakened.'

The traditional view of the Commandos is that their main contribution to the war was psychological, that their buccaneering image – largely borne of propaganda – unnerved German sentries and raised morale at home. It probably did have both those effects, although to what extent it is hard to gauge. But it may also be that the formation's existence undermined the fighting spirit of at least some units on its own side. And those it took from them often saw very little action; they would have been of more use in the daily struggle on the front line. The perception that the Commandos' status bred resentment elsewhere was another reason for reducing their numbers now that peace had come.

In 1945, therefore, the Commando experiment appeared to have largely outrun its usefulness. What was to lead to its unexpected renaissance was the change in the nature of combat in the decades that followed. The founders of the Commando concept – Clarke, Laycock, Stirling and Courtney – had simply been ahead of their time. They may not have won the Second World War, but they would shape many that came after it.

With the drawing down of the Iron Curtain, it had been assumed that the chief threat to Britain would come from the Warsaw Pact. In fact, where force turned out to be needed was in small wars – clashes mainly with insurgents and terrorists against whom flexible methods and specialised skills proved vital. Technological developments also meant that more and more could be accomplished by small detachments of soldiers, often inserted behind enemy lines.

All these principles had been pioneered by the Commandos. And while their heritage would live on in the reformed SAS and SBS, as well as in the Royal Marines, the wartime units had won a wider victory, too. Once, the knowledge, experience and values instilled at Achnacarry had been the preserve of an elite. Their dissemination worldwide since then has made them fundamental to modern military training. Now every soldier is a commando.

Those who had been there at the start were left to reflect on the maelstrom through which they had passed. The medals they had won showed that much had been asked of them. Not all would find the demands of peace any easier.

Many who had temporarily held high rank at a young age knew that it would be years before they reached it again and so left the Army. Bob Laycock, a major general in his thirties, stood unsuccessfully for Parliament before serving as Governor of Malta in the 1950s. David Sutherland, a lieutenant colonel and commander of the SBS at twenty-four, spent the rest of his career with MI5, while keeping up his links with the special forces. He advised the Home Office during the Iranian Embassy siege in 1980.

Peter Young and Jimmy Dunning did stay in the Army. Others were disillusioned with it, and it with them. Roger Courtney was packed off to Somaliland as a colonial administrator even before the war was over. He died there in 1949, aged only forty-six. Unlike David Stirling, the founder of the SAS, Courtney's role in the birth of the SBS has been largely forgotten. His younger brother Gruff, who had commanded 2 SBS, joined the Intelligence Service and later settled in Australia.

Some went on to prosper in business. Tommy Macpherson, taken prisoner during his recce for the Rommel raid, later escaped to Sweden, joined SOE and served with distinction in France and Italy, winning three MCs. He afterwards became president of the Association of European Chambers of Commerce and was knighted.

Ronnie Swayne was similarly honoured for his part in the containerisation revolution that transformed shipping in the 1970s. When he ordered two vessels from a German yard, its managing director turned out to be the first officer of the *Jaguar*, the warship with which he had fought an uneven duel at St Nazaire.

Tommy Langton also tried to become an MP, but the Finchley Conservatives selected Margaret Thatcher instead. Shimi Lovat returned to his Highland estate. Blondie Hasler became the father of modern ocean racing. Bill Sparks, the only other survivor of FRANKTON, worked on the buses. Jack Terry, who had walked out of the desert with Laycock, fulfilled his boyhood ambition of joining the police. Bill Jenkins trained as a teacher, while Jos Nicholl – who received the MC after Comacchio – was ordained as a priest. Eric de la Torre, the veteran of St Nazaire and Vaagso, opened a sporting goods shop. George Peel went back to Norway to give back the little box of bible passages that he thought had kept him safe during ARCHERY. Maurice Tiefenbrunner of the SIG settled in Jerusalem.

Many other commandos did not survive the war, of course. David Russell escaped the debacle at Tobruk only to be murdered while operating undercover with SOE in Romania. Herbert Buck, who had recruited him to the SIG, was released from captivity when Germany surrendered, but was killed a few months later in an air crash while en route to India with the SAS. Nothing, however, could harm 'Mad' Jack Churchill, who in May 1945 walked a hundred miles to freedom over the Tyrolean mountains.

Others seemed to have adapted to a new life but were only concealing an inner emptiness. In 1972, Joe Smale went to the funeral of his former CO, John Durnford-Slater, who had committed suicide having spent almost thirty years as a school bursar and personnel manager. 'It was sad,' Smale revealed later.

> After the war he couldn't live without his excitement. He had failings but you couldn't help liking him . . . I had a look at the wreaths. One was from a couple of soldiers who had served under him. It read: 'To Colonel Durnford-Slater, the man who made No. 3 what it was, from Len and Ginger, No. 5 Troop.' And I thought, well, that says everything, really.

Smale looked back fondly on his time as a commando. 'It was a great life, really,' he thought. 'You were always getting ready for something, being buoyed up, you always had something to look forward to. The bulk of the ordinary Army was just sitting there waiting for D-Day.'

Micky Burn's feelings were more mixed. He became a writer after losing much of his money in a fishery business in which he had tried to replicate the spirit he had found in No. 2 during wartime. Yet he disliked the aura that had come to gather around the Commandos in the years since the war and which did so much to maintain public interest in them:

> One of the absurd situations that I find myself in now is that I am considered three times a war hero on the basis of no danger at all, except for the St Nazaire raid, because I was in the Commandos, because I was at St Nazaire and because I was at Colditz.
>
> Children and people who like war stories, their eyes pop out of their head. My brother was in Atlantic and Arctic convoys the whole way through, my son-in-law was in tanks the whole way through Africa, Italy and Germany. No-one's interested in them. It's the media who have done it. It's quite false.

Another veteran who preferred not to make a fuss about what he had achieved was John Barton. After being withdrawn from the Adriatic following his slaying of the Brac garrison commander, he had joined SOE. There his career had taken a still more extraordinary turn. In November 1944, he had been hand-picked by

Field Marshal Alexander to carry out another assassination. This time, the target was the commander of German forces in Italy, General von Vietinghoff.

Despite not speaking Italian, Barton spent three months in enemy-occupied territory but he was unable to locate the general. In the last weeks of the war, he again parachuted behind the lines to liaise with partisans, and had to shoot his way out on at least one occasion. Based near Ferrara, he was able to confirm the withdrawal of a division from there to Comacchio after ROAST, information regarded by his superiors as 'the most important intelligence item of the campaign'.

Barton was awarded a Bar to his DSO, but after settling in Kenya as a farmer he hardly ever mentioned the war or brought out his medals. When he did wear them to a Remembrance Day service, they were stolen.

Even the man who had started it all, Dudley Clarke, rarely talked about what he had done. He wrote a memoir of his time in the Commandos, but mindful of official secrecy drew a veil over much else that he had accomplished afterwards. He received little credit for his vital deception work, and after retiring from the Army worked for a security firm. Perhaps he would have agreed with the advice of one of those whom his creation had shaped. The German-born George Saunders, of 10 Commando, did not want to dwell on the past: 'Life is today and tomorrow – not yesterday.'

Yet, for many commandos, the war had been the most formative experience of their lives, and the friendships it had forged were those they cherished above all. Civvy Street lacked the comradeship they had found with each other. Among those who treasured it was Joe Patterson, No. 4's medic, who later became a surgeon in Belfast. 'I am glad I saw it through, and even more glad that I had the luck to come home safely,' he wrote. 'It was in fact just a martial interlude, but I had met and known so many remarkable characters that the memory of those years is vivid and forever stimulating.'

'You wouldn't miss that, would you?' agreed Harry Winch. 'It's an experience you can't buy. You were with men.' He regularly attends meetings of the Royal British Legion and the Burma Campaign Fellowship Association, but though they have helped him come to terms with the war, the conversation never turns to its cost. 'I've never heard one of them say they shot anybody, and they went against the Germans, the Italians . . . I never talked about the war. My family didn't know until a few years ago. It's the funny things I shall remember. I talk about them.'

Others were haunted by what they had seen. Dinger Bell buried it deep and only began to feel its impact when he was in his sixties, when he had a breakdown and suppressed memories started to surface. He remembered in particular one scene on the Myebon Peninsula in Burma: 'It was a moonlit night, and we were following up the Japs on patrol. We went over this bank, me and a couple of other blokes, and we suddenly found ourselves in a shallow grave with dead Japanese and coyotes eating them. Think how frightening that is.'

In later life, Vic Ralph also reflected on the cruelty and pointlessness of combat. 'War is a most peculiar thing,' he observed. 'You're shooting men simply because they're wearing a different uniform, they're a different race, they've got different ideals. You don't know them. Possibly you could have been great friends if you'd met under different circumstances.'

Once a year, when the beech leaves turn golden, commandos gather to commemorate the sacrifices claimed by war. A mile uphill from Spean Bridge, where so many took their first steps towards earning a green beret, stands the Commando Memorial. Dedicated in 1952, it takes the form of three woollen-capped soldiers, cast in bronze but seemingly hewn from granite, gazing south towards some of Scotland's highest hills. There, with quiet pride and dignity, the fallen of both past and current battles are remembered, the dwindling band of veterans standing together in the autumn light with the present generation of warriors. For Vic Ralph, theirs was an indestructible bond:

When we march up the hill to the war memorial on the Sunday afternoon, the school pipe and drum band lead us up. You see those men – old men – and some of them are bent over. But when the pipes start to play their shoulders come back and they're eighteen or twenty again. It takes us back.

Apart from marriage, I can't think of any friendship that would last so long.

EPILOGUE

THE COMMANDO PRAYER

Teach us, Good Lord
To serve Thee as Thou deservest
To give and not to count the cost
To fight and not to heed the wounds
To toil and not to seek for rest
To labour and not to ask for any reward
Save that of knowing that we do Thy Holy will
And bearing our part in Thine eternal purpose
Through Jesus Christ Our Lord, Amen

St Ignatius of Loyola

NOTES

Abbreviations

NA National Archives, Kew.
IWM Imperial War Museum (SA: Sound Archive; DD: Department of Documents).
LHCMA Liddell Hart Centre for Military Archives, King's College, London.
REL Papers of Major General Sir Robert Laycock, at LHCMA.

Prologue: CORDITE

xix It was an hour after dusk: I have reconstructed CORDITE chiefly from the accounts given in Courtney, *SBS in World War Two*, pp. 25 et seq., Strutton and Pearson, *The Secret Invaders*, pp. 1–47, and Trenowden, *Stealthily by Night*, pp. 9–17. The main archival sources are: James Sherwood, IWM SA 9783; Private Papers of A.I. Hughes, IWM DD 2222; and Private Papers of Nigel Clogstoun-Willmott, IWM DD 7062.

xxi Yet there was a side to him: Additional information on Willmott's life is from an interview with Jonathan Clogstoun-Willmott, 6 November 2011.

xxiii 'grown-up boy': Sherwood, IWM SA 9783.
Now nearly forty: Courtney, op. cit., pp. 21–24 has the fullest account of Roger Courtney's early life and the origins of the SBS. See also NA DEFE 2/711B.
The Arab Revolt: Courtney, *Palestine Policeman*, p. 13.
'For several nights': Sherwood, IWM SA 9783.

xxiv 'Generally speaking': Hughes, IWM DD 2222.

xxv 'I'd never been': Sherwood, IWM SA 9783.

xxix Roger Courtney was awarded the Military Cross: The citation is in NA WO 373/27.

xxx 'silly fiascos': NA CAB 120/414, 23 July 1940.

1: AMBASSADOR

1 5 June 1940: For Clarke's account of his meeting with Dill and the birth of the Commandos see Clarke, *Seven Assignments*, pp. 205–216. The other main source that I have used is the Private Papers of D.W. Clarke, IWM DD Box 8080. For

those interested in footnotes to history, the uncensored version of his memoir in the papers reveals that his destination in Assignment Five was neutral Dublin.

1 'We must': Dudley Clarke, *The Listener*, 25 November 1948.

2 'With the resources': Clarke, IWM DD Box 8080.

'The completely defensive': NA CAB 120/414, 3 June 1940.

3 'We have got to get': Ibid., 5 June 1940.

4 Five Independent Companies: NA WO 193/384.

5 Anthony Eden: NA CAB 120/414, c.14 June 1940.

6 'specialising in tip and run tactics': NA WO 193/384.

'I was tired': Durnford-Slater, *Commando*, p. 11.

'What I was seeking': Ibid., p. 20.

7 'We'd fought the Germans': John Smale, IWM SA 29819.

'You would be attacking': Ibid.

'We chose a number': Ibid.

9 'wandered around a bit': Ronald Swayne, IWM SA 10231.

'We got everybody off': Ibid.

10 The last group: Clarke's account of the raid at Stella Plage, and the press's response to it, is in *Seven Assignments*, pp. 227–238.

11 'Publicity will play': Clarke, IWM DD Box 8080.

The target was Guernsey: The principal sources for the raid that I have drawn on are Durnford-Slater, op. cit. pp. 22–34, the official report on it, NA WO 106/2958, and 3 Commando's war diary, WO 218/3.

12 An officer originally from the island: See the obituary of Philip Martel, *Daily Telegraph*, 23 March 2012. Martel landed with Desmond Mulholland, hence the choice of password.

'We were completely raw': Smale, IWM SA 29819.

'We weren't remotely ready': Swayne, IWM SA 10231.

13 'There was a bungalow': Smale, IWM SA 29819.

'De Crespigny said': Ibid.

14 'We'd done a swimming test': Ibid.

15 'I sank twice': Smale, www.war-experience.org/collections/land/alliedbrit/smale/default.asp.

'ridiculous, almost comic failure': Durnford-Slater, op. cit., p. 32.

'if that garrison': Smale, IWM SA 29819.

16 'It would be most unwise': NA CAB 120/414, 23 July 1940.

He urged Bourne: Clarke, IWM DD Box 8080. See also Churchill, *The Second World War*, p. 413.

17 'My own judgement': NA CAB 120/414, 7 July 1940.

2: EXPORTER

19 From birth: The major source of information on Laycock, his time with 8 Commando and with Layforce are the thirty-four boxes of personal papers (REL) kept at LHMCA.

'In accordance': REL, Box 9/1/2.

'a society cavalryman': Private Papers of Thomas Macpherson, File 2/18, IWM DD 13335.

20 'a very good type': REL, Box 1/1.

21 'No drive': REL, Box 1/3.

'white hunter': REL, Box 1/2.

21 'we belted out': Sherwood, IWM SA 9783.
22 'the lightning, destructive and ruthless methods': REL, Box 2/5.
'austerity and formality': Evelyn Waugh, 'Commando Raid on Bardia', *Life*, 17 November 1941.
'a completely new world': Smale, IWM SA 29819.
23 'He hadn't, nor had anybody else': Durnford-Slater, op. cit., p. 38. Similar details about the raid, given in Clarke, op. cit., p. 237, are equally fanciful.
'We were gradually': Swayne, IWM SA 10231.
'The average Englishman': REL, Box 2/6.
The Special Training Centre: For its origins see in particular Kemp, *No Colours or Crest*, pp. 18–23, and Allan, *Commando Country*.
24 'He tried to make us': Swayne, IWM SA 10231.
'I knew a man': Papers of Quintin Riley, LHCMA.
Cyril Mackworth-Praed: Macpherson, IWM SA 17912.
'Suddenly at the top': Ronald Hall, www.bbc.co.uk/history/ww2peopleswar/stories/38/a4544138.shtml.
25 'The senior detective': Kemp, op. cit., p. 22.
'Instead of holding': Smale, IWM SA 29819.
'They taught us how': Ibid.
26 Roger Keyes: His career and his attitude to his role at Combined Operations are outlined in Halpern, *The Keyes Papers*, vol. 3. For an internal history of Combined Ops, see NA DEFE 2/1773, as well as Fergusson, *The Watery Maze*.
28 'He was greeted': Colville, *The Fringes of Power*, p. 272, 15 December 1940.
'merely long rows of seats': Sherwood, IWM SA 9783.
29 'No information is available': REL, Box 3/4.
'I saw the last': Halpern, op. cit., p. 146, 3 February 1941.
30 'We had expected': Sherwood, IWM SA 9783.
'Things went badly': There is an account of the raid by Robin Mount in REL, Box 6/26. This also contains material by Jocelyn Nicholls on 7 Commando in North Africa and Crete. More of Nicholls's papers, including material relating to his death in Burma, are in the IWM.
'Our situation is now': REL, Box 6/3.
31 A month earlier: Macpherson, File 1/15, IWM DD 13335. Other details about 11 Commando's training and the raid at Litani are taken from his interview, IWM SA 17912, and memoir, *Behind Enemy Lines*.
32 At one aerodrome: Keyes, *Geoffrey Keyes VC of the Rommel Raid*, p. 143.
33 'determined to do him credit': Ibid., p. 4.
'We had been brought up': Richard Bath, *Scotland on Sunday*, 29 May 2009.
They never managed: Information about Mayne from interview with Gerald Bryan, 3 November 2011.
34 Pedder's plan: Reports on the raid are in NA DEFE 2/349 and Macpherson, IWM DD 13335. See also McHarg, *Litani River*, Keyes, op. cit., and Colin Smith, *England's Last War against France: Fighting Vichy 1940–42* (Weidenfeld & Nicolson, 2009).
35 'The distance was about': Macpherson, *Notes of Left Flank Operations of Litani Landing 1941*, IWM DD 13335.
36 'somewhat handicapped': Ibid. See also his *10 Troop's Withdrawal* in the same file.
38 'Extremely unpleasant': Geoffrey Keyes's diary, containing his observations on the Litani operation, is in NA DEFE 2/349.
40 'My cavaliers': NA DEFE 2/349.

'Whatever else': Macpherson, letter to Gerald Bryan, 9 October 1990, File 1/16, IWM DD 13335.

3: FLIPPER

41 'Am twenty-one today!': Keyes, op. cit., p. 193.
'It's as raiding units': REL, Box 3/17.

42 Evelyn Waugh tried: REL, Box 9/1/1.
'The Commandos have been frittered away': NA CAB 120/414, 20 July 1941.
'in the main of Jews': NA WO 201/731.
'We are thousands of men short': REL, Box 6/4.

43 'I know I am destined': For this exchange of letters see Halpern, op. cit., pp. 198–209.
'For a major': Keyes, op. cit., p. 190.
'It means convincing': Ibid., p. 192.

44 On the night of the 24th: Macpherson recounts this reconnaissance in File 2, IWM DD 13335, and IWM SA 17912.

45 'He raised a scream': Macpherson, File 2, IWM DD 13335.

46 'like a bird': Ibid.

47 'So they were six men short': Fred Birch, IWM SA 9770.
The attraction of Operation FLIPPER: The plan for the raid and subsequent events are set out in NA DEFE 2/349, Laycock's papers in the LHCMA, IWM VC Box 42 and Keyes, op. cit. See also Asher, *Get Rommel*.
'Even if initially successful': Keyes, op. cit., p. 203.

48 'It is dirty work': Ibid. Also in Macpherson, File 2, IWM DD 13335.
'My mate': Birch, IWM SA 9770.

49 David Sutherland: His view of the raid is in *He Who Dares*, pp. 46–49.
Although Keyes was in command: Laycock gives his reasons in a draft report in REL, Box 5/9.

50 Wearing native robes: Citation for Haselden's MC, NA WO 373/23.

51 'Apart from an appalling smell': Keyes, op. cit., p. 224. Campbell's narrative in it is also in Saunders, *The Green Beret*, p. 75 et seq.
'It started to rain': Birch, IWM SA 9770.
'Spirits were sinking': Keyes, op. cit., p. 226.
'The travelling was so bad': Birch, IWM SA 9770.
'As we crouched': Keyes, op. cit., p. 228.

52 'Tell them we are German troops': Ibid., p. 230.

53 'That's what raised the alarm': *The Herald*, 11 November 1997.
'We heard a man': Keyes, op. cit., p. 233.
'As I was standing': Statement by Terry, 9 February 1942, in Macpherson, File 2, IWM DD 13335.
'a stray burst': Ibid. Laycock uses the same adjective in the several versions of his report.
He understood: Private Papers of Robin Campbell, IWM DD 2402. He wrote an article for *Horizon* in 1943 about his time as a PoW. He became Director of Art at the Arts Council and established the Hayward Gallery on London's South Bank. He died in 1985, not in 2001 as Asher has it.

55 'unpleasant': REL, Box 5/9.

56 'Living behind enemy lines': Laycock's memoir of his escape is in REL, Box 9/1/2.

57 'Rommel had left': REL, Box 6/24, 21 March 1947.
Haselden's sources: The allegation about the map is in NA DEFE 2/349.

58 'I was informed by the Arabs': Ibid.
His description of Keyes's heroic death: Compare the sequence of events given in the accounts by Terry, Laycock and Campbell already mentioned. See also Kenneth Hare-Scott, 'The Daring Raid on Rommel's HQ', *The War Illustrated*, vol. 10, no. 247, 6 December 1946, and the citation for Campbell's DSO, NA WO 373/94. Elizabeth Keyes's book about her brother, published in 1956, makes veiled criticisms of Laycock but contains inconsistencies of its own. Only it, for example, claims that Geoffrey Keyes killed a sentry with a knife before entering the villa.
It contains one crucial revelation: The report is dated 18 November 1941 and is in Macpherson, IWM DD 13335.
'was actually what': Macpherson, IWM SA 17912.

59 'I would far rather': Keyes, op. cit., p. 260.

4: ARCHERY

60 None the less, when he took over: See DEFE 2/1773 for conditions at COHQ. Expansion brought new problems. M.R.D. Foot, who worked there, knew of a secretary who sold her security pass to a black marketeer for a bar of chocolate.

61 'negative power': Hansard, House of Commons Debate, 1 July 1942, vol. 381, cc 224–476.
Several factors: Fergusson, op. cit., p 116.

62 'And one of': Smale, IWM SA 29819.
When it exploded: Private Papers of J.C. Haydon, File 2/6, IWM DD Box 2397.
Their destination would be: The official accounts of the raid by the main participants are in NA DEFE 2/83. The 'Summary of Operation' and that by Peter Young are especially useful. See also Buckley, *Norway – The Commandos – Dieppe*.
'At long last': Durnford-Slater, op. cit., p. 70.

63 'The soldiers did rather well': Alan Smallman, IWM SA 16252.
'We ended up': Eric de la Torre, IWM SA 29820.
The administrative arrangements: Smallman, IWM SA 16252.

64 'Charlie was no expert': Ibid. The episode was the subject of a celebrated letter by Evelyn Waugh, which improved still further on the truth of it.
'And then the storm': George Peel, IWM SA 29618.

65 'You knew there were going to be': George Webb, IWM SA 29618 (on the same recording as Peel at the time of writing).

66 'They jumped into the water': Peel, IWM SA 29618.
'Mad Jack': For biographical information on Churchill's early career see in particular an interview, IWM SA 7081/05, and the section on him in the Private Papers of J.E.C. Nicholl, IWM DD 6880.

67 'I think the war coming': John Churchill, IWM SA 7081/05.
'I said if I can': Ibid.
'We went into': Private Papers of J.H. Patterson, File 1/3, IWM DD 13225.
'Frimley': Churchill is usually said to have played 'The March of the Cameron Men' at Vaagso, but the recording of him recreating it is of 'Frimley'. See IWM Music 2526.
'We all knew': De la Torre, IWM SA 29820.
'I and L/Sgt Connelly': Peter Young's account is in NA DEFE 2/83.

68 'Then a stream of tracer': De la Torre, IWM SA 29820.
69 'like all stupid young men': George Peel's reminiscences are in IWM SA 29618.
71 'I was very surprised': Webb, IWM SA 29618.
'Something flew': De la Torre, IWM SA 29820.
One of its officers: Jos Nicholl's memoir, in IWM DD 6880, serves as an anecdotal group history of 2 Commando. It is told from several points of view. Black's may be based on a diary that he kept.
74 'I then ran': NA DEFE 2/83.
'Although I detest': Ibid.
75 'Nein, nein': Ibid.
The sky was filled: Smallman, IWM SA 16252.
76 'It can't be': Peel, IWM SA 29618.
77 'It was a terrible sight': Henriques's account is in Haydon, File 2/6, IWM DD Box 2397.
78 'It brought home': De la Torre, IWM SA 29820.
'As we drew in': Smallman, IWM SA 16252.
'Can you imagine': Peel, IWM SA 29618.
79 'I had been thinking': Durnford-Slater, op. cit., p. 89.
'We'd been blooded': Peel, IWM SA 29618.
'It was a big morale booster': Webb, IWM SA 29618.
'I am basking': Haydon, File 1/3, IWM DD Box 2397.
'It had never': Ibid., File 2/6.
80 'If the British': For the German High Command's reactions to raids, including in Norway, see Bernhard R. Kroener *et al.*, *Germany and the Second World War*, vol. 5/II (Clarendon Press, 2003), pp. 127, 246–247 and 444.
81 'Algy Forrester's performance': Durnford-Slater, op. cit., p. 130.
'John was an artillery officer': Smale, IWM SA 29819.
'the good thing about': Ibid.
82 'quite rightly': Devins, *The Vaagso Raid*, p. 213.
'Before Vaagso': Durnford-Slater, op. cit., p. 88.

5: POSTMASTER

83 'I say, I f-f-feel': J.E.A., *Geoffrey*, p. 41. This memoir by his father is the principal source for Appleyard's early life.
84 'Funny how': Ibid., p. 19.
By the time: NA WO 373/16.
'M-P is a very stout fellow': J.E.A., op. cit., p. 46. For Gus March-Phillipps's early career see also his private papers, IWM DD 14857.
'He was one': Correspondence with M.R.D. Foot, 23 October 2011.
85 'Of course, it's absolutely terrific': J.E.A., op. cit., p. 44.
One rainy afternoon: Obituary of Jan Nasmyth, *The Times*, 26 September 2008.
André Desgranges: His SOE personnel file is NA HS 9/426.
By January 1941: See Foot, *SOE in France*, p. 182 for the original understanding between SOE and Combined Operations that the latter would look after raids involving fewer than thirty men.
Operation SAVANNA: See J.E.A., op. cit., p. 55 et seq., and Foot, *SOE in France*, p. 154.
87 'the weakest character': NA HS 9/888/2.
'Unless I am': Ibid.

88 'they had an 80 per cent': March-Phillipps, IWM DD 14857.
88 a diesel-driven barge, *Bibundi*: Often given as 'Burundi', but this is the vessel's correct name.
89 'Throughout the autumn': SOE's key reports on the raid are in NA HS 3/89 and HS 3/92. See also Private Papers of Desmond Longe, IWM DD 12792.
89 'On a hot afternoon': Longe, IWM DD 12792.
90 'We were very pleased': Ibid.
'Gus's threats': Ibid.
'many of the volunteers': Ibid.
92 'His Majesty's Government': Ibid.
'Will you get': NA HS 3/89. The same file is the source of the other remarks made on the night of the raid and cited here.
94 'The Italian captain': Longe, IWM DD 12792.
96 'I'll take over here': Ibid.
97 'All Post Masters': NA HS 3/87.
'Up til last night': Longe, IWM DD 12792.
'You will be glad': NA HS 3/87.
98 'certain of our seniors': NA HS 3/89.
'It isn't a spirit': J.E.A., op. cit., p. 47.

6: CHARIOT

100 Planning for the raid: Newman's account is in NA DEFE 2/127. The other reports on and assessments of the raid are contained in NA DEFE 2/125–133.
102 Subaltern John Roderick: Nicholl's memoir, IWM DD 6880, has many anecdotes about individual members of 2 Commando.
103 One of his few other officers: Sources for Micky Burn's life include his autobiography, *Turned towards the Sun*, and several interviews in the IWM. See also Stanley, *Commando to Colditz*, and Burn's obituary in the *Daily Telegraph*, 6 September 2010.
'I am ashamed': *The Times*, 29 March 2008.
104 'was developed much more': Michael Burn, IWM SA 9247.
'with the chance of a bit of fun': De la Torre, IWM SA 29820.
105 'We learnt': Swayne, IWM SA 10231.
'I remember': Burn, IWM SA 9247.
106 'I got the biggest': Swayne, IWM SA 10231.
'We were told': De la Torre, IWM SA 29820.
'frightful apprehension': Swayne, IWM SA 10231.
107 'Well, dad, dearest': Quoted in Dorrian, *Storming St Nazaire*, p. 68.
'I was wondering': Nicholl, IWM DD 6880.
108 'Watching till the eyes': Ibid.
'We have at last': Ibid.
'How far could we': NA DEFE 2/127.
109 'From that moment': Ryder's account in the official dispatch, *London Gazette*, 30 September 1947. Also in NA DEFE 2/129.
'Up went her Boche flares': NA DEFE 2/127.
'People often ask': Stuart Chant, IWM SA 2529.
110 'going fast and shooting hard': Curtis's account, NA DEFE 2/133.
'Then as she got': De la Torre, IWM SA 29820.
111 'Shall we pull him': Burn, IWM SA 9247.

114 'I remember beginning': Ibid. The citation for his MC for this exploit is in NA WO 373/46.
115 'I decided': Newman's reminiscences are in NA DEFE 2/127.
116 'I used to have': Burn, IWM SA 9247.
117 'There were two or three': De la Torre, IWM SA 29820.
'It was a scene of chaos': Ibid. See also his obituary in the *Daily Telegraph*, 28 September 2011.
118 'Our engines were untouched': NA DEFE 2/133.
119 'There were outlines': Swayne, IWM SA 10231.
'I saw holes': Ibid.
'I started parleying': Ibid.
121 'We were very depressed': De la Torre, IWM SA 29820.
'When it went up': Ibid.
'We went running': Swayne, IWM SA 10231.
122 'Gloom over town': NA DEFE 2/37.
They broke down: Interview with M.R.D. Foot, 8 December 2011. The raid took place during his first few days at COHQ.
123 'By then': Burn, IWM SA 9247.
Ronnie Swayne remembered: Information from Sir Adrian Swire.
124 'If she had been': De la Torre, IWM SA 29820.
'It must be admitted': The German assessment is in NA DEFE 2/125.

7: JUBILEE

126 'all hell': William Spearman, IWM SA 9796.
129 'You may depend on it': REL, Box 6/6, 2 July 1942.
130 Durnford-Slater's target: The fullest accounts of 3 Commando's part in the raid are in Durnford-Slater's own memoir and Young, *Storm from the Sea*, but Buckley, *Norway – The Commandos – Dieppe*, remains a valuable summary.
'We set off': Patrick Porteous, IWM SA 10060/2.
'It was by far': Young, op. cit., p. 61.
131 'It was going to hit us': Smale's account is published online at www.war-experience.org/collections/land/alliedbrit/smale/default.asp.
'like a collapsed rugger scrum': Durnford-Slater, op. cit., p. 104.
133 'They looked a bit': Young, op. cit., p. 64.
135 'tried to do my thinking': Lovat, *March Past*, p. 239.
Though 4 Commando: The unit's reports on CAULDRON are in NA WO 218/34.
136 'like thieves in an alley': Mills-Roberts, *Clash by Night*, p. 22. Similar verbatim versions of his account also appear in Buckley's and Lovat's books, and in his papers in the LHCMA.
'Are you going to shoot Papa?': Mills-Roberts, op. cit., p. 24.
'We heard the battery': Ibid., p. 25.
137 'It was rather like': Ibid., p. 26.
'I was in charge': James Dunning, IWM SA 19927.
'A blinding flash': NA WO 218/34.
138 Webb had been annoyed: Spearman, IWM SA 9796.
'Before us': Quoted in Lovat, op. cit., p. 259.
139 Captain Roger Pettiward: He accompanied Peter Fleming to the Amazon in the search for the missing explorer Colonel Fawcett, brilliantly sent up by Fleming as *Brazilian Adventure* (1933).

139 'As we got': Porteous, IWM SA 10060/2.
140 'Like a fool': Irving Portman, IWM SA 9766.
141 'Where you had': Spearman, IWM SA 9796.
'and the Very light': Dunning, IWM SA 19927.
'The Germans must have': Spearman, IWM SA 9796.
'It was a stupendous charge': NA WO 218/34.
'It seemed to be': Porteous, IWM SA 9766.
142 'It was total confusion': Spearman, IWM SA 9796.
'I was so excited': Portman, IWM SA 9766.
'Razor-sharp Sheffield steel': Quoted in Lovat, op. cit., p. 260.
143 'The gun sites': NA WO 218/34.
'When a raid is over': Spearman, IWM SA 9796.
144 'When machine-gun fire': Ibid.
145 'with the false dawn': Lovat, op. cit., p. 266.
For Charles Haydon: Haydon, File 2/7, IWM DD 2397.
146 'We at Combined Headquarters': Ibid., File 1/7. Mountbatten was writing in 1962.
'perhaps the most outstanding': *Supplement to the London Gazette*, 12 August 1947.
'from the moment': Porteous, IWM SA 9766.
147 He had been washed: Joe Smale remained a prisoner until the end of the war. He served in the Army until 1958, and died in 2008.
'half-shut knives': Gilchrist's anecdote has been widely quoted, including in Young, *Commando*, p. 128.
The establishment: For the evolution of Commando training methods, see NA WO 33/1668 and DEFE 2/1134.
149 'a guardsman out and out': Dunning, IWM SA 19927.
150 'We thought they': Vic Ralph's impressions are in IWM SA 20614.
151 'Everything was that much tougher': William Jenkins, IWM SA 21186.
'The object was': Ralph, IWM SA 20614.
'We tried to': Jenkins, IWM SA 21186.
152 'Panting for breath': Nicholl, IWM DD 6880.
'On the sound': Ralph, IWM SA 20614.
153 'It was fascinating': Nicholl, IWM DD 6880.
154 'every thought': Ibid.
'It is high time': This exchange is in REL, Box 6/4.
'He couldn't stand bullying': Dunning, IWM SA 19927.
'It was always wet': Ralph, IWM SA 20614.
155 'It's dirty': T. Charles Bell, IWM SA 20309.
'these men': Keyes, op. cit., p. 144.
156 'Kill the Huns': Kellas, *Down to Earth*, p. 63.

8: DRYAD

157 'force the enemy': NA ADM 116/5112.
158 'During Friday's house hunting': J.E.A., op. cit., p. 92.
'I don't regret it': Kemp, IWM SA 9769.
160 'We were a very happy unit': Kemp, op. cit., p. 48.
The target of DRYAD: The reports on the SSRF's raids are in NA DEFE 2/109. The citation for Appleyard's DSO is in WO 373/93.
161 'Although we had': Kemp, op. cit., p. 51.

161 'was a university man': F. Bourne, IWM SA 11721.

163 'I have never seen': J.E.A., op. cit., p. 97.
One of the sleepers: NA DEFE 2/109.

165 'At that time': Correspondence with M.R.D. Foot, 23 October 2011. Foot went on to serve with the SAS behind enemy lines in France, where he was severely wounded.
The aim of the mission: Appleyard's report on AQUATINT is in NA DEFE 2/109. Fournier and Heintz's *If I Must Die* has much additional material on the participants.
'What do you think, chaps?': Variously attributed to having been remembered by Bourne or by Tony Hall. Binney, *Secret War Heroes*, p. 153, favours the latter.
'Gus had that quality': Interview with M.R.D. Foot, 8 December 2011.

167 'We would not have been discovered': NA DEFE 2/365.

169 Over the next few months: Letter of 27 September 1945 from Hayes's mother to March-Phillipps's wife, IWM DD 14857.

170 'the fine spirit': Ibid., letter of 19 September 1942.

171 BASALT is in NA DEFE 2/109.
'As he said to me': Correspondence with M.R.D. Foot, 6 and 8 February 2012. See also his *SOE in France*, p. 186.
'There comes out of the sea': Churchill gave his speech on 7 October 1942.

172 The target was: The description of the events of FAHRENHEIT is taken from Kemp's report, NA DEFE 2/109.

176 'the proposed activities': NA ADM 116/5112.

177 On the night: Appleyard's SOE file has more details about his disappearance, NA HS 9/48/1.
'England has lost': J.E.A., op. cit., pp. 152–153. The most recent account of Appleyard's life, Gordon Brown's *Wartime Courage* (Bloomsbury, 2008), contains several inaccuracies: only Appleyard and the crew were lost, not the parachutists; Appleyard was then serving in the SAS, not the Commandos; and the SSRF was not the predecessor of the SBS.
'was one of the few': Peniakoff's own adventures are recounted in *Popski's Private Army* (Cape, 1950).

178 Peter Kemp: Obituary by M.R.D. Foot, *Independent*, 4 November 1993. Kemp's books, notably *Mine Were of Trouble* (1957), about his experiences in the Spanish Civil War, are hard to obtain and deserve republishing.
'about the slowest witted': Desgranges's interrogation and subsequent service history with SOE is in NA HS 9/426. My thanks are due to the National Archives for agreeing to open it to me.

179 A few months later: NA ADM 1/24288.
For, in April 1946: This material is in Private Papers of L.E. Prout, IWM DD 17255.

180 He continued his military career: Interview with André Heintz, 9 March 2012.
His suspicions: Information from M.R.D. Foot, 23 October and 8 December 2011.

9: MUSKETOON

181 As he lay in bed: Nicholl, IWM DD 6880.
South of Narvik: The principal archive sources are the reports in NA DEFE 2/109, DEFE 2/364 and DEFE 2/365. The dates of events vary in some of the

accounts and I have followed those in DEFE 2/109. Schofield's *Musketoon* has useful detail but much of it is rendered as reconstructed dialogue.

182 'very jolly': Interview with Desirée Roderick, 13 September 2011.
His second-in-command: The newsletter of the Colditz Society, March 2011, contains an outline of Houghton's life. The website of the Commando Veterans Association, www.commandoveterans.org, also has useful information about this raid and about many other Commando operations and personnel.

187 'Are there any Germans': Christiansen's account is in NA DEFE 2/364. One report says that Christiansen shot a Quisling collaborator, not a sentry.

189 Unfortunately, one of the Norwegians: Schofield, op. cit., p. 82 et seq., has the only version of this incident.

191 'He was in much stronger form': O'Brien, Trigg and Fairclough's initial adventures are recounted in the *London Gazette*, 7 January 1943. See also Schofield, op. cit., p. 104 et seq., which is the only source for the later wanderings of O'Brien, the details of which differ from those he gave in his report.

193 Intelligence reports: NA DEFE 2/365.

194 'This operation': The assessment by Laycock and the others is in NA DEFE 2/364.

195 The only ones: The file containing the reports and correspondence on the aftermath of the raid and the fate of the captured men is NA DEFE 2/365. See also NA WO 309/845. There are memorials to them in Sachsenhausen and at Glomfjord.

196 'just been speaking': NA WO 361/420. Tony Davies died in 2006.

197 O'Brien received: NA WO 373/93.
'I have nothing but good': NA DEFE 2/364.
'They admired': Ibid.

10: ANGLO

198 By the summer: The main source for Sutherland's time in 8 Commando and later the SBS is his memoir, *He Who Dares*. His account in it of ANGLO largely parallels his official report in NA WO 201/736. The mission was the basis for the film *They Who Dare* (1954), with Sutherland's role played by Dirk Bogarde.

202 'Two valuable nights': NA WO 201/736.

204 'This was our only way': Ibid.

209 'Our physical condition': Ibid.
Five minutes later: Obituary of St John, *Daily Telegraph*, 22 March 2009.

11: AGREEMENT

211 The Afrika Korps lorry: There is a full description of Buck's escape in his MC citation (by Clarke), NA WO 373/19.

212 Since leaving the Commandos: For more on Clarke's work with Force A in Cairo, including his cross-dressing antics, see Thaddeus Holt, *The Deceivers* (Weidenfeld & Nicolson, 2004).

213 'We are in the process': NA WO 201/732, 1 April 1942. *Special Forces in the Desert War*, published by the National Archives, is a useful summary of the main Commando-style operations there.

214 'My parents': Tiefenbrunner's memoir of his early life and military career, *A Long Journey Home*, is online at http://mtiefenbrunner.blogspot.com. His time with the SIG is also detailed in several articles and a website about the unit by Martin Sugarman. Some of the details about his service that Tiefenbrunner gives are

inaccurate. There was, for instance, no raid by the SIG or other commandos on Rommel's HQ in the summer of 1942, nor does he mention the SIG's last mission, Operation AGREEMENT.

215 'provided Intelligence sources': NA WO 201/727.
Their first major test: Buck's report on the Martuba raid is in NA WO 201/727.

216 'I heard loud explosions': Tiefenbrunner, op. cit., Section 6.

217 'The lorry was immediately surrounded': NA WO 201/727.

218 'consisting of British troops': Ibid.
'not to tell Buck': Ibid.
'The officer': Haselden's SOE file is in NA HS 9/673/2. His MCs are in NA WO 373/18 and 373/23.
'this may well lead': NA WO 201/749. The operation was largely planned by a rising star of the Army, Shan Hackett.

219 'Commando Battalions': NA WO 201/732.
'the critical phase': NA WO 201/749.
Commando training: His own account of the Tobruk raid is in the Private Papers of T.B. Langton, IWM DD 241. His report on it is in NA WO 201/742.

220 'felt no fear': Ibid.
'We were all': William Taylor, IWM SA 21058.

221 'If you go down': Langton's reminiscences of the entry into Tobruk are from his unpublished memoir in IWM DD 241.

222 'There was a stack': Ibid.
'They were all shouting': Taylor, IWM SA 21058.

223 'I turned and clambered': Langton, IWM DD 241.

224 'So I stared back': Ibid.
'I lifted my pistol': Ibid.

225 'It was too dark': Hillman's report is also in NA WO 201/742.

226 'We discussed the situation': Langton, IWM DD 241.
'We wedged ourselves': Ibid.

227 'We changed his name': Ibid.
'There was a little liquid': Langton's account of his walk is taken from his memoir and from a letter he wrote from hospital in November 1942, both in IWM DD 241. He was awarded the MC – NA WO 373/46.

229 David Russell: His escape is described in his report in NA WO 201/742 and in the citation for the MC he received for it, NA WO 373/46.

230 'Many too many': NA WO 201/745.

12: JV AND FRANKTON

233 Perhaps worried: NA DEFE 2/342.
Its targets: The fullest account of the raid is Montanaro's own in File 3 of his papers in the LHCMA, dated 13 April 1942.
'A great deal': Papers of Gerald Montanaro, LHCMA.

234 Then Montanaro returned: This incident comes from Courtney, *SBS in World War Two*, p. 157.

237 'gallant efforts': NA DEFE 2/342. Preece's citation is in NA WO 373/93.
'very dithery': Papers of Gerald Montanaro, LHCMA.
'We have discovered': REL, Box 6/13.

238 The posting therefore: Montanaro's SOE file contains more on this – NA HS 9/1053/3.

238 Even as a boy: The standard source for Hasler's life is Southby-Tailyour, *Blondie*.
239 'eager to engage': The RMBPD war diary is in NA ADM 202/310.
'Special service': Sparks's observations are in IWM SA 8397.
240 In mid-November: NA DEFE 2/218. See also William Sparks, IWM SA 8397.
241 'The chaps': Jock Stewart, IWM SA 8388.
For some time: The plans and reports on FRANKTON are in NA DEFE 2/217 and 2/218.
242 'You are young': Quoted in Neil Tweedie, 'Cockleshell Heroes: The Truth at Last', *Daily Telegraph*, 28 October 2010.
243 'I know it looks foolish': Quoted in David Gerges, 'World War Two marine who sacrificed his life in "suicidal" raid is refused military honour', *Daily Mail*, 4 March 2012.
'a magnificent bunch': NA DEFE 2/218.
'an unpleasant surprise': Ibid. Hasler's report is dated 8 April 1943.
244 'Being with the Major': Sparks, IWM SA 8397.
245 'All that day': Ibid.
'He was rather upset': NA DEFE 2/218.
246 'We were so close': Sparks, IWM SA 8397.
'We were really thankful': Ibid.
247 'We shook hands': Ibid.
'Suddenly we were bathed': Ibid.
'We found we were trapped': Ibid. Sparks's account points up the inaccuracies in the film made of the operation, *The Cockleshell Heroes* (1955), which depicts the attack as having been far more aggressive. It was post-war propaganda such as this that largely (and inaccurately) shaped the perception of the Commandos which still prevails.
248 At first light: For details of their route see NA WO 208/3312.
249 As well as insisting: Foot and Langley, *MI9*, p. 88.
'She was terrible': Sparks, IWM SA 8397.
250 'Few decorations': DEFE 2/217.
Three of the four ships: Ibid.
Bobby Ewart: Heather herself died shortly afterwards from tuberculosis.
251 It also emerged: Foot, *SOE in France*, p. 26.

13: TARBRUSH

252 Of all the secret weapons: Haydon, File 2/6, IWM DD Box 2397. See also Fergusson, op. cit., p. 302.
For instance: Ibid., p. 300.
254 However, a secret memorandum: Part of the Operation STARKEY deception plan.
While Smith: See the Private Papers of I.C.D. Smith, IWM DD 15632, which also contain the reports on the various raids in which he took part.
255 Among the last: The Forfar raids are in NA DEFE 2/208–213.
256 'The shooting was wild': Smith, IWM DD 15632.
257 'He was at pains': Casalonga's report is in IWM DD 15632.
259 'The more I think': NA DEFE 2/957, 27 January 1944.
260 TARBRUSH 3: The official report is in NA WO 205/220. It does not tally exactly with Smith's account. He does not mention his going ashore or the encounter with the trawler. It may be that Smith was supposed to stay in the dory and he agreed with Groom to gloss over the danger into which they had got themselves.

261 'We correctly assumed': Smith, IWM DD 15632.
'We slid quietly': Ibid.
262 'I remember putting': Ibid.
He soon found: Stone's raid was TARBRUSH 8, NA WO 106/4343.
When Robert Laycock: Cited in his 'Raids in the Late War and Their Lessons'.
Most of the commandos: The standard history of 10 Commando remains that by Ian Dear.
263 Lieutenant George Lane: George Lane, IWM SA 13307.
264 Lane joined SOE: His personnel file appears not to have survived.
'a proper person': REL, Box 6/4.
Perhaps the most vivid: Miriam Rothschild, IWM SA 30203.
265 'They were an intellectual group': Ibid.
'apparently corpses': Ibid.
'I really believed': Lane, IWM SA 28406.
266 The night was pitch black: Lane's account is in NA WO 106/4343. The citation for his MC, NA WO 373/98, varies slightly from this.
'Naturally, one was very scared': Lane, IWM SA 13307.
268 'With a rather theatrical gesture': Ibid.
'They told us': Ibid.
269 Surprised as he was: Lane's version of the interview is in IWM SA 13307. Wooldridge's account in NA WO 106/4343 largely matches Lane's.
270 'vital to our impending campaign': Smith, IWM DD 15632. See also NA DEFE 2/612.
Some months later: Fergusson, op. cit., p. 304.

14: FLOUNCED

271 'Bravo!': Barton's accounts of the raid and of his time on Brac are in NA WO 218/64. There is also information about both in Nicholl, IWM DD 6880.
272 'We moved camp': NA WO 218/64.
'When it came': Ibid.
Hauptmann Kunstler: The commandant's name is given in signals traffic in NA WO 204/1527.
Certainly, the fact: Information about Barton's early life from his SOE file, NA HS 9/98/1, and a conversation with Luke Griffiths, 20 October 2011.
The year before: The MC citation is NA WO 373/25.
273 'I gave it a burst': NA WO 218/64.
274 He had already been: Ibid.
'I hadn't realised': John Morris, IWM SA 20808.
275 'We were just': Morris's account of the attack is in IWM SA 20808.
Kicking open the front door: The citation for Hausmann's DCM is in the *London Gazette*, 20 July 1944. Barton's DSO is in NA WO 373/6.
276 'There is no doubt': NA WO 218/64.
This led to more controversy: Barton's name was mentioned, for instance, by the *New York Times* in a description of his exploit published on 13 July 1944. See also 2 Commando's war diary for 20 July 1944, NA WO 218/64.
'We knew we couldn't do much': Morris, IWM SA 20808.
277 'Having one administrative officer': REL, Box 6/4.
In the case of No. 5: Patterson, File 1/3, IWM DD 13225.
278 'It's very surprising': REL, Box 5/27/6.

278 'raiding for the sake of raiding': Ibid., Box 4/20.
'full of self-pity': REL, Box 6/16. The report was by Philip Dunne of 8 Commando.
'done nothing but good': Ibid.
'that feeling': Ibid.
279 'lose their individuality': Ibid., REL Box 6/21.
'The situation, quite bluntly': Ibid.
The order of the day: REL, Box 4/20.
280 'The news of Bob's appointment': Haydon, File 1/3, IWM DD Box 2397.
Other leading candidates: Rear Admiral Sir Philip Vian had refused the post, according to Mountbatten.
For instance: NA CAB 120/414, 10 October 1943.
281 As Laycock: Nicholl, IWM DD 6880.
282 In another man: Patterson, File 1/3, IWM DD 13225.
Churchill once arrived late: Nicholl, IWM DD 6880.
'One of the great things': Churchill, IWM SA 7801/05.
'I demoted myself': Ibid.
On the evening: Saunders, op. cit., p. 189. The name of the village is often rendered incorrectly as Pigoletti. See also Churchill's DSO citation at NA WO 373/4 and *London Gazette*, 13 January 1944.
284 'The tendency': Churchill, IWM SA 9231.
Life with Tito's men: 2 Commando's war diary is in NA WO 218/64.
285 'They were standing': Nicholl, IWM DD 6880.
'the Medical Officer': NA WO 218/64.
'It is about time': These letters are in the Private Papers of T.B.L. Churchill, IWM DD 6387.
286 'I'm very anxious': Churchill, IWM SA 7081/05.
'They ordered me': REL, Box 9/1/2.
'I can't hope': Ibid., Box 6/18.
'an inspiration': Nicholl, IWM DD 6880.
'mentioning incidents': NA WO 218/64.
287 'like cow-bells': Nicholl, IWM DD 6880. His memoir has more on the capture of Jenkins. The main file on the raid is NA WO 204/7577.
'We all got': Morris, IWM SA 20808.
'It was the first time': NA WO 204/7577.
288 'There was a lot': Morris, IWM SA 20808.
289 He wanted to send: Churchill, IWM SA 9231.
'precious little confidence': Ibid.
Despite having organised: Ibid.
None the less, on the night of 1 June: The report on FLOUNCED is at NA WO 204/7290. For 43 Commando's war diary see NA ADM 202/88. See also Nicholl, IWM DD 6880.
290 'To my astonishment': Churchill, IWM SA 9231.
291 'Barbed wire and mines': Ibid.
292 'Manners had only': Churchill's description of events on the hill is in IWM SA 9231.
293 'The bald facts': NA WO 204/7290.
'It was the most stirring': NA WO 218/64.
'His determination': The citation is in NA ADM 1/29691.
294 'I believe it was': REL, Box 9/1/2.

15: OVERLORD

295 'She was looking down': James Kelly, IWM SA 11281.
The 1st Special Service Brigade: For its participation in D-Day at command level, see NA DEFE 2/53.
296 By contrast: The 4th Special Service Brigade's war diary is in NA DEFE 2/46.
297 'It was at tea time': Patterson, File 1/7, IWM DD 13225. For 4 Commando's experiences in Normandy, see in particular McDougall, *Swiftly They Struck*.
'It was a lovely evening': William Millin, IWM SA 11614.
298 'Going across the Channel': Spearman, IWM SA 9796.
'but I was terrified': Kelly, IWM SA 11281.
David Haig-Thomas: Haig-Thomas had been the explorer Wilfrid Thesiger's companion on his first journey in East Africa, and in the late 1930s led expeditions in the Arctic. See his *Tracks in the Snow* (1939).
'Everything seemed to stand out': Warwick Nield-Siddall, IWM SA 19672.
299 'The East Yorks': Patterson, File 1/7, IWM DD 13225. 4 Commando's own war diary is in NA DEFE 2/40.
300 'I took a look around': Patterson, File 1/7, IWM DD 13225.
'Ready on the ramp!': Ibid.
'It came up to': Ibid.
301 'He was submerged': Ibid.
'I was shocked': Spearman, IWM SA 9796.
'It's only a person': Ibid.
302 'As I was doing so': Patterson, File 1/7, IWM DD 13225.
303 'About 200 yards further': Ibid.
'It used to sound': Portman, IWM SA 9766.
'We were under': Spearman, IWM SA 9796.
304 'I lost three men': Portman, IWM SA 9766.
'We had suffered heavily': Patterson, File 1/7, IWM DD 13225.
The landing craft: 41 Commando's war diary for D-Day is in NA ADM 202/103.
305 'The next thing': Kelly, IWM SA 11281.
306 'Who thinks straight': Ibid.
'When that Jeep': Ibid.
307 'I fired one shot': Ibid.
308 'There was shellfire': Millin, IWM SA 11614.
'There he stood': George Saunders, IWM SA 13558.
309 'War, to the uninitiated': Ibid.
'They hunted me': Ibid. For 10 Commando's experiences in Normandy, see NA WO 218/70.
310 'If they had discovered': G. Saunders, IWM SA 13558.
'I was so close': Millin, IWM SA 11614.
311 'It was as if': Ibid.
'We had to move': Interview with Lovat in 1978, available at www.commandoveterans.org/site.
312 'My dear Shimi': REL, Box 6/15.
'Lord Lovat was the perfect leader': Millin, IWM SA 11614.
'We were like a machine': Spearman, IWM SA 9796.
313 'He was a big, beefy man': Millin, IWM SA 11614.
'We thought we'd be': Interview with Lovat in 1978, available at www.commandoveterans.org/site.

313 'It was not really': Spearman, IWM SA 9796.
314 'It was not a role': Portman, IWM SA 9766.
'I don't care': Millin, IWM SA 11614.
'So I gave': Ibid.
315 'The aim was': Kelly, IWM SA 11281.
'The most sleep': Ibid.
'When it started': Ibid.
316 'The whole of Normandy': Spearman, IWM SA 9796.

16: INFATUATE

319 'When they became': Spearman, IWM SA 9796.
320 Under cover: The key reports on INFATUATE are in NA DEFE 2/307. 4 SS Brigade's war diary is in NA ADM 202/407.
'It was clear': Portman, SA 9766.
321 In the very early hours: 4 Commando's extensive war diary is in NA DEFE 2/40. See also McDougall, op. cit., and Brooks, *Walcheren 1944*.
322 '20 or 30 badly scared Germans': NA DEFE 2/40.
'Just before the shelling stopped': Spearman, IWM SA 9796.
'We landed on a jetty': Portman, IWM SA 9766.
323 'To anybody on the British side': NA DEFE 2/40.
'You were constantly': Spearman, IWM SA 9796.
324 'the weakness': NA DEFE 2/40.
325 'You could see': Kaspar Gudmundseth, IWM SA 23218. 10 Commando's war diary for the operation is in NA WO 218/70.
326 'It was the first time': Kelly, IWM SA 11281.
'Then we got one': Gudmundseth, IWM SA 23218.
327 'I wasn't quite sure': Ibid.
'They were having breakfast': Nield-Siddall, IWM SA 19672.
'When we landed': Kelly, IWM SA 11281. 41 Commando's war diary for Walcheren is in NA ADM 202/103.
328 'Out of the top window': Ibid.
'We would go': Gudmundseth, IWM SA 23218.
330 'Whatever hit him': Kelly, IWM SA 11281.
'When I lifted him up': Ibid.
331 'I remember getting slammed': Ibid.
'The locals': NA DEFE 2/40.
332 'You and your fellows': REL, Box 6/21.
333 Bob Laycock was already: His complaint is in NA DEFE 2/307. Even this late in the war, there were criticisms as well of the lack of effective coordination between the naval and Army elements of the force. See Ramsay's memorandum to Eisenhower, NA DEFE 2/309.
'From our point of view': Spearman, IWM SA 9796.

17: TALON

334 'I know all about': Bell, IWM SA 20309.
A handful of veterans: See, for instance, the obituary of Major William Seymour, *Daily Telegraph*, 25 August 2011. His *British Special Forces* remains a useful survey of the operations of the Commandos and other wartime units, such as the SAS.
335 Each of these: Hughes, IWM DD 2222.

336 'So I finally got ashore': Harry Winch, IWM SA 21798.
337 'There was as much mud': Jack Johnson, IWM SA 20516.
'We worked out a plan': Bell, IWM SA 20309.
'These were hardened': Johnson, IWM SA 20516.
338 'The armoured sampan': The COPP recce is noted in Hughes's diary, IWM DD 2222.
339 The Brigade duly followed: Its war diary is in NA DEFE 2/53.
There was no enemy: 1 Commando's war diary covering Kangaw is in NA DEFE 2/37.
'Half-way up': Ralph, IWM SA 20614.
340 'I was lucky': Bell, IWM SA 20309.
'No sooner had': John Webber, IWM SA 20267.
'When the shell': Johnson, IWM SA 20516.
'I had a lance-corporal': Bell, IWM SA 20309.
341 'I remember lifting': Webber, IWM SA 20267.
'When the Japs': Bell's experiences on the hill are in IWM SA 20309.
342 'If you think about it': Johnson, IWM SA 20516.
'We lost 27': Bell, IWM SA 20309.
343 'The Japanese got round': Ibid.
'The first thing': Johnson, IWM SA 20516.
'They thought that': Ibid.
344 'You're in the jungle': Winch's reminiscences are from IWM SA 21798.
'One of the Indian regiments': Ralph, IWM SA 20614.
345 'All at once': Winch, IWM SA 21798.
Despite the danger: The action is described in the Commando war diary and in the recommendation for Knowland's VC, DEFE 2/37. There are more details on his life in IWM VC Box 43 K 40. His deed was commemorated in *The Victor* comic on 8 July 1961.
346 'I don't know whether': Ralph, IWM SA 20614.
'It was hand-to-hand': Winch, IWM SA 21798.
347 'It wasn't frightening': Ralph, IWM SA 20614.
More than 340 Japanese: See Peter Young's account of the action, NA WO 203/1792.
'Much as I like Ken': REL, Box 6/15.
348 'your courage and determination': NA DEFE 2/53.

18: ROAST

349 The SBS patrol: The events described here are reconstructed from Fryforce's reports, NA WO 218/76, and the citation for Lassen's VC. See also Langley, *Anders Lassen*.
350 The plan envisaged: The strategic appreciation and 2 Commando Brigade's war diary for Comacchio are in NA WO 218/76.
351 Each sortie was long: For the COPP recces, see the DSO citation for Lieutenant Richard Fyson, NA ADM 1/30413, and his reports at WO 204/8019.
352 'It was', according to the Brigade's war diary: NA WO 218/76.
353 Captain Jos Nicholl: Recounted in his memoir, IWM DD 6880.
As soon as: 2 Commando's own war diary is in NA WO 218/82.
354 'A solid slab of concrete': Nicholl, IWM DD 6880. His MC citation is in NA WO 373/13.
Once the two lead Troops: 43 Commando's war diary is in NA ADM 202/88.

355 'The Artillery was magnificent': Jenkins, IWM SA 21186. See also his memoir, *Commando Subaltern at War*, p. 111 et seq.

356 'We slogged back': Jenkins, IWM SA 21186.
The Valletta Canal: See NA ADM 202/88, WO 218/76 and the citation for Hunter's VC.

357 'My most vivid memory': David Sutherland and George Jellicoe, IWM SA 26607.
'He was irresistible': Ibid.

358 In July 1943: The citation for the second of Lassen's three MCs is in NA HS 9/888/2.
'The SBS mess': Smith, IWM DD 15632.

359 It was towards midnight: NA WO 218/76. Lassen is buried in the military cemetery in Argenta.
He drove down to Rimini: Sutherland, *He Who Dares*, p. 170.

360 Within a week: For the Argenta Gap offensive, see 2 Commando Brigade's war diary at NA WO 218/76.

361 They were to receive: NA ADM 202/88.
'It was a very inauspicious start': Jenkins, IWM SA 21186. See also Jenkins, op. cit., p. 134 et seq. – his oral and written accounts vary slightly.
'Just as I was rounding': Jenkins, IWM SA 21186.

362 'I reached in my holster': Ibid.
Jenkins was in the lead: His charge is described in his DSO citation, NA WO 373/47, but he omits it from his memoir and interview.

363 'I stood up': Jenkins, IWM SA 21186.
'If they had been a bit braver': Ibid.
'A tall chap': Ibid.

364 A patrol from 2 Commando: NA WO 218/82.

19: ECLIPSE

365 So it was: Dalzel-Job, *From Arctic Snow to Dust of Normandy*, p. 115.
According to one of his comrades: T.J. Glanville in 30 Assault Unit Papers at LHCMA. For more on the history of the organisation, see Glanville's report in NA ADM 223/214 and Major W.G. Cass's summary of 30 Troop's work in NA WO 218/71. See also Glanville and Nutting, *Attain by Surprise*, the manuscript of which is in LHCMA. The most recent account is Rankin, *Ian Fleming's Commandos*.
He was a qualified parachutist: See the obituaries in the *Daily Telegraph*, 16 October 2003, and *Independent*, 28 October 2003. See also the summary given in www.warexperience.org/collections/sea/alliedbrit/dalzel-job/default.asp. His papers in the LHCMA are essentially the draft of his memoir.

366 'authorised looters': 30 Assault Unit Papers, LHCMA.
'It was selected': NA DEFE 2/1107.
'Half of the trouble': Ibid.
'It must be accepted': Papers of Quintin Riley, LHCMA.

367 'It always felt': Ibid.

368 Dalzel-Job's Team 4: See Dalzel-Job, op. cit., p. 146 et seq. for the fullest account of this episode.
'a mess of drunken bits': Bon Royle, in 30 Assault Unit Papers, LHCMA.

369 'Initiative and resourcefulness': Papers of Quintin Riley, LHCMA.
'With the disbandment': REL, Box 4/28. For assessments of the Commandos'

performance, see in particular Buckley, op. cit., p. 164 and Thomas, 'The Importance of Commando Operations in Modern Warfare 1939–82'.

371 'Every platoon': Quoted in Richard Holmes, *Soldiers*, p. 392.

'A few strong toughies': Geoffrey Picot, *Accidental Warrior*, p. 282.

373 Herbert Buck: He died in an air crash on the Blackdown Hills, Somerset, in November 1945.

'It was sad': Smale, IWM SA 29819.

374 'One of the absurd': Burn, IWM SA 9247. He married Mary Booker, who had been the girlfriend of the wartime pilot and author Richard Hillary. The newsreel footage of him at St Nazaire was seen by a Dutch acquaintance, who sent packages to him in Colditz. After his release, he returned the favour by sending her cigarettes which she was able to trade for penicillin, helping to save the life of her young daughter, Audrey Hepburn.

375 Despite not speaking Italian: These SOE missions are in NA HS 6/859. See also the citation for his second DSO, in NA WO 373/6.

'the most important intelligence item': NA HS 9/98/1. Other information from interview with Luke Griffiths, 20 October 2011.

'Life is today': G. Saunders, IWM SA 13558.

'I am glad': Patterson, File 1/3, IWM DD 13225.

'You wouldn't miss that': Winch, IWM SA 21798.

376 'It was a moonlit night': Bell, IWM SA 20309.

'You're shooting men': Ralph, IWM SA 20614.

377 'When we march': Ibid.

BIBLIOGRAPHY

Books and unpublished memoirs

Allan, Stuart, *Commando Country* (National Museums Scotland, 2007)
Asher, Michael, *Get Rommel* (Weidenfeld & Nicolson, 2004)
Binney, Marcus, *Secret War Heroes* (Hodder & Stoughton, 2005)
Brooks, Richard, *Walcheren 1944* (Osprey, 2011)
Buckley, Christopher, *Norway – The Commandos – Dieppe* (HMSO, 1952)
Bull, Stephen, *Commando Tactics* (Pen & Sword, 2010)
Burn, Michael, *Turned towards the Sun* (Michael Russell, 2003)
Chappell, Mike, *Army Commandos* (Osprey, 1996)
Cherry, Niall, *Striking Back* (Helion, 2009)
Churchill, Winston, *The Second World War*, vol. 2: *Their Finest Hour* (Cassell & Co, 1949; Penguin, 2005)
Clarke, Dudley, *Seven Assignments* (Jonathan Cape, 1948)
Colville, John, *The Fringes of Power: Downing Street Diaries 1939–1955* (Weidenfeld & Nicolson, 2004)
Courtney, G.B., *SBS in World War Two* (Robert Hale, 1983)
Courtney, Roger, *Palestine Policeman* (Herbert Jenkins, 1939)
Dalzel-Job, Patrick, *From Arctic Snow to Dust of Normandy* (Nead-an-Eoin, 1991)
Dear, Ian, *10 Commando* (Pen & Sword, 1987)
Devins, Joseph, *The Vaagso Raid* (Chilton, 1968)
Dorrian, James, *Storming St Nazaire* (Leo Cooper, 1998)
Duggan, Sally, *Commando* (Channel 4 Books, 2001)
Dunning, James, *It Had to Be Tough* (The Pentland Press, 2000)
—— *The Fighting Fourth* (Sutton, 2003)
—— *When Shall Their Glory Fade?* (Frontline Books, 2011)
Durnford-Slater, John, *Commando* (William Kimber, 1953)
Fergusson, Bernard, *The Watery Maze* (Collins, 1961)
Foot, M.R.D., *SOE in France* (HMSO, 1966)
Foot, M.R.D. and Langley, J.M., *MI9* (The Bodley Head, 1979)
Ford, Ken, *St Nazaire 1942* (Osprey, 2001)
Fournier, Gérard and Heintz, André, *If I Must Die* (Orep Editions, 2nd edn, 2006)
Fowler, Will, *The Commandos at Dieppe: Rehearsal for D-Day* (Collins, 2002)

Gilchrist, Donald, *Castle Commando* (Oliver & Boyd, 1960)
Halpern, Paul G. (ed.), *The Keyes Papers*, vol. 3: *1939–1945* (Publications of the Naval Records Society, vol. 122; George Allen & Unwin for the Naval Records Society, 1981)
Hampshire, A. Cecil, *The Secret Navies* (William Kimber, 1978)
Henriques, Robert, *The Commander* (Viking, 1968)
—— *Red over Green* (Collins, 1956)
Holmes, Richard, *Soldiers* (Viking, 2011)
J.E.A. [J.E. Appleyard], *Geoffrey* (Whitehead & Miller, 1945)
Jenkins, W.G., *Commando Subaltern at War* (Greenhill Books, 1996)
Keene, Thomas Edward, 'Beset by Secrecy and Beleaguered by Rivals: The Special Operations Executive and Military Operations in Western Europe 1940–1942 with Special Reference to Operation Frankton' (unpublished thesis, University of Plymouth, 2011)
Kellas, Arthur, *Down to Earth* (The Pentland Press, 1990)
Kemp, Peter, *No Colours or Crest* (Cassell, 1958)
Keyes, Elizabeth, *Geoffrey Keyes VC of the Rommel Raid* (George Newnes, 1956)
Ladd, James, *Commandos and Rangers of World War II* (Macdonald and Jane's, 1978)
Landsborough, Gordon, *Tobruk Commando* (Cassell, 1956)
Langley, Mike, *Anders Lassen* (New English Library, 1988)
Lodwick, John, *The Filibusters* (Methuen, 1947)
Longden, Sean, *T-Force* (Constable & Robinson, 2009)
Lovat, Lord, *March Past* (Weidenfeld & Nicolson, 1978)
Lucas Phillips, C.E., *The Greatest Raid of All* (William Heinemann, 1958)
Macpherson, Tommy with Bath, Richard, *Behind Enemy Lines* (Mainstream, 2010)
McDougall, Murdoch C., *Swiftly They Struck* (Odhams Press, 1950)
McHarg, Ian, *Litani River* (Club Books, 2011)
Messenger, Charles, *The Commandos 1940–1946* (William Kimber, 1985)
—— *The Middle East Commandos* (William Kimber, 1988)
Michelli, Alison, *Commando to Captain-General* (Pen & Sword, 2007)
Miller, Russell, *The Commandos* (Time-Life Books, 1981)
Mills-Roberts, Derek, *Clash by Night* (William Kimber, 1956)
Ministry of Information, *Combined Operations* (HMSO, 1943)
Moreman, Tim, *British Commandos 1940–46* (Osprey, 2006)
National Archives, *Special Forces in the Desert War 1940–1943* (Crown Copyright, 2008)
Neillands, Robin, *By Sea and Land* (Pen & Sword, 1987)
Nicholl, J.E.C., 'Untitled' (unpublished memoir, *c.* 1978)
Parker, John, *Commandos* (Headline, 2000)
Pettiward, Roger, *The Last Cream Bun* (Chatto & Windus and The Hogarth Press, 1984)
Picot, Geoffrey, *Accidental Warrior* (Book Guild, 1993)
Pitt, Barrie, *Special Boat Squadron* (Century, 1983)
Rankin, Nicholas, *Ian Fleming's Commandos* (Faber & Faber, 2011)
Saunders, Hilary St George, *The Green Beret* (Michael Joseph, 1949)
Schofield, Stephen, *Musketoon* (Jonathan Cape, 1964)
Scott, Stan, *Fighting with the Commandos* (Pen & Sword, 2008)
Seymour, William, *British Special Forces* (Sidgwick and Jackson, 1985)
Smith, Ian, 'The Happy Amateur' (unpublished memoir, 2006)
Smith, Peter C., *Massacre at Tobruk* (William Kimber, 1987)
Southby-Tailyour, Ewen, *Blondie* (Leo Cooper, 1998)

Stanley, Peter, *Commando to Colditz* (Pier 9, 2009)
Strutton, Bill and Pearson, Michael, *The Secret Invaders* (Popular Press, 1958)
Sutherland, David, *He Who Dares* (Leo Cooper, 1998)
Tiefenbrunner, Monju, 'A Long Way Home' (unpublished memoir, 2009)
Trenowden, Ian, *Stealthily by Night* (Crecy Books, 1995)
US Department of War, *British Commandos* (Military Library Research Service, 2004)
Van der Bijl, Nick, *No. 10 (Inter-Allied) Commando 1942–45* (Osprey, 2006)
—— *Commandos in Exile* (Pen & Sword, 2008)
Van der Bijl, Nick and Hannon, Paul, *The Royal Marines 1939–93* (Osprey, 1994)
Waugh, Evelyn, *Diaries of Evelyn Waugh* (ed. Michael Davie, Weidenfeld & Nicolson, 1976)
—— *The Letters of Evelyn Waugh* (ed. Mark Amory, Ticknor & Fields, 1980)
Young, Peter, *Storm from the Sea* (William Kimber, 1958)
—— *Commando* (Pan/Ballantine, 1974)

Articles

Gallagher, Donat, 'Misfire: Reassessing the Legacy of General Robert Laycock', *Journal of the Royal United Services Institute*, vol. 153, February 2008
Garrod, Martin, 'Amphibious Warfare: Why?', *Journal of the Royal United Services Institute*, vol. 133, Winter 1988
Greenhous, Brereton, 'Operation Flodden: The Sea Fight off Berneval and the Suppression of the Goebbels Battery, 19 August 1942', *Canadian Military Journal*, vol. 4, no. 3, Autumn 2003
Kerr, Carol, 'So Fine and Honourable an Englishman: Capt. Joseph Houghton MC', *Newsletter of the Colditz Society*, no. 46, March 2011
Laycock, Robert, 'Raids in the Late War and Their Lessons', *Journal of the Royal United Services Institute*, vol. 92, November 1947
Reed, John, 'Myebon–Kangaw 1945', *War Monthly*, no. 51, April 1978
Sugarman, Martin, 'The SIG', *Jewish Historical Society of England*, vol. 35, 1996–8
Thomas, David, 'The Importance of Commando Operations in Modern Warfare 1939–82', *Journal of Contemporary History*, vol. 18, no. 4, October 1983
Waugh, Evelyn, 'Commando Raid on Bardia', *LIFE*, 17 November 1941

INDEX